FOOD SCIENCE AND TECHNOLOGY

MUSHROOMS

CULTIVATION, ANTIOXIDANT PROPERTIES AND HEALTH BENEFITS

FOOD SCIENCE AND TECHNOLOGY

Additional books in this series can be found on Nova's website
under the Series tab.

Additional e-books in this series can be found on Nova's website
under the e-book tab.

Food Science and Technology

Mushrooms

Cultivation, Antioxidant Properties and Health Benefits

Grégoire Pesti
Editor

New York

Copyright © 2014 by Nova Science Publishers, Inc.

All rights reserved. No part of this book may be reproduced, stored in a retrieval system or transmitted in any form or by any means: electronic, electrostatic, magnetic, tape, mechanical photocopying, recording or otherwise without the written permission of the Publisher.

For permission to use material from this book please contact us:
Telephone 631-231-7269; Fax 631-231-8175
Web Site: http://www.novapublishers.com

NOTICE TO THE READER

The Publisher has taken reasonable care in the preparation of this book, but makes no expressed or implied warranty of any kind and assumes no responsibility for any errors or omissions. No liability is assumed for incidental or consequential damages in connection with or arising out of information contained in this book. The Publisher shall not be liable for any special, consequential, or exemplary damages resulting, in whole or in part, from the readers' use of, or reliance upon, this material. Any parts of this book based on government reports are so indicated and copyright is claimed for those parts to the extent applicable to compilations of such works.

Independent verification should be sought for any data, advice or recommendations contained in this book. In addition, no responsibility is assumed by the publisher for any injury and/or damage to persons or property arising from any methods, products, instructions, ideas or otherwise contained in this publication.

This publication is designed to provide accurate and authoritative information with regard to the subject matter covered herein. It is sold with the clear understanding that the Publisher is not engaged in rendering legal or any other professional services. If legal or any other expert assistance is required, the services of a competent person should be sought. FROM A DECLARATION OF PARTICIPANTS JOINTLY ADOPTED BY A COMMITTEE OF THE AMERICAN BAR ASSOCIATION AND A COMMITTEE OF PUBLISHERS.

Additional color graphics may be available in the e-book version of this book.

Library of Congress Cataloging-in-Publication Data

Mushrooms : cultivation, antioxidant properties and health benefits / editors, Grigoire Pesti.
    pages cm. -- (Food science and technology)
  Includes index.
  ISBN: 978-1-63117-521-3 (hardcover)
  1. Mushrooms--Therapeutic use. 2. Maitake--Therapeutic use. 3. Medicinal plants. I. Pesti, Grigoire, editor of compilation.
  RM666.M87M87 2014
  615.3'296--dc23
               2014007727

Published by Nova Science Publishers, Inc. † *New York*

CONTENTS

Preface		**vii**
Chapter 1	Biological Significance and Medicinal Properties of the Maitake Mushroom *Sensuke Konno*	**1**
Chapter 2	The Use of Edible Mushroom Extracts as Bioactive Ingredients to Design Novel Functional Foods with Hypocholesterolemic Activities *Alicia Gil-Ramírez and Cristina Soler-Rivas*	**43**
Chapter 3	Mushrooms: Biological Characterization, Antioxidant Properties and Interactions with Human Health *Patrícia Molz, Joel Henrique Ellwanger, Daniel Prá and Silvia Isabel Rech Franke*	**75**
Chapter 4	Phytochemistry, Traditional Uses and Health Benefits of the Mushroom Inonotus obliquus (Chaga) *Haixia Chen and Jia Wang*	**93**
Chapter 5	Immunomodulatory Effects of Mushroom Extracts and Compounds *Tzi Bun Ng and Charlene Cheuk Wing Ng*	**119**
Chapter 6	An Insight into Anti-Diabetic Effects of Mushrooms *Bin Du and Baojun Xu*	**141**
Chapter 7	Protective Effects of Mushrooms against Tissue Damage with Emphasis on Neuroprotective, Hepatoprotective and Radioprotective Activities *Tzi Bun Ng and Charlene Cheuk Wing Ng*	**157**
Chapter 8	Effects of Mushroom Extracts and Compounds on Experimental Diabetes *Tzi Bun Ng and Charlene Cheuk Wing Ng*	**175**
Chapter 9	Antihyperlipidemic Effects of Mushroom Extracts and Compounds *Tzi Bun Ng and Charlene Cheuk Wing Ng*	**189**

vi Contents

Chapter 10 Mushroom Proteins with Antibacterial, Antifungal, Antiviral,
Anti-Parasite and Anti-Insect Activities **199**
Jack Ho Wong and Tzi Bun Ng

Chapter 11 Micronutrients Benefits of Consumption of the Sclerotium (Tuber)
of Pleurotus tuber-regium (Ósū) Mushroom in Southeastern Nigeria **209**
Innocent C. Nnorom

Chapter 12 Valorization of Coffee-Grounds Supplemented with Wheat Straw
by Cultivation of a Pleurotus ostreatus Local Strain **227**
*Malika Mansour-Benamar, Souhila Aoudia
and Nadia Ammar-Khodja*

Index **243**

PREFACE

Many of the vast number of mushroom species are available worldwide. They are valued in gourmet traditions around the world for their unique taste, aroma, nutritional value, and medicinal potentials. Many mushroom species are also used in traditional medicines in many countries around the world, including China, Japan, Nigeria, Tibet, etc. Additionally, mushrooms are highly appreciated by many in most communities. Because they are considered as valuable health foods, have acceptable texture and flavor, have low energy content, high proportion of indigestible fiber, and antioxidant constituents. They have good medicinal values, and they contain significant amounts of vitamins, and minerals. This book discusses the cultivation of mushrooms along with the antioxidant properties mushrooms have. The book also provides information on the health benefits edible mushrooms may have on the human body.

Chapter 1 - Maitake mushroom (*Grifola frondosa*) is an edible, medicinal mushroom. It has been extensively studied for the past 30 years, revealing numerous medicinal properties that could provide great health benefits. Those include various physiological benefits ranging from immunomodulatory and antitumor activities to treatment for diabetes, hypertension, hypercholesterolemia, viral infections (hepatitis B and human immunodeficiency virus), and obesity. Two distinct bioactive extracts have been obtained from maitake and are called "maitake D-fraction" and "maitake SX-fraction". A number of scientific studies have been performed on these two maitake derivatives, which are thus well characterized. Maitake D-fraction consists of proteoglucan (protein-bound polysaccharide), or more specifically known as β-glucan. This β-glucan is an active component of D-fraction and its two major biological activities, *immunomodulatory* and *antitumor*, have been the main target for scientific and clinical research. Various *in vitro*, *in vivo*, and clinical studies showed that D-fraction was capable of modulating immunologic and hematologic parameters, significantly inhibiting or regressing the cancer cell growth, and even improving the quality of life of cancer patients. In addition, the synergistic potentiation of D-fraction with vitamin C demonstrated *in vitro* is rather interesting and has clinical implication, because such combination therapy could be performed solely or be used as an adjuvant regimen with current therapies to improve the overall efficacy. As far as the safety of D-fraction is concerned, it has been exempted from a Phase I toxicology test by the US Food and Drug Administration (FDA) and also approved for the Investigational New Drug (IND) application for a Phase II pilot study on patients with advanced cancers. Thus, its safety has been well granted. In contrast, maitake SX-fraction is a water-soluble glycoprotein and has been shown to primarily have hypoglycemic (glucose-lowering), hypotensive (blood pressure-lowering), and cholesterol/lipids-lowering effects in various study settings, implying potential prevention or treatment of metabolic disorders, diabetes, and cardiovascular diseases. Particularly, the hypoglycemic effect of SX-fraction has been demonstrated in type 2 diabetic patients and its hypoglycemic mechanism, involving the insulin signal transduction pathway, has also been adequately delineated. Moreover, no adverse effects of SX-fraction have yet been seen in any patients or participants involved in such studies. D-fraction and SX-fraction are described in detail herein, suggesting that maitake is indeed a promising medicinal mushroom with great therapeutic potential.

Chapter 2 - Coronary heart disease (CHD) is the leading cause of death in the Western world after cancer according to World Health Organization. Many studies have established that high total-cholesterol levels and low-density lipoprotein (LDL) cholesterol levels are risk factors for CHD and mortality.

In public health terms, achieving a reduction in cholesterol by dietary advice is of limited effectiveness. Thus, many investigators have been exploring the possibility of increasing components in the diet which have hypocholesterolaemic effects such as the use of plant sterols (phytosterols) or cereal β-glucans creating new food products with higher levels of these compounds.

Both functional products are able to lower cholesterol in serum by reducing its absorption. However, it has been shown that in subjects who were administered β-glucan, the cholesterol biosynthetic pathway was stimulated compared with control subjects. Thus, in order to design a really effective functional food it might be necessary to combine inhibitors of the cholesterol absorption with inhibitors of the cholesterol synthesis. Edible mushrooms are good sources of phytosterol-like structures such as ergosterol, fungisterol, ergosterol peroxides and many other derivatives sharing similar bioactivities as cholesterol displacers during digestion. Moreover, mushrooms also contain specific β-glucans with glycosidic bounding 1-3, 1-6 instead of the typical 1-3, 1-4 of the cereal β-glucans but able to scavenge bile acids as one of the mechanism of action proposed for cereal β-glucans to impair cholesterol absorption. Moreover, some mushroom species also contained specific compounds able to impair the endogenous synthesis of cholesterol by inhibiting the 3-hydroxy-3-methyl-glutaryl CoA reductase (a key-enzyme in the cholesterol metabolism) or acting as reducers by other more complexes mechanisms.

Chapter 3 - The cultivation of mushrooms as food and for medicinal use began thousands of years ago. Since then, mushrooms have become among the finest culinary items and most appreciated ingredients worldwide. Furthermore, mushrooms have been viewed as a functional food because they present several previously ignored biological properties. Of the many known edible species of mushrooms, only 20 are cultivated on a large scale worldwide. The production of these species exceeds 6 million tons per year. Information about the composition of foods has become increasingly important to evaluate the quality of the foods. In terms of quality, mushrooms are a demonstrably healthy food, low in calories but high in protein, vitamins, minerals and fiber. The popularity of mushrooms has been demonstrated by the interest of many researchers who have endeavored to study the nutritional and medicinal effects of mushrooms. In this context, the discovery of a variety of biological activities has highlighted the antioxidant power of mushrooms. However, the literature reports adverse effects, side effects and toxicity in animals and in clinical trials related to the species of mushrooms marketed for human consumption. It is known that edible mushrooms do not pose risks to human health if they are adequately stored, processed and properly cultivated and if due care is taken to identify species that can be safely ingested. Additional randomized clinical trials are needed to prove the effectiveness and safety of mushrooms and to identify beneficial doses to be used in the prevention and treatment of various diseases or in health promotion. In this chapter, the authors will present and discuss the biological characteristics, antioxidant properties and interactions with human health of the mushrooms most frequently consumed by humans.

Chapter 4 - Mushroom *Inonotus obliquus*, a well-known folk medicine, has multiple health benefits such as treating malignant tumors, diabetes, cardiovascular disease, tuberculosis, liver diseases, ascariasis, and AIDS. Modern phytochemistry and pharmacological experiments had proved that polysaccharides, triterpenoids and polyphenols were the major active ingredients in *Inonotus obliquus* and they had been demonstrated to have various important biological activities including immunomodulation, antitumor, antioxidant, anti-inflammatory, hypoglycemic and antiviral activity. The purpose of this chapter is to summarize previous and current information available on the structural characterization and biological activities of the main compounds from *Inonotus obliquus* and to explore its health benefits and future research opportunities. The outcome of the studies on *Inonotus obliquus* will further expand the existing health benefits potential of mushroom *Inonotus obliquus* and provide a convincing support to its future use in modern medicine and functional foods.

Chapter 5 - The following is a list of mushrooms and mushroom products with immunostimulatory activity: *Agaricus bisporus* 2-amino-3H-phenoxazin-3-one, *Agaricus blazei. Agaricus brasiliensis* β-glucans, *Antrodia camphorata* mycelial fraction and culture filtrate, *Antrodia camphorata* immunomodulatory protein, *Calocybe indica* polysaccharide, *Cordyceps taii* polysaccharide, protein-bound polysaccharide (PSK) and polysaccharopeptide (PSP) from *Coriolus versicolor, Calocybe indica* polysaccharide, *Cordyceps taii* polysaccharide, *Cryptosporus volvatus, Cordyceps militaris,* Der p 2-Fve fusion protein, *Flammulina velutipes* fungal immunomodulatory protein, *Flammulina velutipes* hemagglutinin, *Ganoderma capense* lectin, *Ganoderma lucidum* fungal immunomodulatory protein, *Ganoderma lucidum* immunomodulating substance, *Nectria haematococca* fungal immunomodulatory protein, *Grifola frondosa* ergosterol peroxide, extracts of mycelia and culture filtrate, *Pleurotus citrinopileatus, P. australis,* and *P. pulmonarius* polysaccharides, polysaccharide, *Hypsizigus marmoreus* water-soluble extracts, *Inonotus obliquus* polysaccharide, N-benzoylphenylisoserinates of Lactarius sesquiterpenoid alcohols, *Lentinula edodes* polysaccharide, *Lentinus squarrosulus* polysaccharide, *Lentinus polychrous* compounds, *Macrolepiota dolichaula* glucan, *Morchella conica* polysaccharide, *Pleurotus Florida* polysaccharide, (1-->6)-beta-d-glucan from somatic hybrid between *Pleurotus Florida* and *Volvariella volvace,* glucan from a hybrid mushroom (backcross mating between PfloVv12 and *Volvariella volvacea*) , polysaccharide from somatic hybrid between *Pleurotus florida* and *Calocybe indica,* glucan from a hybrid mushroom of *Pleurotus florida* and *Lentinula edodes, Inonotus obliquus* water extract, hybrid of *Pleurotus florida* and *Lentinus squarrosulus:* water-soluble heteroglycan, *Pleurotus ostreatus* proteoglycan fractions, *Pleurotus ostreatus* pleuran-β-glucan, *Pleurotus ostreatus* protein fraction (Cibacron blue affinity purified protein), *Rubinoboletus ballouii* compounds, *Russula albonigra* glucan, *Trametes versicolor* glucan extracts, *Tricholoma crassum* polysaccharide, *Tricholoma matsutake* polysaccharides, *Tricholoma matsutake* alpha-D-glucan, *Tricholoma mongolicum* polysaccharide-peptide, *Volvariella volvacea* fungal immunomodulatory protein and *Volvariella volvacea* lectin.

Chapter 6 - Mushrooms have been valued as flavorful foods and as medicinal substances. Mushrooms are also recognized as functional foods for their bioactive compounds which offer multiple beneficial impacts on human health. Diabetes mellitus (DM) is a common metabolic disease characterized by high blood glucose levels. It is caused by insulin deficiency or functional disturbance of the receptors, which leads blood glucose to rise and induce metabolization disorders. Natural bioactive compounds, including polysaccharides, proteins, dietary fibres, and many other biomolecules isolated from mushrooms, have been shown to be effective in diabetes treatment as biological anti-hyperglycemic agents.

Over the past decade, numerous studies have demonstrated that mushrooms possess anti-diabetic effects, in particular, blood glucose lowering effect, glucose-stimulated insulin secretion, antioxidant, digestive enzymes (α-amylase and α-glycosidase) inhibitory effects and tyrosine kinase inhibitory effects. This chapter focuses on the anti-diabetic effects of mushrooms in both *in vitro* and *in vivo* studies and potential mechanisms of action. Future prospective for this field of research and the constraints that may affect the development of potential drug products from mushrooms are also reviewed.

Chapter 7 - Many mushrooms protect against damage induced by noxious chemicals and organisms. *Agaricus bisporus, Agaricus blazei, Antrodia cinnamomea, Coprinus comatus, Ganoderma. lucidum, Ganoderma tsugae, Inonotus xeranticus, Lentinus edodes, Morchella esculenta, Panellus serotinus, Panus giganteus, Pholiota dinghuensis, Pleurotus cornucopiae, Pleurotus florida, Pleurotus ostreatus* and *Tremella mesenterica* had hepatoprotective effects. *Pleurotus porrigens* offered protection against gentamicin- induced nephrotoxicity. *Antrodia camphorata, Cordyceps sinensis Cordyceps militaris Dictyophora indusiata, Ganoderma. lucidum, Grifola frondosa, Inonotus obliquus, Paxillus curtisii, Paxillus panuoides, Phellinus linteus* and *Phellinus rimosus* exhibited neuroprotective effects. *Hericium erinaceus* has neurotrophic effect. *Ganoderma. lucidum* exhibited cardioprotective effect. *Agaricus brasiliensis* protected against pulmonary inflammation. *Grifola frondosa Lactarius deterrimus and Castanea sativa*: demonstrated protective effects on pancreatic β-cells. *Hericium erinaceus* protected against *Salmonella typhimurium. Ganoderma lucidum* had protective effects against malaria. *Pleurotus ostreatus laccase* manifested protection against hepatitis C virus. *Phellinus baumii* offers protection against bovine collagen type II induced arthritis. *Hohenbuehelia serotina, Phellinus rimosus* and *Tremella mesenterica* displayed radioprotective effects.

Chapter 8 - Diabetes mellitus is a disease that afflicts an innumerable number of people worldwide. There has been much effort dedicated to ascertain natural products with antidiabetic potential. Mushroom species with antihyperglycemic activity comprise Agaricus bisporus, Agaricus blazei, Agaricus brasiliensis, Coriolus versicolor, Ganoderma applanatum, Grifola frondosa, Hericium erinaceus, Inonotus obliquus, Lentinus edodes, Lentinus strigosus, Mycoleptodonoides aitc hisonii, Panellus serotinus, Phellinus baumii, Phellinus linteus, Phellinus rimosus, Pleurotus ostreatus, Pleurotus cystidiosus, Tremella aurantialba, Tremella fuciformis and Tremella mesenterica. In some cases the active principles have been identified to be polysaccharides. Aldose reductase inhibitors have been identified in some mushrooms.

Chapter 9 - A diversity of mushroom species including *Agaricus bisporus, A. blazei, Ganoderma lucidum, Grifola frondosa, Hericium erinaceus, Lentinus edodes, Pholiota nameko, Pleurotus citrinopileatus P. eryngii, P. florida, P.ostreatus, P. sajor-caju sajor-caju* and *P. confluens* are able to lower blood levels of cholesterol and/or triglyceride. In an investigation, *Omphalotus olearius* OBCC 2002 and *Pleurotus ostreatus* OBCC 1031 were found to produce the largest amount of the hydroxymethylglutaryl coenzyme A reductase inhibitor lovastatin which competitively inhibits the key enzyme on the cholesterol biosynthetic pathway. Chitosan and fiber of mushroom origin can reduce blood lipid levels.

Chapter 10 - Mushrooms are a rich source of potentially exploitable proteins. Antibacterial proteins are produced by *Clitocybe sinopica, Pseudoplectanus nigrella,* and *Pleurotus eryngii.* Antifungal proteins are produced by *Agrocybe cylindracea, Armillaria mellea, Cordyceps militaris Pleurotus eryngii, Ganoderma lucidum, Hypsizygus marmoreus, Lentinus edodes, Lyophyllum shimeji, Pleurotus ostreatus, Polyporus alveolaris,* and *Tricholoma giganteum.* Antiviral proteins are produced by *Rozites caperata* and *Pseudoplctanus nigrella.* Anti-insect proteins are produced by *Clitocybe nebularis* and *Xerocomus chrysenteron.* Anti-parasite proteins are produced by *Lentinus edodes, Agaricus blazei, Agrocybe cylindracea, Boletus edulis, Ganoderma lucidum, Tricholoma mongolicum* and *Xylaria hypoxylon.*

Chapter 11 - In Nigeria and around the world, edible mushrooms are valued for their nutritional value, aroma and unique taste. Many edible mushroom species are also used in traditional medicines. For instance, in Nigeria, P. tuber-regium is commonly used in alleviating headache, stomach pain fever, cold, and constipation. Mushrooms of the genus *Pleurotus* are among the very popular edible varieties. They have rapid growth and are easy to cultivate. The mushroom species, *Pleurotus tuber-regium,* also known as the 'king tuber oyster' or 'tiger milk,' is a saprotroph, found on dead woods, and native to the tropical and subtropical regions of the world. The fungus infects dry wood, producing the sclerotium or storage tuber, which is usually buried within the decaying wood tissues or in the underlying soil. Both the sclerotia and the fruiting bodies that emerge from it are edible. The sclerotia are mostly spherical or ovoid in shape, and from dark brown to black on the surface, with a white underneath. The tuber of *Pleurotus tuber-regium* is a rich source of food nutrients, and is used in preparing foods considered delicacies in Nigeria. This chapter discusses the micronutrient benefits of the consumption of the tuber of *Pleurotus tuber-regium.* From the nutritional point of view, the sclerotia of *P. tuber-regium* would serve as a good dietary source of many essential elements to humans. The estimated elements intakes are compared with regulatory limits for the elements such as the provisional tolerable weekly intake (PTWI).

Chapter 12 - Valorization of both local agro-wastes and local biological resources by edible mushroom cultivation is a stake for many countries. Coffee-grounds has previously been shown to be a cultivation substrate for a local Algerian strain of *Pleurotus ostreatus* but the yields were low. In order to improve the process, the addition of wheat straw in mixture with coffee-grounds was studied in the present chapter. The pH of the substrates was optimized by the addition of 2 % calcium carbonate. By using a low-tech and inexpensive cultivation process at an experimental scale, improved yields were measured in mixture of coffee-grounds and wheat straw reaching biological efficiency to 102% and 153% with a local strain and a commercial strain of *P. ostreatus* respectively, when they were measured in a mixture of 50% coffee-grounds and 50% wheat straw supplemented with calcium carbonate. Analysis of physic-chemical parameter in cultivation substrates revealed that the two strains had the same behavior for substrate transformation. Coffee grounds is a waste having a good potential as component of cultivation substrates for the production of *Pleurotus* mushrooms.

In: Mushrooms
Editor: Grégoire Pesti

ISBN: 978-1-63117-521-3
© 2014 Nova Science Publishers, Inc.

Chapter 1

BIOLOGICAL SIGNIFICANCE AND MEDICINAL PROPERTIES OF THE MAITAKE MUSHROOM

Sensuke Konno, Ph.D. [*]
Department of Urology, New York Medical College, Valhalla, NY, US

ABSTRACT

Maitake mushroom (*Grifola frondosa*) is an edible, medicinal mushroom. It has been extensively studied for the past 30 years, revealing numerous medicinal properties that could provide great health benefits. Those include various physiological benefits ranging from immunomodulatory and antitumor activities to treatment for diabetes, hypertension, hypercholesterolemia, viral infections (hepatitis B and human immunodeficiency virus), and obesity. Two distinct bioactive extracts have been obtained from maitake and are called "maitake D-fraction" and "maitake SX-fraction". A number of scientific studies have been performed on these two maitake derivatives, which are thus well characterized. Maitake D-fraction consists of proteoglucan (protein-bound polysaccharide), or more specifically known as β-glucan. This β-glucan is an active component of D-fraction and its two major biological activities, *immunomodulatory* and *antitumor*, have been the main target for scientific and clinical research. Various *in vitro*, *in vivo*, and clinical studies showed that D-fraction was capable of modulating immunologic and hematologic parameters, significantly inhibiting or regressing the cancer cell growth, and even improving the quality of life of cancer patients. In addition, the synergistic potentiation of D-fraction with vitamin C demonstrated *in vitro* is rather interesting and has clinical implication, because such combination therapy could be performed solely or be used as an adjuvant regimen with current therapies to improve the overall efficacy. As far as the safety of D-fraction is concerned, it has been exempted from a Phase I toxicology test by the US Food and Drug Administration (FDA) and also approved for the Investigational New Drug (IND) application for a Phase II pilot study on patients with advanced cancers. Thus, its safety has been well granted. In contrast, maitake SX-fraction is a water-soluble glycoprotein and has been shown to primarily have hypoglycemic (glucose-lowering), hypotensive (blood pressure-lowering), and cholesterol/lipids-lowering effects in various

---

[*] Correspondence: Sensuke Konno, Ph.D. New York Medical College, Department of Urology, BSB, Room A03, Valhalla, NY 10595 USA, Tel: (914) 594-3745, Fax: (914) 594-4428, E-mail: sensuke_konno@nymc.edu.

study settings, implying potential prevention or treatment of metabolic disorders, diabetes, and cardiovascular diseases. Particularly, the hypoglycemic effect of SX-fraction has been demonstrated in type 2 diabetic patients and its hypoglycemic mechanism, involving the insulin signal transduction pathway, has also been adequately delineated. Moreover, no adverse effects of SX-fraction have yet been seen in any patients or participants involved in such studies.

D-fraction and SX-fraction are described in detail herein, suggesting that maitake is indeed a promising medicinal mushroom with great therapeutic potential.

INTRODUCTION

The maitake mushroom (*Grifola frondosa*) is an edible and tasty mushroom, which literally means *dancing mushroom*. Besides its great taste, maitake can be also considered one of the medicinal mushrooms that are believed to provide health benefits and are often used for therapeutic purposes. Unlike many mushrooms, maitake has been extensively studied in the past 30 years, revealing numerous medicinal properties that could provide remarkable health benefits. In particular, it has been shown to have immunomodulatory and antitumor activities and other physiological benefits, including diabetes, hypertension, hypercholesterolemia, hepatitis B infection and obesity [1-9]. It is also noteworthy that the antiviral activity of maitake against human immunodeficiency virus (HIV)/AIDS (acquired immune deficiency syndrome) was confirmed by the U.S. National Cancer Institute (NCI) in 1992 [10].

The majority of maitake research described above has been performed using its bioactive extract, namely "Maitake D-fraction (DF)", while other studies have been performed with a different preparation, named "SX-fraction (SXF)", from the same maitake. In other words, two distinct bioactive extracts are obtained from maitake and they are quite different in their physical/chemical characteristics and medicinal properties, such as potential prevention and/or treatment of various diseases and disorders. They are unique and promising natural agents with diverse potential, and further investigations are currently underway. The biological significance and medicinal properties of D-fraction and SX-fraction are described in detail and also discussed herein.

MAITAKE D-FRACTION (DF)

Maitake D-fraction (DF) is the protein-bound polysaccharide or *proteoglucan*, consisting of *β-glucan* (either β-1,6-linked glucan with β-1,3 branches or β-1,3-linked glucan branched with β-1,6 glucosides; *see* Figure 1) as a main polysaccharide backbone to which a few *uncharacterized protein units* are attached. In other words, D-fraction is *not* a pure form of β-glucan that is yet a core constituent but is a "proteoglucan" having both β-glucan (major) *and* protein (minor) portions. This is a huge proteoglucan with a molecular weight of ~1 x 10^6 dalton [1, 11], having acid-insoluble, alkali-soluble and a hot water-extractable nature [1]. In addition, the biological activities of D-fraction have been shown to stem primarily from "β-glucan", which was thus considered a bioactive component of D-fraction [1, 3, 5, 7-11]. Particularly, its two major biological activities, such as *immunomodulatory* and *antitumor* [1, 5, 11], have been well documented implying its clinical and therapeutic uses.

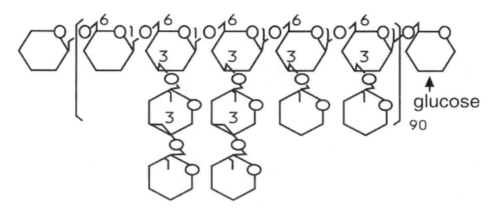

Figure 1. Schematic structure of DF (with β-linkages).

Immunomodulatory Activity of D-Fraction

The innate immune system is the first line of defense against microbial invasion, immediately recognizing and coping with such infections. Although various *β-glucans* have been known to commonly exhibit immunomodulatory activity for a long time [12], such underlying cellular and molecular mechanisms have not been fully defined but are currently being unveiled. Since D-fraction has a core β-glucan structure for its inherent bioactivities, all immunomodulatory activities demonstrated with β-glucans would be substantially relevant to those exhibited by D-fraction. Such immunomodulations by β-glucans include mitogenecity and activation of immune effector cells such as lymphocytes, macrophages, dendritic cells, and natural killer (NK) cells, stimulating the production of various cytokines and chemokines, such as interleukins (IL-1β, IL-6, IL-8, IL-12 etc.), tumor necrosis factor-α (TNF-α), and interferon-γ (IFN-γ) [13, 14]. However, the first step in triggering the immune-modulating effects by β-glucans requires the specific cellular receptors that recognize and bind to them. In fact, a number of "β-glucan receptors" have been identified on both immune and non-immune cells, including macrophages, NK cells, monocytes, neutrophils, endothelial cells, fibroblasts and so forth [15]. Those receptors include complement receptor 3 (CR3), lactosyl ceramide, scavenger receptors, and Dectin-1 [16]. Particularly, Dectin-1 appears to be the most interesting receptor, predominantly found on macrophage/monocyte and neutrophil lineages, and can recognize soluble and particulate β-glucans [17]. It then mediates a variety of cellular immune-modulating effects, such as phagocytosis, endocytosis, and the oxidative burst, and also induces the production of pro-inflammatory cytokines/chemokines including TNF-α, IL-12, and macrophage-inflammatory protein-2 (MIP-2) [16-18], although they could work in a positive or negative manner, depending on the microenvironments where they are regulated or interact with certain/specific factors. Nevertheless, β-glucans would activate a wide variety of innate host defenses against infections with fungal, protozoal, bacterial, and viral pathogens as well as preventing cancer development (carcinogenesis). This well represents how various β-glucans (including D-fraction) would induce the immunomodulatory effects: i.e., binding of β-glucans to specific receptors, triggering activation of immune effector cells, stimulating production of cytokines/chemokines, and targeting and attacking foreign pathogens and (cancer) cells.

The following studies describe various immunologic and hematologic aspects of D-fraction; however, it should be noted that D-fraction used in some of those studies were *essentially* all the same, but not exactly the same or identical, due to changes in suppliers/manufacturers of D-fraction or maitake extracts during the past 30 years. Nonetheless, all data obtained from the studies used D-fraction or "similar maitake extracts" are fully relevant.

A) Effects of D-Fraction on Hematopoietic Stem Cells

The maitake extract, similar to D-fraction, has been reported to enhance proliferation of mouse bone marrow cells (BMCs) and their differentiation into granulocytes-macrophages (GMs) [19]. In addition, this extract has protected the colony formation unit (CFU) response of GMs (CFU-GM response) from doxorubicin (DOX)-induced hematopoietic suppression [19]. Similar results were obtained from a separate study using human umbilical cord blood (CB) cells: the extract also induced differentiation of CB cells into CFU-GM and reduced DOX-induced hematopoietic toxicity [20]. Thus, these results suggest that maitake extract might be capable of inducing hematopoietic cell differentiation and protecting them from the toxic effects of chemotherapy. In particular, maitake extract or D-fraction may have clinical implications in treatment of myelosuppression and other hematopoietic disorders/diseases.

B) Effects of D-Fraction on Immune System In Vitro or In Vivo

To assess the immunomodulatory activity of D-fraction or its actual effects on the immune system, a number of studies have been conducted *in vitro* (cell cultures) as well as *in vivo* (animals and humans). In animal study, possible antibacterial activity of D-fraction through stimulating the host immune system has been investigated in *Listeria*-infected mice. *Listeria monocytogenes* are the gram-positive, food-mediated bacteria, causing the listeria [21], and vancomycine (VCM) is usually the primary therapeutic modality but its high dose is known to cause various side effects. It is then possible if the VCM dose could be reduced once combined with D-fraction, alleviating side effects while improving the efficacy. Such combination of D-fraction and VCM resulted in the longer/better survival rate (60%) of *Listeria*-infected mice than those treated with VCM alone [22]. However, all of non-treated control mice died in 3 days after the inoculation. Moreover, macrophages and T cells in D-fraction/VCM-treated mice exhibited 2.7 times higher IL-1 production and 2.6 times greater bactericidal activity, respectively, than those in control mice [22]. Thus, these findings suggest an adjuvant role of D-fraction in antibacterial treatment for patients in a high-risk group.

The macrophage-mediated immune response is mediated through activation of inducible nitric oxide synthase (iNOS) with nitric oxide (NO) production [13]. The recognition of microbes by macrophages would lead to phagocytosis, activating several enzymes including iNOS that facilitates the production of bactericidal reactive oxygen intermediates and NO [13]. Accordingly, whether D-fraction would induce iNOS-mediated NO production in RAW264.7 cells, a murine macrophage cell line was examined. Such study showed that D-fraction was capable of inducing iNOS-mediated NO production by RAW cells, leading to the significant reduction in cell viability of human hepatoma-derived huH-1 cells [23]. This antitumor effect of RAW cells is thus due to activation of iNOS by D-fraction, not to direct cytotoxic activity of D-fraction on huH-1 cells, demonstrating the macrophage-mediated antitumor effect. In addition, D-fraction has demonstrated immune enhancement in tumor-bearing mice in the early study [24]: immune effector cells and cytokines including NK cells, T lymphocytes (CTL), lymphokine-activated killer cells, and IL-1 and IL-2 were all activated 1.5-2.2 fold (compared to controls) following the D-fraction treatment in mice. Concurrently, the rate of cancer proliferation was significantly reduced with D-fraction, demonstrating its antitumor activity. Thus, these results suggest that D-fraction appears to be a potent immunomodulator, which is capable of inhibiting or slowing down the cancer cell proliferation through its immune-modulating effects.

NK cells are a class of lymphocytes that rapidly respond to intracellular infections with viruses or bacteria, killing those infected cells and producing the macrophage-activating cytokines. However, NK cells do not express T-cell receptors that recognize specific peptides presented on the major histocompatibility complex (MHC), but they can recognize the surface changes that occur on infected cells or a variety of cancer cells [25]. NK cells are also known to have two relevant functions [26]. One of them is cytotoxicity, mediated through the recognition and lysis of target cells such as virus- or bacteria-infected cells. The other function is to produce various cytokines such as IFN-γ, TNF-α, and granulocyte/macrophage-colony-stimulating factor (GM-CSF), which can modulate natural and specific immune responses. Hence, potential effects of D-fraction on NK cells have been investigated in cancer patients and mice. A limited number of clinical trials of D-fraction showed that cytotoxic activity of NK cells in 8 cancer patients were elevated by 1.2-2.7 times with the D-fraction treatment and even sustained for one year [27]. To elucidate the mechanism of such sustained NK activity with D-fraction, further studies were performed in mice as well as cell cultures. C3H/HeN mice were implanted with MM-46 breast carcinoma cells and received D-fraction intraperitoneally (i.p.) for 19 days. The results then showed that the levels of TNF-α and IFN-γ released from spleen cells, and TNF-α expression in NK cells, were significantly increased in tumor-bearing mice receiving D-fraction (compared to control mice without D-fraction), as their tumor growths were also markedly suppressed [27]. This increased TNF-α and IFN-γ release is typically indicative of activation of NK cells. Moreover, the increased IL-12 secretion from macrophage RAW 264.7 cells was also detected following the D-fraction treatment [27]. Since IL-12 is critical to the functions of NK and T cells, the long-term NK cytotoxicity with D-fraction could be at least in part attributed to the increased IL-12 release from macrophages. Indeed, NK cells can be even more activated by IFN-γ released from them, as well as activated T cells. Similarly, in a separate study, activation of peripheral blood NK cells and their sustained cytotoxicity with D-fraction was observed in patients with lung, breast, and liver cancer [28].

Besides the innate immune response primarily involving NK cells and macrophages, there is another one called the adaptive immune response that comprises T and B cells. T cells or CTL include T-helper (Th) cells and cytotoxic T (Tc) cells. Th cells activate B cells to secrete antibodies targeting foreign antigens (known as the antibody response), while Tc cells attack and destroy infected host cells with pathogens (as the cell-mediated immune response) [29]. Th cells can be also classified into Th-1 and Th-2 cells according to the types of cytokines they produce. Th-1 cells produce IL-2, IFN-γ, and TNF-β (introducing cellular immunity to the organisms), while Th-2 cells produce IL-4, IL-5, IL-6, IL-10 and IL-13 (activating humoral immunity) [30]. One study showed that D-fraction decreased B cell activation but increased Th-1 cell activation in tumor-bearing C3H/HeN mice, resulting in enhanced cellular immunity. D-fraction also stimulated the production of IFN-γ, IL-12p70, and IL-18, but suppressed IL-4 production [31]. These results suggest that D-fraction may establish Th-1 dominance that induces cellular immunity in the population with Th-2 dominance due to carcinoma.

It was yet of interest to perform the same study above using "BALB/c" mice (instead of C3H/HeN mice), because they have been genetically altered to have a "Th-2" dominant response. Such study revealed that D-fraction was capable of inducing the differentiation of tumor-bearing BALB/c mice with the Th-2 response into the Th-1 dominant response, mediated through enhancement of IL-12p70 production by dendritic cells (DCs), which were antigen-presenting cells (APCs) with a unique ability to activate both Th and Tc cells and produce IL-12 and INF-γ [32, 33]. These results thus suggest that D-fraction may stimulate DCs, through activation of macrophages and NK cells, inducing innate T cells into Th-1 cells.

C) Effects of Maitake Extract or D-Fraction on Immunologic or Hematologic Parameters in Cancer Patients or Normal Subjects in Controlled Clinical Trials

It has been recently reported that the maitake extract (similar to D-fraction) was used in a Phase I/II trial of breast cancer patients to assess its immunologic effects. Thirty-four postmenopausal breast cancer patients, free of disease after the initial treatment, followed an oral regimen of this maitake extract for 3 weeks and various immunologic parameters were analyzed [34]. No apparent toxicity of the extract was observed but there was a statistically significant association between the extract and immunologic function: some immunologic parameters were up-regulated with the extract while others were down-regulated. For example, depending upon the dosage of the extract given, $CD3^+/CD25^+$, $CD4^+/CD25^+$, IL-2, or IL-10 was significantly increased but IFN-γ production was decreased – *this* is indicative of the modulation of cell-mediated immunity with the extract. Thus, these results show that oral administration of the extract indeed *modulates* immunologic parameters in these cancer patients, so that they should be aware that it could stimulate as well as depress their immune function.

This study may then raise the question on how such maitake extract or D-fraction would affect "healthy individuals", and such study has also been conducted. Twenty-eight healthy subjects participated in a randomized double-blinded trial of D-fraction for a month. Various hematologic parameters including complete blood count, serum glucose, total cholesterol and high-density lipoprotein (HDL), bilirubin, creatinine, hepatic enzymes, etc. were evaluated before and after a 1-month D-fraction regimen [35]. All hematologic data were subjected to statistical analysis. First of all, no participants presented palpable ailments or adverse effects during the trial. Second, no substantial and clear differences/changes in 24 parameters tested were seen between the control and the D-fraction groups after this 1-month trial. However, the *statistically* significant differences ($p < 0.05$) in hemoglobin, hematocrit, eosinophils, mean corpuscular volume (MCV), alkaline phosphatase, glutamic-pyruvic transaminase/ alanine aminotransferase (GPT/ALT), glutamic-oxaloacetic transaminase/aspartate aminotransferase (GOT/AST), cholesterol, triglycerides, and creatinine, were seen in between the D-fraction and placebo groups [35]. In addition, although the differences may not be clearly significant, those in red blood cells (RBC), lymphocytes, mean corpuscular hemoglobin (MCH), mean corpuscular hemoglobin concentration (MCHC), and HDL were *nearly* statistically significant (0.05< p <0.1) [35]. Moreover, there was the possible *time* trend (prediction) that the differences in some parameters could become significant in the long-term (i.e., longer than one month of this trial). One may then make some speculations; for example, the decreased creatinine concentration with D-fraction could indicate improved renal function, while the reduced levels of GPT/ALT and GOT/AST indicate improved liver function with reduced hepatic cell injury. Similarly, the decreased cholesterol and triglyceride levels could be indicative of improved lipid metabolism, preventing potential adverse sequels associated with cardiovascular disease. Apart from these speculations, this study yet confirms that D-fraction undoubtedly has certain hematologic effects on normal subjects and larger randomized studies are thus required for demonstrating its potential health benefits.

Antitumor/Anticancer Activity of D-Fraction

It has been known that many pure β-glucans extracted from mushrooms were less effective when given *orally* to animals bearing cancers, although they could be effective or exhibit antitumor activity when administered *intravenously* or *intraperitoneally* [36]. However, a number of studies have then demonstrated antitumor activity of orally administered D-fraction *in vivo*, which was mainly associated with immunomodulatory activity described above.

When an allogeneic Sarcoma-180 tumor was implanted into ICR-nu/nu mice (lacking matured T cells), orally administered D-fraction was capable of inhibiting the tumor growth by 88% compared to control mice (received no D-fraction) [37]. Similar results were also obtained from the studies using different mice bearing some syngeneic tumors. Following oral D-fraction administration, C3H/HeN mice bearing MM-46 carcinoma (breast cancer), CDF1 mice with IMC carcinoma (skin cancer), and C57BL/6 mice with B-16 melanoma (skin cancer) showed the tumor inhibition of 64%, 75%, and 27%, respectively [37] (Table 1). It is thus practical that *oral* administration of D-fraction would allow its easy intake for a clinical utility.

Table 1. Antitumor effect of DF on tumor-bearing mice

Tumors	Host Mice	Growth Inhibition (%)[a]
Sarcoma 180	ICR-nu/nu	88%
MM-46 (Breast carcinoma)	C3H/HeN	64%
IMC (Skin carcinoma)	CDF1	75%
B-16 (Melanoma)	C57BL/6	27%

[a] The percent (%) relative to control mice received no DF (0% inhibition).
Abbreviations: DF, D-fraction.

Another interesting study was to assess if D-fraction might prevent carcinogenesis in normal cells, i.e., anti-carcinogenic activity. A known carcinogen, N-nitrosodi-n-butylamine (NDBA), was given to mice with food: the control group received only normal feed (with NDBA) while the D-fraction group received food (with NDBA) and oral D-fraction supplement. After 60 days, the number of tumors appeared or developed in the liver was determined. The cancer incidence rate in the D-fraction group was merely ~10% compared to that in the control group (100% as the number of cancer cells found) [38]. A similar study using another known carcinogen, 3-methylcholanthrene (3-MCA), on mice has also been conducted. An injection of 3-MCA (suspended in olive oil) was given to the back of mice (n=10/group) once, and on the 15th day, D-fraction or saline solution (control) was orally administered for 15 consecutive days. After 30 days, the number of mice with cancer was ~93% in the control group but only 31% in the D-fraction group [39]. These findings suggest that D-fraction appears to significantly prevent carcinogenesis or may have anti-carcinogenic activity.

A critical issue following carcinogenesis is to slow down cancer progression or inhibit cancer metastasis, and such anti-metastatic activity of D-fraction has been investigated using tumor-bearing mice. MM-164 liver carcinoma was injected into the left rear footpad of mice, which was then amputated after 2 days. Either normal food alone (control) or that with D-fraction was given to (amputated) mice daily, and after 30 days the number of tumor foci metastasized to the liver was determined.

Compared to the control group, cancer metastasis to the liver was remarkably prevented by over 90% in the D-fraction group [38]. In another study, MM-46 breast carcinoma was intraperitoneally implanted in C3H/HeN mice and subsequently the palpable tumor formed (~7 mm in diameter) and was surgically removed. D-fraction or saline (control) was then given to mice for 10 consecutive days and the tumor foci spread to other organs were assessed in sacrificed mice. The tumor metastasis (the number of metastasized tumor foci found) was inhibited by 92% in the D-fraction group whereas no such inhibition (0%) was seen in the control group [39]. Thus, D-fraction appears to have anti-metastatic activity, presumably activating immunocompetent cells that would then necrotize tumor cells present in the blood and/or lymphatic vessels.

Additionally, the combination of D-fraction and mitomycin C (MMC), a chemotherapeutic drug, demonstrated the augmented antitumor activity *in vivo*. Tumor (MM-164)-bearing mice that received D-fraction alone showed greater tumor growth inhibition (~80%) than that (~45%) in those that received MMC alone. When D-fraction and MMC were given together (by cutting each initial dose by half) to mice, the tumor growth was almost completely (98%) inhibited [24].

This enhanced antitumor effect of D-fraction/MMC combination could be explained by the stimulated immune response with D-fraction (as an immunomodulatory) accompanied by the cytotoxic effect of MMC. The similar study of D-fraction/MMC combination was performed in mice bearing MM-46 breast tumor [40]. MMC alone had antitumor activity but with immunosuppression; however, its combination with D-fraction enhanced antitumor activity and alleviated immunosuppression, perhaps due to the increased immunocompetent cell proliferation.

Further studies then revealed that such combination led to the increased CD28 expression on CD8[+] T cells as well as the increased IL-12 production (through activated macrophages), indicating enhancement of the Th1-dominant response. Thus, these results suggest that D-fraction is capable of ameliorating potential side effects of chemotherapeutic drugs and providing better clinical outcomes for cancer patients. It further supports the notion that D-fraction could be used as an adjuvant agent for chemotherapy in those patients with cancer.

Clinical Trials of D-Fraction on Cancer Patients

Regarding clinical trials of D-fraction, not many human trials have been performed and little information is available. Yet, a non-randomized clinical study of D-fraction on 165 patients with various types of advanced cancers has been conducted in Japan [24]. Such study showed that tumor regression or significant symptomatic improvements with D-fraction were observed in 73% of breast cancer patients, 67% of lung cancer patients and 47% of liver cancer patients. When D-fraction was given to the patients receiving chemotherapy, the response rates have improved from 12 to 28%. Overall, this study illustrated that the clinical status of patients with breast, prostate, lung, and liver cancers was significantly improved with D-fraction, while less effective on those with bone and stomach cancers or leukemia [24, 41]. In addition, interestingly various side effects of chemotherapy on all types of cancer patients were ameliorated with D-fraction administration. It is well known that chemotherapy often lowers or damages the immune system, but D-fraction may help maintain optimal activities of key immunocompetent cells, minimizing such side effects. In fact, adverse symptoms such as nausea, hair loss, and leucopenia were all alleviated in 90% of those patients, while a reduction in pain was reported in 83% of patients [24]. Thus, D-fraction appears to improve quality of life in patients and might be considered a useful adjuvant in ongoing cancer chemotherapy.

In addition, once D-fraction was exempted from a Phase I toxicology test by the FDA, it was also approved for the Investigational New Drug (IND) application for a Phase II pilot study on patients with advanced breast and prostate cancer [42]. It would be worthwhile to briefly mention some of FDA-sanctioned D-fraction studies on prostate cancer patients [43]. Those patients have orally received the appropriate amounts (calculated from the body weight) of D-fraction daily with 2,000 mg VC and were evaluated for general condition, blood chemistry, and immune status (e.g., activities of NK cells and CTL). Additionally, the levels of serum prostate-specific antigen (PSA), a widely used biochemical marker for prostate cancer, have also been measured for assessing the disease status of these patients.

Case 1: A 68-year-old patient was diagnosed for prostate cancer with an initial PSA of 20 ng/ml (a normal PSA range: <4.0 ng/ml) in 1998. His PSA steadily went up every year until year 2000, indicating a possible progression of disease. After he started taking D-fraction with VC in 2001, his PSA came down significantly in 3 months and all other parameters also looked stable. Thus, this report suggests that cancer progression might have been slowed down or stopped by D-fraction.

Case 2: The initial PSA of 7 ng/ml (in 1995) in a 72-year-old patient declined to 1.7 ng/ml by year 2000 following primary hormonal therapy. He appeared to be in disease *remission*, but his PSA started rising again in June of 2001 and further went up to 3.9 ng/ml by September, indicating a possible recurrence or progression of cancer. He was immediately placed on a D-fraction regimen and his PSA gradually came down to 2.2 ng/ml within 3 months. This report also suggests that D-fraction may slow down or stop cancer progression.

Case 3: This is rather an interesting case with a high Gleason score of 7 (with PSA of 8 ng/ml) in a 65-year-old patient. The "Gleason score" is a pathological grading system of 1-10 based on the histological examination of biopsy specimen [44], helping us assess a probability of having cancer metastasis – in general, the higher score indicates the greater risk of metastasis. Since his initial PSA had not notably come down in 2 years, he decided to have surgery (radical prostatectomy) in 2001. His PSA went down significantly to 2 ng/ml within a month after his surgery, although we were still concerned about possible metastasis because of his high Gleason score. As a precaution, he then started taking D-fraction and his PSA further declined to <0.1 ng/ml in 6 months. His prognosis was good with all parameters being normal. This report suggests that D-fraction may also suppress metastatic disease or stop cancer progression to a fatal hormone-refractory state, although it is possible that surgery could have completely removed the tumor before metastasis started up.

These case studies suggest that D-fraction may help lower the serum PSA levels in prostate cancer patients and probably slows down or prevents disease progression or metastasis. We also found that D-fraction appeared to sustain the high levels of NK cell and CTL activities, indicating an alert immune surveillance, and to improve physical and/or mental soundness, and quality of life of these patients. Taken all together, D-fraction is indeed safe to cancer patients (as well as healthy subjects [35]) and may also offer some health benefits, comfort, and hope to those patients.

Synergistic Potentiation of D-Fraction with Vitamin C

Vitamin C (VC) or ascorbic acid could be the most popular nutritional supplement known and taken by numerous people worldwide. VC is a water-soluble antioxidant that can scavenge free radicals, thereby protecting the cells from lethal oxidative stress [45]. Interestingly, VC may also act as a *pro-oxidant* to generate free radicals, particularly through the reduction of metal ions such as iron or copper – this is known as the Fenton reaction [46]. In other words, VC has a *dual* role that can act as an antioxidant or a pro-oxidant, depending upon its cellular concentrations and the availability/presence of cellular iron. Besides such redox properties of VC, it has been well documented that VC also has an anticancer effect on various cancer cells *in vitro*, due to its pro-oxidant activity generating free radical (hydrogen peroxide, H_2O_2) rather than its popular antioxidant action [47]. Yet, another important question is if VC could actually induce such generation of free radicals (particularly H_2O_2) *in vivo*. Actually, it has been shown that a measurable or significant amount of H_2O_2 was generated with the high serum concentrations of VC achieved through its intravenous (i.v.) administration in mice [48]. The exact mechanism(s) is not completely understood but it may likely involve or interact with some protein-bound metal cations. In addition, this VC-mediated H_2O_2 production *in vivo* appears to only take place in extracellular fluids, not in blood, since antioxidant enzymes (e.g., catalase, glutathione peroxidase etc.) present in erythrocytes could efficiently remove or scavenge H_2O_2 [49].

VC has also been reported to promote the efficacy of several chemotherapeutic drugs *in vivo* [50]; however, the *oral* administration of VC (6,100 mg) had no effects on patients undergoing chemotherapy [51] and even the higher VC dose (10 g) was ineffective on patients with advanced cancer [52]. Moreover, pharmacokinetic studies revealed that the oral administration of VC would not achieve its plasma concentrations higher than 50-100 µM [53]. However, the Phase I trial of i.v. administration of VC to cancer patients has reported that the high-dose VC instillation demonstrated an anticancer effect. In this study, the i.v. infusion of VC allowed the injection of extremely high VC doses, up to 1.5 g/kg (body weight), to cancer patients, raising its plasma concentrations >10 mM for over 4 h, which were previously shown to be sufficient to induce cancer cell death *in vitro* [54]. This new approach of i.v. administration of VC allows it to achieve the therapeutic (effective) plasma level but yet remains controversial, requiring sufficient clinical data. Thus, further clinical studies are warranted to adequately address the true efficacy of VC in cancer therapy.

Synergism: Enhanced D-Fraction Activity with VC

Apart from various aspects of VC described above, it was interesting for us to learn that VC had been postulated to enhance bioactivity of mushroom extract or specifically β-glucans [55], although the exact mechanism needs to be yet defined. Since D-fraction has β-glucan as its major bioactive element, mentioned earlier, and could be potentiated with VC, it was reasonable that VC was included in the D-fraction regimen for prostate cancer patients described above, although the actual effects of VC with D-fraction have not yet been addressed. To examine such combined effects of D-fraction and VC on cancer cells, we performed the *in vitro* study using human prostate cancer PC-3 cells as our experimental model. This study was published previously [56], but it should be noted that the concentrations of D-fraction used in *all studies* have been *normalized* in the following studies described because the stock D-fraction concentrations had varied with some modifications made on formulating D-fraction by the manufacturer.

A) Effects of D-Fraction or VC on PC-3 Cell Growth

Prostate cancer is the second-leading cause of cancer death in elderly men in the United States. Several conventional therapies such as androgen ablation, chemotherapy, brachytherapy (radioactive seeds implant), radiotherapy, immunotherapy, surgery, etc. are currently available; however, none of them has yet been able to achieve the expected level of efficacy [57, 58]. To explore a more effective modality for prostate cancer, we investigated if D-fraction might inhibit or slow down the growth of human prostate cancer PC-3 cells, derived from a patient with bone metastasis [59].

PC-3 cells were cultured with varying concentrations (0-1,000 µg/ml) of D-fraction and cell number/viability was assessed in 72 h. This dose-response study showed that no effects of D-fraction were seen up to 250 µg/ml but the significant 19% and 65% growth reductions were observed at 500 and 1,000 µg/ml, respectively (Figure 2). When cells were cultured with the varying concentration (0-700 µM) of VC for 72 h, no apparent effects were seen up to 200 µM but the 12%, 36% and 80% reductions in cell viability were attained with 300, 500 and 700 µM, respectively (Figure 3). Thus, these results show that D-fraction is capable of inhibiting cell growth at concentrations ≥500 µg/ml and VC can also induce the significant cell viability reduction at ≥300 µM.

B) Synergistic Effects of D-Fraction Combined with VC on PC-3 Cell Growth

Since it would be practical if the relatively high concentration of D-fraction required could be *lowered* without losing its potency, we next examined whether VC might help augment D-fraction potency as it has been postulated above [55]. PC-3 cells were treated for 24 h with relatively low, ineffective concentrations (0-250 µg/ml) of D-fraction in combination with similarly ineffective concentrations (0-200 µM) of VC. Among various combinations tested, particularly the combination of 200 µg/ml D-fraction and 200 µM VC resulted in ~95% cell death in 24 h (Figure 4).

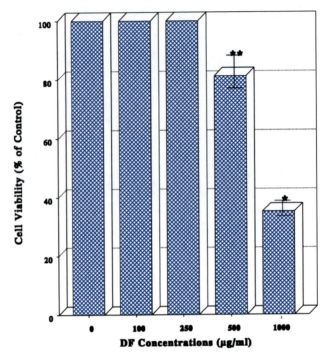

Figure 2. Effect of DF on PC-3 cell viability. PC-3 cells were cultured with varying concentrations of DF (0-1,000 µg/ml) for 72 h, and cell viability was determined by MTT assay. All data are mean ± SD (standard deviation) from three separate experiments [*p <0.02 and **p <0.05 versus DF (0 µg/ml)].

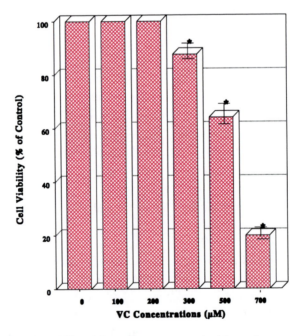

Figure 3. Effect of VC on cell viability. After cells were treated with varying concentrations of VC (0-700 µM), cell viability in 72 h was determined by MTT assay. All data are mean ± SD from three independent experiments [*p <0.05 versus VC (0 µM)].

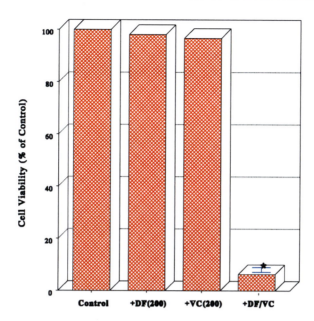

Figure 4. Effects of DF/VC combination on cell viability. PC-3 cells were treated for 24 h with the ineffective concentrations (0-250 µg/ml) of DF in combination with the similarly ineffective concentrations (0-200 µM) of VC. Particularly, the combination of 200 µg/ml DF and 200 µM VC resulted in ~95% cell death (*p <0.01 versus control) as shown here.

Since neither 200 µg/ml D-fraction nor 200 µM VC alone showed any effects on cell growth/viability, such profound (~95%) cell death induced by this particular combination is more likely attributed to a synergistic potentiation of these two agents. It is then plausible that VC may primarily serve as an adjuvant factor to augment the D-fraction activity. Thus, this finding suggests that the relatively low concentrations of D-fraction with no cytotoxic activity could be yet synergistically potentiated with VC to become highly cytotoxic to PC-3 cells.

C) Oxidative Stress Exerted by D-Fraction/VC Combination

Lipid peroxidation (LPO) assay is often used for assessing damage or perturbation in the plasma membrane due to oxidative stress, by measuring the amount of malondialdehyde (MDA) formed, an end product from peroxidation of polyunsaturated fatty acids [61]. This assay was then performed on the cells exposed to the combination of D-fraction (200 µg/ml) and VC (200 µM) for 3 h, which was sufficient to exert oxidative stress. Such analyses revealed that the MDA level in D-fraction/VC-exposed cells was almost 2-fold higher than those in the control, sole D-fraction- or sole VC-exposed cells (Figure 5). These results indicate that significant plasma membrane damage through oxidative stress has been made in D-fraction/VC-exposed cells, ultimately leading to cell death [62]. Thus, these findings support the notion that D-fraction/VC-induced cell death is at least in part due to oxidative stress, presumably through generated H_2O_2.

However, one may raise some concern for a clinical utility of D-fraction/VC combination because their cytotoxic mechanism appears to be primarily attributed to oxidative stress. It is conceivable that such resulting oxidative stress could cause a non-specific random damage to even normal cells as well as cancer cells. Interestingly, cancer cells have been shown to be *more vulnerable* to oxidative stress than normal cells [63]. Although the reason(s) for such a different susceptibility is not fully understood, several evidences point to the inherent difference in *antioxidant enzymes* whose primary function is to scavenge harmful free radicals. For example, two common antioxidant enzymes, catalase and glutathione peroxidase, were often found to be deficient or have a significantly low activity in cancer cells [64]. Moreover, the reduced expressions of catalase and superoxide dismutase were also detected in prostate cancer specimens, compared to those in normal or benign prostatic hyperplasia specimens [65]. Thus, a difference in cellular antioxidant enzymes may at least account for a different susceptibility (to oxidative stress) between normal and cancer cells. It is then plausible that oxidative stress exerted by a D-fraction/VC combination could be severe enough to kill *cancer* cells (with a *low* antioxidant enzyme activity) but might *not* be severe enough to even harm normal cells (with a *high* enzyme activity). In other words, the D-fraction/VC combination would kill only cancer cells but normal cells may remain intact. Therefore, D-fraction/VC combination appears to effectively and selectively target cancer cells, implying its clinical/therapeutic utility.

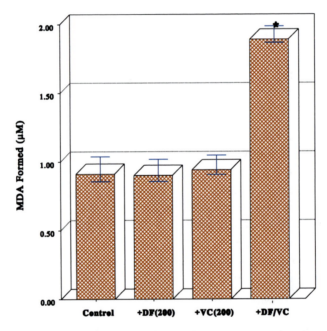

Figure 5. Assessment of oxidative stress by LPO assay. Cells were exposed to the combination of DF (200 µg/ml) and VC (200 µM) for 3 h, and the amount of malondialdehyde (MDA) formed in control, DF alone-, VC alone-, and DF/VC-exposed cells was determined for comparison. The data are mean ± SD from three separate experiments (*p <0.01 versus control).

D) Induction of Apoptosis by D-Fraction/VC Combination

The next valid question is exactly how PC-3 cells would die from the D-fraction/VC treatment – whether they may die with necrosis or apoptosis (programmed cell death). Despite a drastic reduction (~95%) in cell viability induced by the D-fraction/VC combination, cell fragmentation or disintegration was rarely observed, indicating that such cell death would be unlikely due to necrosis. Accordingly, we performed an *in situ* hybridization (ISH) assay to test possible induction of apoptosis by the D-fraction/VC combination. ISH analyses then revealed that the cells treated with the combination of D-fraction (200 μg/ml) and VC (200 μM) for 24 h exhibited a positive brown staining while a negative staining was seen in control cells. Since distinctly fragmented DNA can be stained *brown* with ISH assay, this positive staining is indicative of apoptotic cell death [66]. Thus, these results suggest that D-fraction/VC-induced cell death most likely results from apoptosis or follows the apoptotic pathway.

Combined Effects of D-Fraction and Chemotherapeutic Drugs

It was of interest to further examine whether cytotoxic activity of D-fraction/VC combination could be comparable to that of chemotherapeutic drugs, and VC or D-fraction might also act as the adjuvant agents to potentiate those drugs. As prostate cancer has been known to be highly resistant to chemotherapy [67], it would certainly be beneficial if such a poor efficacy of these drugs could somehow be improved.

Accordingly, PC-3 cells were treated solely with various chemotherapeutic drugs, including carmustine (BCNU, 50 μM), vinblastine (VBL, 100 nM), 5-fluorouracil (5FU, 5 μg/ml), methotrexate (MTX, 100 μM), etoposide (VP16, 100 nM), cisplatin (CPL, 100 μM), cyclophosphamide (CyP, 300 μg/ml), and mitomycin C (MMC, 300 nM), or in combination with VC (200 μM) or D-fraction (200 μg/ml). To attain the optimal efficacy of each drug *in vitro*, the concentrations of drugs used here were the estimated maximum or above physiologically tolerable levels. Cell viability at each condition was then assessed in 72 h and the results are summarized in Table 2. Although some of those drugs (BCNU, VBL, 5FU, and MTX) were solely capable of inducing a ~50% growth reduction, little improvements in their cytotoxic activity were observed with D-fraction, except for a ~90% cell viability reduction with the BCNU/D-fraction combination. VP16, CPL, CyP, or MMC alone or in combination with D-fraction had no effects whatsoever.

Table 2. Comparison of cytotoxic effects of chemotherapeutic drugs alone or in combination with DF in PC-3 cells

Additions	Cell Viability (%)[a]		Differences Between Groups
	No additions	DF (200 μg/ml)	
No additions	100%	100%	N/S[b]
+BCNU (50 μM)	49 ± 3.6	10 ± 2.2	*p*<0.01
+VBL (100 nM)	53 ± 3.2	50 ± 3.9	N/S
+5FU (5 μg/ml)	51 ± 4.1	52 ± 2.8	N/S
+MTX (100 μM)	50 ± 4.4	48 ± 4.3	N/S
+VP16 (100 nM)	100	97 ± 1.7	N/S
+CPL (100 μM)	100	95 ± 2.3	N/S
+CyP (300 μg/ml)	100	100	N/S
+MMC (300 nM)	100	96 ± 2.1	N/S
+VC (200 μM)	97 ± 1.7	6.3 ± 1.2	*p*<0.001

[a] All cell viability data (%) are mean ± standard deviation (SD) of three separate experiments.

[b] N/S indicates that differences in cell viability between "No additions" and "DF" are not statistically significant.

Abbreviations: DF, D-fraction; BCNU, 1,3-bis(2-chloroethyl)-1-nitrosourea; VBL, vinblastine; 5FU, 5-fluorouracil; MTX, methotrexate; VP16, etoposide; CPL, cisplatin; Cyp, cyclophosphamide; MMC, mitomycin C.

Nonetheless, D-fraction/VC combination led to a ~95% viability reduction, which was far better than all dugs tested except BCNU. Therefore, these results suggest that the D-fraction/VC combination appears to be more effective than various chemotherapeutic drugs currently being used in clinical cases. It is also possible that potentiation of BCNU cytotoxicity with D-fraction may imply its selective chemo-sensitizing effect, capable of improving the efficacy of certain chemotherapeutic drugs.

Possible Potentiation of Other Natural Products with VC

Although no chemotherapeutic drugs seem to be potentiated with VC as seen above, we further explored if any other natural products/agents besides D-fraction might work on VC. The following 9 products were commercially obtained and used in this study:

- ABE: Agaricus blazei Murill mushroom extract
- HMM: Himematsutake extract
- LEE: Shiitake (Lentinus edodes) mushroom extract
- GLE: Reishi (Ganoderma lucidum) mushroom extract
- AHC: Mycelial extracts of several mushrooms
- MSK: Mixed powder of 3 different mushrooms and 3 herbs
- ASC: Mixed powder of Agaricuc blazei Murill and shark cartilage
- ARBX: Arabinoxylan from rice bran
- YCW: Yeast cell wall extract (supplemented with vitamin C)

PC-3 cells were cultured with the varying concentrations (0-1,000 µg/ml) of these extracts with or without VC (200 µM) and their effects on cell growth were assessed in 72 h (Table 3).

D-fraction (200 µg/ml) was also included serving as a positive control, capable of inducing ~95% cell death with VC. Six products, such as ABE, HMM, AHC, MSK, ASC, and ARBX, had no effects on PC-3 cell growth even at a maximal dose of 1,000 µg/ml, whereas LEE and GLE at 300 µg/ml showed a ~15% and ~40% reduction in cell viability, respectively. Unexpectedly, *YCW* led to a >95% viability reduction at "20 µg/ml" (based on the β-glucan content); however, it must be noted that such a profound cytotoxicity of YCW could have been due primarily to "VC" supplemented in this product. For PC-3 cells, VC by itself was found to have significant cytotoxic effects when its concentrations went beyond 300 µM (Figure 3).

According to our calculation, "20 µg/ml (β-glucan)" of YCW used here actually contained *2,400 µM* of VC, which was apparently a lethal dose for PC-3 cells. It is thus feasible that YCW-induced cytotoxicity is most likely attributed to the excess amount of VC supplement, not to its active ingredient (β-glucan). Since *pure* β-glucan (present in YCW) must be required for testing its direct cytotoxic effect on PC-3 cells, YCW has been dismissed from this study.

Biological Significance and Medicinal Properties of the Maitake Mushroom   17

Table 3. Effects of various natural agents and their combination with VC on PC-3 cells

Natural Agents	Cell Growth/Viability (%)	
	No additions	+VC (200 µM)
ABE	100%	100%
HMM	100	100
LEE[a]	~85	~40
GLE[a]	~60	~10
ASC	100	100
MSK	100	100
AHC	100	100
ARBX	100	100
YCW[c]	<5	N/A
DF[b]	100	~5

[a] Three hundred µg/ml each of LEE and GLE was used solely while the rest of agents (excluding YCW) were tested up to a maximum concentration of 1,000 µg/ml.

[b] DF (200 µg/ml) alone and its combination with VC was also included as a positive control.

[c] Concentration of YCW used here was 20 µg/ml based on the amount of β-glucan, but it also contained the estimated, lethal dose of 2,400 µM VC. Hence, YCW has been dismissed from this study and *see* the text for further explanation.

Abbreviations: DF, D-fraction; VC, vitamin C; ABE, *Agaricus blazei Murill* mushroom extract; HMM, Himematsutake extract; LEE, Shiitake (*Lentinus edodes*) mushroom extract; GLE, Reishi (*Ganoderma lucidum*) mushroom extract; ASC, Mixed powder of *Agaricuc blazei Murill* and shark cartilage; MSK, Mixed powder of 3 different mushrooms and 3 herbs; AHC, Mycelial extracts of several mushrooms; ARBX, Arabinoxylan from rice bran; YCW, Yeast cell wall extract; N/A, not applicable.

When these 8 extracts were combined with VC (200 µM), most of them failed to show any enhanced cytotoxicity, except for LEE and GLE (at 300 µg/ml) exhibiting ~60% and ~90% cell viability reduction, respectively (Table 3). Thus, the combination of D-fraction and VC appears to yet have the most potent cytotoxic effect on PC-3 cells, inducing ~95% cell viability reduction; however, enhanced cytotoxicity of LEE and GLE with VC suggests that some other natural agents/products could be also potentiated with VC. Moreover, it should be noted that the effectiveness of various mushroom extracts (glucans or polysaccharides) is known to be *cancer-specific* despite their structural and functional similarities [68]. Some other natural extracts besides mushrooms are also shown to have cancer specificity. Thus, we cannot rule out the possibility that some of natural agents tested above with little effects could be highly effective on certain malignancies besides prostate cancer. Studies of such natural agents on a variety of cancer cells are warranted.

Cytotoxic Effect of D-Fraction/VC Combination on Other Cancer Cells

Although the combination of D-fraction and VC was highly effective on prostate cancer, it was of interest to examine whether such a combination could be also effective on other human cancers. This possibility was tested using various human cancer cells such as bladder (T24), kidney (ACHN), breast (MCF-7), lung (A549), stomach (AGS), liver (HepG2), brain

(U-89), and leukemia (HL-60) cells. In addition to these human cancers, whether the D-fraction/VC combination may have the anticancer effect on "non-human" cancers was also examined, using three *canine* cancer cells such as mammary gland (CF33), connective tissue (CF21), and lymphoma (CL-1) cells, in this study.

A) D-Fraction/VC Effects on Human Cancer Cells

All human cancer cells were cultured with D-fraction (200 µg/ml) alone or in combination with VC (200 µM) and cell number/viability was determined at 24 h (Table 4). No effects of D-fraction alone were seen in most of cancer cells, except for U-87 and HL-60 cells. Both U-87 and HL-60 cells were exceptionally susceptible to D-fraction, resulting in a ~90% and >90% cell death (determined by cell viability assay), respectively. No further tests of a combination of D-fraction and VC were performed in these cells.

Table 4. Effects of DF alone and its combination with VC on various cancer cells

Cancer Cells	Cell Growth/Viability (%)	
	+ DF (200 µg/ml)	+DF/VC (200 µM)
T24 (bladder)	100	<10
ACHN (kidney)	100	10
MCF-7 (breast)	100	<10
A549 (lung)	100	30
AGS (gastric)	100	10
HepG2 (liver)	100	<10
U-87 (brain)	~10	N/A
HL-60 (leukemia)	<10	N/A

Abbreviations: DF, D-fraction; VC, vitamin C; N/A, not applicable and see the text for further explanation.

The rest of the 6 cancer cells were then cultured with the combination of D-fraction (200 µg/ml) and VC (200 µM) for 24 h to assess any apparent effects on their proliferation status. After 24 h, the significant (≥90%) cell viability reductions (due to cell death) were detected in nearly all cancer cells, except for A549 cells with a 30% viability reduction (Table 4). Our pilot study already confirmed that 200 µM VC alone had no effects on these 6 cancer cells used here, and 200 µg/ml D-fraction alone had no effects either. Thus, these results also show that D-fraction and VC can work *synergistically* to exert a cytotoxic effect on these 6 cancer cells (besides PC-3 cells), implying that this combination may commonly work on a variety of human cancer cells.

B) D-Fraction /VC Effects on Canine Cancer Cells

Three types of canine cancer cells, canine mammary gland cancer (CF33), connective tissue cancer (CF21), and lymphoma (CL-1) cells [69], were cultured with varying concentrations (0-1,000 µg/ml) of D-fraction alone to assess their dose-dependent profiles (Table 5). After 24 h, no apparent effects of D-fraction were seen in CF33 and CF21 cells but CL-1 cells were highly susceptible to D-fraction, resulting in a ~20% and >90% cell viability reduction (due to cell death) with 500 and 1,000 µg/ml D-fraction, respectively. In 72 h, 500 and 1,000 µg/ml of D-fraction led to ~40% and ~65% growth reduction in CF33 cells while

Biological Significance and Medicinal Properties of the Maitake Mushroom 19

~30% and ~70% growth reduction in CF21 cells, respectively. Thus, these results suggest that D-fraction can induce the growth inhibition or cell death in all three canine cancer cells, although relatively high concentrations (≥500µg/ml) of D-fraction are required to be effective.

Table 5. Effects of DF alone and its combination with VC on canine cancer cells

Canine Cancer Cells	Growth/Viability Reduction (%)		
	+DF[a]		+DF/VC[b]
	24 h	72 h	(24 h)
CF33 (mammary gland)	N/E	~40% (500 µg/ml) ~65% (1,000)	~90%
CF21 (connective tissue)	N/E	~30% (500) ~70% (1,000)	~90%
CL-1 (lymphoma)	~20% (500) >90% (1,000)	N/A	~100%

[a] Effective concentrations of DF tested (0-1,000 µg/ml) are shown.
[b] Combination of DF (200 µg/ml) and VC (200 µM) was used.
Abbreviations: DF, D-fraction; VC, vitamin C; N/E, no effects; N/A, not applicable.

When these 3 cancer cells were cultured with the combination of D-fraction (200 µg/ml) and VC (200 µM) for 24 h, both CF33 and CF21 cells showed a ~90% viability reduction while CL-1 cells were completely dead (Table 5). It should be noted that D-fraction at 200 µg/ml had no effects on CF33 and CF21 cells in a dose-dependent study above, so that the combination of D-fraction and VC again illustrates the synergistic potentiation of cytotoxic activity. Therefore, D-fraction alone or its combination with VC demonstrates significant anti-proliferative or cytotoxic activity on 3 canine cancer cells, implying that D-fraction may work on human cancers as well as canine and other veterinary cancers crossing a species barrier.

Antiviral Activity of D-Fraction

In addition to two major biological significance of D-fraction, immunomodulatory and antitumor/anticancer activities, *antiviral* activity could be another significant potential of D-fraction. Unlike bacterial infections, no antibiotics would work for viral infections, so that effective drugs/agents need to be found or developed, although a few antiviral drugs are currently available. Hence, potential antiviral activity of D-fraction may have clinical implications in several serious viral infections such as HIV/AIDS, hepatitis B, influenza and so forth.

AIDS with HIV is one the major epidemic viral infections and will require no further description. As a great number of AIDS research projects are underway worldwide, we are obtaining a better understanding and finding an improved therapeutic approach for this deadly infection. Incidentally, D-fraction is considered a potential anti-HIV agent for controlling or treating HIV infection. In 1992, the report on an *in vitro* anti-HIV screening test for D-fraction conducted by the NCI showed that D-fraction was highly effective against HIV, preventing the HIV-mediated destruction of Th (CD4$^+$) cells up to 97% [10]. Additionally, D-fraction was found to be as effective or powerful as azidothymidine (AZT), which is a common AIDS drug but with certain side effects. These findings are significant because evaluating CD4$^+$ cells in AIDS patients is considered a benchmark in monitoring the progression of HIV. Following this report, one study of D-fraction on AIDS patients [70] showed that oral administration of D-fraction led to an increase in CD4$^+$ cell counts to 1.4-1.8 folds and the improvements in other clinical parameters in AIDS patients. These good outcomes are believed to result from anti-HIV activity of D-fraction with direct inhibition of HIV replication and stimulation of the body's defense system against HIV [70]. Overall, ~85% of all patients treated with D-fraction were reported to have an increased sense of well-being regarding various symptoms and secondary diseases caused by HIV. Thus, it is conceivable that D-fraction could be a promising agent, encouraging its further trials on patients with HIV/AIDS.

Hepatitis can be caused by several different viruses. Among them, nearly 300 million people worldwide are estimated to suffer from hepatitis B caused by the hepatitis B virus (HBV) [71]. For the primary therapy, cytokines (interferon-α2b etc.) are used to directly inactivate intracellular HBV and activate T cells to destroy the infected hepatocytes to control HBV infection [72]. However, this immunomodulatory therapy has many limitations with a poor efficacy, incapable of eradicating HBV from the body. Since no other viable options are currently available, a search for more effective anti-HBV drugs/agents or therapeutic modalities is required. As D-fraction has been shown to stimulate macrophages and dendritic cells that could attack and destroy HBV, the possible inhibitory effects of D-fraction and its combination with interferon-α2b (IFN) were examined on HBV. Such study [9] showed that D-fraction or IFN alone significantly inhibited HBV with the 50% inhibitory concentration (IC$_{50}$) of 0.59 mg/ml and 1,399 IU/ml, respectively. Yet, when D-fraction and IFN were combined, the anti-HBV activity of IFN increased by 9-fold (IC$_{50}$ = 154 IU/ml), suggesting that D-fraction might synergize with IFN. Thus, these results suggest that the combination of D-fraction and IFN may offer a more effective therapeutic modality for HBV infections.

Furthermore, there is a very common infection, which is not as severe or fatal as HIV/AIDS or hepatitis, but it is a pandemic influenza infection. Without a doubt, influenza can still become serious and fatal with other complications. Both macrophages and monocytes are susceptible to the influenza virus [73] and an infection triggers the production of several inflammatory cytokines such as IL-1, IL-6, and TNF-α [74]. Interestingly, TNF-α was initially described as a tumor cell-killing factor but is also known to play a key role in the inflammatory response and host-resistance to pathogens [75, 76]. In fact, it has been shown that TNF-α was capable of inhibiting the replication of various viruses including vesicular stomatitis virus, encephalomyocarditis virus, herpes simplex virus, influenza virus etc., presumably preventing cytopathic effects [77]. Since D-fraction is known to stimulate the production of certain cytokines including TNF-α [14], whether it could induce such TNF-α production in macrophages, ultimately inhibiting the influenza virus growth, was investigated. Several different forms (based on molecular weights) of D-fraction, a murine macrophage cell line (D1), and the Madin-Darby canine kidney (MDCK) cell line as a host, were prepared and used in this study [78]. Influenza virus-infected MDCK cells with direct treatment of various D-fractions showed no inhibitory effects on the virus growth, indicating no cytotoxic activity in these D-fractions. However, after D1 cells were first treated with different D-fractions for 10 h and those conditioned media were added to the infected cells, the virus growth was inhibited at the different degrees. A conditioned medium with the highest (~40%) inhibitory growth effect was from one of the D-fractions with molecular weights ranging from 30 Kd to 100 Kd, which also induced the highest production of TNF-α from D1 cells.

Addition of TNF-α antibody (anti-TNF-α) to this medium entirely diminished the inhibitory growth activity, confirming that TNF-α is primarily responsible for such an antiviral effect. Thus, D-fraction may not have a direct cytotoxic effect on the influenza virus but can stimulate macrophages for the production of TNF-α, which will then kill or destroy the virus. This is a typical case of host-mediated antiviral activity, implying D-fraction to be a preventative and therapeutic agent for influenza virus infection.

Summary

A number of *in vitro* and *in vivo* studies and limited clinical studies have demonstrated potent immunomodulatory and antitumor activities of Maitake D-fraction, implying its great potential in cancer treatment and prevention. Particularly synergistic potentiation of D-fraction with VC may further help improve the efficacy of currently ongoing treatments for various cancers. Although i.v. administration of VC could be an interesting and useful procedure, more clinical studies are required for assessing its safety and efficacy in cancer patients. It is also interesting that D-fraction may not only alleviate various side effects and improve quality of life of patients under chemotherapy but also have possible chemosensitizing effects to improve the efficacy of chemotherapy.

Moreover, the potential antiviral activity of D-fraction may have broad clinical implications in prevention and/or treatment of serious viral infections including AIDS, hepatitis, influenza, etc. Its stimulation of macrophages for TNF-α production to execute antiviral activity is particularly interesting and deserves further studies.

Nevertheless, more comprehensive and controlled studies are required for the clinical demonstration of D-fraction. It is thus advised that physicians and professional health care providers actively participate in such studies to adequately and timely evaluate the clinical significance of D-fraction.

MAITAKE SX-FRACTION (SXF)

Maitake SX-fraction (SXF) is a water-soluble bioactive glycoprotein with a ~20,000-dalton molecular weight, exhibiting hypoglycemic, hypotensive, anti-hypercholesterolemic, and anti-diabetic activities [79]. Particularly, its hyperglycemic or blood glucose-lowering activity has been demonstrated on diabetic mice and limited clinical studies of type 2 diabetic patients [80, 81]. Diabetes or *diabetes mellitus* is a metabolic disorder of persistent *high* blood glucose (hyperglycemia) affecting over 16 million people (yet excluding *undetected* patients) in the US [82]. The prevalence of diabetes is increasing by 4-5% every year with an estimated 40-45% of people over 65 years old at risk [83]. Currently, diabetes is classified into two types: type 1 (insulin-dependent) and type 2 (non-insulin-dependent) diabetes [84].

Type 1 diabetes is caused primarily by insulin deficiency (due to dysfunction of pancreatic β-cells) and represents <20% of all cases of diabetes [85], while type 2 diabetes with a >80% incidence rate involves multiple factors such as defects in insulin secretion, insulin resistance at peripheral sites (muscle and adipose tissue), and elevated hepatic glucose production [85, 86]. Hence, type 2 diabetes has a higher prevalence with complex etiologies compared to type 1. Additionally, the incidence of type 2 diabetes is frequently associated with obesity and aging (over 40 years old), although the exact reason remains largely unknown.

A chronically high blood glucose level in all diabetic patients could cause serious clinical complications, such as retinopathy, neuropathy, nephropathy and lead to blindness, renal failure, amputation, coma, and death [84, 85]. Type 1 diabetes is more manageable through insulin injection, whereas the primary problem with type 2 diabetes is not insulin deficiency but *insulin resistance*, making it more difficult to treat/control [86]. In fact, due to this insulin resistance, current oral therapy using sulfonylurea derivatives [87], which primarily stimulate insulin secretion from pancreatic β-cells, often failed to achieve the expected level of efficacy. Nevertheless, to enhance peripheral insulin sensitivity, pharmaceuticals such as troglitazone [88] and metformin [89] have also been developed. Some improved glycemic control with these drugs has been reported, but potential adverse effects had to be advised [90]. For instance, metformin may cause lactic acidosis, presenting as impairment of renal function, cardiogenic or septic shock, or liver failure [90]. Moreover, troglitazone has been taken off the U.S. market, due to severe hepatotoxicity. These issues then demand safe and alternative means to overcome such insulin resistance. As SX-fraction is a natural agent with little adverse effects, it may offer a safer and more effective modality for prevention and/or treatment of patients with type 2 diabetes.

It should be noted that SX-fraction has gone through the chronological transition since it was originally introduced as "X-fraction" nearly 20 years ago. Strictly speaking, the physical/chemical compositions of SX-fraction are somewhat different from the original X-fraction, presenting the extensive physiological effects/benefits [79]. Hence, different names (from SX-fraction) such as *maitake extract* or *maitake* would be used in some of the following studies. Nonetheless, the outcomes of such studies (with different names) are practically relevant and comparable to those with SX-fraction.

Anti-diabetic Effects of Maitake Extract in Animals

In one study [3], the diabetic mice were divided into two groups: one group had control mice fed with a regular chow diet and the other group had mice fed with a chow diet and maitake extract. After 8 weeks, compared to the control group, the maitake extract group (mice fed with maitake extract) showed significant (p <0.01) improvements in three parameters of diabetes, such as the blood glucose, insulin, and triglyceride levels (Table 6). To confirm this finding, two experimental conditions have been *reversed*: the former control group now receives maitake extract while the former maitake extract group serves as the control (no more SX-fraction). This reverse-study [3] was continued for 4 weeks to assess if maitake extract would be primarily responsible for the outcomes. Even after 1 week, maitake extract was indeed responsible for improvements in the three parameters and the results were completely *reversed* (Table 7). All three parameters of the mice in the converted maitake extract group (the former control) have declined to the normal levels, while those in the control (the former maitake extract) mice have now risen to the abnormally high (diabetic) levels. Therefore, these results confirm that maitake extract was capable of positively regulating the blood glucose, insulin, and triglyceride levels, suggesting that it may act as a potential anti-diabetic agent.

Table 6. Effects of maitake extract[a] on parameters of diabetes in mice

Parameters	Control mice	Maitake-fed mice
Blood Glucose (mg/dl)	400	200[b]
Insulin (μU/ml)	1,200	220[b]
Triglyceride (mg/dl)	780	410[b]

[a] Eight-week period.
[b] $p < 0.01$.

Table 7. Changes in parameters after 1 week of *feed-switch* in mice (reverse study)

Parameters	Control → Maitake	Maitake → Control
Blood Glucose (mg/dl)	400 → 155[a]	180 → 365[a]
Insulin (μU/ml)	790 → 20[a]	120 → 990[a]
Triglyceride (mg/dl)	560 → 125[a]	230 → 620[a]

[a] $p < 0.01$.

In another study, a dose- and time-dependent study of maitake extract was also performed in diabetic mice [2].

Again, the mice were divided into two groups: the control group (mice fed with a chow diet) and the maitake extract group (mice fed with a chow diet and maitake extract). After those mice were fed with a single dose (28 mg) of maitake extract, their glucose levels were significantly lowered in a time-dependent manner.

Interestingly, this dosage was effective up to ~16 h but the (lowered) glucose levels subsequently returned to the initial high levels by 24 h. To sustain or prolong such a hypoglycemic effect of maitake extract, a *higher* dose (70 mg) of maitake extract was then given to mice *twice* a day for 7 days. Even after 4 days, blood analysis revealed that the levels of both glucose and insulin were significantly ($p < 0.05$) lower than those of controls (no maitake extract fed).

After all, the glucose levels in the maitake extract group have declined from 241 (Day 0) to 171 mg/dl (Day 7) and the insulin levels also decreased from 5.9 (Day 0) to 2.5 ng/ml (Day 7) (Table 8). For comparison, an additional study was performed using an oral diabetic medication, glipizide. It was found that glipizide had no significant effects on the glucose and insulin levels, although there was a trend toward a decrease in glucose level [2]. This indicates that maitake extract may have better control of glucose/insulin metabolism than glipizide in a long-term trial.

Table 8. Effects of maitake extract and glipizide on serum glucose and insulin in mice[a]

	Days	
	0	7
Serum glucose (mg/dl):		
Control	225	211
Maitake-fed	241	171[b]
Glipizide-fed	229	186
Serum insulin (ng/ml):		
Control	3.8	4.2
Maitake-fed	5.9	2.5[b]
Glipizide-fed	4.1	2.9

[a] Data are mean of 7-9 mice tested per group.
[b] $p < 0.05$.

A similar study was also performed to assess if SX-fraction might enhance insulin sensitivity in rats [91], and pioglitazone, a drug capable of improving insulin sensitivity [92], was used as a positive control. Insulin sensitivity was actually evaluated by the glucose tolerance and insulin challenge tests. Briefly, the rats were divided into the control, SX-fraction, and pioglitazone groups, and glucose (1.5 g/Kg body weight) was intraperitoneally injected to *all* rats for the glucose tolerance test, followed by injecting insulin (0.6 unit/Kg body weight) after 7.5 min for the insulin challenge test. The blood glucose levels were then monitored for next 3 h. After 30 min, the glucose levels (~50 mg/dl) in both SX-fraction and pioglitazone groups were quite similar and significantly lower than that (~160 mg/dl) of the control group. Moreover, at the 7.5 min mark (just before the insulin challenge), the circulating insulin concentrations in both SX-fraction and pioglitazone groups were also significantly lower than that in the control. Thus, these results suggest that SX-fraction (as well as pioglitazone) appears to improve glucose tolerance, enhancing insulin sensitivity in the rats. Taken together, the SX-fraction could be an alternative natural agent for the effective treatment of type 2 diabetic patients by improving insulin sensitivity.

Hypoglycemic Effect of Maitake/SX-Fraction in Type 2 Diabetic Patients

Encouraged by animal studies, the hypoglycemic effect of maitake has been studied in type 2 diabetic patients and such a study is also currently being performed on a volunteer basis. One closely watched case study [80] involved a 44-year-old male who was newly diagnosed with type 2 diabetes; a follow-up is summarized in Table 9.

His initial fasting blood glucose (FBG) value was 248 mg/dl (normal FBG range: 55-115 mg/dl) with glycosylated hemoglobin (HbA_{1c}) level of 11.5% (normal HbA_{1c} range: 5-7.5%). No retinopathy, neuropathy or other diabetes-related complications had yet developed. He was immediately placed on glyburide (GLB; oral 2.5 mg daily) therapy and his FBG level declined to ~180 mg/dl in next 2 days.

He also started taking a maitake caplet (500 mg) three times a day with GLB on the 3rd day. His FBG on the next day (4th day) went down to 83 mg/dl, followed by a quick rise to ~120 mg/dl, and then the FBG levels gradually decreased to ~100 mg/dl in next 10 days.

After this short "adjustment" period, his FBG levels remained 80-90 mg/dl for the next 3 months and HbA$_{1c}$ was also down to 5.2%, indicating that his FBG and HbA$_{1c}$ are back to normal. GLB was then reduced to 1.25 mg with two maitake caplets a day, and his FBG levels still remained at 80-90 mg/dl for the following 2 months. Eventually, GLB was completely withdrawn but he was kept on daily two maitake caplets. Yet, his FBG and HbA$_{1c}$ levels remained at ~90 mg/dl and 5.6%, respectively, over 6 months. Even during his "GLB-free" period, a daily "two maitake regimen" was also halted for 2 weeks. During this "wash-out" interval, his FBG rose slightly to 120 mg/dl but returned to ~80 mg/dl once his two maitake regimen was resumed. Since then, he has been free of any medications except for two maitake caplets daily. It has been over 13 years since his initial diagnosis but he still remains normoglycemic (normal FBG).

Table 9. Hypoglycemic effect of maitake on newly diagnosed type 2 diabetic patient

Diagnosis/Prognosis	Average FBG (mg/dl)	HbA$_{1c}$ (%)
Initial diagnosis	248	11.5
3rd month prognosis (with 2.5 mg GLB and Maitake)	80-90	5.2
5th month prognosis (with 1.25 mg GLB and Maitake)	80-90	N/D
9th month to present prognosis (with Maitake only)	~90	5.6

Abbreviations: FBG, fasting blood glucose; HbA$_{1c}$, glycosylated hemoglobin A$_{1c}$; GLB, glyburide; N/D, not determined.

In another study [93], 7 patients with type 2 diabetes were instructed to take an SX-fraction caplet three times a day. Although most of patients (6 of 7) were taking oral medications at that time, their FBG levels were somewhat controlled but were still *higher* than the normal levels.

They were then instructed to take those medications with SX-fraction caplets (without any contraindications). After 2 weeks, blood analysis for FBS revealed that all 7 patients already showed the apparent improvements (decline) in their FBG levels, and by 4 weeks they all exhibited more than a 30% (30-63%) decline in their FBG levels under this SX-fraction regimen (Table 10). Additionally, none of participants presented palpable ailments or adverse effects linked to SX-fraction (with medications) during the trial, confirming its safety as well as no drug contraindications. Thus, this study demonstrates that SX-fraction is indeed capable of lowering the blood glucose levels in type 2 diabetic patients in the relatively short periods (2-4 weeks).

Although SX-fraction seems to work well for type 2 diabetes, one may ask how it would work for *type 1* diabetes. It is a valid question and there is the study of SX-fraction on type 1 diabetes using an animal model [94]. It has been established that injection of streptozotocin (STZ) into rats would induce a type 1 diabetic condition by injuring the pancreatic β cells (producing insulin) [95].

Table 10. Hypoglycemic effects of SXF on type 2 diabetic patients

| Patients Age (yrs.) | Sex | Average FBS (mg/dl)[a] | | % of FBG Declined with SXF[b] |
		Before SXF	After SXF	
44	M	~260	90-100	~63
75	F	~200	110-130	~40
25	F	150-180	110-120	~30
37	M	180-200	120-140	~32
41	M	~210	100-110	~50
64	F	~220	130-150	~37
53	F	170-190	100-110	~42

[a] As all patients were under oral medications, their average FBG levels *before* SXF were with medications while those *after* SXF were with both medications and SXF.
b The values (%) of FBG declined reflect how much their glycemic control is improved with SXF.
Abbreviations: SXF, SX-fraction; FBG, fasting blood glucose; M, male; F, female.

In this study, the effects of SX-fraction were examined in SZT-induced diabetic rats (using Sprague-Dawley rats). SX-fraction showed enhanced insulin sensitivity, lowered circulating glucose levels, and lowered blood pressure (SBP) in SZT diabetic rats. These results thus suggest that even type 1 diabetic conditions appear to be improved by SX-fraction, although how this insulin-dependent diabetes, in contrast to insulin resistant form (type 2), would be positively managed requires further studies.

Possible Hypoglycemic Mechanism of SX-Fraction

It appears that SX-fraction is capable of significantly lowering the blood glucose levels in animals and humans, implying its potential prevention and treatment of diabetes. However, the hypoglycemic mechanism of the SX-fraction or how it would work has not been yet fully understood. We then hypothesized that the SX-fraction might enhance *insulin sensitization* by acting on the insulin signal transduction pathway.

Currently, how or why insulin-targeted tissues/organs would become insulin-resistant remains unknown, but it has been postulated that the insulin receptor (IR) might have a primary clue. The IR is a heterotetrameric glycoprotein consisting of two α-subunits and two β-subunits [96]. The binding of insulin to the α-subunits of the IR induces a conformational change that leads to trans-autophosphorylation of tyrosine residues on the *β*-subunits, activating their tyrosine kinase activity [96, 97]. One of such specific phosphorylated tyrosine residues, i.e., tyrosine 972, serves as a binding site for the phospho-tyrosine binding domains of *insulin receptor substrate 1* (IRS-1) whose tyrosine residues are then phosphorylated [96, 98]. This tyrosine-phosphorylated IRS-1 acts as a *docking* site/molecule that binds to and activates phosphatidylinositol 3-kinase (PI3K), which in turn activates serine/threonine kinase Akt (protein kinase B) [96, 97, 99,100]. Activated Akt induces the translocation of glucose transporter 4 (GLUT4) to the plasma membrane, ultimately promoting glucose-uptake by insulin responsive cells [97, 99, 101]. This is rather a simplified scheme of the insulin signal transduction pathway, which is triggered by activation of the IR (with insulin) and undergoes a cascade of biochemical events described above. As two other insulin signal pathways have also been postulated [98, 99], it is indeed a complex biochemical process and more studies are required for further elaboration. Nonetheless, insulin resistance (of the IR) developed by the undefined (acquired and inherited) causes would block the signal pathway, resulting in an accumulation of glucose in the circulation. This prolonged hyperglycemic milieu may further keep inactivating or insensitizing the IR/IRS-1, thereby developing into the chronic hyperglycemic state known as diabetes. Thus, one rational approach to overcome such insulin resistance would be to *(re)activate* the IR/IRS-1 to successfully execute the entire signal pathway.

Accordingly, we investigated the effects of glucose (Glc) on the insulin signal transduction pathway (ISTP) to learn if the hypoglycemic action of the SX-fraction would actually target this pathway. We focused on the effects of Glc and/or SX-fraction on the *phosphorylation status* of IR, IRS-1, and Akt, which would adequately indicate their *activation status*. In addition, the Glc uptake study [101, 102] was performed to assess the potential improvement in such Glc uptake with SX-fraction. Although this study has been published elsewhere [93], the key findings are briefly described herein.

The skeletal muscle L6 cells were used as an excellent *in vitro* model in this study [102] and possible effects of the SX-fraction were examined on some key biochemical parameters involved in the ISTP. Such biochemical alterations were then analyzed on ELISA (enzyme-linked immunosorbent assay). First of all, L6 cells must be differentiated to *myotubes*, which can then express IR, IRS-1 and other biochemical parameters [102]. In other words, L6 cells cannot simply be used for experiments, due to a lack of key parameters to be studied. Cells were allowed to grow until they reached at ~90% confluence (usually took 3 days). After discarding spent medium, fresh medium (with low serum concentration) was added to cells, which were incubated until they were differentiated to *myotubes* expressing IR, IRS-1, and other parameters. This differentiation process usually completes in 7-10 days.

Myotubes or differentiated L6 cells were first treated with *Glc* (35 mM) for 24 h and then treated with *SX-fraction* (300 µg/ml) or *insulin* (100 nM) for 15 min. All harvested cells were then subjected to ELISA to assess *activities* of several biochemical parameters indicated by the phosphorylation state of specific amino acid residues (tyrosine or serine). Compared to control cells (no exposure to Glc), this high Glc was indeed capable of reducing the IR activity by ~15%. However, after 24-h Glc treatment, when cells were exposed to SX-fraction for 15 min, the reduced IR activity went up to ~10% higher than controls or ~30% greater than the Glc-suppressed cell group (Figure 6A). Nearly the same IR activation was also attained with insulin, which was run as a positive control. Although Glc also inactivated IRS-1 by ~12%, SX-fraction was capable of re-activating or reversing such Glc-suppressed IRS-1 as seen with insulin. Similarly, Akt was considerably (~42%) inactivated by Glc but its reduced activity was then significantly (~2-fold) augmented by SX-fraction as well as insulin. In addition, the reduced (~25%) Glc uptake with Glc exposure was facilitated or increased by ~45% or it was even ~20% higher than that in control cells (Figure 6B). This stimulated Glc uptake was also demonstrated by insulin (slightly better than SX-fraction). As it is known that the amount/rate of Glc uptake reflects the outcome of the ISTP, the *increased* Glc uptake indicates the successful completion of the ISTP while the *decreased* uptake indicates the interrupted, incomplete ISTP. Taken all together, these results suggest that SX-fraction may re-activate Glc-*inactivated* IR, triggering the ISTP to consequently facilitate Glc uptake by the cells. In other words, high Glc alone can inactivate the IR/IRS-1, interrupt the ISTP by inactivating or inhibiting other parameters, and will result in a decreased Glc uptake.

However, SX-fraction (or insulin) re-activates the Glc-suppressed IR/IRS-1, carries out the ISTP by activating or stimulating those parameters, and leads to an increased Glc uptake. Therefore, the SX-fraction appears to act on the insulin signal transduction pathway (ISTP), particularly, overcoming insulin resistance by activating IR/IRS-1 to trigger the pathway and implement the subsequent signaling events. This may then account for the hypoglycemic action of SX-fraction.

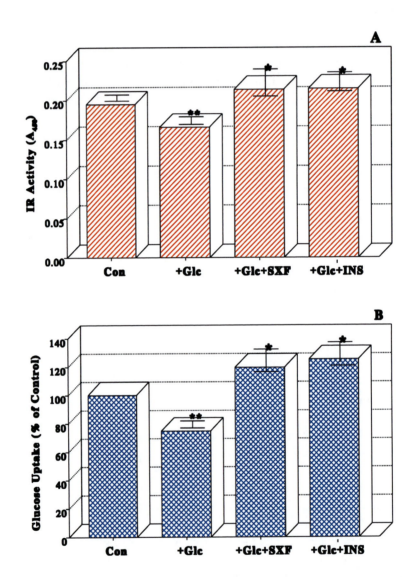

Figure 6. Effects of SXF or INS on IR phosphorylation or glucose uptake under high Glc (35 mM). (A) After a 24-h Glc treatment, followed by a 15-min exposure of cells to SXF (300 μg/ml) or INS (100 nM), the IR phosphorylation status was assessed by ELISA. All data are mean ± SD from three independent experiments (*p <0.04 versus Glc-treated or **p <0.05 versus control). (B) Following a 24-h Glc treatment and a 15-min SXF/INS exposure, glucose uptake was measured using a radioactive ligand and expressed by the % relative to control (100%). The data are mean ± SD from three separate experiments (*p <0.03 versus Glc-treated or **p <0.05 versus control).

Effects of Maitake Extract/SX-Fraction on Hypertension and Hyperlipidemia

Epidemiologically, obesity and hypertension are found concomitantly in the same individual [103]. Obesity is frequently linked to glucose/insulin disturbances, which are commonly seen in patients with hypertension, which is more prevalent among diabetics [104, 105]. It is then plausible that hypertensive patients will more likely be obese and have a higher fasting insulin level [104], while diabetic patients will have perturbations in glucose/insulin metabolism and blood pressure [103, 105]. Or simply, diabetic patients tend to become hypertensive while hypertensive patients tend to become diabetics.

As mentioned above, the SX-fraction has the hypoglycemic effect through possible activation of the insulin signal transduction pathway, lowering the FBG levels in (type 2) diabetic patients. It is interesting to study whether the SX-fraction may also have the hypotensive or blood pressure lowering effect on patients with hypertension. Actually, such studies have also been performed in animals and patients.

In an early animal study [7], hypertensive rats (the blood pressure increasing with aging) were placed on a normal diet with or without maitake extract. After 4 days, blood pressure in the rats fed with maitake extract was lowered from 230 mmHg to 170 mmHg (i.e., 60 mmHg decline). Additionally, total cholesterol decreased while HDL (high-density lipoprotein) remained stable. In the next experiment, when the rats fed with maitake extract were placed only in a normal diet *without* maitake extract, their blood pressure rapidly went up. However, once they were placed back on the feed with maitake extract, their blood pressure declined again. These results thus illustrate that maitake extract appears to be capable of lowering blood pressure (in these hypertensive rats). In the similar study, the effects of SX-fraction were examined in diabetic Zucker fatty rats (ZFR), which were often used as a model for insulin resistance and type 2 diabetes [106]. The SX-fraction significantly lowered systolic blood pressure (SBP) and fasting blood glucose in ZFR over the 3 to 6 weeks of study. This finding suggests that the SX-fraction could be useful in lowering high SBP associated with type 2 diabetes.

In the clinical setting (unpublished), 30 hypertensive patients were scheduled to take SX-fraction as instructed for two months. As their blood pressure was measured weekly, there was a mean decrease in systolic (maximal) blood pressure of ~14 mmHg as well as a mean decrease in diastolic (minimal) blood pressure of ~8 mmHg. No adverse effects were reported by any of the patients but actually they all felt well during the trial. In addition, although some patients on medication often showed fluctuating or unstable blood pressure, their blood pressure became stable and gradually decreased toward normalcy (120/80) once they started taking SX-fraction. Thus, this study also supports the notion that the SX-fraction may effectively lower blood pressure in hypertensive patients.

Hyperlipidemia or the high levels of cholesterol and triglycerides are indicators of increased risk for cardiovascular disease and are also partly linked to diabetes-related clinical complications [107]. For instance, LDL (low-density lipoprotein) can contribute to coronary artery disease, in which the blood vessels are narrowed by deposits of a fatty tissue called *atheromas* made up largely of cholesterol. Such narrowing of the coronary arteries by atheromas can then cause angina (severe pain in the chest spreading to the shoulders, arms, and neck), and this could further increase the risk of artery blockage by a blood clot [108]. In addition to high blood cholesterol, the high level of triglycerides is also associated with the increased risk for heart disease. Triglycerides are normally moved into the liver for storage (for later use) in a healthy person. However, the high levels of triglycerides can lead to a formation of smaller, denser LDL particles, which will then promote the obstructions in the blood vessels that can trigger heart attack [109]. Thus, it should be important to understand that an excess amount of blood triglycerides (hypertriglyceridemia) is deadly with a serious medical condition.

For prevention or treatment of people with high levels of cholesterol and/or triglycerides, several drugs are currently available as they can lower those levels and also play a crucial role in life-threatening situations [110]. However, in the area of preventive medicine, natural agents with cholesterol/triglycerides-lowering effects could be a wiser choice since the long-term effects of those drugs have not been clarified. As SX-fraction is such a safe natural agent, its potential effects on hyperlipidemia have been investigated. Nearly two decades ago, maitake extract was tested on the rats with hyperlipidemia induced by cholesterol feed [4]. The levels of cholesterol and triglycerides were compared between cholesterol-fed rats (control) and rats-fed with cholesterol *and* maitake extract in specified time points. Even after 12 days, the values of both cholesterol and triglycerides were significantly (~43%) *lower* in maitake-fed rats than those in control rats. In 24 days, it was apparent that body weight, liver weight, body fat, and serum phospholipid levels were all lower in maitake-fed rats (compared to controls). Thus, maitake extract might be able to alter lipid metabolism by inhibiting the accumulation of liver lipids as well as the elevation of serum lipids. Several similar rat/mouse studies also consistently showed lowered lipid and/or cholesterol levels and improved lipid metabolism with maitake-feed [6, 111-114]. Furthermore, although controlled clinical trials of maitake extract are required for assessing its cholesterol/lipids-lowering effects on actual patients, some volunteer-based studies have already been conducted showing the encouraging data.

In summary, the present data suggest that maitake extract or SX-fraction appears to have hypotensive and cholesterol/lipids-lowering effects, which may presumably help prevent cardiovascular diseases.

Effects of Maitake/SX-Fraction on Syndrome X or Metabolic Syndrome

As described above, diabetes, hypertension, and hyperlipidemia all seem to be linked together. For instance, obesity, high blood pressure, and high blood glucose all tend to appear *together* (at the same time) in some people, increasing their risk for diabetes, heart disease, possible cancer, and other various diseases [103-105]. A new term, *Syndrome X*, has been coined for a *cluster* of disease-causing conditions/symptoms, which might indicate a predisposition to diabetes, hypertension, heart disease, and other life-threatening diseases of aging [115]. For example, diabetes can be considered an (age-related) metabolic disorder since Syndrome X is also associated with "insulin resistance". Due to such *acquired* insulin resistance, those insulin-responsive cells (e.g., muscles and fats) will stop responding to insulin or become resistant to insulin for blood glucose uptake. As a result, glucose circulating in the blood accumulates and elevates while more and more insulin is released from the pancreas to stimulate the cells [86]. This disturbance will create two adverse physiological conditions, hyperglycemia (high blood glucose) and hyperinsulinemia (high blood insulin), which is then known as *diabetes*. That's how Syndrome X and diabetes (type

2) are tightly linked and have much in common. Syndrome X may also indicate a cluster of risk factors for heart disease associated with insulin resistance, including hypertension, hyperlipidemia, high blood LDL (low HDL), hyperglycemia, and hyperinsulinemia, which are all linked to cause a variety of life-threatening diseases [115, 116]. These diseases, in particular, include coronary heart disease, heart failure, stroke, diabetes, and certain cancers [117, 118]. Thus, Syndrome X is a serious medical concern that demands further investigations.

Earlier, maitake has been shown to positively control various symptoms of Syndrome X or metabolic syndrome in animal and human studies. Potential effects of SX-fraction on the metabolic syndrome were examined in diabetic Zucker fatty rats (ZFR) [119]. The control ZFR lost nearly 50 g body weight (average 858 g) over 6 weeks, indicating a declining state of health. As *body weight* is a vital marker of health status in rats, significant weight losses are associated with failing health and sickness. In contrast, ZFR receiving SX-fraction lost only 16 g body weight with lowered blood pressure as well as circulating glucose, urea, and creatinine, indicating good or improved health. In addition, other health parameters such as oxidative stress (assessed by lipid peroxidation) and DNA damage were also shown to be significantly lowered/minimized in SX-fraction given ZFR. Thus, these results demonstrate that SX-fraction is capable of ameliorating high blood pressure, insulin resistance, and other metabolic parameters linked to the aging process.

Moreover, a similar study of SX-fraction focusing on age-associated metabolic perturbations was performed in *aging* rats [120]. A normotensive strain of Sprague-Dawley rats (SD) was employed and found to show a gradual rise in blood pressure (SBP) to the hypertensive levels (>150 mmHg) with a diet containing 20% sucrose over the 4 months of study. The inclusion of sucrose in a diet was to assure that a regular feed (for SD) contained a virtually similar portion of refined carbohydrates (in calories) as the normal American Diet [121], simulating the age-related hypertension often seen in humans. After 4 months, SX-fraction has restored age-related metabolic disturbances such as progressive elevation of blood pressure and disordered glucose metabolism. Those SD (received SX-fraction) showed lowered SBP, decreased activity of the renin-angiotensin system (RAS), enhanced insulin sensitivity, and lowered TNF-α level. As the RAS can regulate blood pressure (and water balance), its decline would result in lowered SBP. The reduced level of circulating TNF-α is indicative of lessened inflammation. Thus, SX-fraction appears to ameliorate age-related hypertension (partly through the RAS activity), perturbed glucose-insulin metabolism, and cytokine (TNF-α)-associated inflammation, leading to a longer, healthier life span.

Although the etiologies of Syndrome X or metabolic syndrome have not yet been fully understood, there are many *factors* commonly associated with it: aging, lifestyle factors (diet and physical inactivity), biological factors (abdominal obesity, hypertension, hyperglycemia and inflammation), and elevated oxidative stress (production of reactive oxygen species) [118, 122] as partially described above. Epidemiologically, in addition to what was mentioned earlier, metabolic syndrome with *obesity* and insulin resistance are often found in countries with an industrialized, strong economic status, including the US [123]. For example, many Americans are enjoying a great lifestyle with abundant food supplies; however, in many ways, so many of them are now suffering from *overnutrition* with too much sugar, too many fats, and too many calories. In fact, an estimated 72.5 million American adults are obese (a body mass index, BMI, ≥ 30 kg/m^2) and nearly 1 in 3 children are overweight or obese [124, 125]. In addition, due to their busy lifestyle, most people don't get adequate exercise. It is thus plausible that a high calorie diet and lack of exercise will make many of them overweight or obese. Presumably, *obesity* could be the first sign of insulin resistance that will lead to metabolic syndrome linked to diabetes and other serious age-related diseases.

It has been shown that "obesity" in mice and participants was improved with maitake supplements, resulting in significant *weight loss*. In an animal study, rats weighing 120-130 g were divided into the control group with normal feed and the maitake group with normal feed and maitake. After one month, the control rats gained weight up to 240 g (from 120g), while the maitake group showed only 20-30 g weight gain (i.e., 140-160 g) [126], suggesting the preventive effect of maitake on weight gain. It was of interest to also examine how maitake would affect those *obese* rats (~350 g). The control rats (without maitake) steadily gained weight up to nearly 400 g in 18 weeks; however, the maitake group actually lost weight down to ~315 g (i.e., ~35 g loss). Thus, maitake appears to be capable of inducing or facilitating weight loss as it also prevents/suppresses weight gain. One clinical study showed that 30 obese participants were instructed to take a given amount of maitake daily for 2 months without changing their regular diets and daily routines. In 2 months, *all* of the participants lost weight with an average loss of 11-13 pounds [127]. This study thus suggests that maitake may have a weight-control potential regardless of one's regular diet pattern. In other words, it is rather convenient for people to lose weight without making major adjustments to their diets. Taken together, maitake may effectively control or improve the (adverse) metabolic processes, especially glucose and cholesterol/lipids metabolisms, aiding weight control.

Therapeutic Use of SX-Fraction in Patients with Polycystic Ovary Syndrome

There are potential beneficial effects of SX-fraction on patients with polycystic ovary syndrome (PCOS), which is one of the most common endocrine disorders in 7-8% of reproductive women [128]. PCOS is clinically characterized by menstrual dysfunction, hyperandrogenism, and metabolic complications, leading to menstrual irregularities, infertility, and obesity [128, 129]. Additionally, PCOS is often associated with insulin resistance and hyperinsulinemia that could result in diabetes and cardiovascular diseases [128, 129]. Hence, PCOS can cause serious adverse effects on reproductive aged women. Women who are expecting to have children should be concerned with PCOS since it could complicate pregnancy. First of all, to become pregnant, women must ovulate following a regular menstrual cycle, but those with PCOS often have no ovulation and menstruation. The following clinical study [130] has been conducted to assess if SX-fraction would induce ovulation in PCOS patients.

PCOS patients were first divided randomly into two groups: one group was assigned to receive SX-fraction for 12 weeks while another group received clomiphene citrate (CC). It should be noted that CC is the first-line standard medication used to induce ovulation in PCOS patients [131] and was included as a positive control in this study. The results showed that ovulation was observed in 20 of 26 patients treated with SX-fraction (the ovulation rate of 76.9%) and 29 of 31 patients with CC (93.5%). However, there were 15 patients who failed to respond to monotherapy with either SX-fraction (7 cases) or CC (8 cases) (Table 11). These patients then underwent combination therapy using SX-fraction combined with CC. In this therapy, 7 of 7 patients (100%) that failed in sole SX-fraction treatment and 6 of 8 (75%) that failed in sole CC treatment resulted in ovulation (Table 11). Hence, this study demonstrates that SX-fraction is capable of inducing ovulation in PCOS patients. The ovulation rate of 76.9% with SX-fraction is indeed impressive even compared to that in the CC (93.5%). It is more impressive that *combination* therapy of SX-fraction and CC can lead to the markedly improved ovulation rate of 87% (13/15) in those patients who previously failed with either SX-fraction or CC monotherapy. Therefore, it is promising that SX-fraction may have clinical implications in a better, improved therapeutic modality for women with PCOS. However, the positive effect of SX-fraction on infertility requires further studies for addressing its actual efficacy. Such studies are currently in progress.

Table 11. Effects of SXF or CC alone or their combination on ovulation in PCOS patients

	Patients (n)	Ovulated (n)	Rate of Ovulation (%)
Monotherapy (SXF or CC):			
SXF alone	26	20	76.9 %
CC alone	31	29	93.5%
Combination (SXF + CC) therapy:			
SXF-failed	7	7	100%
CC-failed	8	6	75%

Abbreviations: SXF, SX-fraction; CC, clomiphene citrate; PCOS, polycystic ovary syndrome.

A similar study of SX-fraction on PCOS patients was performed [132]. Thirty Japanese women (21-37 years old) with newly diagnosed PCOS were divided into two groups: the control group (n=15) received SKT (a common herbal medicine prescribed for PCOS) and the SX-fraction group (n=15) received SX-fraction. After a three-month treatment, ovulation was assessed by the change in basal body temperature and ultrasonography. The results showed that 66.7% and 30.8% of the patients ovulated in the SX-fraction and the control groups, respectively; however, the difference was not statistically significant ($p = 0.0581$). On the other hand, the "ovulation cycle rate" (% of menstrual cycles with ovulation) showed 48.9% for the SX-fraction group and 15.4% for the control group, indicating the statistically significant difference ($p = 0.0011$). Thus, SX-fraction appears to be more effective than SKT (control) in inducing ovulation in these PCOS patients. Moreover, additional hormonal and metabolic changes/profiles of these patients revealed that the estradiol level and the estradiol/testosterone ratio were significantly ($p < 0.04$) increased in those with the SX-fraction regimen. These findings suggest that SX-fraction could promote aromatization of testosterone to estradiol in granulose cells, presumably inducing ovulation. After all, this study also supports the notion that using SX-fraction may indeed provide an improved therapeutic modality for women with PCOS.

EPILOGUE

Two bioactive extracts from maitake mushroom, D-fraction and SX-fraction, have been shown to have a variety of medicinal properties. D-fraction has two major biological activities, immunomodulatory and anticancer/antitumor and a potential antiviral activity. Its immunomodulatory activity involves the innate immune system comprising NK cells, macrophages, dendritic cells etc. and the adaptive immune system primarily comprises T and B cells. As a result, D-fraction may provide us with protection against infections (bacterial, viral, protozoal, and fungal pathogens) as well as prevention/protection against cancer development, growth, progression, or metastasis.

Practically, immunomodulatory and anticancer activities of D-fraction must work with coordination: D-fraction would induce the immunomodulatory effects by activating immune effector cells and also stimulating production of cytokines/chemokines, ultimately targeting and attacking foreign pathogens and cancer cells. As a part of such immunomodulatory activity, D-fraction may stimulate the specific cytokine production for exerting its antiviral activity against a variety of viruses. Thus, D-fraction appears to build up the best possible defense system in the body. Since the FDA has granted the safety of D-fraction, it can be taken by patients as well as healthy (normal) people.

Another maitake extract, namely SX-fraction, is substantially different from D-fraction in terms of medicinal or physiological properties. It primarily plays a beneficial role in the glucose and lipid metabolisms, particularly exhibiting its lowering/reducing effects on high blood glucose, insulin, blood pressure, lipids, cholesterol, triglycerides, etc. Hence, it is believed to help prevent/treat diabetes, hypertension, metabolic syndrome, and cardiovascular diseases. In addition, it is worthwhile mentioning the possible hypoglycemic mechanism of the SX-fraction (in diabetes).

As seen in the study of type 2 diabetic patients (Table 10), the hypoglycemic effect of SX-fraction appears to be attributed to its ability to restore the insulin signal transduction pathway (ISTP), overcoming insulin resistance. SX-fraction demonstrated re-activation of the *inactive* insulin receptor (IR) (linked to insulin resistance), triggering and carrying out a cascade of signaling events. Consequently, a successful execution of ISTP will end with the increased glucose uptake, presumably leading to the *lowered* blood glucose level (in diabetic patients). Thus, SX-fraction may specifically act on the ISTP to sensitize the IR (to insulin), overcoming insulin resistance and improving glucose metabolism. Moreover, animal and clinical studies have also confirmed no adverse or side effects of SX-fraction, warranting its safety.

After all, both D-fraction and SX-fraction are indeed promising natural agents with great biological significance and medicinal properties. More studies on these agents may further unveil other unknown or unidentified potentials.

ACKNOWLEDGMENTS

I would like to thank Mr. Mike Shirota (Mushroom Wisdom, Inc.) for generously providing D-fraction and SX-fraction as well as his personal support. I am also indebted to Dr. Muhammad Choudhury, our Department Chairman, for his understanding and commitment to support the entire project.

REFERENCES

[1] Mizuno T, Zhuang C. Maitake, *Grifola frondosa*: pharmacological effects. *Food Rev. Int.* 1995;11:135-149.

[2] Manohar V, Talpur NA, Echard BW, Lieberman S, Preuss HG. Effects of a water-soluble extract of maitake mushroom on circulating glucose/insulin concentrations in KK mice. *Diabetes Obes. Metab.* 2002;4:43-48.

[3] Kubo K, Aoki H, Nanba H. Anti-diabetic activity present in the fruit body of *Grifola frondosa* (maitake). *Biol. Pharm. Bull.* 1994;17:1106-1110.

[4] Kubo K, Nanba H. The effect of maitake mushrooms on liver and serum lipids. *Altern Ther Health Med.* 1996;2:62-66.

[5] Jones K. Maitake, a potent medicinal food. *Altern Complement Ther.* 1998;4:420-429.

[6] Kabir Y, Yamaguchi M, Kimura S. Effect of shiitake (Lentinus edodes) and maitake (Grifola frondosa) mushrooms on blood pressure and plasma lipids of spontaneously hypertensive rats. *J. Nutr. Sci. Vitaminol. (Tokyo).* 1987;33:341-346.

[7] Adachi K, Nanba H, Otsuka M, Kuroda H. Blood pressure-lowering activity present in the fruit body of *Grifola frondosa*. *Chem Pharm Bull.* 1988;36:1000-1006.

[8] Nakai R, Masui H, Horio H, Ohtsuru M. Effect of maitake (Grifola frondosa) water extract on inhibition of adipocyte conversion of C3H10T1/2B2C1 cells. *J. Nutr. Sci. Vitaminol. (Tokyo).* 1999;45:385-389.

[9] Gu CQ, Li JW, Chao FH. Inhibition of hepatitis B virus by D-fraction from Grifola frondosa: synergistic effect of combination with interferon-α in HepG2 2.2.15. *Antiviral. Res.* 2006;72:162-165.

[10] Developmental Therapeutics Program, National Cancer Institute. *In-vitro* anti-HIV drug screening results. *NSC: F19500.* Jan 1992.

[11] Nanba H, Hamaguchi A, Kuroda H. The chemical structure of an antitumor polysaccharide in fruit bodies of *Grifola frondosa* (maitake). *Chem. Pharm. Bull.* 1987;35:1162-1168.

[12] Wasser SP. Medicinal mushrooms as a source of antitumor and immunomodulating polysaccharides. *Appl. Microbiol. Biotechnol.* 2002;60:258-274.

[13] Lull C, Wichers HJ, Savelkoul HF. Antiinflammatory and immunomodulating properties of fungal metabolites. *Mediators Inflamm.* 2005;2:63-80.

[14] Williams DL, Mueller A, Browder W. Glucan-based macrophage stimulators. *Clin. Immunother.* 1996;5:392-399.

[15] Brown GD, Gordon S. Fungal beta-glucans and mammalian immunity. *Immunity.* 2003;19:311-315.

[16] Brown GD, Gordon S. Immune recognition of fungal β-glucans. *Cell. Microbiol.* 2005;7:471-479.

[17] Taylor PR, Brown GD, Reid DM, et al. The beta-glucan receptor, Dectin-1, is predominantly expressed on the surface of cells of the monocyte/macrophage and neutrophil lineages. *J. Immunol.* 2002;269:3876-3882.

[18] Brown GD, Herre J, Williams DL, Willment JA, Marshall AS, Gordon S. Dectin-1 mediates the biological effects of beta-glucan. *J. Exp. Med.* 2003;197:1119-1124.

[19] Lin H, She YH, Cassileth BR, Sirotnak F, Cunningham Rundles S. Maitake beta-glucan MD-fraction enhances bone marrow colony formation and reduces doxorubicin toxicity in vitro. *Int. Immunopharmacol.* 2004;4:91-99.

[20] Lin H, Cheung SWY, Nesin M, Cassileth BR, Cunningham Rundles S. Enhancement of umbilical cord blood cell hematopoiesis by maitake beta-glucan is mediated by granulocyte colony-stimulating factor production. *Clin. Vaccine Immunol.* 2007;14: 21-27.

[21] de Chastellier C, Berche P. Fate of *Listeria monocytogenes* in murine macrophages: evidence for simultaneous killing and survival of intracellular bacteria. *Infect. Immun.* 1994;62:543-553.

[22] Kodama N, Yamada M, Nanba H. Addition of maitake D-fraction reduces the effective dosage of vancomycin for the treatment of *Listeria*-infected mice. *Jpn. J. Pharmacol.* 2001;87:327-332.

[23] Sanzen I, Imanishi N, Takamatsu N, et al. Nitric oxide-mediated antitumor activity induced by the extract from *Grifola frondosa* (Maitake mushroom) in a macrophage cell line, RAW264.7. *J. Exp. Clin. Cancer Res.* 2001;20:591-597.

[24] Nanba H. Maitake D-fraction: healing and preventive potential for cancer. *J. Orthomol. Med.* 1997;12:43-49.

[25] Miller JS. Biology of natural killer cells in cancer and infection. *Cancer Invest.* 2002;20:405-419.

[26] Sepulveda C, Puente J. Natural killer cells and the innate immune system in infectious pathology. *Rev. Med. Chil.* 2000;128:1361-1370.

[27] Kodama N, Komuta K, Sakai N, Nanba H. Effects of D-fraction, a polysaccharide from *Grifola frondosa*, on tumor growth involve activation of NK cells. *Biol. Pharm. Bull.* 2002;25:1647-1650.

[28] Kodama N, Komuta K, Nanba H. Effect of Maitake (*Grifola frondosa*) D-fraction on the activation of NK cells in cancer patients. *J. Med. Food.* 2003;6:371-377.

[29] Kodama N, Murata Y, Nanba H. Administration of a polysaccharide from *Grifola frondosa* stimulates immune function of normal mice. *J. Med. Food.* 2004;7:141-145.

[30] Mosmann TR, Sad S. The expanding universe of T-cell subsets: Th1, Th2 and more. *Immunol Today.* 1996;17:138-146.

[31] Inoue A, Kodama N, Nanba H. Effect of Maitake (*Grifola frondosa*) D-fraction on the control of the T lymph node Th-1/Th-2 proportion. *Biol Pharm Bull.* 2002;25:536-540.

[32] Kodama N, Harada N, Nanba H. A polysaccharide, extract from *Grifola frondosa*, induces Th-1 dominant responses in carcinoma-bearing BALB/c mice. *Jpn. J. Pharmacol.* 2002;90:357-360.

[33] Harada N, Kodama N, Nanba H. Relationship between dendritic cells and the D-fraction-induced Th-1 dominant response in BALB/c tumor-bearing mice. *Cancer Lett.* 2003;192:181-187.

[34] Deng G, Lin H, Seidman A, et al. A phase I/II trial of a polysaccharide extract from *Grifola frondosa* (Maitake mushroom) in breast cancer patients: immunological effects. *J. Cancer Res. Clin. Oncol.* 2009;135:1215-1221.

[35] Glauco S, Jano F, Paolo G, Konno S. Safety of maitake D-fraction in healthy patients: assessment of common hematologic parameters. *Altern. Complement Ther.* 2004;10:228-230.

[36] Ohno N, Iino K, Takeyama T, et al. Structural characterization and antitumor activity of the extracts from matted mycelium of cultured Grifola frondosa. *Chem. Pharm. Bull.* 1985;33:3395-3401.

[37] Nanba H. Antitumor activity of orally administered D-fraction from maitake mushroom. *J. Naturopathic Med.* 1993;4:10-15.

[38] Nanba H.: Activity of Maitake D-fraction to inhibit carcinogenesis and metastasis. *Ann NY Acad Sci.* 1995;768:243-245.

[39] Nanba H. Effect of Maitake D-fraction on cancer prevention. *Ann. NY Acad. Sci.* 1997;833:204-207.

[40] Kodama N, Murata Y, Asakawa A, et al. Maitake D-fraction enhances antitumor effects and reduces immunosuppression by mitomycin-C in tumor-bearing mice. *Nutrition.* 2005;21:624-629.

[41] Nanba H. Results of non-controlled clinical study for various cancer patients using Maitake D-fraction. *Explore.* 1995;6:19-21.

[42] Maitake Products Inc. Maitake D-fraction obtained IND for clinical study (corporate publication). Feb 1998.

[43] Konno S. Maitake D-fraction: a potent mushroom extract product against human malignancies. *Townsend Lett.* 2002;233:96-100.

[44] Gleason DF, Mellinger GT. Prediction of prognosis for prostatic adenocarcinoma by combined histological grading and clinical staging. *J. Urol.* 1974;111:58-64.

[45] Carr A, Frei B. Does vitamin C act as a pro-oxidant under physiological conditions? *FASEB J.* 1999;13:1007-1024.

[46] Buettner G, Jurkiewicz B. Catalytic metals, ascorbate and free radicals: combinations to avoid. *Radit. Res.* 1996;145:532-541.

[47] Clement M, Ramalingam J, Long L, Halliwell B. The in vitro cytotoxicity of ascorbate depends on the culture medium used to perform the assay and involves hydrogen peroxide. *Antioxid Redox. Signal.* 2001;3:157-163.

[48] Chen Q, Espey MG, Sun AY, et al. Ascorbate in pharmacologic concentrations selectively generates ascorbate radical and hydrogen peroxide in extracellular fluid in vivo. *Proc. Natl. Acad. Sci. USA.* 2007;104:8749-8754.

[49] Chen Q, Espey MG, Krishna MC, et al. Pharmacologic ascorbic acid concentrations selectively kill cancer cells: action as a pro-drug to deliver hydrogen peroxide to tissues. *Proc. Natl. Acad. Sci. USA.* 2005;102:13604-13609.

[50] Taper H, de Gerlache J, Lans M, Roberfroid M. Non-toxic potentiation of cancer chemotherapy by combined C and K3 vitamin pre-treatment. *Int. J. Cancer.* 1987;40:575-579.

[51] Pathak A, Bhutani M, Guleria R, et al. Chemotherapy alone vs. chemotherapy plus high dose multiple antioxidants in patients with advanced non-small cell lung cancer. *J. Am. Coll Nutr.* 2005;24:16-21.

[52] Creagan ET, Moertel CG, O'Fallon JR, et al. Failure of high-dose vitamin C (ascorbic acid) therapy to benefit patients with advanced cancer: a controlled trial. *N. Engl. J. Med.* 1979;301:687-690.

[53] Levine M, Conry-Cantilena C, Wang Y, et al. Vitamin C pharmacokinetics in healthy volunteers: evidence for a recommended dietary allowance. *Proc. Natl. Acad. Sci. USA.* 1996;93:3704-3709.

[54] Hoffer LJ, Levine M, Assouline S, et al. Phase I clinical trial of i.v. ascorbic acid in advanced malignancy. *Ann. Oncol.* 2008;19:1969-1974.

[55] Morishige F. The role of vitamin C in tumor therapy (human). In: Meyskens FI Jr, Parasad KN editors. Vitamins and Cancer: Human Cancer Prevention by Vitamins and Micronutrients. Clifton: Humana Press; 1986: pp 399-427.

[56] Fullerton SA, Samadi AA, Tortorelis DG, et al. Induction of apoptosis in human prostatic cancer cells with β-glucan (maitake mushroom polysaccharide). *Mol. Urol.* 2000;4:7-13.

[57] Zerbib M, Zelefsky MJ, Higano CS, Carroll PR. Conventional treatments of localized prostate cancer. *Urology.* 2008;72:25-35.

[58] Kreis W. Current chemotherapy and future directions in research for the treatment of advanced hormone-refractory prostate cancer. *Cancer Invest.* 1995;13:296-312.

[59] Kaighn ME, Narayan KS, Ohnuki Y, Lechner JF, Jones LW. Establishment and characterization of a human prostate carcinoma cell line (PC-3). *Invest. Urol.* 1979;17:16-23.

[60] Malorni W, Iosi F, Mirabelli F, Bellomo G. Cytoskeleton as a target in menedione-induced oxidative stress in cultured mammalian cells: alterations underlying surface bleb formation. *Chem. Biol. Interact.* 1991;80:217-236.

[61] Dargel R. Lipid peroxidation: a common pathogenetic mechanism? *Exp. Toxicol. Pathol.* 1992;44:169-181.

[62] De Laurenzi V, Melino G, Savini I, Annicchiarico-Petruzzelli M, Finazzi-Agro A, Avigliano L. Cell death by oxidative stress and ascorbic acid regeneration in human neuroectodermal cell lines. *Eur. J. Cancer.* 1995;31A:463-466.

[63] Leung PY, Miyashita K, Young M, Tsao CS. Cytotoxic effect of ascorbate and its derivatives on cultured malignant and nonmalignant cell lines. *Anticancer Res.* 1993;13:475-480.

[64] Sinha BK, Mimnaugh EG. Free radicals and anticancer drug resistance: oxygen free radicals in the mechanisms of drug cytotoxicity and resistance by certain tumors. *Free Radic. Biol. Med.* 1990;8:567-581.

[65] Baker AM, Oberley LW, Cohen MB. Expression of antioxidant enzymes in human prostatic adenocarcinoma. *Prostate.* 1997;32:229-233.

[66] Gavrieli Y, Sherman Y, Ben-Sasson SA. Identification of programmed cell death in situ via specific labeling of nuclear DNA fragmentation. *J. Cell Biol.* 1992;119:493-501.

[67] Theyer G, Hamilton G. Role of multidrug resistance in tumors of the genitourinary tract. *Urology.* 1994;44:942-950.

[68] Borchers AT, Stern JS, Hackman RM. Mushrooms, tumors and immunity. *Proc. Soc. Exp. Biol. Med.* 1999;221:281-293.

[69] Konno S. Potential growth inhibitory effect of maitake D-fraction on canine cancer cells. *Vet. Ther.* 2004;5:263-271.

[70] Nanba H, Kodama N, Schar D, Turner D. Effects of maitake (*Grifola frondosa*) glucan in HIV-infected patients. *Mycoscience.* 2000;41:293-295.

[71] Kao JH, Chen DS. Global control of hepatitis B virus infection. *Lancet Infect. Dis.* 2002;2:395-403.

[72] Menesis EK, Hadziyannis SJ. Interferon α treatment and retreatment of hepatitis B e antigen-negative chronic hepatitis B. *Gastroenterology.* 2001;121:101-109.

[73] Hofmann P, Sprenger H, Kaufmann A, et al. Susceptibility of mononuclear phagocytes to influenza A virus infection and possible role in the antiviral response. *J. Leukoc. Biol.* 1997;61:408-414.

[74] Jakeman KJ, Bird CR, Thorpe R, Smith H, Sweet C. Nature of the endogenous pyrogen (EP) induced by influenza viruses: lack of correlation between EP levels and content of the known pyrogenic cytokines, interleukin 1, interleukin 6 and tumor necrosis factor. *J. Gen. Virol.* 1991;72:705-709.

[75] Seo SH, Webster RG. Tumor necrosis factor alpha exerts powerful anti-influenza virus effects in lung epithelial cells. *J. Virol.* 2002;76:1071-1076.

[76] Abbas AK, Lichtman AH, Pober JS. Cellular and molecular immunology. 4th ed. Philadelphia: WB Sanders Company; 1991: pp 235-269.

[77] Mestan J, Digel W, Mittnacht S, et al. Antiviral effects of recombinant tumor necrosis factor in vitro. *Nature.* 1986;323:816-819.

[78] Obi N, Hayashi K, Miyahara T, et al. Inhibitory effect of TNF-α produced by nacrophages stimulated with Grifola frondosa extract (ME) on the growth of influenza A/Aichi/2/68 virus in MDCK cells. *Am. J. Chin. Med.* 2008;36:1171-1183.

[79] Maitake Products Inc. US Patent 7,214,778 B2. May 2007.

[80] Konno S, Tortorelis DG, Fullerton SA, Samadi AA, Hettiarachchi J, Tazaki H. A possible hypoglycaemic effect of maitake mushroom on type 2 diabetic patients. *Diabet. Med.* 2001;18:1010.

[81] Preuss HG, Echard B, Bagchi D, Perricone NV, Zhuang C. Enhanced insulin-hypoglycemic activity in rats consuming a specific glycoprotein extracted from maitake mushroom. *Mol. Cell. Biochem.* 2007;306:105-113.

[82] Alper J. New insights into type 2 diabetes. *Science.* 2000;289:37-39.

[83] Wagman AS, Nuss JM. Current therapies and emerging targets for the treatment of diabetes. *Curr. Pharm. Des.* 2001;7:417-450.

[84] American Diabetes Association (ADA). Standards of medical care in diabetes 2011. *Diabetes Care.* 2012;34:S11-S63.

[85] Caro JF. Effects of glyburide on carbohydrate metabolism and insulin action in the liver. *Am. J. Med.* 1990;89:17S-25S.

[86] Groop LC. Insulin resistance: the fundamental trigger of type 2 diabetes. *Diabetes Obes. Metab.*1999;1:S1-S7.

[87] Groop LC. Sulfonylureas in NIDDM. *Diabetes Care.* 1992;15:737-754.

[88] Nolan JJ, Ludvik B, Beerdsen P, Joyce M, Olefsky J. Improvement in glucose tolerance and insulin resistance in obese subjects treated with troglitazone. *N. Engl. J. Med.* 1994;331:1188-1193.

[89] DeFronzo RA, Goodman AM. Efficacy of metformin in patients with non-insulin-dependent diabetes mellitus. The Multicenter Metformin Study Group. *N. Engl. J. Med.* 1995;333:541-549.

[90] Bailey CJ. Biguanides and NIDDM. *Diabetes Care.* 1992;15:755-772.

[91] Preuss HG, Echard B, Bagchi D, Perricone NV, Zhuang C. Enhanced insulin-hypoglycemic activity in rats consuming a specific glycoprotein extracted from maitake mushroom. *Mol. Cell. Biochem.* 2007;306:105-113.

[92] Lawrence JM, Reckless JP. Pioglitazone. *Int. J. Clin. Pract.* 2000;54:614-618.

[93] Konno S, Alexander B, Zade J, Choudhury M. Possible hypoglycemic action of SX-fraction targeting insulin signal transduction pathway. *Int. J. Gen. Med.* 2013;6:181-187.

[94] Preuss HG, Echard B, Fu J, et al. Fraction SX of maitake mushroom favorably influences blood glucose levels and blood pressure in streptozotocin-induced diabetic rats. *J. Med. Food.* 2012;15:1-8.

[95] Rerup CC. Drugs producing diabetes through damage of the insulin secreting cells. *Pharmacol. Rev.* 1970;22:485-518.

[96] Youngren JF. Regulation of insulin receptor function. *Cell. Mol. Life Sci.* 2007;64:873-891.

[97] Biddinger SB, Khan CR. From mice to men: insight into insulin resistance syndromes. *Annu. Rev. Physiol.* 2006;68:123-158.

[98] Boura-Halfon S, Zick Y. Phosphorylation of IRS proteins, insulin action, and insulin resistance. *Am. J. Physiol. Endocrinol. Metab.* 2009;296:E581-E591.

[99] Saltiel AR, Khan CR. Insulin signaling and the regulation of glucose and lipid metabolism. *Nature.* 2001;414:799-806.

[100] Gual P, Le Marchand-Brustel Y, Tanti JF. Positive and negative regulation of insulin signaling through IRS-1 phosphorylation. *Biochimie.* 2005;87:99-109.

[101] Kohn AD, Summers SA, Birnbaum MJ, Roth RA. Expression of a constitutively active Akt Ser/Thr kinase in 3T3-L1 adipocytes stimulates glucose uptake and glucose transporter 4 translocation. *J. Biol. Chem.* 1996;271:31372-31378.

[102] Mitsumoto Y, Burdett E, Grant A, Klip A. Differential expression of the GLUT1 and GLUT4 glucose transporters during differentiation of L6 muscle cells. *Biochem. Biophys. Res. Commun.* 1991;175:652-659.

[103] Colosia AD, Palencia R, Khan S. Prevalence of hypertension and obesity in patients with type 2 diabetes mellitus in observational studies: a systematic literature review. *Diabetes Metab. Syndr. Obes.* 2013;6:327-338.

[104] Davy KP, Hall JE. Obesity and hypertension: two epidemics or one? *Am. J. Physiol. Regul Integr Comp Physiol.* 2004;286:R803-R813.

[105] Sowers JR. Insulin resistance and hypertension. *Am. J. Physiol. Heart Circ. Physiol.* 2004;286:H1597-H1602.

[106] Talpur N, Echard B, Dadgar A, et al. Effects of maitake mushroom fractions on blood pressure of Zucker fatty rats. *Res. Commun. Mol. Pathol. Pharmacol.* 2002;112:68-82.

[107] Peter R, Bajwa H, Anthony S. Hyperlipidaemia and cardiovascular disease: newer antihyperglycaemic agents and cardiovascular disease. *Curr. Opin. Lipidol.* 2013;24:189-190.

[108] Shanmugam N, Roman-Rego A, Ong P, Kaski JC. Atherosclerotic plaque regression: fact or fiction? *Cadiovasc. Drugs Ther.* 2010;24:311-317.

[109] Kasai T, Miyauchi K, Yanagisawa N, et al. Mortality risk of triglyceride levels in patients with coronary artery disease. *Heart.* 2013;99:22-29.

[110] Berthold HK, Gouni-Berthold I. Hyperlipoproteinemia(a): clinical significance and treatment options. *Atheroscler. Suppl.* 2013;14:1-5.

[111] Mori K, Kobayashi C, Tomita T, Inatomi S, Ikeda M. Antiantherosclerotic effect of the edible mushroom Pleurotus eryngii (Eringi), Grifola frondosa (Maitake), and Hypsizygus marmoreus (Bunashimeji) in apolipoprotein E-deficient mice. *Nutr. Res.* 2008;28:335-342.

[112] Talpur N, Echard BW, Fan AY, Jaffari O, Bagchi D, Preuss HG. Antihypertensive and metabolic effects of whole maitake powder and its fractions in two rat strains. *Mol. Cell. Biochem.* 2002;237:129-136.

[113] Fukushima M, Ohashi T, Fujiwara Y, Sonoyama K, Nakano M. Cholesterol-lowering effects of maitake (Grifola frondosa) fiber, shiitake (Lentinus edodes) fiber, and enokitake (Flammulina velutipes) fiber in rats. *Exp. Biol. Med. (Maywood).* 2001;226: 758-765.

[114] Kubo K, Nanba H. Anti-hyperliposis effect of maitake fruit body (Grifola frondosa) I. *Biol. Pharm. Bull.* 1997;20:781-785.

[115] Cameron AJ, Shaw JE, Zimmet PZ. The metabolic syndrome: prevalence in worldwide populations. *Endocrinol. Metab. Clin. N Am.* 2004;33:351-375.

[116] Wilson PWF, D'Agostino RB, Parise H, Sullivan L, Meigs JB. Metabolic syndrome as a precursor of cardiovascular disease and type 2 diabetes mellitus. *Circulation.* 2005;112:3066-3072.

[117] Malnick SDH, Knobler H. The medical complications of obesity. *QJM.* 2006;99:565-579.

[118] Gallagher EJ, LeRoith D. Epidemiology and molecular mechanisms tying obesity, diabetes, and the metabolic syndrome with cancer. *Diabetes Care.* 2013;36:S233-S239.

[119] Talpur N, Echard B, Yasmin T, Bagchi D, Preuss HG. Effects of niacin-bound chromium, maitake mushroom fraction SX and (-)-hydroxycitric acid on the metabolic syndrome in aged diabetic Zucker fatty rats. *Mol. Cell Biochem.* 2003;252:369-377.

[120] Preuss HG, Echard B, Bagchi D, Perricone NV. Maitake mushroom extracts ameliorate progressive hypertension and other chronic metabolic perturbations in aging female rats. *Int. J. Med. Sci.* 2010;7:169-180.

[121] Bray GA. Soft drink consumption and obesity: it is all about fructose. *Curr. Opin. Lipidol.* 2010;21:51-57.

[122] Roberts CK, Sindhu KK. Oxidative stress and metabolic syndrome. *Life Sci.* 2009;84:705-712.

[123] Ford ES, Mokdad AH. Epidemiology of obesity in the Western hemisphere. *J. Clin. Endodrinol. Metab.* 2008;93:S1-S8.

[124] Garber AJ. Obesity and type 2 diabetes: which patients are at risk? *Diabetes Obes Metab.* 2012;14:399-408.

[125] Cho SS, Qi L, Fahey GC, Klurfeld DM. Consumption of cereal fiber, mixtures of whole grains and bran, and whole grains and risk reduction in type 2 diabetes, obesity, and cardiovascular disease. *Am. J. Clin. Nutr.* 2013;98:594-619.

[126] Ohtsuru M. Anti-obesity activity exhibited by orally administered powder of maitake (*Grifola frondosa*). *Anshin.* 1992;July:198-200.

[127] Yokota M. Observatory trial of anti-obesity activity of maitake (*Grifola frondosa*). *Anshin.*1992; July:202-203.

[128] Azziz R, Woods KS, Reyna R, Key TJ, Knochenhauer ES, Yildiz BO. The prevalence and features of the polycystic ovary syndrome in an unselected population. *J. Clin. Endocrinol. Metab.* 2004;89:2745-2749.

[129] Randeva HS, Tan BK, Weickert MO et al. Cardiometabolic aspects of the polycystic ovary syndrome. *Endocr. Rev.* 2012;33:812-841.

[130] Chen JT, Tominaga K, Sato Y, Anzai H, Matsuoka R. Maitake mushroom (*Grifola frondosa*) extract induces ovulation in patients with polycystic ovary syndrome: a

possible monotherapy and a combination therapy after failure with first-line clomiphene citrate. *J. Altern. Complement Med.* 2010;16:1295-1299.

[131] Kar S. Clomiphene citrate or letrozole as first-line ovulation induction drug in infertile PCOS women: a prospective randomized trial. *J. Hum. Reprod. Sci.* 2012;5:262-265.

[132] Tominaga K, Tsuchida M, Hayashi M, Asahi A, Inui H. Ovulatory effects of an extract from maitake mushroom in patients with polycystic ovary syndrome. *J. Reprod. Engineer.* 2011;14:7-12.

In: Mushrooms
Editor: Grégoire Pesti

ISBN: 978-1-63117-521-3
© 2014 Nova Science Publishers, Inc.

Chapter 2

THE USE OF EDIBLE MUSHROOM EXTRACTS AS BIOACTIVE INGREDIENTS TO DESIGN NOVEL FUNCTIONAL FOODS WITH HYPOCHOLESTEROLEMIC ACTIVITIES

Alicia Gil-Ramírez and Cristina Soler-Rivas*
CIAL -Research Institute in Food Science (UAM-CSIC),
Department of Production and Characterization of Novel Foods,
Madrid, Spain

ABSTRACT

Coronary heart disease (CHD) is the leading cause of death in the Western world after cancer according to World Health Organization. Many studies have established that high total-cholesterol levels and low-density lipoprotein (LDL) cholesterol levels are risk factors for CHD and mortality.

In public health terms, achieving a reduction in cholesterol by dietary advice is of limited effectiveness. Thus, many investigators have been exploring the possibility of increasing components in the diet which have hypocholesterolaemic effects such as the use of plant sterols (phytosterols) or cereal β-glucans creating new food products with higher levels of these compounds.

Both functional products are able to lower cholesterol in serum by reducing its absorption. However, it has been shown that in subjects who were administered β-glucan, the cholesterol biosynthetic pathway was stimulated compared with control subjects. Thus, in order to design a really effective functional food it might be necessary to combine inhibitors of the cholesterol absorption with inhibitors of the cholesterol synthesis.

Edible mushrooms are good sources of phytosterol-like structures such as ergosterol, fungisterol, ergosterol peroxides and many other derivatives sharing similar bioactivities as cholesterol displacers during digestion. Moreover, mushrooms also contain specific β-glucans with glycosidic bounding 1-3, 1-6 instead of the typical 1-3, 1-4 of the cereal β-

---

* Corresponding author: alicia.gil@uam.es.

glucans but able to scavenge bile acids as one of the mechanism of action proposed for cereal β-glucans to impair cholesterol absorption. Moreover, some mushroom species also contained specific compounds able to impair the endogenous synthesis of cholesterol by inhibiting the 3-hydroxy-3-methyl-glutaryl CoA reductase (a key-enzyme in the cholesterol metabolism) or acting as reducers by other more complexes mechanisms.

INTRODUCTION

Cardiovascular diseases (CVD) are still leading the cause of death in industrialized countries around the world after cancer. Only in the last years, advertisements and publicity giving dietary advice (increase consumption of vegetable and fruits) achieved certain reduction in the percentages of CVD incidence and prevalence but still the quantitative numbers are high [1, 2].

Many studies have established that high total-cholesterol levels and particularly, high low-density lipoprotein (LDL)-cholesterol levels are risk factors for CVD and mortality. Thus, the food industry has been exploring the possibility of increasing components in the diet which have hypocholesterolemic effects and nowadays there are already marketed products with EFSA, FDA, FOSHU etc. approved health claims [3-5].

All the marketed products claiming a reduction in the cholesterol levels in serum are able to perform their beneficial effect by reducing cholesterol absorption. However, it has been shown that in subjects who were administered some of them (depending on genetic polymorphisms), the cholesterol biosynthetic pathway was stimulated compared with control subjects [1]. Thus, it could be convenient to combine inhibitors of the cholesterol absorption with inhibitors of the cholesterol synthesis in order to increase the product efficiency.

Exogenous Cholesterol Absorption

The exogenous cholesterol is coming from 3 different sources: diet, bile and intestinal epithelial sloughing. In diets from people from industrialized areas the average daily intake is approximately 300 – 500 mg. Bile provides 800 mg – 1200 mg cholesterol per day to the intraluminal pool. The turnover of intestinal mucosal epithelium is the third source of intraluminal cholesterol, and it is estimated to contribute with 300 mg cholesterol per day [6, 7].

In humans, digestion of cholesterol-containing foods (diet) begins with the cephalic phase in which saliva is produced in the mouth to break down mainly polysaccharides. The stomach continues to breaking down the alimentary bolus by mechanically and chemically action through the churning of the stomach and mixing with low pH acids, pepsin and some gastric lipases. At this step, mainly proteins and some lipidic compounds are degraded. Further on in the intestinal track, the presence of lipids in the duodenum stimulates the secretion of bile salts, phosphatidylcholine and cholesterol from the gall bladder and pancreatic fluids (containing pancreatic lipases/co-lipases) from the pancreas. Lipases binds at the surface of the oil droplets formed by the gall bladder emulsifiers hydrolyzing lipids into their digestion products and generating a series of colloidal species including micelles, mixed micelles, vesicles and emulsion droplets. Lipophilic compounds will be absorbed by intestinal enterocytes only if they are inside or forming part of dietary mixed micelles (DMM) membranes [8]. The micellated cholesterol molecule should pass the mucoid barrier of enterocytes and enter by protein binding inside the cell. Then, it will be further transformed, processed and immediately transported to lymph.

After entering the enterocytes, approximately half of the cholesterol molecules move to the endoplasmic reticulum where they are esterified by the acyl-CoA: cholesterol acyltransferase (ACAT) before incorporation into nascent chylomicron particles (Figure 1). ACAT showed two isoforms ACAT1 and ACAT2. ACAT2 is expressed mainly in liver and small intestine and is responsible for esterification of cholesterol absorbed from the intestine. However, the ACAT is not the only factor influencing the cholesterol absorption. The Niemann-Pick C1-like 1 protein (NPC1L1) is a sterol influx transporter located at the apical membrane of the enterocyte, which facilitate the uptake of cholesterol [9]. Other proteins such as ABCG5 and ABCG8 (ATP-binding cassette transporters) promote active efflux of cholesterol and plant sterols from the enterocyte into the intestinal lumen for excretion. The combined regulatory effect of NPC1L1, ABCG5/8 (heterodimer) and perhaps ABCA1 (another transporter but located at the basolateral enterocyte side and related with the HDL formation) may play a critical role in modulating the amount of esterified cholesterol that will be integrated in the chylomicrons (with the assistance of the apolipoporotein B48 (apoB48), the microsomal triglyceride transfer protein (MTTP) and the diacylglicerol-o-acyltransferase (DGAT1/2)) to reach the lymph [10].

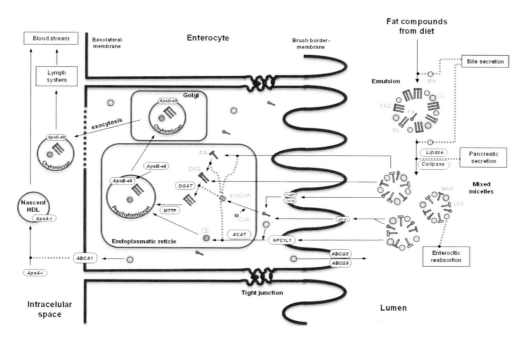

Figure 1. Fat digestion and absorption pathway. BA: bile acids, CL: cholesterol, TAG: triacylglycerol, PL: phospholipids, FA: fatty acids, MAG: monoacylglycerols, LPA: lysophosphatidic acid, CE: cholesterol esters, CoA: coenzyme A, acylCoA: acyl coenzyme A, PA: phosphatidic acid, DAG: diacylglycerol, ABCG5, ABCG8 and ABCA1: ABC membrane transporters, NPC1L1: Niemann-Pick C1-like protein, **ACAT**: acetyl-CoA acetyltransferase, MTTP: microsomal triglyceride transfer protein large subunit, DAGT: diacylglycerol O-acyltransferase, ApoB48: apolipoprotein B and ApoA1: apolipoprotein A-I.

Moreover, there are other molecules involved in the regulation of cholesterol homeostasis such as the liver X receptor α (LXRα), the farnesoid X receptor (FXR) and regulatory element-binding proteins (SREBP-2). For instance, the transcription factor LXR senses cholesterol overload and restricts its accumulation by upregulating the transcription of genes involved in its cellular elimination, hepatic delivery (lipoprotein lipase, cholesteryl ester transfer protein), and intestinal or biliary excretion [11, 12].

Endogenous Cholesterol Synthesis

As previously indicated, cholesterol is not only obtained from the diet, but synthesized *de novo* in the liver. The synthesized endogenous cholesterol can reach up to 1000-1600 mg per day although this rate is highly dependent of the cholesterol amount absorbed from the dietary sources. Reduction of cholesterol absorption in the gut can not only reduce total serum cholesterol level, but also increase the ratio of high-density lipoproteins (HDL) to low-density lipoproteins (LDL) in blood and that is the reason why nutritionists emphasize the importance of dietary intake of low-cholesterol food, mono- and polyunsaturated fats, dietary fibres, fruits and vegetables helps to normalize blood cholesterol level [13].

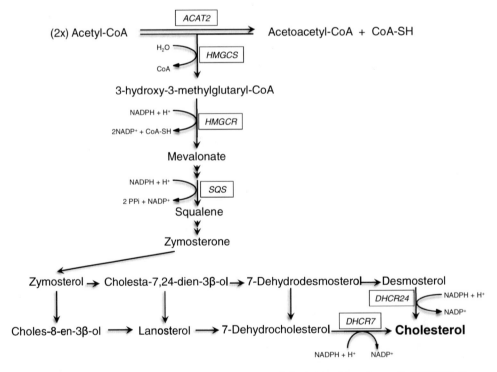

Figure 2. Cholesterol biosynthetic pathway. ACAT2: acetyl-CoA acetyltransferase 2, HMGCS: 3-hydroxy-3-methylglutaryl-CoA synthase, HMGCR: hydroxymethylglutaryl-CoA reductase, SQS: Squalene synthase, DHCR24: 24-dehydrocholesterol reductase, DHCR7: 7-dehydrocholesterol reductase.

When an excess of exogenous cholesterol is absorbed and reach the liver, it triggers the inhibition of cholesterol synthesis and inhibits the expression of the receptor for low density lipoproteins (LDL-R) resulting in discrete increase of cholesterolemia. The low density lipoprotein (LDL) is the major carrier of cholesterol in the blood and the LDL receptor (LDL-R) remove LDLs by binding to apolipoproteins. Apolipoprotein B (apoB) contains the ligand-binding domain for binding of LDL to LDL-R site, which enables the removal of LDL from circulation [14].

The second mentioned regulation point to maintain the cholesterol homeostasis is at the level of the 3-hydroxy 3-methylglutaryl co-enzyme A reductase (HMG CoA reductase) since it is the key enzyme in the endogenous synthesis of cholesterol (Figure 2). This enzyme is regulated at several levels: transcriptional (gene expression), translational (via interaction with specific elements such as the SREBPs) and later by modification of the enzyme susceptibility to proteolytic degradation or its catalytic kinetics [15].

MARKETED FUNCTIONAL FOODS CONTAINING HYPOCHOLESTEROLEMIC COMPOUNDS

Moderate to severe hypercholesterolemia is usually treated with several drugs acting as inhibitors of endogenous cholesterol biosynthesis or impairing exogenous cholesterol absorption. These pharmacological compounds lower cholesterol levels in serum following different mechanisms of actions, for instance:

1. Natural or synthetic statins (lovastatin, atorvastatin etc.) are HMGCoA reductase inhibitors thus, they inhibit the cholesterol biosynthesis.
2. Bile acid scavengers (i.e., cholestyramine, etc.) reduce cholesterol absorption via interruption of the enterohepatic circulation of bile acids and results in a secondary increase in the hepatic LDL receptor activity.
3. Inhibitors of the intestinal ACAT and the cholesterol ester transfer protein as well as compounds able to interfere with the apolipoproteins and chylomicron formation (i.e., gemfibrozil, etc.).
4. Other compounds showed a potential to alter the NPC1L1 or ABC transporter activity in the intestine (i.e., ezetimibe, etc.).
5. Specific pancreatic lipase inhibitors (i.e., orlistat etc.) may also suppress cholesterol absorption by blocking the degradative process within the gastro-intestinal lumen which results in a decreased solubility of cholesterol during the critical stage of intestinal diffusion.

People with incipient hypercholesterolemia can prevent or delay the pharmaceutical treatment by taking a few functional foods already available at the supermarkets. At the present, many supplements are indicated by herbalists because they might help against CVD such as garlic extracts, soy preparations, ω3 oils, etc. However, only two types of compounds are nowadays authorized by most of the industrialized countries to bear the health claim ¨hypocholesterolemic properties¨ in their label and they are marketed under many different brands by the food industry: plant sterols and β-glucans.

Phytosterols

This group of compounds gained much attention in the last decade since, in 1999 a sitostanol-containing margarine was launched in the market [16, 17]. A few years later, other sterols such as esterified phytosterols and not free sterols were utilized to functionalize foods because the esterification increases their solubility in fat and improved their bioavailability [18, 19].

Cholesterol absorption from dietary and biliary sources is significantly reduced in the presence of plant sterols. Their mechanism of action is related to their structural similarity since they appear to compete with dietary cholesterol absorption displacing it from the dietary mixed micelles formed during intestinal digestion and then, the unabsorbed cholesterol is excreted in the faeces [6]. Apparently, phytosterols become more efficiently incorporated into micelles in the intestinal lumen, displace the cholesterol, and lead to its precipitation with other, nonsolubilized phytosterols. Furthermore, competition between cholesterol and plant sterols was also observed for their transfer through the brush border membrane and within the cell, for the ACAT. More recent publications suggested other mechanisms such as inhibition of the gene expression of proteins such as NPC1L1, ABC transporters [6], regulation by acting as LXRα agonists etc. [12].

β-Glucans

More recently, β-glucans containing foods such as oat or barley products have also been launched in the market claiming up to 15% cholesterol reduction after regular consumption [1]. Many epidemiological studies have demonstrated a reduced CVD risk for consumers of high amounts of dietary fibre. The $(1 \rightarrow 3)$, $(1 \rightarrow 4)$-β-glucans are believed to perform many biological functions and one of them is the ability to lower serum cholesterol (LDL) levels [20]. Water soluble β-glucan are thought to act via their capacity to form viscous gels in the intestinal tract. The increase in viscosity (water binding capacity in the chyme) might leads to a reduced diffusion rate of bile acids, which cannot be reabsorbed by the body being then excreted [21]. The possible mechanism by which the water-insoluble polysaccharides lower cholesterol could be a more direct binding of bile acids and cholesterol (from ingested food) [22]. As the fibres bind bile acids, micelle formation is altered and reabsorption of bile acids is subsequently impaired resulting in the excretion of the fibre-bile complex through the faeces and stimulating the transformation of cholesterol into bile acids. Moreover, certain barley β-glucans were able to down-regulate the expression of a few genes involved in the lipidic metabolism including regulators such as SREBP1 and 2 [23].

Chitosan

Chitosan, a de-N-acetylated derivative of chitin, is a heteropolysaccharide consisting of linear β-1-4-linked glucosamine and N-acetyl-D-glucosamine units and it is included in the list of approved health claims according to FOSHU regulations with the claim ¨helps lower cholesterol level¨. At the present (2011) in Japan, there are 142 marketed products including powdered or soft drinks containing chitosan. This compound is obtained from chitins extracted from crustacean shell wastes, insect skeletons, mushrooms and other fungi or bacteria [24]. A particular enterprise is conducting double-blind studies with animals and it is scheduled to begin with human clinical tests next year to submit a specific preparation for FOSHU approval. The preparation includes a mushroom-derived chitosan combined with β-glucans.

The hypocholesterolemic action of chitosan might be due to its ability to decrease cholesterol absorption and interfere with bile acid absorption following a mechanism similar to those explained for the other above mentioned β-glucans [25] since both the water-soluble and water-insoluble chitosan fractions were able to lower cholesterol in a clinical trial with 60 elderly hyperlipidemic patients. Total cholesterol significantly declined by 7.5% in the water-soluble and by 8.9% in the water-insoluble chitosan groups over 8 weeks [26]. Other studies carried out on rat groups fed on a diet rich in cholesterol found that chitosan hydrolysates with different molecular weights and viscosity were also effective and that the lower the molecular weight, the better its cholesterol-lowering potential [27, 28].

EVIDENCES OF THE HYPOCHOLESTEROLEMIC PROPERTIES OF MUSHROOMS

Edible mushrooms should also contain compounds able to lower cholesterol levels in serum since already for years, many works have been published pointing some mushrooms species as source of hypocholesterolemic compounds although many of them did not identified the responsible molecules because most of the studies were animal or clinical tests using the complete fruiting body (sporophore) or certain specific extracts or fractions.

Animal Testing

In vivo studies in Wistar rats, Syrian hamsters and Chinchilla rabbits demonstrated the ability of oyster mushrooms (*Pleurotus ostreatus*) to lower the cholesterol levels. Rats with hereditary enhanced sensitivity to alimentary cholesterol were fed with 4% fruiting bodies in a diet containing 1% cholesterol. Mushroom consumption prevented serum cholesterol increase after 4 weeks and after 7 weeks the cholesterolemia was lowered by 40% compared with control animals. This effect was due to a decrease in the concentrations of very low density lipoproteins (VLDL) and LDL [29] and to an induced delay in cholesterol absorption [30, 31]. A 50% increase in the HDL and activation of antioxidative enzymes was also observed [32]. Similar results were observed using Chinchilla rabbits (fed with 10% *P. ostreatus*) where a decrease in total serum cholesterol was also detected primarily affected by the reduction (70%) of the VLDL-cholesterol. An increase by a factor of 3 in the HDL was also observed [33]. However, the hypocholesterolemic effect was dependent on the amount of dietary oyster mushroom administrated, 1% was ineffective while doses of 5% induced a significantly reduction in normal rats [34]. The ethanol extracts obtained from the same mushroom were less efficient with increasing concentrations of ethanol than the whole body or its water extract. The latter and the extracts including 30 and 60% ethanol were also able to reduce the cholesterol and triacylglycerol levels in hamsters serum and liver (reduction of 34% cholesterol and 48% triacylglycerols). The consumption of the water and 30% ethanol extracts reduced the VLDL fraction [30]. Another extract obtained from its mycelium with dichloromethane and 95% ethanol lowered cholesterol levels in liver of normal rats [35] but, a β-glucan fraction extracted from the fruiting bodies was unable to affect cholesterols levels in both serum and liver [32].

Supplementation of a high-fat-diet given to hyperlipidemic rats with *Pleurotus citrinopileatus* fruiting bodies, a hot-water extract and two specific fractions obtained by eluting from a silica gel column with ethyl acetate and methanol at different doses showed that serum triglycerides and total cholesterol levels were significantly lower and HLD significantly higher in the groups supplemented with the highest dosage of the two eluted fractions as compared with the control groups with no mushroom addition. The major constituents of the eluted fractions were ergosterol in one of them and nicotinic acid in the other [36].

Other species from the same genera such as *Pleurotus eryngii* reduced the plasma total cholesterol, triglyceride, LDL, total lipid, phospholipids and LDL/HDL ratio by 24, 46.3, 62.5, 24.6, 19.2 and 57.1% respectively and showed no adverse effects when they were added as supplement (5%) to hypercholesterolemic Sprague-Dawley albino rats. Feeding mushrooms increased total lipid and cholesterol excretion in faeces [37]. Its water extracts showed hypolipidemic and hypocholesterolemic effects in fat-loaded mice. The low fat absorption provoked was due to its lipase inhibitory activity. Apparently, the water extract might prevent the interactions between lipid emulsions and pancreatic lipase [38]. The remarkably reduction of lipid levels, total cholesterol, total triglyceride and LDL-cholesterol and increase in HDL-cholesterol was because of its water-soluble polysaccharides [39].

Ganoderma lucidum is considered by the Asiatic culture as a medicinal mushroom because of its many different beneficial properties. Several of these properties have been confirmed by scientific studies [40, 41] including its hypocholesterolemic effects in hamsters and minipigs [42]. The organic fractions containing oxygenated lanosterol derivatives inhibited cholesterol synthesis in T9A4 hepatocytes. In hamsters, 5% supplementation did not affect LDL but decreased 9.8% total cholesterol, 11.2% HDL and had effects on several faecal neutral sterols and bile acids. It also reduced hepatic microsomal *ex-vivo* HMGCoA reducase activity but not its gene expression [43]. In minipigs, 2.5% supplementation decreased 20% total cholesterol, 27% LDL and 18% HDL-cholesterol and increased faecal cholestanol and coprostanol and decreased cholate. Results also indicated that *G. lucidum* reduced LDL cholesterol *in vivo* through various mechanisms [42].

Similar studies with the white button mushroom (*Agaricus bisporus*) indicated that they were able to lowers blood glucose and cholesterol levels in diabetic and hypercholesterolemic Sprague-Dawley rats fed with hypercholesterolemic diets for 3 or 4 weeks [44]. Hypercholesterolemic rats significantly decreased their levels of plasma total cholesterol and LDL (22.8 and 33.1% respect.) and their hepatic levels of cholesterol and triglycerides (36.2 and 20.8% respect.) increasing significantly their plasma HDL concentrations. Apparently, these effects might have been induced by the presence of *A. bisporus* fibres because when rats were fed with these compounds, the serum total cholesterol, VLDL, IDL (intermediate density lipoprotein) and LDL were lower than control rats while the HDL were lower. These observations could be caused by the overexpression of the hepatic LDL receptor since its mRNA level was significantly higher than in the control rats [45].

The Use of Edible Mushroom Extracts as Bioactive Ingredients ...   51

After these results, the fibre fraction from other edible mushrooms was also investigated. Rats were fed with the fibre fraction from *Grifola frondosa* (maitake), *Lentinula edodes* (Shiitake) and *Flammulina velutipes* (enokitake mushrooms) for 4 weeks and compared with cellulose as control. The total cholesterol in serum was significantly lower in rats fed with *G. frondosa* and *F. velutipes* than in those rats fed with cellulose. The VLDL, IDL and LDL levels were also lower when the rats ate any of the three mushrooms whereas only the HDL of the *F. velutipes* group was significantly lower than the others. The LDL receptor mRNA levels were only significantly higher in the *F. velutipes* group, thus, *F. velutipes* lowered cholesterol in serum by enhancement of hepatic LDL receptor mRNA while the other mushroom fibres enhanced the faecal cholesterol excretion [46]. Moreover, *G. frondosa* and two other mushroom species such as *P. eryngii*, and particularly *Hypsizygus marmoreus* also showed antiatherosclerotic effects in atherosclerosis-susceptible C57BL/6J, apolipoprotein E– deficient (apoE–/–) mice [47].

Auricularia auricular (tree-ear mushroom) and *Tremella fuciformis* (white jelly-leaf mushroom) fruiting bodies were also capable of reducing total cholesterol in serum (5% fed Sprague-Dawley rats) after 4 weeks (17 and 19% reduction respect.) by decreasing the LDL-cholesterol levels but with no significant differences in the HDL levels nor total lipids or cholesterol in liver [48]. However, the hypocholesterolemic properties of the mushrooms were effective when the animals consumed the fruiting bodies in regular basis and for long terms because when the cholesterol levels were determined 3 or 6 h after in taking, although the glycemic levels were decreased no statistical differences were observed in cholesterol levels in Wistar rats administrated with water or methanol extracts obtained from *Lentinula lepideus*, *Calvatia cyathiformis* and *Ganoderma applantum* [49].

Clinical Trials

In a clinical investigation carried out on 17 diabetic subjects eating *Pleurotus ostreatus* for 24 days, it was concluded that mushrooms significantly reduced blood glucose, blood pressure, triglycerides and cholesterol of diabetic subject without any deleterious effect on liver and kidney. The mushroom diet modified particularly the total cholesterol leaving unaffected the HDL levels [50]. A similar trial was performed by Schneider et al. (2011) but using healthy volunteers [51]. They drank an oyster mushroom soup as part of a diet followed by 20 subjects (9 male, 11 female 20-34 years old) during 21 days. After the treatment, the volunteers showed a significant decrease in triacylglycerol concentrations and oxidized-LDL and a tendency in lowering total cholesterol values with no effect on HDL or LDL levels. They attributed the beneficial effects to the presence of linoleic acid, ergosterol and ergosta-derivatives showing antioxidant activities.

A few more edible mushrooms were tested with human trials such as *Ganoderma lucidum* (Lingzhi or reishi mushroom) [52] and *Cordyceps* sp. [53] to investigate, besides other parameters, their hypocholesterolemic effects. Both were double-blinded, placebo-controlled studies and results indicated that those mushrooms could help treating hyperlipidemia. Specific extracts obtained from *L. edodes* also induced significant decrease in serum cholesterol in young women and people older than 60 years in Japan [24]. Recently, Poddar et al. (2013) demonstrated that substitution of meat by mushrooms (*Agaricus bisporus*) improved energy intake, reduced body weight and improved the lipid (including LDL) and inflammatory profile among 73 obese adults in a short and 1 yearlong trials [54].

FUNGAL COMPOUNDS POTENTIALLY ABLE TO IMPAIR CHOLESTEROL ABSORPTION

After the above mentioned studies it seems possible to conclude that edible mushrooms should contain bioactive compounds responsible for the observed hypocholesterolemic effects. Some of them have been already investigated in detail, however for some others, results are still inconclusive, contradictory or with no physiological significance although their *in vitro* tests were promising.

Ergosterol and Other Derivative Fungal Sterols

Edible mushrooms are good sources of cholesterol-like structures such as ergosterol, (ergosta-5,7,22-trien-3β-ol), fungisterol (ergosta-7-enol), ergosterol peroxides and many other derivatives (Figure 3) [55-58] so these molecules could also act as plant sterols or even better because some of them are more hydrophobic.

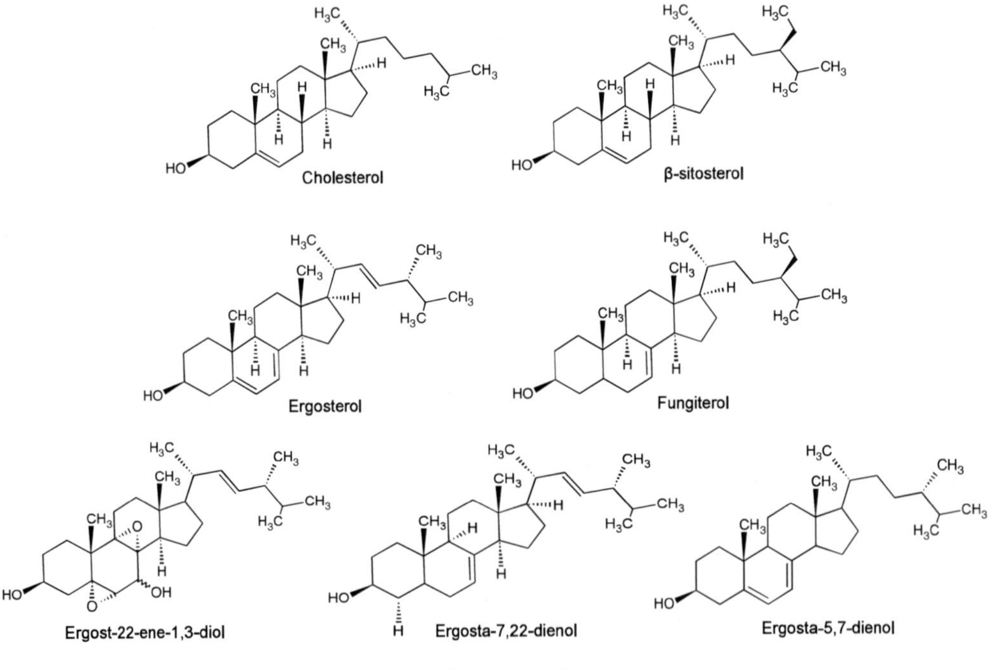

Figure 3. Cholesterol, β-sitosterol (a plant sterol) and fungal sterol structures.

In fact many of them showed interesting bioactive properties such as antioxidant, antimicrobial, antitumor activities etc. [58]. But, two of their biological activities can be particularly interesting because of their relation with the cholesterol metabolism such that the ability of ergosterol derivatives (ergost-22-ene-1,3-diol, ergosta-5,7-dien-3b-ol, (22E)-ergosta-1,4,6,22-tetraen-3-one, etc.) that were pointed as a potent agonists for LXR able to induce the expression of ABC transporters [59]. Moreover, ergosterol was a competitive inhibitor (showing Ki values = 36.8 µM) of the enzyme that catalyzes the reduction of the double bond at C-24 in the cholesterol-biosynthesis pathway (C24-reductase). Ergosterol together with other sterols such as stigmasterol and brassicasterol were efficient because of its double bond at C-22 in the side chain of their structure [60].

These sterols were unable to inhibit other key enzymes such as the HMGCoA reductase [61] but recent studies indicated that ergosterol and particularly specific SFE ergosterol-enriched extracts were able to displace cholesterol from de DMM more efficiently than β-sitosterol using an *in vitro* digestion model were the DMM fraction was isolated [62].

The major fungal sterol, ergosterol, is abundant in all mushrooms species since it is a constitutive compound of the hyphae membranes and it is known as a vitamin D_2 (ergocalciferol) precursor. This compound might represent 53 up to 98% of the fungal sterols. Some mushroom species such as *Chantharellus cibarius* and *Craterellus cornucopioides* showed almost exclusively ergosterol, other species showed more ergosta-5,7-dienol than fungisterol (i.e., *Lyophyllum shimeji*, *Pleurotus ostreatus* etc.) (Table 1), other showed specific derivatives such as *Flammulina velutipes* which according to some reports contained high amount of ergosta 5,8,22-trien3β-ol, etc. Ergosterol concentrations ranged from 0.2 up to almost 10 mg/g dw being the most commonly cultivated mushrooms the species with the highest levels. This is probably because mushroom growers cultivate them with specific substrates containing all the nutritive requirements and harvest the fruiting bodies at their optimal developmental stage while when they grow wild in the woods they do not always flush at the optimal environmental conditions. Ergosterol is utilized as a biomarker of optimal fungal growth since high production of this constituent by the fungal hyphae indicates that the mycelia are elongated and the mushroom is properly growing [24].

Moreover, besides the influence of the different analytical methodologies utilized, the observed differences between publications are normal because of the typical variability depending on the mushroom strain, mushroom variety and other cultivation parameters such as flush number, type of casing soil and developmental stages.

Within the sporophore tissues, veil and gills and the lower part of the stipe (usually considered as by-product and discarded) of strains such as *A. bisporus*, showed higher ergosterol content than skin, flesh and upper stipe [70]. Similarly, in species such as *C. cibarius, C. tubaeformis* and *L. trivialis* the ergosterol levels were higher in the gills except for *B. edulis* with similar ergosterol concentrations in the cap and gills [55].

Mushroom from the first flush contained higher amount of fungal sterols than second or latter flushes since the substrate nutrients disappear during the cultivation. During the mushroom fructification, pin-heads showed lower amount of ergosterol and derivatives than immature mushrooms and when they become more mature their sterol concentrations were again reduced because of their senescence [70].

Table 1. Fungal sterol content in mushroom species (mg/g dw)

Mushroom specie	A	B	C	D	E	F	G	H	Reference
Agaricus bisporus	3.06	0.67	0.65	0.67					[63]
	8.92 (44.6*)	0.18 (0.9*)	0.38 (1.9*)	0.38 (1.9*)					[56]
	6.42								[64]
	7.8								[65]
	6.54	0.26	0.15	0.94					[55]
Agaricus blazeii	1.73	0.75	1.06	0.6					[63]
Agrocybe aegerita	5.11	ND	ND	1.01					[63]
Amanita caesarea	3.81	1.09	1.05	1.15					[63]
	8.25			1.75					[66]
Amanita ponderosa	1.65	0.62	ND	0.6					[63]
Boletus edulis	5.69	0.87	1.21	0.93					[63]
	4.89								[55]
	38.4 (192.2*)	3.28 (16.4*)	2.24 (11.2*)	2.5 (12.5*)					[56]
	4.00								[64]
Calocybe gambosa	3.61								[64]
Clitocybe maxima	6.42								[68]
Clitocybe nebularis	6.38	1.04							[57]
Catathelasma ventricosum	6.51								[[68]
Cantharellus cibarius	2.61								[63]
	3.04								[55]
	4.94 (24.7*)	0.04 (0.2*)	0.08 (0.4*)	0.08 (0.4*)					[56]
	0.23								[64]
Cantharellus tubaeformis	1.73								[57]
	3.36 (16.8*)	0.24 (1.2*)	0.36 (1.8*)	0.9 (4.5*)					[56]
	3.77								[55]

Mushroom specie	A	B	C	D	E	F	G	H	Reference
Craterellus cornucopioides	3.27								[68]
	0.79	ND	ND	ND					[63]
	0.44								[64]
Coprinus atramentarius	2.45			7.55					[66]
Flamulina velutipes	0.68								[65]
	4.53		1.41	1.05	3.01				[66]
Ganoderma lucidum	0.69	0.25	0.59	0.17					[63]
	0.705								[67]
Ganoderma sinense	0.0801								[67]
Grifola frondosa	3.24	0.61	0.57	ND					[63]
	0.32								[64]
	1.85 (9.25*)	0.204 (1.02*)	0.104 (0.52*)	0.01 (0.05*)		0.01 (0.05*)	0.011 (0.56*)	0.004 (0.02*)	[69]
Lactarius sangruifluus	3.6 (18*)	0.26 (1.32*)	0.19 (0.97*)	0.008 (0.04*)		0.008 (0.04*)	0.102 (0.51*)	0.008 (0.04*)	[69]
lactarius semisanguifluus	2.12 (10.58*)	0.26 (1.3*)	0.174 (0.87*)	0.012 (0.06*)		0.014 (0.07*)	0.11 (0.57*)	0.01 (0.05*)	[69]
Lactarius trivialis	2.96								[55]
Lampteromyces japonicus	4.56			5.44					[66]
Laccaria amethystea	6.37								[68]
Lentinula edodes	5.51	0.43	0.4	ND					[63]
	21.58 (107.9*)	1.82 (9.1*)	1.7 (8.5*)	1.4 (7.0*)					[56]
	3.64								[64]
	6.05								[65]
	6.79	0.63	0.17	0.28					[55]
Lepiota procera	2.57	0.64	0.67	ND					[63]
Leucopaxillus giganteus	8.59			0.73					[66]
Lyophyllum shimeji	4.64	0.68	ND	1.55					[63]
Marasmius oreades	3.85	0.57	0.54	0.59					[63]
Hydnum repandum	6.28	0.85							[57]
Hygrophorus marzuolus	6.81								[64]

Table 1. (Continued)

Mushroom specie	A	B	C	D	E	F	G	H	Reference
Hypsizygus marmoreus	10.56 (52.8*)								[47]
Hygrocybe punicea	7.88			2.12					[66]
Pleurotus ostreatus	3.75	0.51	0.79	0.98					[63]
	12.14 (60.7*)	1.24 (6.2*)	0.64 (4.7*)	1.18 (5.9*)					[56]
	3.31								[64]
	4.4								[65]
	6.74	0.18	0.15	0.83					[55]
Pleurotus eryngii	1.4	0.22	0.2	0.25					[63]
	9.1 (45.5*)								[47]
Pleurotus cystidus	4.35								[65]
	9.86 (49.3*)								[47]
Russula cyanoxantha	6.32	1.28							[57]
Russula xerampelina	6.55	1.12							[57]
Russula delica	2.5 (12.51*)	0.38 (1.90*)	0.266 (1.33*)	0.034 (0.17*)		0.048 (0.24*)	0.12 (0.61*)	0.014 (0.07*)	[69]
Russula foetens	7.09			2.91					[66]
Russula senecis	8.45								[66]
Russula nigricans	8.38			1.62					[66]
Suillus granulatus	7.02	0.8							[57]
Suillus luteus	6.62	0.83							[57]
Suillus bellinii	2.46 (12.31*)	0.298 (1.49*)	0.14 (0.70*)	0.076 (0.38*)		0.094 (0.47*)	0.054 (0.27*)	0.01 (0.05*)	[69]
Stropharia rugoso-annulata	7.89								[68]

ND = no detected, * in the original article the value was expressed in fresh weigh (value between bracket in mg/100g fw) but it is here converted into dry weight assuming an average 95% r.h.

A: ergosterol, B: fungisterol, C: ergosta-7,22-dienol, D: ergosta-5,7-dienol, E: ergosta-5,8,22-trien-3ol, F: lanosterol, G: lanosta-8,24-dienol, H: 4α-methylzymosterol.

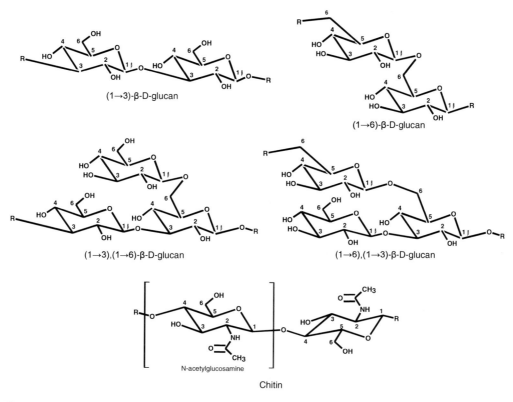

Figure 4. Typical fungal β-glucans molecular structures (including chitin).

Dietary Fibres (Soluble Polysaccharides, Beta-glucans, Chitins etc.)

Edible mushrooms also contain interesting polysaccharides such as β-glucans (Figure 4). Their molecular structure is different than those present in cereals since their branching profiles are (1→3) and (1→3)(1→6) but they share many biological activities such as antioxidant, antitumoral and immunomodulatory activities including the capability of lowering serum cholesterol levels [20, 48, 71] and those are the reason for the detailed studies carried out on many particular fungal β-glucans such as lentinan from shiitake mushrooms (*Lentinula edodes*), schizophyllan from *Schizophyllum commune*, grifolan from *G. frondosa*, and other from *Agaricus blazei, G. lucidum, P. ostreatus* as well as the (1→3) β-glucans and glucuronoxylomannans from *Auricularia polytricha* and *Tremella fuciformis,* etc. [72, 73]. The viscous and gel-forming properties of some of these compounds could lower the cholesterol absorption by inhibiting the formation of micelles in the small intestine. The anionic charged functional groups such as in glucuronoxylomannan may also interfere with the absorption of cholesterol from the digestive tract in a way similar to the ion-exchange resins. Furthermore, these dietary fibre and possibly other components from the mushrooms might interact with the bile acids similarly as explained for cereal β-glucans. This would lead to an increase in faecal bile acids excretion and the organism would response by increasing hepatic conversion of cholesterol to bile acids. Indeed, recent investigations indicated that β-glucans extracts from *P. ostreatus, A. bisporus* and *L. edodes* were able to scavenge bile acids in an *in vitro* digestion model although at slightly lower ratios than a cereal polysaccharide extract [62].

Some reports indicated that the biologically active β-glucans were those with a similar structure, such as a main chain of (1-3)-β-linked glucans to which some side chains were randomly connected by (1-6)-β-linkages with a range of DB (degree of branching) about 0.2-0.3, since polysaccharides such as lentinan, shizophyllan and a few others with those moieties showed high antitumour activity. Obviously, the tertiary structure varies with the linkage degree because β-glucans with few or no β-(1-6)-linkages mainly have a single helix structure while those with higher degrees of β-(1-6)-glycosidic bonds form a triple helix [74]. Other reports indicated that triple helix structure together with the molecular mass positively affected the biological activity of the β-glucans [75]. However, the more polysaccharides are studied the least correlation between structure and function can be drawn [76]. This conclusion applies also to the hypocholesterolemic properties, some studies indicated that the immunomodulatory activities of the β-glucans were mainly due to the water soluble glucans while the capability of impairing cholesterol absorption were due to the water insoluble polysaccharides. Other reports pointed the degradation products of the β-glucans as more bioactive than larger molecules. Thus, until now the precise structural requirements for the observed hypocholesterolemic action of fungal β-glucans remains unclear and further studies are necessary [76].

The main problem with finding the correlations between structures and functions within the β-glucans are the different extraction procedures followed to obtain polysaccharides enriched extracts. For instance, traditional β-glucan extraction protocols included: hot water extraction, ethanol precipitation, alkali/acid treatments, enzymatic degradations, washing with Sevag or other reagents etc., yielding fractions with completely different composition difficult to characterize or quantify. According to some publications mushroom species such as *G. Lucidum, P. ostreatus, L. edodes, Agrocybe aegerita* and *Lactarius deliciosus* showed high levels of β-glucans (38 - 65 mg/100mg) [63]. But, they were almost 10 fold higher quantities than previously reported [77-79]. In those earlier publications the described β-glucan contents ranged from 0.14 to 0.53 mg/100 mg in similar strains such as *Pleurotus pulmonarius, P. ostreatus, P. eryngii, B. edulis, A. aegerita* and *L. edodes*. Other more recent publications estimated the total β-glucan levels between 2.6 - 13.4 mg/100mg dw for *A. bisporus, F. Velutipes, L. edodes, P. ostreatus* and *P. eryngii* using other analytical determinations thus, the values were intermediate between the other two described ranges [75, 80]. An example of these wide quantitative differences can be noticed in the table 2.

A particular type of β-glucans which is lately getting interest is chitin and chitins derivatives such as the previously mentioned chitosans and their degradation products (low molecular weight polymers generated from chitin/chitosan hydrolysis (LMWC) or chitooligosaccharides). Chitin is a water-insoluble β-(1→4)-glucan of N-acetylglucosamine monomers and chitosan can be obtained from chitin by de-N-acetylation, both are considered as dietary fiber [25]. The immunomodulatory and antitumor properties seemed to be more related to the water soluble fraction including the oligomers and low molecular weight polymers generated from chitin hydrolysis (LMWC) [81] while their effect as prebiotic and hypocholesterolemic compounds might be due to their water-insoluble β-glucans (chitins and protein-bound glucans) [71] although as previously indicated for other type of β-glucans, results are largely different depending on report [27].

The Use of Edible Mushroom Extracts as Bioactive Ingredients ... 59

Table 2. Fungal β-glucan content in mushroom species (mg/100mg dw) according to different authors indicating those that were quantified as chitins (mg/100 mg dw)

Mushroom specie	β-glucan content mg/100mg dw	Reference	Chitin content (mg/100mg dw)	Reference
Cantharellus cibarius	17.8	[63]	5.19	[62]
Cantharellus lutescens			6.37	[62]
Craterellus cornucopioides	21.8	[63]	5.74	[62]
Agaricus bisporus	12.3	[63]	4.86	[62]
	58.2	[83]	4.69	[75]
			8.68-6.17	[84]
Agaricus blazei (or A. brasiliensis)	14.5	[63]	7.10	[62]
	22.8	[83]		
Lepiota procera	11.2	[63]	8.22	[62]
Pleurotus ostreatus	41.8	[63]	3.32	[62]
	0.38-0.24	[77]	0.76	[75]
			5.46-2.42	[84]
Pleurotus eryngii	27.5	[63]	5.69	[62]
	0.38-0.29	[77]	3.16	[75]
Marasmius oreades	15.9	[63]	8.62	[62]
Lentinula edodes	38.2	[63]	4.61	[62]
	0.2	[77]	1.87	[75]
			8.07-5.36	[84]
Amanita ponderosa	20.4	[63]	8.42	[62]
Amanita caesaria	23.6	[63]	7.40	[62]
Lyophyllum shimeji	29.0	[63]	4.74	[62]
Morchella esculenta	12.2	[63]		
Morchella conica	20.8	[63]	6.38	[62]
Flammulina veluttipes	21.2	[63]	5.23	[62]
	3.2	[80]	9.83	[75]
Boletus edulis	22.1	[63]	8.16	[62]
Lactarius deliciosus	36.5	[63]	3.94	[62]
Agrocybe aegerita	37.6	[63]	4.13	[62]
Ganoderma lucidum	64.4	[63]	4.78	[62]
	1.2	[83]		
Grifola frondosa	32.3	[63]	7.04	[62]
	33.5	[80]		
Auricularea judea	48.6	[63]		
Pholiota nameko	29.8	[63]	4.88	[62]
	32.8	[80]		
Phellinus linteus	21.8	[83]		
Pleurotus pulmonarius	0.53	[77]	6.09	[62]
Panellus serotinus	19.6	[80]		
Calocybe gambosa			7.14	[62]
Hypsizygus marmoreus	13.7	[80]		
Hydum repandum			5.78	[62]
Pleurotus cornucopiae	7.5	[80]		
Armillaria mellea	5.8	[80]		
Hypsizygus tessulatus			0.39	[75]

Some indicated that chitin itself was unable of lowering cholesterol levels in serum if it is not transformed into chitosan or degraded in smaller products [25]. However, specific extracts obtained by advance technologies (see later) containing chitins and other β-glucans were able to scavenge bile acids in an *in vitro* digestion model. Moreover, these β-glucan enriched fractions obtained from *P. ostreatus* reduced total cholesterol levels of Winstar mice that were administrated simultaneously with a hypercholesterolemic diet for 4 weeks [82]. Perhaps, the presence of other β-glucan (which are not chitins, could be proteoglucans) enhanced their hypocholesterolemic effect or stimulated certain synergy between polysaccharides.

Chitin concentrations were more similar between different publications than those values described for β-glucans if the same or similar analytical methods were utilized (Table 2). Many authors determined chitin by the amount of N-glucosamine residues present in the samples [84] while others quantify them by the amount of non-protein nitrogen content detected with Keldar [80, 85, 86].

Inhibitors of the Pancreatic Lipase

Inhibiting the pancreatic lipase (PL) during digestion can be considered as an indirect mechanism of lowering cholesterol because if this enzyme cannot generate properly the DMMs, less lipids are absorbed as well as less cholesterol since this molecule should also be included in the micelles for enterocyte absorption.

A few different PL inhibitors were isolated from edible fungi, two of them were β-lactones with unusual configurations named percyquinin (obtained from *Stereum complicatum*) and vibralactone (*Boreostereum vibrans*) with similar IC_{50} (0.4 μg/mL). Several publications and particularly Slanc et al. [85, 87, 88] screened more than 60 edible and non-edible fungi species and found that some of them exhibited PL inhibitory activities ranging from 1% till 97% depending on the specie considered. Later on, Palanisamy et al. [89] also found interesting PL activity in the extracts obtained with methanol, water and methanol:water (1:1) from *Lepiota procera*, *Grifola frondosa*, *Pleurotus eryngii* and *Lyophyllum shimeji*. However, when the PL inhibitory activity was evaluated using an *in vitro* digestion model mimicking gut conditions, none of the selected mushroom extracts were able to inhibit PL activity. Thus, only the report from Mizutani et al. [38] managed to record PL inhibitory activity *in vivo* (for *P. eryngii*).

FUNGAL COMPOUNDS POTENTIALLY ABLE TO INHIBIT CHOLESTEROL METABOLISM

Actually, no functional food able to inhibit the cholesterol synthesis have been designed, there are only drugs prescribed for people with cholesterol levels in serum reaching pathological levels. However, edible mushrooms might contain several types of compounds able to perform such a task via different mechanisms.

Inhibitors of the HMGCoA Reductase

According to several authors, oyster mushrooms species such *as P. ostreatus, P. sapidus, P. eryngii* and *P. cornucopiae*, contain lovastatin (mevinolin), a statin able to inhibit the HMGCoA reductase [90, 91]. In lower quantities, statins were also described in other species such as *A. bisporus, B. edulis, Clitocybe maxima, Hipsizigus marmoreus* etc. [39, 92]. The statin levels were high in the spores and widely distributed through the complete fruiting body and they were present during all the developmental stages [91]. Statins or vastatins were in fact isolated for the first time from fungi by the pharmaceutical industry. They can act as competitive inhibitors of the enzyme substrate, the 3-hydroxy-3-methylglutaryl-coenzyme A, since they can bind to the enzyme with higher affinity (KM≈nM) than its own substrate (Km≈μM) [15].

However, other authors found no statins [42, 51, 93, 94] but other compounds such as lanosteroids, ganoderols etc. in *G. lucidum* able to reduce the mRNA expression of the HMGCoA reducase. Gil-Ramírez et al. [93, 94] also failed detecting statins but still high HMGCoA inhibitory activity using *in vitro* tests. The latter publication suggested the implication of proteo/glucans in the observed inhibitory activity since the fractions with higher molecular weight showed higher inhibitory activity than small molecules [94]. Although, there could be more than one type of inhibitor since results were different depending on the mushroom specie considered [93]. For instance, the water extracts obtained from *Lentinula edodes* and *Amanita ponderosa* showed high HMGCoA-reductase inhibitory activity while the methanol: water (1:1) extracts obtained from the fruiting bodies of *Agaricus bisporus* and *Cantharellus lutescens* were more effective inhibitors than their aqueous or methanol extracts [93].

Inhibitors of Other Enzymes Involved in the Cholesterol Synthesis

Nowadays, the main pharmaceutical target to inhibit the cholesterol biosynthesis in hypercholesterolemic patients is the enzyme HMG-CoA reductase. Inhibitors of this key enzyme (i.e., statins) are well tolerated, having little collateral effects. However, when this enzyme is blocked, other important metabolic pathways are affected such as ubiquinone, dolichol and isoprenylated protein synthesis [95, 96]. Thus, new hypocholesterolemic drugs are at the present being developed to inhibit other enzymes down-stream in the cholesterol biosynthetic pathway such as the squalene synthase. This enzyme also named farnesyl-diphosphate:farnesyl-diphosphate farnesyl transferase catalyzes the reductive dimerization of two molecules of farnesyl pyrophosphate to form squalene at the final branch point of the cholesterol biosynthetic pathway (Figure 2). Inhibition of squalene synthase could therefore avoid any potential adverse effect associated with reduced synthesis of isoprenylated metabolites by the inhibitors of HMG-CoA reductase.

Only a few inhibitors of this enzyme have been studied in detail, one is the synthetic RPR 107393 compound (3-hydroxy-3-[4-(quinolin-6-yl)phenyl]-1-azabicyclo [2-2-2]octane dihydrochloride) [97] but others are called zaragozic acids and they are obtained from the liquid broth of certain ascomicetes able to form macroscopic fruiting bodies [98]. These types of compounds might also be found in the basidiomycota family where most of the macrofungi are included (together with the ascomycota). At the present, only inhibition of the squalene synthase gene expression has been recently reported by A. *bisporus* extracts [62].

Moreover and as previously indicated, ergosterol was able to inhibit another enzyme related with the cholesterol metabolic pathway such as the C24-reductase, the enzyme that catalyzes the reduction of the double bond at C-24 (Figure 2) [60].

Bobek et al., (1998) also suggested that the reduction in the cholesterol biosynthesis found in rats was not only due to the suppression of the hepatic HMGCoA reducase activity but also by accelerating the cholesterol catabolism by up-regulating hepatic cholesterol 7α-hydroxylase (Bobek et al. 1994) [31, 34].

Modulators of the Phospholipid Metabolism

Lentinula edodes was able to induce hypocholesterolemia and reduce the triacylglycerol levels in rats due to its content in eritadenine (2(R), 3(R),-dihydroxy-4-(9-adenyl)-butyric acid, lentinacin or lentysine) a specific compound with S-adenosylhomocysteine hydrolase (SAHH) inhibitory activity able to modify the hepatic phospholipid metabolism [99]. Rats supplemented with eritadenite significantly decreased the phosphatidylcholine: phosphatidylethanolamine ratio in liver microsomes and the S-adenosylmethionine:S-adenosylhomocysteine ratio in the liver in addition to the plasma cholesterol concentration suggesting that the hypocholesterolemic action of this compound might be associated with a modification of hepatic phospholipid metabolism [100]. Moreover, eritadenine also decreased in a dose-dependent manner levels of VLDL, LDL and HDL, increased the hepatic S-adenosylhomocysteine (SAH) level and decreased the ratio of S-adenosylmethionine (SAM) to SAH indicating that the hypocholesterolemic action of eritadenine might be elicited through an alteration of the hepatic phospholipid metabolism that resulted from an inhibition of phosphatidylethanolamine N-methylalion due to a decreased SMA/SAH ratio in the liver [100].

Modulators of the Thyroid Hormones Metabolism

Another important factor in the cholesterol regulation is via thyroid. Triiodothyronine (T3) is a thyroid hormone directly involved in the regulation of LDL-R gene expression. A 20% of this hormone is secreted directly by thyroid but the major amount is produced from thyroxine (T4) (produced exclusively in the thyroid) by 5′-deiodination in peripheral tissues. This reaction is catalyzed by the selenoprotein, type-I 5′-iodothyronine deiodinasein (DIO1 and 2). Other related selenoprotein is the glutathione peroxidase (GSH-Px) since the reduced expression of GSH-Px has been shown to increase cell-mediated oxidation of LDL [14].

Mushrooms contain selenium and can be easily Se-fortified by addition of sodium selenite to their cultivation substrates. This supplementation can modify their biological properties [101]. Moreover, selenium supplementation combined with statins therapy was proved to be significantly beneficial to lipid therapy. The observed upregulation of LDL-R expression by selenium supplementation might have offered more receptor sites for LDL binding and its clearance from the circulation. One ppm Se supplementation on rats decreased the total cholesterol and LDL levels, increased T3 levels due to increased DIO2 expression, decreased the apoB and HMG CoA reductase mRNAs expression [14].Thus, it could be assumed that if an statin-producer mushroom strains could be Se-fortified during its cultivation, it might enhance their hypocholesterolemic effect. However, when *Agaricus bisporus* strains showing HMGCoA reductase inhibitory activities were Se-fortified (31.6 µg/g, 10 fold higher concentrations than normal mushrooms) no significant increase in their inhibitory activities were observed. Moreover, when their methanol: water (1:1) extracts were also applied to Caco2 cell cultures no differences were observed in the gene expression profile of mRNAs involved in the cholesterol metabolism [62]. Perhaps, the fact that no lovastatin was detected in these samples or that the selenium concentration was insufficient might be the cause of the failure in the enhancing of the HMGCoA reductase inhibition expected.

ADVANCED TECHNOLOGIES TO OBTAIN BIOACTIVE FUNGAL EXTRACTS

In the past, most of the biological activities described for edible mushrooms were observed in the whole fruiting body or in easily prepared water or organic extracts. However, in more recent publications new and more advance technologies have been used in order to extract bioactive fractions from several mushroom species to be used as ingredients to design functional foods.

Pressurized Solvent Technologies

Supercritical fluids extractions (SFE) are environmentally-friendly advance technologies utilized for the extraction of specific fractions of interest for the food industry [102]. These technologies are nowadays encouraged because they are considered as GRAS since they used usually CO_2 as extraction solvent. Then, it can easily evaporate after the extraction and depressurization leaving no solvent trace in the extract. CO_2-SFE were utilized to obtain triterpenoids from *G. lucidum*, carboxylic and fatty acids from *Agaricus* spp., antioxidant and antimicrobial compounds from the fruiting bodies of *L. edodes,* antitumoral fractions from *Cordyceps sinensis* mycelia and immune-modulators polysaccharides from *G. lucidum* [103-108]. Ergosterol could also be efficiently extracted from both fruiting bodies and the lower part of the stipe (considered as by product of cultivation and wasted during harvesting) of *A. bisporus* using moderated extraction conditions such as 40°C and 9 to 30 MPa yielding fractions containing on average 60% of sterols (mainly ergosterol, fungisterol, ergosta-7,22-dienol and ergosta-5,7-dienol) [70].

Pressurized liquid extractions (PLE) also called accelerated solvent extractions (ASE) can also be ecological and interesting technologies since under pressure they can improve the extraction capabilities of nontoxic solvents such as water or ethanol. PLE was also utilized to obtain certain fatty acids from *Cordyceps* spp. [109] and to extract fungal sterols although with lower yields than SFE. PLE using ethanol as solvent at 10.7 MPa (50°C and 100°C) after 5 cycles of 5 min extraction (mixing in the extraction cell the sample with sand in a ratio 1:4) yielded extracts with respectively. 5 and 2.9% sterols [70]. However, PLE was more effective to selectively isolate polysaccharides from several fungal species [110-113].

A high content β-glucans extracts could be obtained from cultivated mushrooms (*A. bisporus*, *L. edodes, P. ostreatus* and *G. lucidum*) and wild mushrooms, (*B. edulis*) using water as extraction solvent and 200°C, 5 cycles of 5 min each at 10.3 MPa. The crude polysaccharide (PSC) fractions, isolated from the PWE extracts contained mainly β-glucans (including N-glucosamine-containing compounds deriving from chitin hydrolysis), β-glucans and other PSCs (hetero-/proteo-glucans) depending on the extraction temperature and mushroom strain considered [111, 114]. Some of the obtained fractions showed bile acid binding capacities [62]. PLE was also utilized to obtain aqueous fractions from *L. edodes* and *P. ostreatus* with high HMGCR inhibitory activity by selecting 10.7 MPa and 25°C as common extraction conditions and 5 cycles of 5 min each for *P. ostreatus* fruiting bodies and 15 cycles of 5 min for *L. edodes* [103]. Higher extraction temperatures (>100°C) were deleterious since the inhibitors appeared to be heat sensitive.

Microwave and Ultrasonic-assisted Extractions

A wide variety of polysaccharides with different structures and biological activities have also been obtained from edible mushrooms using other advance technologies included ultrasonic-assisted (UAE) [86, 115, 116] and microwave assisted (MAE) [39] extractions or combinations of both technologies [117], and specific devices such as high-throughput dynamic microwave-assisted extraction (HTDMAE) [118] to extract other compounds.

Ultrasound-assisted extraction (UAE) extracted higher amounts of polysaccharide–protein (PSP) complexes than conventional hot-water extractions when *G. frondosa* and *L. edodes* were utilized as starting material but lower when *C. versicolor* was used. The obtained PSPs fractions had higher protein but lower carbohydrate contents than those extracted by a conventional method, the PSP obtained fractions also showed different molecular weight profiles and exhibited higher antioxidant activities than the conventional method [116]. Tian et al. [119], optimized an specific UAE method to extract polysaccharides from *A. bisporus*, the optimal extraction conditions were obtained by selecting an ultrasonic power of 230 W, temperature 70°C during 62 min and W/M ratio 30 ml/g. Under these conditions a polysaccharide yield of 6.02% was achieved including polysaccharides of 158 kDa constituted mainly by Glc with β-type glycosidic bond and high antioxidant activity.

Antioxidant polysaccharides were also extracted using microwave-assisted extraction (MAE) from *Auricularia auricula*. The obtained fraction included a heteropolysaccharide (composed of glucose, galactose, mannose, arabinose and rhamnose at the molar ratio of 37.53:1:4.32:0.93:0.91) with the molecular weight of 2.77×10^4 Da with $(1 \rightarrow 3)$ linked [117]. However, none of these methods were used to obtain hypocholesterolemic extracts.

CONCLUSION

Edible mushrooms hold an interesting potential as bioactive ingredients to functionalize foods not only because of their hypocholesterloremic properties but for many other health beneficial activities. Perhaps, the fruiting bodies by themselves do not contain some of the bioactive responsible compounds in enough quantities to provoke a significant physiological effect *in vivo* but, nowadays there are extraction technologies, traditional and more innovative, able to generate fungal extracts or fractions enriched in those biologically active compounds which could be integrated into food matrices to design new functional foods. These potentially mushroom-containing novel foods able to lower cholesterol levels in serum might be more effective than those products actually found at the supermarkets since they showed two mechanisms of action, they were able of impairing the exogenous cholesterol absorption and inhibiting the endogenous cholesterol synthesis.

ACKNOWLEDGMENTS

The review was supported by AGL2010-21537 national R+D program from the Spanish Ministry of Science and Innovation and ALIBIRD-C M S2009/AGR-1469 regional program from the Community of Madrid (Spain).

REFERENCES

[1] Chen, J; Huang, XF. The effect of diets enriched in beta-glucans on blood lipoprotein concentrations. *Journal of Clinical Lipidology*, 2009 3, 154-158.

[2] Uemura K; Pisa Z. Trends in cardiovascular disease mortality in industrialized countries since 1950. *World Health Statistics Quarterly*, 1988 41, 155-78.

[3] EFSA Panel on Dietetic Products, Nutrition and Allergies (NDA). Scientific Opinion on the substantiation of a health claim related to 3 g/day plant stanols as plant stanol esters and lowering blood LDL-cholesterol and reduced risk of (coronary) heart disease pursuant to Article 14 of Regulation (EC) No 1924/2006. *EFSA Journal*, 2012 10, 2692.

[4] EFSA Panel on Dietetic Products, Nutrition and Allergies (NDA). Scientific Opinion on the substantiation of a health claim related to oat beta-glucan and lowering blood cholesterol and reduced risk of (coronary) heart disease pursuant to Article 14 of Regulation (EC) No 1924/20061. *EFSA Journal*, 2010 8, 1885.

[5] EFSA Panel on Dietetic Products, Nutrition and Allergies (NDA). Scientific Opinion on the substantiation of a health claim related to barley beta-glucans and lowering of blood cholesterol and reduced risk of (coronary) heart disease pursuant to Article 14 of Regulation (EC) No 1924/20061. *EFSA Journal*, 2011 9, 2471.

[6] Wilson, MD; Rudel, LL. Review of cholesterol absorption with emphasis on dietary and biliary cholesterol. Journal of Lipid Research, 1994 35, 943-955.

[7] Ginter, E. Cardiovascular Disease Prevention in Eastern Europe. *Nutrition*, 1998 14, 452-457.

[8] Porter, CJH; Pouton, CW; Cuine, JF; Charman, WN. Enhancing intestinal drug solubilisation using lipid-based delivery systems. *Advance Drug Delivery Reviews*, 2008 60, 673-691.

[9] Davis, HR; Zhu, L; Hoos, LM et al. Niemann-Pick C1 like 1 (NPC1L1) is the intestinal phytosterol and cholesterol transporter and a key modulateor of whole-body cholesterol homeostasis. *Journal of Biological Chemistry*, 2004 279, 33586-33592.

[10] Lammert, F; Wang, DQH. New insights into the genetic regulation of intestinal cholesterol absorption. *Gastroenterology*, 2005 129, 718–734.

[11] Cummins, CI; Hangelsdorf, DJ. Liver X receptors and cholesterol homeostasis: spotlight on the adrenal gland. *Biocheistry Society Transcations*, 2006 34, 1110-1113.

[12] Calpe-Berdiel, L; Escolá-Gil, JC; Blanco-Vaca; F. New insight into the molecular actions of plant sterols and stanols in cholesterol metabolism. *Athersclerosis*, 2009 203, 18-3.

[13] Gylling, H; Miettinen, TA. Cholesterol absorption: Influence of body weight and the role of plant sterols. *Current Atherosclerosis Reports*, 2005 7,466-471.

[14] Dhingra, S; Bansal, MP. Modulation of hypercholesterolemia-induced alterations in apolipoprotein B and HMG-CoA reductase expression by selenium supplementation. *Chemico-Biological Interactions*, 2006 161, 49–56.

[15] Istvan, E. Statin inhibition of HMG-CoA reductase: a 3-dimensional view. *Atherosclerosis Supplements*, 2003 4, 3-8.

[16] Ling, WH; Jones, PJH. Minireview of dietary phytosterols: a review of metabolism, benefits and side effects. *Life Sciences*, 1995 57, 195-206.

[17] Thurnham, DI. Functional foods: cholesterol-lowering benefits of plant sterols. *British Journal of Nutrition*, 1999 82, 255-256.

[18] Miettinen, TA; Puska, P; Gylling, H et al. Reduction of serum cholesterol by sitostanol-ester margarine in a mildly hypercholesterolemic population. *The New England Journal of Medicine*, 1995 333, 1308-1312.

[19] Heinemann, T; Leiss, O; Von Bergmann, K. Effect of low-dose sitostanol on serum cholesterol in patients with hypercholesterolemia. *Atherosclerosis*, 1986 61, 219-223.

[20] Schepetkin, IA; Quinn, MT. Botanical polysaccharides: Macrophage immunomodulation and therapeutic potential. *Inernational Immunopharmacology*, 2006 6, 317-333.

[21] Zacherl, C; Eisner, P; Engel, KH. In vitro model to correlate viscosity and bile acid-binding capacity of digested water-soluble and insoluble dietary fibers. *Food Chemistry*, 2011 126, 423-428.

[22] Jeon, YJ; Shahidi, F; Kim, SK. Preparation of chitin and chitosan oligomers and their applications in physiological functional foods. *Food Reviews International*, 2000 16, 159-176.

[23] Drozdowski, LA; Reimer, RA; Temelli, F et al. β-Glucan extracts inhibit the in vitro intestinal uptake of long-chain fatty acids and cholesterol and down-regulate genes involved in lipogenesis and lipid transport in rats. *The Journal of Nutritional Biochemistry*, 2010 21, 695-701.

[24] Cheung, PCK. Mushrooms as functional foods. New Jersey: John Wiley & Sons, Inc., publications. 2008.

[25] Prashanth, KVH; Tharanathan, RN. Chitin/chitosan: modifications and their unlimited application potential – an overview. *Trends in Food Science and Technology*, 2007 18, 117-131.

[26] Liaoa, FH; Shieha, MJ; Changb, NC; Chiena, YW. Chitosan supplementation lowers serum lipids and maintains normal calcium, magnesium, and iron status in hyperlipidemic patients. *Nutrition Research*, 2007 27, 146– 151.

[27] Sugano, M; Watanabe S; Kishi, A et al. Hypocholesterolemic action of chitosans with different viscosity in rats. *Lipids*, 1988 23, 187.

[28] Ylitalo, R; Lehtinen, S; Wuolijoki, E. et al. Cholesterol-lowering properties and safety of chitosan. *Drug Research*, 2002 1, 1- 7.

[29] Bobek, P; Ginter, E; Jurcovicova, M; Kuniak, L. Cholesterol-lowering effect of the mushroom *Pleurotus ostreatus* in hereditary hypercholesterolemic rats. *Annals of Nutrition and Metabolism*, 1991 35, 191-195.

[30] Bobek, P; Kuniak, L; Ozdin, L. The mushroom *Pleurotus ostreatus* reduces secretion and accelerates the fractional turnover rate of very-low-density lipoproteins in the rat. *Annals of Nutrition and Metabolism*, 1993 37, 142-14.

[31] Bobek, P; Ozdin, L; Kuniak, L. Mechanism of hypocholesterolemic effect of oyster mushroom (*Pleurotus ostreatus*) in rats: Reduction of cholesterol absorption and increase of plasma cholesterol removal. Zeitschriftfur. *Ernahrungswissennschaft*, 1994 33, 44-50.

[32] Bobek, P; Ozdín, L; Kuniak, L. Effect of oyster mushroom and isolated β-glucan on lipid peroxidation and on the activities of antioxidative enzymes in rats fed the cholesterol diet. *Nutritional Biochemistry*, 1997 8, 469-471.

[33] Bobek, P; Galbavý, S. Hypocholesterolemic and antiatherogenic effect of oyster mushroom (*Pleurotus ostreatus*) in rabbits. *Nahrung.*, 1999 43, 339-42.

[34] Bobek, P; Ozdin, L; Galbavy, S. Dose- and time-dependent. hypocholesterolemic effect of oyster mushroom (*Pleurotus ostreatus*) in rats - in vitro and in vivo studies. *Nutrition*, 1998 14, 282-286.

[35] Opletal, L; Jahodar, L; Chobot, V. et al. Evidence for the anti-hyperlipidaemic activity of the edible fungus *Pleurotus ostreatus*. *British Journal of Biomedical Science*, 1997 54, 240–243.

[36] Hu, SH; Liang, ZC; Chia,YC. et al. Antihyperlipidemic and antioxidant effects of extracts from *Pleurotus citrinopileatus*. *The journal of Agricultural and Food Chemistry*, 2006 54, 2103-2110.

[37] Alam, N; Yoon, KN; Lee, JS et al. Dietary effect of *Pleurotus eryngii* on biochemical function and histology in hypercholesterolemic rats. *Saudi Journal of Biological Sciences*, 2011 18, 403-409.

[38] Mizutani, T; Inatomi, S; Inazu, A; Kawahara, E. Hypolipidemic effect of *Pleurotus eryngii* extract in fat-loaded mice. *Journal of nutritional science and vitaminology*, 2010 56, 48-53.

[39] Chen, SY; Ho, KJ; Hsieh, YJ et al. Contents of lovastatin, γ-aminobutyric acid and ergothioneine in mushroom fruiting bodies and mycelia. *LWT - Food Science and Technology*, 2012 47, 274-278.

[40] Kabir, Y; Kimura, S; Tamura, T. Dietary effect of *Ganoderma lucidum* mushroom on blood pressure and lipid levels in spontaneously hypertensive rats (SHR). *Journal of nutritional science and vitaminology*, 1988 34, 433-8.

[41] Russell, R; Paterson, M. Ganoderma – A therapeutic fungal biofactory. *Phytochemistry*, 2006 67, 1985–2001.

[42] Berger, A; Rein, D; Kratky, E. et al. Cholesterol-lowering properties of *Ganoderma lucidum* in vitro, ex vivo, and in hamsters and minipigs. *Lipids in Health and Disease*, 2004 3, 2.

[43] Seto, SW; Lam, TY; Tam, HL. et al. Novel hypoglycemic effects of *Ganoderma lucidum* water-extract in obese/diabetic (+db/+db) mice. *Phytomedicine*, 2009 16, 426–436.

[44] Jeong, SC; Jeong, YT; Yang, BK. et al. White button mushroom *(Agaricus bisporus)* lowers blood glucose and cholesterol levels in diabetic and hypercholesterolemic rats. *Nutrition Research*, 2010 30, 49-56.

[45] Fukushima, M; Nakano, M; Morii, Y. et al. Hepatic LDL receptor mRNA in rats Is Increased by dietary mushroom (*Agaricus bisporus*) fiber and sugar beet fiber. *The Journal of Nutrition*, 2010 130, 2151-2156.

[46] Fukushima, M; Ohashi, T; Fujiwara, Y. et al. Cholesterol-lowering effects of Maitake (*Grifola frondosa*) fiber, Shiitake (*Lentinus edodes*) fiber, and Enokitake (*Flammulina velutipes*) fiber in rats. *Experimental Biology and Medicine*, 2001 226, 758-765.

[47] Mori, K; Kobayashi, C; Tomita, T. et al. Antiatherosclerotic effect of the edible mushrooms *Pleurotus eryngii* (Eringi), *Grifola frondosa* (Maitake), and *Hypsizygus marmoreus* (Bunashimeji) in apolipoprotein E–deficient mice. *Nutrition Research*, 2008 28, 335–342.

[48] Cheung, P. The hypocholesterolemic effect of two edible mushrooms: *Auricularia auricula* (tree-ear) and *Tremella fuciformis* (white jelly-leaf) in hypercholesterolemic rats. *Nutrition Research*,1996 16, 1721-1725.

[49] Tamez de la O, E. J; Garza-Ocañas, L; Zanatta-Calderón, MT. et al. Hypoglycemic and hypocholesterolemic effects of aqueous and methanolic extracts of *Lentinus lepideus*, *Calvatia cyathiformis* and *Ganoderma applanatum*, from Northeastern Mexico, in Wistar rats. *Journal of Medicinal Plants Research* 7, 2013, 661-668.

[50] Kathun, K; Mahtab, H; Khanam, P. et al. Oyster mushroom reduced blood glucose and cholesterol in diabetic subjects. *Mymensingh Medical Journal*, 2007 16, 94-99.

[51] Schneider, I; Kressel, G; Meyer, A. et al. Lipid lowering effects of oyster mushroom (*Pleurotus ostreatus*) in humans. *Journal of Functional Foods*, 2011 3, 17–24.

[52] Wachtel-Galor, S; Tomlinson, B; Benzie, IF. *Ganoderma lucidum* ("Lingzhi"), a Chinese medicinal mushroom: biomarker responses in a controlled human supplementation study. *British Journal of Nutrition*, 2004 91, 263-269.

[53] Shao, G. Treatment of hyperlipidemia with cultivated *Cordyceps*--a double-blind, randomized placebo control trial. *Medicinal Mushrooms*, 1985 11, 652-65.

[54] Poddar, KH; Ames, M; Hsin-Jen, C. et al. Positive effect of mushrooms substituted for meat on body weight, body composition, and health parameters. A 1-year randomized clinical trial. *Appetite*, 2013 71, 379-387.

[55] Mattila, P; Lampi, AM; Ronkainen, R. et al. Sterol and vitamin D2 contents in some wild and cultivated mushrooms. *Food Chemistry*, 2002 76, 293-298.

[56] Teichmann, A; Dutta, PC; Staffas, A. et al. Sterol and vitamin D2 concentrations in cultivated and wild grown mushrooms: Effects of UV irradiation. *LWT - Food Science and Technology*, 2007 40, 815-822.

[57] Kalac, P. Chemical composition and nutritional value of European species of wild growing mushrooms: A review. *Food Chemistry* 2009 113, 9-16.

[58] Kobori, M; Yoshida, M; Ohnishi-Kameyama, M; H Shinmoto. Ergosterol peroxide from an edible mushroom suppresses inflammatory responses in RAW264.7 macrophages and growth of HT29 colon adenocarcinoma cells. *British Journal of Pharmacology*, 2007 150, 209-219.

[59] Kaneko, E; Matsuda, M; Yamada, Y. et al. Induction of Intestinal ATP-binding cassette transporters by a phytosterol-derived liver X receptor agonist. *The Journal of Biological Chemistry*, 2003 278, 36098-36098.

[60] Fernandez, C; Suarez, Y; Ferruelo, AJ. Et al. Inhibition of cholesterol biosynthesis by Delta-22-unsaturated phytosterols via competitive inhibition of sterol Delta-24-reductase in mammalian cells. *Biochemical Journal*, 2002 366, 109-119.

[61] Clavijo, C; Gil-Ramírez, A; Soler-Rivas, C. et al. Inhibitors of the 3-hydroxy-3-methyl-glutaryl CoA reductase in *Agaricus bisporus L.* (Imbach) fruiting bodies, in Proceedings of the 18th Congress of the International Society for Mushroom Science. 2012 Pekín (China).

[62] Gil-Ramírez, A. Nuevos alimentos bioactivos obtenidos a partir de hongos comestibles capaces de reducir los niveles de colesterol en sangre (Novel bioactive food from edible mushrooms able of lowering serum cholesterol levels). PhD thesis. 2014. Universidad Autónoma de Madrid.

[63] Gil-Ramirez, A; Clavijo, C; Palanisamy, M. et al. Edible mushrooms as potential sources of new hypocholesterolemic compounds, in Proceedings of the 7th International Conference on Mushroom Biology and Mushroom Products, ed. by Jean-Michel Savoie,Marie Foulongne-Oriol, Mich`ele Largeteau, G´erard Barroso. Conference was held in Arcachon (France) 4–7 October 2011. Publisher: INRA, UR1264, Mycology and Food Safety.

[64] Villares, A; Mateo-Vivaracho, L; García-Lafuente, A; Guillamón, E. Storage temperature and UV-irradiation influence on the ergosterol content in edible mushrooms. *Food Chemistry*, 2014 147, 252–256.

[65] Jasinghe, VJ; Perera, CO. Distribution of ergosterol in different tissues of mushrooms and its effect on the conversion of ergosterol to vitamin D2 by UV irradiation. *Food Chemistry*, 2005 92, 541-546.

[66] H. Yokokawa, H; Mitsushashi, T. The sterol composition of mushrooms. *Phytochemistry*, 1981 20, 1349-1351.

[67] Guang-Ping, L; Jing, Z; Jin-Ao, D. et al. Comparison of sterols and fatty acids in two species of *Ganoderma. Chemistry Central Journal*, 2012 6, 10.

[68] Liu, YT; Sun, J; Luo, ZY. et al. Chemical composition of five wild edible mushrooms collected from Southwest China and their antihyperglycemic and antioxidant activity. *Food and Chemical Toxicology*, 2012 50, 1238–1244.

[69] Kalogeropoulos, N; Yanni, AE; Koutrotsios, G; Aloupi. M. Bioactive microconstituents and antioxidant properties of wild edible mushrooms from the island of Lesvos, Greece. *Food and Chemical Toxicology*, 2013 55, 378–385.

[70] Gil-Ramírez, A; Aldars-García, L; Palanisamy, M. et al. Sterols enriched fractions obtained from *Agaricus bisporus* fruiting bodies and by-products by compressed fluid technologies (PLE and SFE). *Innovative Food Science and Emerging Technologies*, 2013 18, 101-107.

[71] Aida, FMNA; Shuhaimi, M; Yazid, M; Maaruf AG. Mushroom as a potential source of prebiotics: a review. *Trends in Food Science & Technology*, 2009 20, 567-575.

[72] Gonzaga, MLC; Ricardo, NMPS; Heatley, F; Soaresa, S. Isolation and characterization of polysaccharides from *Agaricus blazei* Murill. *Carbohydrate Polymers*, 2005 60, 43-49.

[73] Zhang, M; Cheung, PC; Zhang, L. Evaluation of mushroom dietary fiber (nonstarch Polysaccharides) from sclerotia of *Pleurotus tuber-regium* (Fries) singer as a potential antitumor agent. *Journal of Agricultural and Food Chemistry*, 2001 49, 5059-5062.

[74] Synytsya, A; Novak, M. Structural diversity of fungal glucans. *Carbohydrate Polymers*, 2013 92, 792-809.

[75] Nitschke, J; Modick, H; Busch E; Rekowski, RW. A new colorimetric method to quantify β-1,3-1,6-glucans in comparison with total β-1,3-glucnas in edible mushrooms. *Food Chemistry*, 2011 127, 791-796.

[76] Ramberg, JE; Nelson, ED; Sinnott, RA. Immunomodulatory dietary polysaccharides: a systematic review of the literature. *Nutrition Journal*, 2010 9, 54-76.

[77] Manzi, P; Pizzoferrato, L. Beta-glucans in edible mushrooms. *Food Chemistry*, 2000 68, 315-318.

[78] Manzi, P; Aguzzi, A; Pizzoferrato, L. Nutritional value of mushrooms widely consumed in Italy. *Food Chemistry*, 2001 73, 321-325.

[79] Manzi, P; Marconi, S; Aguzzi, A; Pizzoferrato, L. Commercial mushrooms: nutritional quality and effect of cooking. *Food Chemistry*, 2004 84, 201-206.

[80] Lee, JS; Oka, K; Watanabe, O. et al. Immunomodulatory effect of mushrooms on cytotoxic activity and cytokine production of intestinal lamina propria leukocytes does not necessarily depend on β-glucan contents. *Food Chemistry*, 2011 126, 1521-1526.

[81] Rop, O; Mlcek, J; Jurikova, T. Beta-glucans in higher fungi and their health effects. *Nutritional reviews*, 2009 67, 624-631.

[82] Caz, V; Soler-Rivas, C; Tabernero, M. et al. Oyster mushroom (*Pleurotus ostreatus*) decreases blood cholesterol levels in biet-induced hypercholesterolemia mice, in Proceedings of 20th International Congress of Nutrition. Conference was held in Granada (Spain) 15–20 September, 2013. PO2804.

[83] Kozarski, M; Klaus, A; Niksic, M. et al. Antioxidative and immunomodulating activities of polysaccharide extracts of the medicinal mushrooms *Agaricus bisporus, Agaricus brasiliensis, Ganoderma lucidum* and *Phellinus linteus*. *Food Chemistry*, 2011 129, 1667–1675

[84] Vetter, J. Chitin content of cultivated mushrooms *Agaricus bisporus, Pleurotus ostreatus* and *Lentinula edodes*. *Food Chemistry*, 2007 102, 6–9.

[85] Liu, DZ; Wang, F; Liao, TG. Et al. Vibralactone: a lipase inhibitor with an unusual fused β-lactone produed by cultures of the basidiomycete *Boreostereum vibrans*. *Organic letters*, 2006 8, 5749-5752.

[86] Cheung, YC; Siu, KC; Liu, YS; Wu, JY. Molecular properties and antioxidant activities of polysaccharide–protein complexes from selected mushrooms by ultrasound-assisted extraction. *Process Biochemistry*, 2012 47, 892-895.

[87] Birari, RB; Bhutani, KK. Pancreatic lipase inhibitors from natural sources: unexplored potential. *Drug Discovery Today*, 2007 12, 879-89.

[88] Slanc, P; Doljak, B; Mlinari, A; Ítrukel, B. Screening of wood damaging fungi and macrofungi for inhibitors of pancreatic lipase. *Phytotheraphy Research*, 2004 18, 758-762.

[89] Palanisamy, M; Gil-Ramírez, A; Ruíz-Rodríguez, A. et al. Testing edible mushrooms ability to inhibit the pancreatic lipase activity by an in vitro digestion model. *International Journal Food Science and Technology*, 2012 47, 1004-1010..

[90] Gunde-Cimerman, N; Plemenitas, A; Cimerman, A. *Pleurotus* frungi produce mevinolin, an inhibitor of HMGCoA reductase. *FEMS Microbiology Letters*, 1993 113, 333-338.

[91] Gunde Cimerman, N; Cimerman, A. *Pleurotus* fruiting bodies contain the inhibitor of 3-hydroxy-3-methylglutaryl-coenzyme A reductase - lovastatin. *Experimental Mycology*, 1995 19, 1-6.

[92] Gunde-Cimerman, N.; Friedrich, J.; Cimerman, A., Benichi, N. (1993a) Screening fungi for the production of an inhibitor of HMGCoA reductase: production of mevinolin by the fungi of the genus *Pleurotus*. *FEMS Microbiology Letters* 111, 203-206.

[93] Gil-Ramírez, A; Clavijo, C; Palanismy, M. et al. Screening of edible mushrooms and extraction by pressurized water (PWE) of 3-hydroxy-3-methyl-glutaryl CoA reductase inhibitors. *Journal of Functional Foods*, 2013 5, 244-250.

[94] Gil-Ramírez, A; Clavijo, C; Palanisamy, M. et al. Study on the 3-hydroxy-3-methyl-glutaryl CoA reductase inhibitory properties of *Agaricus bisporus* and extraction of bioactive fractions using pressurized solvent technologies (ASE and SFE). *Journal of the Science of Food and Agriculture*, 2013 93, 2789-2796.

[95] Folkers, K; Langsjoen, P; Willis, R. et al. Lovastatin decreases coenzyme Q levels in humans. *Proceedings of the National Academy of Sciences*, 1990 87: 8931–8934.

[96] Willi, RA; Folkers, K; Tucker, JL. et al. Lovastatin decreases coenzyme Q levels in rats. *Proceedings of the National Academy of Sciences*, 1990 87, 8928–8930.

[97] Amin, D; Rutledge, R; Needle, S. et al. A potent squalene synthase inhibitor and orally effective cholesterol-lowering agent: comparison with inhibitors of HMG-CoA reductase. *The Journal of Pharmacology and Experimental Therapeutics*, 1997 2, 746–752.

[98] Hosoya, T; Tanimoto, T; Onodera, K. et al. Zaragozic acids production from discomycetes. *Mycoscience*, 1197 38, 305-311.

[99] Yamada, T; Komoto, J; Lou, K. et al. Structure and function of eritadenine and its 3-deaza analogues: potent inhibitors of S-adenosylhomocysteine hydrolase and hypocholesterolemic agents. *Biochemical Pharmacology*, 2007 73, 981-989.

[100] Sugiyama, K; Akachi, T; Yamakawa, A. Eritadenine-induced alteration of hepatic phospholipid metabolism in relation to its hypocholesterolemic action in rats. *Nutritional Biochemistry*, 1995 6, 80-87.

[101] Spolar, MR; Schaffer, EM; Beelman, RB. et al. Selenium-enriched *Agaricus bisporus* mushrooms suppress 7,12-dimethlybenz[a] anthracene bioactivation in mammary tissue. *Cancer Letters*, 1999 138, 145-150.

[102] Mendiola, JA; Herrero, M; Cifuentes, A; Ibañez, E. Use of compressed fluids for sample preparation: Food applications. *Journal of Chromatography A*, 2007 1152, 234–246.

[103] Huang, SQ; Ning, ZX. Extraction of polysaccharide from *Ganoderma lucidum* and its immune enhancement activity. *International Journal of Biological Macromolecules*, 2010 47, 336-341.

[104] Hsu, RC; Lin, BH; Chen, CW. The Study of Supercritical Carbon Dioxide Extraction for *Ganoderma Lucidum*. *Industrial & Engineering Chemistry Research*, 2001 40, 4478-4481.

[105] Ibrahim Abdullah, M; Young, JC; Games, DE. Supercritical fluid extraction of carboxylic and fatty acids from *Agaricus spp.* mushrooms. *Journal of Agricultural and Food Chemistry*, 1994 42, 718–722.

[106] Kitzberger, CSG; Smania, A; Pedrosa, RC; Ferreira, SRS. Antioxidant and antimicrobial activities of shiitake (*Lentinula edodes*) extracts obtained by organic solvents and supercritical fluids. *Journal of Food Engineering*, 2007 80, 631–638.

[107] Kitzberger, CSG; Lomonaco, RH; Michielin, EMZ. et al. Supercritical fluid extraction of shiitake oil: Curve modeling and extract composition. *Journal of Food Engineering*, 2009 90, 35–43.

[108] Wang, BJ; Won, SJ; Yu, ZR; Su, CL. Free radical scavenging and apoptotic effects of *Cordyceps sinensis* fractionated by supercritical carbon dioxide. *Food and Chemical Toxicology*, 2005 43, 543-552.

[109] Yang, FQ; Feng, K; Zhao, J; Li, SP. Analysis of sterols and fatty acids in natural and cultured *Cordyceps* by one-step derivatization followed with gas chromatography–mass spectrometry. *Journal of Pharmaceutical and Biomedical Analysis*, 2009 49, 1172-1178.

[110] Fan, X; Li, X; Chu, C. et al. Optimization of technology for pressurized solvent extraction of lentinan by response surface method. *Journal of Chinese Institute of Food Science and Technology*, 2012 12, 98-104.

[111] Aldars-García, L; Palanisamy, M; Gil-Ramírez, A. et al. Extracción acelerada con disolventes (ASE) de polisacáridos de *Boletus edulis*, in proceedings of the VI Reunión de Expertos en Tecnología de Fluidos Comprimidos (FLUCOMP). Conference was held in Madrid (Spain), 2013.

[112] Di, X; Chan, KKC; Leung ,HW; Huie, CW. Fingerprint profiling of acid hydrolyzates of polysaccharides extracted from the fruiting bodies and spores of Lingzhi by high-performance thin-layer chromatography. *Journal of Chromatography A*, 2003 1018, 85-95.

[113] Lo, TCT; Tsao, HH; Wang, AY; Chang, CA. Pressurized water extraction of polysaccharides as secondary metabolites from *Lentinula edodes*. *Journal of Agriculture and Food Chemistry*, 2007 55, 4196-4201.

[114] Palanisamy, M; Gil-Ramírez, A; Aldars-García, L. et al. Pressurized water extraction of bioactive β-glucans from the medicinal mushroom *Ganoderma lucidum*, in proocedings of the XVI Jornadas Nacionales de Nutrición Practica. Conference was held in Madrid (Spain), 2012.

[115] Zhang, M; Cui, SW; Cheung, PCK; Wang, Q. Antitumor polysaccharides from mushrooms: a review on their isolation process, structural characteristics and activity. *Trends in Food Science and Technology*, 2007 18, 4-19.

[116] Pan, Y; Hao, Y; Chu, T. et al. Ultrasonic-assisted extraction, chemical characterization of polysaccharides from Yunzhi mushroom and its effect on osteoblast cells. *Carbohydrate Polymers*, 2010 80, 922-926.

[117] Zeng, WC; Zhang, Z; Gao, H. et al. Characterization of antioxidant polysaccharides from *Auricularia auricular* using microwave-assisted extraction. *Carbohydrate Polymers*, 2012 89, 694-700.

[118] Wang, H; Zhao, Q; Song, W. et al. High-throughput dynamic microwave-assisted extraction on-line coupled with solid-phase extraction for analysis of nicotine in mushroom. *Talanta*, 2011 85, 743-748.

[119] Tian, Y; Zeng, H; Xu, Z. et al. Ultrasonic-assisted extraction and antioxidant activity of polysaccharides recovered from white button mushroom (*Agaricus bisporus*). *Carbohydrate Polymers*, 2012 88, 522-529.

In: Mushrooms
Editor: Grégoire Pesti

ISBN: 978-1-63117-521-3
© 2014 Nova Science Publishers, Inc.

Chapter 3

MUSHROOMS: BIOLOGICAL CHARACTERIZATION, ANTIOXIDANT PROPERTIES AND INTERACTIONS WITH HUMAN HEALTH

*Patrícia Molz[1], Joel Henrique Ellwanger[2], Daniel Prá[1] and Silvia Isabel Rech Franke[*1]*

[1]Programa de Pós-Graduação em Promoção da Saúde,
Universidade de Santa Cruz do Sul (UNISC), Santa Cruz do Sul, RS, Brasil
[2]Programa de Pós-Graduação em Biologia Celular e Molecular, Universidade Federal do
Rio Grande do Sul (UFRGS), Porto Alegre, RS, Brasil

ABSTRACT

The cultivation of mushrooms as food and for medicinal use began thousands of years ago. Since then, mushrooms have become among the finest culinary items and most appreciated ingredients worldwide. Furthermore, mushrooms have been viewed as a functional food because they present several previously ignored biological properties. Of the many known edible species of mushrooms, only 20 are cultivated on a large scale worldwide. The production of these species exceeds 6 million tons per year. Information about the composition of foods has become increasingly important to evaluate the quality of the foods. In terms of quality, mushrooms are a demonstrably healthy food, low in calories but high in protein, vitamins, minerals and fiber. The popularity of mushrooms has been demonstrated by the interest of many researchers who have endeavored to study the nutritional and medicinal effects of mushrooms. In this context, the discovery of a variety of biological activities has highlighted the antioxidant power of mushrooms. However, the literature reports adverse effects, side effects and toxicity in animals and in clinical trials related to the species of mushrooms marketed for human consumption. It is known that edible mushrooms do not pose risks to human health if they are adequately stored, processed and properly cultivated and if due care is taken to identify species that can be safely ingested. Additional randomized clinical trials are needed to prove the

---

* Correspondence to: Dr. SIR Franke. Universidade de Santa Cruz do Sul. Programa de Pós-Graduação em Promoção da Saúde. Av. Independência, 2293, sala 4206. CEP: 96815900. Santa Cruz do Sul, RS, Brasil. E-mail: silviafr@unisc.br.

effectiveness and safety of mushrooms and to identify beneficial doses to be used in the prevention and treatment of various diseases or in health promotion. In this chapter, we will present and discuss the biological characteristics, antioxidant properties and interactions with human health of the mushrooms most frequently consumed by humans.

1. INTRODUCTION

The Fungi are a unique group consisting of completely different organisms whose characteristics and individual groupings are extremely variable, with various shapes, colors and sizes (Chang; Miles, 1992). Recent estimates suggest that there are as many as 5.1 million fungal species worldwide (Blackwell, 2011).

Mushrooms are eukaryotic heterotrophic organisms belonging to a special group of macroscopic fungi (Blackwell, 2011). A mushroom is the fleshy fruiting body of a fungus. Also known as macrofungi, fruiting bodies show characteristic forms that are visible to the naked eye (Falandysz; Borovička, 2013). Taxonomically, the mushrooms are classified into two different groups: Basidiomycetes, comprising many of the known genera, and Ascomycetes (Poppe; Griensven, 2000).

More than 14,000 species of mushrooms are known. Of these species, approximately 2,000 are identified as edible (Chang; Buswell, 2008). These edible mushrooms are divided into 30 genera and 270 species (Wasser, 2002).

Several of these species have therapeutic potential or can contain preventive agents that can contribute to the welfare of humans (Wasser, 2002). Mushrooms have been used by humans for thousands of years and in areas as diverse as food, medicine and ornamentation (Mattila; Suonpaa; Piironen, 2000; Cheung, 2010; Leskosek-Cukalovic et al., 2010). The first record of the use of mushrooms as food is from China (ca. 900 B. C.) (De Roman, 2010). As a food, mushrooms have become one of the finest culinary items, as they have an unequaled flavor, aroma and texture (Mattila; Suonpaa; Piironen, 2000; Valentao et al., 2005; Grangeia et al., 2011).

Throughout human history, mushrooms have been used as a medically beneficial therapeutic food for humans. Currently, mushrooms are used in the prevention of many diseases, serving as a source for the development of pharmaceuticals and nutraceuticals (foods with pharmaceutical properties) (Barros, L. et al., 2007).

2. KEY EDIBLE MUSHROOMS IN THE HUMAN DIET

According to The Food and Agriculture Organization Corporate Statistical Database (FAOSTAT), the total world production of mushrooms, including truffles, was almost 6 million metric tons in 2010. China was by far the largest producer (Kalac, 2013). The increasing trend of mushroom production is expected to continue into the future (Cheung, 2010). Among the more than 20 cultivated species, *Agaricus bisporus* (button mushroom, champignon, common mushroom, white mushroom, brown mushroom, mushroom of Paris or Portobello mushroom) dominates world production, followed by *Lentinula edodes* (often called by its Japanese name of Shiitake) and *Pleurotus* spp. (particularly *P. ostreatus,* the oyster mushroom or hiratake varieties) (Kalac, 2013). These 3 species of mushrooms will be further discussed in this chapter.

The mushroom *Agaricus bisporus* (Mushroom of Paris) (Figure 1) is the leading cultivated edible mushroom and is consumed worldwide. It is commonly sold as button mushrooms when small and Portobello mushrooms when larger and is used in salads, soups and many other dishes. Its original form has a brownish cap and dark brown gills, but more familiar forms have a white cap, stalk and flesh and brown gills (Ghorai et al., 2009).

Figure 1. *Agaricus bisporus*.

The mushroom *Lentinula edodes* (Figure 2) is the second most widely cultivated edible mushroom. It has good nutritional properties and shows several functional properties (e.g., antitumor and hypocholesterolemic activity) as well as antimicrobial and antioxidant effects. They are traditionally grown on natural logs. For their intensive cultivation, blocks of sawdust supplemented with nutrients are used (Chen, 2005).

Figure 2. *Lentinula edodes*.

The third most frequently cultivated edible mushroom worldwide, *Pleurotus ostreatus* (Figure 3), popularly known as Shimeji, offers economic value and ecological and medicinal properties. Its culture has changed to allow its production in combination with other mushrooms. The substrate used for its cultivation does not require special treatment. However, its cultivation requires a degree of environmental control. Its fruiting bodies are seldom attacked by pests or diseases. These species require a shorter growth period than other edible mushrooms and can be grown simply and inexpensively (Bonatti et al., 2004). All of these characteristics make Shimeji an excellent alternative for mushroom production compared with other mushrooms (Sanchez, 2010).

Figure 3. *Pleurotus ostreatus*.

3. Nutritional Properties of Edible Mushrooms

Edible mushrooms can be a source of many types of nutraceuticals, as they can contain unsaturated fatty acids, phenolic compounds, tocopherols, ascorbic acid and carotenoids. Thus, they can be used directly in the diet and to promote health, furnishing the additive and synergistic effects of all the bioactive compounds (Reis et al., 2012).

The first reports on the chemical composition of macrofungal fruiting bodies appeared more than 100 years ago, in descriptions by Zellner in 1907. However, reliable data became available with the development of validated analytical methods and advanced instruments, especially after the 1970s (Falandysz; Borovička, 2013).

Knowledge of the chemical composition, nutritional value and beneficial health effects of mushrooms has expanded dynamically in recent years. As large variations in the nutritional value of mushrooms occur among species, this value has been reassessed (Gunc *Ergonul* et al., 2013; Kalac, 2013). The usual content of protein, lipid and ash ranges from 38.7-416.0, 5.0-92.3 and 52.7-120.0 g kg^{-1}, respectively, and the carbohydrate content is also variable. The amount of energy is low, usually between 303-772 kcal kg^{-1}. The content of protein appears to be overestimated; however, data derived from previous measurements indicate that mushrooms provide limited of essential amino acids proportion (Kalac, 2013). Generally, the lipid content is low in mushroom species. In particular, cholesterol levels are low, whereas several unsaturated fatty acids and polyunsaturated fatty acids (PUFA) occur at elevated levels (Gunc Ergonul et al., 2013). The content of fat is characterized by low levels of linoleic acid, and the proportion of n-3 fatty acids is nutritionally marginal. The major carbohydrates are chitin, glycogen, trehalose and mannitol. Information on the content and composition of the fiber is limited (Kalac, 2013), but fungi have considerable value as a source of dietary fiber in human nutrition (Cheung, 1997; Cheung, 2013). A serving of 100 g of mushrooms can provide 9 to 40% of the daily recommendation of dietary fiber (Manzi; Aguzzi; Pizzoferrato, 2001), and 80 g of mushrooms represents one portion in terms of the advice to eat 5 portions of fruit and vegetables a day (Sadler, 2003). Table 1 shows the chemical composition of the mushroom species *Agaricus bisporus*, *Lentinula edodes* and *Pleurotus ostreatus*.

Table 1. Chemical composition of the most frequently consumed mushrooms*

	Agaricus bisporus	*Lentinula edodes*	*Pleurotus ostreatus*
Dry matter[1]	87.3	202.2	108.3
Protein[1]	140.8	44.0	70.2
Lipid[1]	21.8	17.3	14.0
Ash[1]	97.4	67.3	57.2
Carbohydrates[1]	740.0	871.4	858.6
Total fiber[2]	1.98	11.5	4.10
Soluble fiber[2, 3]	0.32	-	0.43
Insoluble fiber[2]	1.66	-	3.67
Energy[1]	325	772	416

* dry matter (g kg^{-1}), proximate composition (g kg^{-1} DM), fiber (g/100 g) and energy (kcal kg^{-1}FM). Source: [1]Kalac (2013), [2]Manzi, Aguzzi and Pizzoferrato (2001), [3]Sadler (2003).

Mushroom protein is considered by the Food and Agriculture Organization (FAO) to be superior to most plant proteins (Fao, 1991). Therefore, edible mushroom species are highly nutritive and have been compared to meat, eggs and milk because they reveal an amino acid composition similar to that of animal proteins (Grangeia et al., 2011). The amino acid composition of mushrooms is equivalent to or superior to that of soy proteins, and it is similar to that of hens' eggs for certain species of mushrooms (Yin; Zhou, 2008). With a few exceptions, the amount of essential amino acids in mushroom proteins ranges from 30 to 50 g/100 g protein dry weight (DW). Mushrooms are relatively rich in arginine (37–140 mg/g protein DW), aspartic acid (91–120 mg/g protein DW %), glutamic acid (130–240 mg/g protein DW), threonine (41–95 mg/g protein DW) and valine (36–89 mg/g protein DW) and poor in methionine (1.2–22 mg/g protein DW) and cysteine (16–19 mg/g protein DW) (Cheung, 2010).

Edible mushrooms can also provide nutritionally significant amounts of vitamins, particularly cobalamin, folic acid, nicotinic acid, pantothenic acid, pyridoxine, riboflavin and thiamine, as well as other vitamins, such as biotin, ergosterol and tocopherols (Sadler, 2003; Sanmee et al., 2003; Reis et al., 2012). Data on cultivated mushrooms show that they contain several vitamins, including riboflavin (vitamin B2), niacin, and folates, varying within a range of 0.6-0.8, 31–65, and 0.30–0.64 mg/100 g DW, respectively (Mattila et al., 2001). The riboflavin content of mushrooms is higher than that generally found in vegetables, and the amount of folates is generally similar to that found in vegetables (Cheung, 2010). Vitamin D is almost entirely absent in cultivated mushrooms, but the level of ergosterol, the provitamin of ergocalciferol, is relatively high (400–600 mg/100 g DW) (Mattila et al., 2002). For certain groups (vegetarians or persons allergic to fish), mushrooms can thus represent an important dietary source of this vitamin (Outila et al., 1999). The commonly consumed mushrooms can be an important source of vitamins (Table 2). Shimenji has notable levels of folic acid and niacin.

Table 2. Vitamin and provitamin content in the most commonly consumed mushrooms (mg or µg/100 g)*

	Agaricus bisporus	*Lentinula edodes*	*Pleurotus ostreatus*
Vitamin C (mg)	17	25	20
Vitamin B$_1$(mg)	0.6	0.6	0.9
Vitamin B$_2$ (mg)	5.1	1.8	2.5
Folic acid (µg)	450	300	640
Niacin (mg)	43	31	65
Vitamin B$_{12}$ (µg)	0.8	0.8	0.6
Ergosterol	654	679	674

* dry weight. Source: Mattila *et al.* (2001).

Fungi contain a wide variety of minerals (aluminum, calcium, chlorine, copper, fluorine, iodine, iron, manganese, magnesium, mercury, phosphorus, potassium, sodium, sulfur and zinc) (Sadler, 2003; Rudawska; Leski, 2005). Their low sodium content is of great benefit to the consumer (Seeger; Trumpfheller; Schweinshaut, 1983; Vetter, 2003). The level of minerals in fungi depends, among other things, on the species and age of the mushrooms, on the diameter of the pilei and on the substratum (Demirbaş, 2001). Common edible mushrooms, such as *A. bisporus*, *L. edodes* and *P. ostreatus*, have been reported to contain various levels of potassium (2700–4700 mg/100 g DW), phosphorus (500–1400 mg/100 g DW), magnesium (20–200 mg/100 g DW), zinc (4.7–9.2 mg/100 g DW), and copper (0.50–3.5 mg/100 g DW) (Cheung, 2010). In particular, *A. bisporus* contains a high level of selenium (30–90 mg/110 g fresh weight) (Falandysz, 2008). In 2007, Çağlarırmak studied the mineral content of *L. edodes* and *Pleurotus* species and found values similar to those in the literature for magnesium, phosphorus and zinc. These elements in the studied mushrooms could contribute to human nutrition and are a good source of these elements in terms of the recommended daily intake. Moreover, as a good balance between high content of potassium and low content of sodium was found, the studied mushrooms could have beneficial effects on hypertension. However, the studied mushrooms were considered inadequate as a dietary source of calcium (Çağlarırmak, 2007).

The nutritional and medicinal value of *A. bisporus* is usually considered to be less than that of other cultivated mushrooms that are frequently grown. Nevertheless, due to its nutritional value, with a low content of calories, purine, carbohydrate and sodium as well as a high content of several vitamins, potassium, phosphorus and several trace elements, *A. bisporus* is considered a valuable component of the human diet, especially by health-conscious people. Recent studies have furnished evidence that *A. bisporus* contains high levels of substances of possible medicinal importance, such as tyrosinase, aromatase inhibitors and immunomodulating and antitumor polysaccharides, and that it shows antioxidant activity (Savoie; Minvielle; Largeteau, 2008).

The Shiitake mushroom is also low in calories and highly nutritious, with large amounts of vitamins, proteins and minerals. It also contains several elements essential to human nutrition, e.g., calcium, copper, phosphorus, manganese, magnesium and zinc (Molz et al., 2014).

The Shimeji mushroom is highly appreciated for its delicious taste. It is low in fat and contains high levels of carbohydrates, proteins and vitamins, especially vitamin B1, B2 and B3, and it also contains high levels of minerals, including calcium, phosphorus and iron (Bonatti et al., 2004).

4. FACTORS THAT AFFECT THE NUTRITIONAL COMPOSITION OF EDIBLE MUSHROOMS

Many factors can influence the nutritional value of mushrooms, including the species, strain and variety, the type of substrate used and the type and degree of maturity, as well as the storage and conservation process (Manzi et al., 1999; Ragunathan; Swaminathan, 2003; Banik; Nandi, 2004).

The nutritional benefits of mushrooms are closely related to their cultivation. Cultivation of mushrooms is considered both a science, which is developed through research, and an art, which is perfected through curiosity and practical experience (Cheung, 2008). The cultivation of edible mushrooms is a biotechnological process that is useful for organic waste recycling, combining the production of protein-rich food with the reduction of environmental pollution (Beetz; Greer, 1999) and involving growth under a variety of climatic conditions on inexpensive, readily available waste materials (Sanchez, 2010). The cultivation of mushrooms involves several operations (Figure 4). Each species must be grown under specified conditions to allow differentiated production. Currently, various cultivation techniques are being employed in the production of mushrooms to furnish better flavor, appearance, texture, nutritional qualities and medicinal properties at low cost (Sanchez, 2004). Cultivation can be performed on a wide variety of plant substrates, allowing the use of industrial agri-food waste (Poppe; Griensven, 2000). However, few studies have evaluated the effects of production processes on the nutritional composition of mushrooms. Thus, it is important to perform further studies to determine the effects of the production process on the chemical composition of mushrooms.

Processing and storage are essential to the success of the product. New techniques are being used to increase the shelf life of mushrooms. These techniques can offer a good alternative for mushroom storage (Barron et al., 2002).

Mushrooms can be cooked for consumption in several ways, each of which affects their nutritional composition (Falandysz; Borovička, 2013). Certain forms of preparation are more effective than others for maintaining the nutritional value of mushrooms. For example, in their review, Wang et al. (2014) reported that people in China have a traditional method of cooking called "urgent fire stir fry" that helps to preserve vitamin B2. Note that the methods used by different authors to assign a nutritional value to certain mushroom species should also be considered because different quantitative methods result in values that can be highly variable (Falandysz; Borovička, 2013).

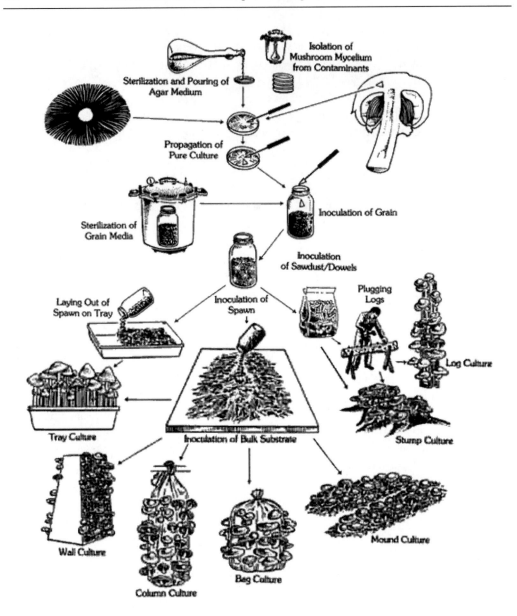

Figure 4. Mushroom cultivation.

5. HEALTH BENEFITS OF EDIBLE MUSHROOMS

Due to the medicinal importance of mushrooms, the Romans viewed them as the "food of the gods", and the Chinese viewed them as an "elixir of life" (Mattila; Suonpaa; Piironen, 2000). The benefits of mushroom compounds for different clinical conditions have attracted the interest of the scientific community in the past decade, resulting in efforts to understand the molecular mechanisms responsible for the health benefits of mushrooms (Wasser, 2011).

Studies conducted over the past few decades have shown that mushrooms have a number of nutritional and functional properties that could make a notable contribution to the design of healthy eating patterns (Chang, 1996; Kalogeropoulos et al., 2013). In recent years, to unravel unanswered questions about mushrooms, especially those used in traditional medicine, mushrooms are being investigated due to the many ethnomycological claims for their medicinal value (Chang; Buswell, 2008). This topic has contributed to the great increase in the cultivation of varieties, as many of these varieties are sold as medicines in capsule form (e.g., *A. blazei*).

Mushrooms contain significant amounts of bioactive substances, such as vitamins and precursors to vitamins, minerals, trace elements and beta-glucans. Moreover, the specific antioxidant properties of mushrooms are attributed primarily to their phenolic content (Kalogeropoulos et al., 2013). Among the potential therapeutic uses of mushrooms are those linked to the anti-tumor activity of many species, as well as other benefits such as antioxidant activity, anti-inflammatory activity, antiviral activity, immunomodulatory activity, the lowering of cholesterol levels and beneficial effects on hypertension and diabetes. Moreover, mushrooms may be used against autoimmune diseases, such as rheumatoid arthritis and lupus (Smith; Rowan; Sullivan, 2002).

As mushrooms represent a source of compounds with pharmacological properties that show potential for the prevention of these diseases, we present several of the principal activities associated with the health effects of mushrooms:

a) **Anti-tumor:** there is evidence that mushrooms, as a food, play a role in cancer chemoprevention. Although the mechanism of antitumor action is not yet fully known, researchers believe that anticancer activity is associated with cell wall polysaccharides in the fruiting body (fruit) that can stimulate the formation of antibodies that inhibit tumor growth. In this case, the most important known polysaccharide is beta-glucan, which enhances the immune system by increasing the natural defenses of the body (Manzi; Pizzoferrato, 2000; Smith; Rowan; Sullivan, 2002).

b) **Diabetes:** components derived from mushrooms have been shown to have an effect in the control of diabetes by regulating various pathophysiological pathways related to the onset of the disease (Li et al., 2011; Xiao et al., 2011; Huang et al., 2012). Several antihyperglycemic mechanisms associated with medicinal mushrooms have been investigated, including the improvement of β cells and insulin-releasing activity, antioxidant defenses, the pathways of carbohydrate metabolism and α-glucosidase inhibitory activity of aldose reductase, but more conclusive data are needed (De Silva et al., 2012).

c) **Hypertension**: several types of mushrooms have shown hypotensive effects when blood pressure is already high (Guillamon et al., 2010). One of these possible effects is related to the low concentration of sodium and the high concentration of potassium (182–395 mg/100 g) in mushrooms (Manzi et al., 1999). Several studies have investigated the anti-hypertensive effects of certain edible mushroom species, e.g., *L. edodes, Ganoderma lucidum, Pleurotus narbonensis* and *G. frondosa* (Guillamon et al., 2010).

d) **Cholesterol**: in general, the intake of edible mushrooms reduces cardiovascular risk due to the occurrence of specific substances and other bioactive compounds

(Guillamon et al., 2010). Although the mechanism of action is unclear, the anti-triglyceride and anti-total cholesterol activities of edible mushrooms may be attributable to the fermentation of dietary fiber. Short-chain fatty acids, such as propionate, generated by the bacterial fermentation of dietary fibers have been shown to inhibit hepatic cholesterol synthesis (Chen; Anderson; Jennings, 1984; HARA et al., 1998). It has been suggested that dietary fiber from mushrooms might bind bile acids, reducing their entry into the enterohepatic circulation. This mechanism then produces an increase in gut bile acid secretion (Cheung, 1996). As a result, the liver responds by increasing the hepatic conversion of cholesterol into bile acids, reducing the circulating levels of cholesterol (Jeong et al., 2010). Several studies have shown lipid peroxidation inhibition and a suppression of the activity of HMG-CoA reductase in both normocholestolemic and hypercholesterolemic animal models (Guillamon et al., 2010).

e) **Anti-inflammatory:** certain species of fungi are known to produce significant anti-inflammatory effects (Jose; Ajith; Janardhanan, 2004; Kim et al., 2004; Lull; Wichers; Savelkoul, 2005), and natural anti-inflammatory substances have been isolated from certain edible mushrooms. In addition, it has been reported that ergosterol and ergosterol peroxide from edible mushrooms can inhibit inflammatory processes (Guillamon et al., 2010).

f) **Immune-modulatory:** several classes of mushroom compounds, such as proteins, polysaccharides, lipopolysaccharides and glucoproteins, have been classified as molecules that have potent effects on the immune system. They may restore and augment the immunological responses of the host immune effector cells, but they have no direct cytotoxic effect on tumors. The regular intake of mushrooms may enhance the immune response of the human body, thereby increasing resistance to disease and, in certain cases, causing regression of the disease state (Chang; Buswell, 2003; Wasser, 2011).

Medicinal mushrooms present an excellent opportunity for the development of new types of therapies and have been valued for their potential healing properties for centuries (Liu et al., 2012; Pereira et al., 2012). Additional evidence on the beneficial effects of medicinal mushrooms has been obtained through in vitro and animal studies (Badole et al., 2006; Ding et al., 2010). Safety issues in terms of the long-term consumption of mushrooms and inter-crossing or interactions with other drugs also need further clarification. Therefore, future investigations of these topics are necessary to rationalize the use of mushrooms and their products as drugs or nutritional supplements used in potential diabetes treatments (De Silva et al., 2012).

6. ANTIOXIDANT PROPERTIES

A number of edible mushrooms have been reported to have high antioxidant activity (Wang et al., 2014). It has been reported that the antioxidant activity of mushroom extracts is a strong inhibitor of lipid peroxidation, occurring in most cases at high concentrations of the extracts (Cheung; Cheung, 2005). The possible mechanisms of antioxidant activity of mushroom extracts include the scavenging of free radicals, possibly through hydrogen-holding capacity, and oxidation by peroxy radicals (Puttaraju et al., 2006).

Mushrooms have also been shown to accumulate a variety of secondary metabolites, e.g., phenolic compounds, polypeptides, terpenes and steroids. Mushroom phenolics have been found to be an excellent antioxidant and to possess synergistic action (Li et al., 2005).

Mushrooms contain various polyphenolic compounds that are recognized as excellent antioxidants due to their ability to scavenge free radicals by single-electron transfer (Hirano et al., 2001). Additionally, flavonoids and phenols have been shown to possess substantial antioxidant activity toward these radicals. This activity is principally based on the redox properties of their phenolic hydroxyl groups and on the relationships between different parts of their chemical structure (Barros, Lillian et al., 2007)

Phenolic compounds could be the foremost contributors to the antioxidant activity of edible macrofungi (Guo et al., 2012) through caffeic acid, catechin, gallic acid, p-coumaric acids and quercetin (WANG et al., 2014). The amount of ergothioneine ranges from 48 to 2851 mg kg^{-1} DM for 29 species of mushrooms (Chen et al., 2012), Thus, the abundant ergothioneine can enhance the antioxidant capacity of the food (Wang et al., 2014).

It is also well known that methanolic extracts of mushroom species show significant antioxidant activity against various antioxidant systems in vitro. The various antioxidant mechanisms responsible for the effects of the extracts may be based on strong hydrogen-donating ability, metal-chelating ability and effectiveness as good scavengers of superoxide and free radicals (Elmastas et al., 2007). Another study has shown that nitric oxide fumigation might have a potential application to enhancing the bioactive compounds and improving the antioxidant activity of mushrooms (Dong et al., 2012).

Beyond these antioxidant activities, other factors contribute, in part, to the antioxidant properties of edible mushrooms. Based on this evidence, phenolic compounds appear to be the main components responsible for the known antioxidant activity. Mushroom species can be used as an easily accessible source of natural antioxidants and as a possible food supplement (Li et al., 2005; Elmastas et al., 2007; Guo et al., 2012).

7. Caveats on Consumption

Mushrooms are a part of the human diet, but they can accumulate high concentrations of certain types of elements and also have the variable and highly specific ability to take several trace elements (metals, metalloids and halogens) from soil and accumulate them in their fruiting bodies (Kalač; Svoboda, 2000; Cheung, 2010; Falandysz; Borovička, 2013). These mechanisms for absorbing and accumulating trace elements from the substrate could be used to produce mineral-enriched food and nutritional supplements (Nunes et al., 2012). However, the consumption of such mushrooms must be controlled, particularly if their chemical composition and/or source is unknown. Consuming mushrooms that are produced according to high standards of quality from soil known to be free of pollutants is an appropriate way to avoid this problem.

Data on the changes in the components of mushrooms under various conditions of preservation and culinary treatments are also fragmented, and knowledge about the bioavailability of nutrients is even more limited (Kalac, 2013). Despite the high toxicity of certain elements, especially cadmium, mercury and lead, whose bioaccumulation may represent a significant potential risk to humans, many elements, such as iron, zinc, manganese, chromium and selenium, are essential for human metabolism at low concentrations because they are enzyme activators. These elements become toxic only at increased concentrations (Garcia; Alonso; Melgar, 2013).

The process of heavy metal accumulation in mushrooms is species-dependent (Falandysz et al., 2012). Instead of the direct use of mushrooms as a food alternative, more studies on the environmental monitoring of mushrooms should be developed. Although the major factors contributing to the accumulation of metals in mushrooms have not been identified, the absorption of metals is determined by various conditions, specifically, the properties of the environment (e.g., the concentration of metals in the soil, water and air, pH and substrate composition) and genetic properties (e.g., ecology, species, and the morphological part of the mushroom) (Garcia; Alonso; Melgar, 2013).

Given this evidence, it is important to monitor the content of toxic metals and metalloids in conjunction with the marketing of mushrooms. Furthermore, it is necessary to exercise care in the use of mushrooms artificially enriched with trace elements. Note, however, that mushrooms, like most other foods consumed by the world's population, should be included in proper proportions in the diet. Following the recommendation that quality products (produced in places with healthy soil) should be selected will ensure the consumption of mushrooms that do not offer significant health risks.

CONCLUSION

The consumption of mushrooms has increased due to not only the pleasant taste and aroma of culinary mushrooms but also (and primarily) the search for natural products that are free of pesticides and can be considered nutraceuticals or functional foods with high nutritional values as well as bioactive activities. These characteristics have already been assessed to identify remedies for disease and healthy natural foods for thousands of years.

Studies by many researchers tend to show that mushrooms have properties that may be beneficial to humans and can promote health as a result of the regular consumption of mushrooms. Furthermore, there is a need to study the potential of mushrooms to elucidate the mechanisms of activity associated with the effects of mushrooms, and there is a need for clinical trials. Until now, these effects have been extensively studied *in vitro* and *in vivo* through animal testing. However, human studies are needed in addition to the identification of additional varieties of mushrooms with properties that may function medically in prevention or therapy. Mushrooms are a promising alternative food source and will be increasingly important in medicine and biotechnology in the future due to their unique biosynthetic capabilities and metabolic products.

REFERENCES

Badole, S. L. et al. Hypoglycemic Activity of Aqueous Extract of *Pleurotus pulmonarius*. in Alloxan-Induced Diabetic Mice. *Pharmaceutical biology,* v. 44, n. 6, p. 421-425, 2006.

Banik, S.; Nandi, R. Effect of supplementation of rice straw with biogas residual slurry manure on the yield, protein and mineral contents of oyster mushroom. *Industrial Crops and Products,* v. 20, n. 3, p. 311-319, 2004.

Barron, C. et al. Modified Atmosphere Packaging of Cultivated Mushroom (*Agaricus bisporus L.*) with Hydrophilic Films. *Journal of Food Science,* v. 67, n. 1, p. 251-255, 2002.

Barros, L. et al. Effects of Conservation Treatment and Cooking on the Chemical Composition and Antioxidant Activity of Portuguese Wild Edible Mushrooms. *Journal of Agricultural and Food Chemistry,* v. 55, n. 12, p. 4781-4788, 2007.

Barros, L. et al. Total phenols, ascorbic acid, β-carotene and lycopene in Portuguese wild edible mushrooms and their antioxidant activities. *Food Chemistry,* v. 103, n. 2, p. 413-419, 2007.

Beetz, A.; Greer, L. Mushroom Cultivation and Marketing Horticulture Production Guide. *Appropriate technology transfer for Rural Areas, Fayetteville,* 1999.

Blackwell, Meredith. The Fungi: 1, 2, 3 ... 5.1 million species? *American Journal of Botany,* v. 98, n. 3, p. 426-438, 2011.

Bonatti, M. et al. Evaluation of *Pleurotus ostreatus* and *Pleurotus sajor-caju* nutritional characteristics when cultivated in different lignocellulosic wastes. *Food Chemistry,* v. 88, n. 3, p. 425-428, 2004.

Çağlarırmak, Necla. The nutrients of exotic mushrooms (*Lentinula edodes* and *Pleurotus* species) and an estimated approach to the volatile compounds. *Food Chemistry,* v. 105, n. 3, p. 1188-1194, 2007.

Chang, Raymond. Functional Properties of Edible Mushrooms. *Nutrition Reviews,* v. 54, n. 11, p. 91-93, 1996.

Chang, S.-T.; Buswell, J. A. Development of the world mushroom industry: Applied mushroom biology and international mushroom organizations. *International Journal of Medicinal Mushrooms,* v. 10, n. 3, p. 195-208, 2008.

Chang, S.; Buswell, J. Medicinal mushrooms-A prominent source of nutriceuticals for the 21st century. *Current Topics in Nutraceutical Research,* v. 1, p. 257-280, 2003.

Chang, S. T.; Miles, P. G. Mushroom biology — a new discipline. *Mycologist,* v. 6, n. 2, p. 64-65, 1992.

Chen, A. W. What is shiitake? In: Gush, R. (Ed.). *Shiitake cultivation.* Korea: MushWord, v. 1, p. 3-31, 2005.CHEN, S.-Y. et al. Contents of lovastatin, γ-aminobutyric acid and ergothioneine in mushroom fruiting bodies and mycelia. *LWT-Food Science and Technology,* v. 47, n. 2, p. 274-278, 2012.

Chen, W. J. L.; Anderson, J. W.; Jennings, D. Propionate may mediate the hypocholesterolemic effects of certain soluble plant fibers in cholesterol-fed rats. *Proceedings of the Society for Experimental Biology and Medicine,* v. 175, n. 2, p. 215-218, 1984.

Cheung, L.; Cheung, P. C. Mushroom extracts with antioxidant activity against lipid peroxidation. *Food Chemistry,* v. 89, n. 3, p. 403-409, 2005.

Cheung, Peter. C. K. The nutritional and health benefits of mushrooms. *Nutrition Bulletin,* v. 35, n. 4, p. 292-299, 2010.

Cheung, Peter. C. K. *Mushrooms as functional foods.* John Wiley and Sons, New York, 2008.

Cheung, Peter. C. K. The hypocholesterolemic effect of two edible mushrooms: *Auricularia auricula* (tree-ear) and *Tremella fuciformis* (white jelly-leaf) in hypercholesterolemic rats[1]. *Nutrition Research,* v. 16, n. 10, p. 1721-1725, 1996.

Cheung, Peter. C. K. Dietary Fibre Content and Composition of Some Edible Fungi Determined by Two Methods of Analysis. *Journal of the Science of Food and Agriculture,* v. 73, n. 2, p. 255-260, 1997.

Cheung, Peter. C. K. Mini-review on edible mushrooms as source of dietary fiber: Preparation and health benefits. *Food Science and Human Wellness,* v. 2, n. 3-4, p. 162-166, 2013.

De Roman, Miriam. The contribution of wild fungi to diet, income and health: A world review. In: Rai M, Kovics G. (Ed.). *Progress in mycology:* Springer, 2010. p.327-348.

De Silva, D. D. et al. Medicinal mushrooms in prevention and control of diabetes mellitus. *Fungal Diversity,* v. 56, n. 1, p. 1-29, 2012.

Demirbaş, Ayhan. Concentrations of 21 metals in 18 species of mushrooms growing in the East Black Sea region. *Food Chemistry,* v. 75, n. 4, p. 453-457, 2001.

Ding, Z. et al. Hypoglycaemic effect of comatin, an antidiabetic substance separated from *Coprinus comatus* broth, on alloxan-induced-diabetic rats. *Food Chemistry,* v. 121, n. 1, p. 39-43, 2010.

Dong, J. et al. Nitric oxide fumigation stimulates flavonoid and phenolic accumulation and enhances antioxidant activity of mushroom. *Food Chemistry,* v. 135, n. 3, p. 1220-1225, 2012.

Elmastas, M. et al. Determination of antioxidant activity and antioxidant compounds in wild edible mushrooms. *Journal of Food Composition and Analysis,* v. 20, n. 3-4, p. 337-345, 2007.

Falandysz, Jerzy. Selenium in edible mushrooms. *Journal of Environmental Science and Health Part C,* v. 26, n. 3, p. 256-299, 2008.

Falandysz, J.; Borovička, J. Macro and trace mineral constituents and radionuclides in mushrooms: health benefits and risks. *Applied Microbiology and Biotechnology,* v. 97, n. 2, p. 477-501, 2013.

Falandysz, J. et al. Mineral constituents in Common Chanterelles and soils collected from a high mountain and lowland sites in Poland. *Journal of Mountain Science,* v. 9, n. 5, p. 697-705, 2012.

Joint Fao—Who Expert Consultation.. *Protein quality evaluation. Food and Nutrition Paper 151Food and Agriculture Organization of the United Nations*, Rome, 1991.

Ganeshpurkar, A.; Rai, G.; Jain, A. Medicinal mushrooms: Towards a new horizon. *Pharmacognosy Reviews,* v. 4, n. 8, p. 127-135, 2010.

García, M. A.; Alonso, J.; Melgar, M. J. Bioconcentration of chromium in edible mushrooms: Influence of environmental and genetic factors. *Food Chemical Toxicology,* v. 58, p. 249-54, 2013.

Ghorai, S. et al. Fungal biotechnology in food and feed processing. *Food Research International,* v. 42, n. 5-6, p. 577-587, 2009.

Giraud, T.; Gladieux, P.; Gavrilets, S. Linking the emergence of fungal plant diseases with ecological speciation. *Trends in Ecology & Evolution,* v. 25, n. 7, p. 387-395, 2010.

Grangeia, C. et al. Effects of trophism on nutritional and nutraceutical potential of wild edible mushrooms. *Food Research International,* v. 44, n. 4, p. 1029-1035, 2011.

Guillamón, E. et al. Edible mushrooms: Role in the prevention of cardiovascular diseases. *Fitoterapia*, v. 81, n. 7, p. 715-723, 2010.

Günç Ergönül, P. et al. Fatty Acid Compositions of Six Wild Edible Mushroom Species. *The Scientific World Journal*, v. 2013, 4 pages, 2013.

Guo, Y.-J. et al. Antioxidant capacities, phenolic compounds and polysaccharide contents of 49 edible macro-fungi. *Food & Function*, v. 3, n. 11, p. 1195-1205, 2012.

Hara, H. et al. Fermentation Products of Sugar-Beet Fiber by Cecal Bacteria Lower Plasma Cholesterol Concentration in Rats. *The Journal of Nutrition*, v. 128, n. 4, p. 688-693, 1998.

Hirano, R. et al. Antioxidant ability of various flavonoids against DPPH radicals and LDL oxidation. *Journal of Nutritional Science and Vitaminology*, v. 47, n. 5, p. 357-362, 2001.

Huang, A. et al. Exacerbation of endothelial dysfunction during the progression of diabetes: role of oxidative stress. *American Journal of Physiology - Regulatory, Integrative and Comparative Physiology*, v. 302, n. 6, p. R674-681, Mar 15 2012.

Jeong, S. C. et al. White button mushroom (*Agaricus bisporus*) lowers blood glucose and cholesterol levels in diabetic and hypercholesterolemic rats. *Nutrition Research*, v. 30, n. 1, p. 49-56, 2010.

Jose, N.; Ajith, T. A.; Janardhanan, K. K. Methanol extract of the Oyster mushroom, *Pleurotus florida*, inhibits inflammation and platelet aggregation. *Phytotherapy Research*, v. 18, n. 1, p. 43-46, 2004.

Kalač, P. A review of chemical composition and nutritional value of wild-growing and cultivated mushrooms. *Journal of the Science of Food and Agriculture*, v. 93, n. 2, p. 209-218, 2013.

Kalač, P.; Svoboda, L. R. A review of trace element concentrations in edible mushrooms. *Food Chemistry*, v. 69, n. 3, p. 273-281, 2000.

Kalogeropoulos, N. et al. Bioactive microconstituents and antioxidant properties of wild edible mushrooms from the island of Lesvos, Greece. *Food and Chemical Toxicology*, v. 55, p. 378-385, 2013.

Kim, S.-H. et al. Anti-inflammatory and related pharmacological activities of the *n*-BuOH subfraction of mushroom *Phellinus linteus*. *Journal of Ethnopharmacology*, v. 93, n. 1, p. 141-146, 2004.

Leskosek-Cukalovic, I. et al. *Ganoderma lucidum* - Medical mushroom as a raw material for beer with enhanced functional properties. *Food Research International*, v. 43, n. 9, p. 2262-2269, 2010.

Li, L. et al. Correlation of Antioxidant Activity with Content of Phenolics in Extracts from the Culinary-Medicinal Abalone Mushroom*Pleurotus abalones* Han, Chen et Cheng (Agaricomycetideae). *International Journal of Medicinal Mushrooms*, v. 7, n. 1 & 2, p. 237-242, 2005.

Li, T. H. et al. Anti-Hyperglycemic Properties of Crude Extract and Triterpenes from Poria cocos. *Evidence-Based Complementary and Alternative Medicine* v. 2011, 8 pages, 2011.

Liu, Y.-T. et al. Chemical composition of five wild edible mushrooms collected from Southwest China and their antihyperglycemic and antioxidant activity. *Food and Chemical Toxicology*, v. 50, n. 5, p. 1238-1244, 2012.

Lull, C.; Wichers, H. J.; Savelkoul, H. F. J. Antiinflammatory and Immunomodulating Properties of Fungal Metabolites. *Mediators of Inflammation*, v. 2005, n. 2, p. 63-80, 2005.

Manzi, P.; Aguzzi, A.; Pizzoferrato, L. Nutritional value of mushrooms widely consumed in Italy. *Food Chemistry*, v. 73, n. 3, p. 321-325, 2001.

Manzi, P. et al. Nutrients in edible mushrooms: an inter-species comparative study. *Food Chemistry*, v. 65, n. 4, p. 477-482, 1999.

Manzi, P.; Pizzoferrato, L. Beta-glucans in edible mushrooms. *Food Chemistry*, v. 68, n. 3, p. 315-318, 2000.

Mattila, P. et al. Contents of Vitamins, Mineral Elements, and Some Phenolic Compounds in Cultivated Mushrooms. *Journal of Agricultural and Food Chemistry*, v. 49, n. 5, p. 2343-2348, 2001.

Mattila, P. et al. Sterol and vitamin D $_2$ sub contents in some wild and cultivated mushrooms. *Food Chemistry*, v. 76, n. 3, p. 293-298, 2002.

Mattila, P.; Suonpää, K.; Piironen, V. Functional properties of edible mushrooms. *Nutrition*, v. 16, n. 7-8, p. 694-696, 2000.

Molz, P. et al. A metabolomics approach to evaluate the effects of shiitake mushroom (*Lentinula edodes*) treatment in undernourished young rats. *Nuclear Instruments and Methods in Physics Research Section B: Beam Interactions with Materials and Atoms*, v. 318, Part A, p. 194-197, 2014.

Nunes, R. G. F. L. et al. Selenium Bioaccumulation in Shiitake Mushrooms: A Nutritional Alternative Source of this Element. *Journal of Food Science*, v. 77, n. 9, p. C983-C986, 2012.

Outila, T. A. et al. Bioavailability of vitamin D from wild edible mushrooms (*Cantharellus tubaeformis*) as measured with a human bioassay. *The American Journal of Clinical Nutrition*, v. 69, n. 1, p. 95-98, 1999.

Pereira, E. et al. Towards chemical and nutritional inventory of Portuguese wild edible mushrooms in different habitats. *Food Chemistry*, v. 130, n. 2, p. 394-403, 2012.

Poppe, J.; Griensven, L. V. Use of agricultural waste materials in the cultivation of mushrooms. In: Van Griensven L. J. L. D. (E.d.). Science and Cultivation of Edible Fungi. *Proceedings of the 15th International Congress on the Science and Cultivation of Edible Fungi, Maastricht, Netherlands*, 15-19 May, 2000., 2000, AA Balkema. p.3-23.

Puttaraju, N. G. et al. Antioxidant Activity of Indigenous Edible Mushrooms. *Journal of Agricultural and Food Chemistry*, v. 54, n. 26, p. 9764-9772, 2006.

Ragunathan, R.; Swaminathan, K. Nutritional status of *Pleurotus* spp. grown on various agro-wastes. *Food Chemistry*, v. 80, n. 3, p. 371-375, 2003.

Reis, F. S. et al. Chemical composition and nutritional value of the most widely appreciated cultivated mushrooms: An inter-species comparative study. *Food and Chemical Toxicology*, v. 50, n. 2, p. 191-197, 2012.

Rudawska, M.; Leski, T. Macro-and microelement contents in fruiting bodies of wild mushrooms from the Notecka forest in west-central Poland. *Food Chemistry*, v. 92, n. 3, p. 499-506, 2005.

Sadler, Michele. Nutritional properties of edible fungi. *Nutrition Bulletin*, v. 28, n. 3, p. 305-308, 2003.

Sanchez, Carmen. Modern aspects of mushroom culture technology. *Applied Microbiology and Biotechnology*, v. 64, n. 6, p. 756-762, 2004.

Sanchez, Carmen. Cultivation of *Pleurotus ostreatus* and other edible mushrooms. *Applied Microbiology and Biotechnology*, v. 85, n. 5, p. 1321-1337, 2010.

Sanmee, R. et al. Nutritive value of popular wild edible mushrooms from northern Thailand. *Food Chemistry,* v. 82, n. 4, p. 527-532, 2003.

Savoie, J. M.; Minvielle, N.; Largeteau, M. L. Radical-scavenging properties of extracts from the white button mushroom, *Agaricus bisporu*s. *Journal of the Science of Food and Agriculture,* v. 88, n. 6, p. 970-975, 2008.

Seeger, R.; Trumpfheller, S.; Schweinshaut, P. On the occurrence of sodium in fungi. *Deutsche Lebensmittel-Rundschau,* v. 79, n. 3, p. 80-87, 1983.

Smith, J. E.; Rowan, N.; Sullivan, R. *Medicinal mushrooms: their therapeutic properties and current medical usage with special emphasis on cancer treatments.* Cancer Research UK, 2002.

Valentao, P. et al. Quantitation of Nine Organic Acids in Wild Mushrooms. *Journal of Agricultural and Food Chemistry,* v. 53, n. 9, p. 3626-3630, 2005.

Vetter, Janos. Data on sodium content of common edible mushrooms. *Food Chemistry,* v. 81, n. 4, p. 589-593, 2003.

Wang, X.-M. et al. A mini-review of chemical composition and nutritional value of edible wild-grown mushroom from China. *Food Chemistry,* v. 151, p. 279-285, 2014.

Wasser, Solomon. P. Medicinal mushrooms as a source of antitumor and immunomodulating polysaccharides. *Applied Microbiology and Biotechnology,* v. 60, n. 3, p. 258-274, 2002.

Wasser, Solomon. P. Current findings, future trends, and unsolved problems in studies of medicinal mushrooms. *Applied Microbiology and Biotechnology,* v. 89, n. 5, p. 1323-1332, 2011.

Xiao, C. et al. Inhibitory effects on alpha-glucosidase and hypoglycemic effects of the crude polysaccharides isolated from 11 edible fungi. *Journal of Medicinal Plants Research,* v. 5, p. 6963-6967, 2011.

Yin, J. Z.; Zhou, L. X. Analysis of nutritional components of 4 kinds of wild edible fungi in Yunnan. *Food Research and Development*, v. 29, p. 133-136, 2008.

In: Mushrooms
Editor: Grégoire Pesti

ISBN: 978-1-63117-521-3
© 2014 Nova Science Publishers, Inc.

Chapter 4

PHYTOCHEMISTRY, TRADITIONAL USES AND HEALTH BENEFITS OF THE MUSHROOM *INONOTUS OBLIQUUS* (CHAGA)

Haixia Chen and Jia Wang*
Tianjin Key Laboratory for Modern Drug Delivery & High-Efficiency,
School of Pharmaceutical Science and Technology,
Tianjin University, Tianjin, China

ABSTRACT

Mushroom Inonotus obliquus, a well-known folk medicine, has multiple health benefits such as treating malignant tumors, diabetes, cardiovascular disease, tuberculosis, liver diseases, ascariasis, and AIDS. Modern phytochemistry and pharmacological experiments had proved that polysaccharides, triterpenoids and polyphenols were the major active ingredients in Inonotus obliquus and they had been demonstrated to have various important biological activities including immunomodulation, antitumor, antioxidant, anti-inflammatory, hypoglycemic and antiviral activity. The purpose of this chapter is to summarize previous and current information available on the structural characterization and biological activities of the main compounds from Inonotus obliquus and to explore its health benefits and future research opportunities. The outcome of the studies on Inonotus obliquus will further expand the existing health benefits potential of mushroom Inonotus obliquus and provide a convincing support to its future use in modern medicine and functional foods.

Keywords: *Inonotus obliquus*, biological activities, active constituents, health benefits

---

* Correspondence author:Haixia Chen, Tianjin Key Laboratory for Modern Drug Delivery & High-Efficiency, School of Pharmaceutical Science and Technology, Tianjin University, Tianjin, 300072, P. R. China. Telephone: 86-22-27401483; Fax: 86-22-27892025; E-mail address: chenhx@tju.edu.cn.

1. INTRODUCTION

Inonotus obliquus (Pers.: Fr.) Pil. (= Fuscoporia obliqua (Pers.: Fr.) Aoshima), commonly known as kabanoanatake in Japan and chaga or tchaga in Russia, is a white-rot fungus belonging to the eumycophyta, basidiomycotina, hymenomycetes, aphyllophorales, polyporaceae, poriahypobrunnea petch families and is widely distributed at latitudes of 45 °N-50°N, in North America, Finland, Poland, Russia (Western Siberia, partial regions in the Far East, Kamchatka peninsula), China (Heilongjiang province, Changbai mountain area of Jilin province), Japan (Hokkaido), etc. (Hawksworth et al., 1995 ; Zhong et al., 2009). *Inonotus obliquus* is a fungal parasite of living trees, growing primarily on branch stubs on birches, but sometimes on elm, alder, or beech trees (Cui et al., 2005). This fungus is usually found as a sterile conk (sclerotia) called Chaga on Betula species (Campbell et al., 1938) and traditionally it has been used to treat gastrointestinal cancer, cardiovascular disease and diabetes since the 16th century in Russia (Huang et al., 2002) and it also has been used to alleviate worms, tuberculosis, stomach ailments, and also as an internal cleansing agent. As with many other natural herbs, the modern scientific community is coming to understand that supplements like Chaga, offer a complex balance of compounds, a delivery of powerful phytonutrients that function as adaptogens and support a healthy immune system. However, its pharmacological actions have not been well documented and numerous attempts to elucidate the therapeutic potential of *Inonotus obliquus* preparations for the treatment of certain diseases gave rather ambiguous results. This chapter presents an attempt at systematizing available published data on the chemical nature of components isolated from *Inonotus obliquus*, their pharmacological activity, and the mechanism of biological action.

2. PHYTOCHEMISTRY

The components of *Inonotus obliquus* mainly include polysaccharides, triterpenoids, polyphenol, steroids, protein, lignin, etc.

2.1. Polysaccharides

The physiochemical and structural features of a kind of polysaccharide are defined by molecular weight, monosaccharide composition, sequence of monosaccharide, configuration and position of glycosidic linkages, type and polymerization degree of branch, spatial configuration, etc. (Jin et al., 2011; Nie et al., 2011). Five polysaccharides (IOP1b, IOP2a, IOP2c, IOP3a and IOP4) were isolated and purified from *Inonotus obliquus* by DEAE-Sepharose fast flow and Sepharose CL-6B column chromatography (Huang et al., 2012). The monosaccharide compositions and average molecular weight were analyzed by GC and HPGPC, respectively. The results showed that IOP1b was only consisted of glucose with the molecular weight of 1.5×10^5 Da. IOP2a, with the molecular of 9.3×10^4 Da, was composed of Rha, Man and Glu in the molar ratios of 1.0:2.3:1.7. IOP2c was composed of Man, Glu and Gal in a molar ratio of 1.0:2.9:0.8 with the molecular weight of 2.3×10^5 Da. The IOP3a was detected to be glycoprotein and the protein and carbohydrate were linked by O-linkage, after alkali treatment, it was composed mainly of Rha, Man, Glu and Gal in a molar ratio of 0.3:4.6:2.3:1.0, with the molecular weight of 4.4×10^4 Da. The IOP4 with the molecular of 1.0×10^5 Da, was composed mainly of Man and Glu in a molar ratio of 1.8:1.0.

Our previous study (Ma et al., 2012) concerning the molecular modifications of polysaccharides of *Inonotus obliquus* had demonstrated that the physicochemical and antioxidant activities were changed by chemical modification. The monosaccharide compositions and average molecular weight of polysaccharides with different chemical modification were analyzed, the Un-IOPS (native polysaccharide) was composed of Rha, Ara, Xyl, Man, Glc, Gal in the molar ratios of 2.67:3.20:6.57:2.16:48.00:17.90, with the molecular weight of 1.2×10^5 Da, and Su-IOPS, with the molecular weights of 5.22×10^4 Da , was composed of the Rha, Ara, Xyl, Man, Glc, Gal in the proportions of 1.57:0.84:5.65:12.90:77.90:1.16; Ac-IOPS and Ca-IOPS consisted of the above monosaccharide compositions in the ratio of 1.64:1.68:4.95:16.60:73.20:1.95 and 0.39:0.41:27.60:11.60:59.20:0.76, with the molecular weight of 1.03×10^5 Da and 2.68×10^4 Da, respectively. In accordance with the decrease of the molecular weight, the intrinsic viscosity of all Un-IOPS derivatives decreased.

In our previous study (Ma, et al., 2013), the effects of different drying methods including freeze drying, hot air drying, and vacuum drying on the physicochemical and antioxidant properties of polysaccharide from *Inonotus obliqus* (IOPS) were investigated. The monosaccharide compositions and average molecular weight were analyzed and it showed that the conformation of the monosaccharides and molecular weight were changed, the IOPS-F(freeze drying treatrment) was composed of Rha, Ara, Man, GalA, Glc in the molar ratios of 32.5:0.8:3.4:28.1:35.1, with the peak molecular weights of 25.11×10^4, 8.78×10^4, 4.36×10^4, 2.16×10^4, and 1.12×10^4 Da, whereas IOPS-H (hot air drying treatment) consisted of Rha, Ara, Man, GalA, Glc in the molar ratios of 33.4:1.7:4.5:25.8:34.1, with the peak molecular weights of 38.52×10^4, 6.69×10^4, 3.32×10^4 and 1.47×10^4 Da , and IOPS-V, with the peak molecular weights of 30.50×10^4, 13.47×10^4, 7.51×10^4, 2.95×10^4 and 1.03×10^4 Da, was composed of the above monosaccharide in the proportions of 12.8: 1.6:4.3:21.5:9.7. The high molecular weight peaks in the IOPS-H and IOPS-V indicated that the polysaccharide molecules were easier to aggregate at the higher temperature conditions. The molecular weight, intrinsic viscosity, molecular shape related parameter was calculated and the value of α for IOPS-F, IOPS-V and IOPS-H was 0.47, 0.53 and 0.48, respectively, which indicated that there were many branches in the backbone structures of IOPS-H and IOPS-F compared to IOPS-V.

In the studies of Zhang et al. (2013), thermal treatment, ultrasonic treatment, acid and alkali hydrolysis were used to modify the polysaccharide which isolated and purified from *Inonotus obliquus*. The contents of neutral sugar and uronic acids were changed to various degrees upon the treatment under different conditions due to the glycosidic linkages of neutral sugar and uronic were different. The monosaccharide compositions and molecular weight of these polysaccharides were analyzed by gas chromatography and size exclusion chromatography analysis, respectively. The IOPS-2 (native polysaccharide) was composed of Rha, Ara, Xyl, Man, Glc, Gal in the ratios of 2.67:3.20:6.57:48.00:17.9, with the molecular weight of 12.20×10^4 Da, the Ac-IOPS(acid hydrolysis), with the molecular weight of 9.79×10^4 Da and 3.01×10^4 Da, was in the ratios of 5.08:4.42:17.60:15.80:42.70:14.40, the Al-IOPS (alkali hydrolysis) was in the ratios of 4.82:4.41:8.21:21.40:42.00:19.20, with the molecular weight of 9.15×10^4 Da and 0.31×10^4 Da, Th-IOPS (thermal treatment) and Ul-

IOPS (ultrasonic treatment) were consisted of the above monosaccharide compositions in the ratios of 8.06:1.47:4.83:39.00:43.80:2.90 and 3.69:4.92:7.03:16.10:33.60:34.60 with the molecular weight of 6.39×10^4 Da ,2.22×10^4 Da and 6.88×10^4 Da, 2.98×10^4 Da, respectively. The molecular weight distributions of polysaccharides with the above physical modifications were decreased, the cleavage of protein and the rupture of main chain might be accounted for the decrease, and the results were in agreement with the changes on the viscosity.

The endo-polysaccharide was extracted from *Inonotus obliquus* mycelia cultivated in a 300-l pilot fermenter, followed by hot water extraction and ethanol precipitation. Purification was achieved by DEAE-cellulose ion-exchange chromatography and gel-permeation chromatography. FII-1 and FII-2 were hetero-glycans consisting of mannose, glucose, fucose, and glucosamine in the ratios of 70.8:1.6:0.8:0.1 and 74.4:2.6:0.7:0.1, respectively. The molecular weight of FII-1 was estimated to be 1000 kDa and the ^{1}H and ^{13}C NMR analyses revealed nine anomeric proton signals, along with the coupling constants of anomeric protons, indicated that the purified endo-polysaccharide was an α-linkage fucoglucomannan (Kim et al., 2006). Although it was difficult to correlate polysaccharide structure with their biological activities, some relationships could be inferred. Wasser et al. (2002) reported that mannan was the major component of some active hetero-polysaccharides, the previously reported FII-1, which showed anticancer activity, was a fucoglucomannan composed primarily of mannose with small amounts of glucose, fucose, and glucos amine (Kim et al. 2006). While in the studies of Kim et al. (2005), the immuno-stimulating activities of water-soluble endo-polysaccharides of *Inonotus obliquuus* was high when it was composed of rhamnose, arabinose, galactose, glucose, xylose, and mannose. The activity was maintained when rhamnose and xylose disappeared. The polysaccharide lost most of its activity, when only glucose and mannose were detected. The results showed that the major component sugars were glucose and mannose, but small amounts of xylose, galactose, and arabinose were also considered to be essential for high activities. The biological activities of polysaccharides are also closely related to molecular mass. Polysaccharide fractions of >50 kDa molecular mass showed the highest activity However, other fractions of < 50 kDa showed low activities. It might be due to the glucose content of the > 50 kDa polysaccharide was decreased whereas the levels of galactose, xylose and mannose were highly increased (Kim et al., 2005). The polysaccharide linkage type is another important factor. The FII-1 (Kim et al. 2006) consists of α -linkages, according to ^{1}HNMR analysis. The immuno-stimulating and anti-tumor effect was considered to depend chiefly on the backbone structure of α-(1→3)-D-mannans (Gao et al., 1996; Vinogradov et al., 2004). It was different from other known immuno-stimulating β-glucans (Usui et al., 1981; Mizuno et al., 1992). The further structural and activity relationship studies are needed.

2.2. Triterpenoids

It was reported that 34 triterpenoids isolated from the sclerotia of *Inonotus obliquus* up to date. The isolated compounds are as follows. Inotodiol (1) (Ludwiczak et al., 1962), 3β-hydroxylanosta-8,24-dien-21-al (2) (Kahlos et al., 1984), Lanosterol (3), Trametenolic acid (4), 3β-Hydroxy-8,24-dien-lanosta-21,23-lactone (5), 21,24-Cyc-lopenta-3β,21,25-triol-8-ene

(6), 3β,22,25-Trihydroxy-Lanosta-8-ene (7) (Yusoo et al., 2001), inonotsuoxides A (11), B (12) (Nakata et al., 2007). Taji S group isolated inonotsulides A (8), B (9), C (10) (Taji et al., 2007), lanosta-8,23E-diene-3β, 22R,25-triol (13), lanosta-7:9(11), 23E-triene-3β, 22 R, 25-triol (14), lanosta-8,24-dien-3β,21-diol (15) (Taji et al., 2008a), Inonotsutriols A (16), B (17), C (18) (Taji et al., 2008b). Inoterpenes A-F (21-26) was obtained by Nakamura et al. (2009). Seven triterpenoids compounds: spiroinonotsuoxodiol (27), inonotsudiol A (28), inonotsuoxodiol A (29) (Handa et al. 2010), inonotsuoxodiol B (30), C (31), epoxyinonotsudiol (32), methoxyinonotsutriol (33) (Handa et al., 2012) were identified by Handa group. In 2011, inonotsutriols D (19), E (20) (Tanaka et al., 2011), betulin (34) (Kim et al., 2011) were isolated and evaluated for their anticancer activities. The names, pharmacological properties and corresponding references are included in Table1 and their structures are shown in Figure 1.

2.3. Polyphenol

Lee et al. (2007) had isolated six polyphenol ingredients including Inonoblins A (1), B (2), C (3) and phelligridins D (4), E (5), G (6) from the methanolic extract of *Inonotus obliquus*. Seven Low molecular weight phenolics, 4-hydroxy-3,5-dimethoxy benzoic acid 2-hydroxy-l-hydroxymethyl ethyl ester, protocatechic acid, caffeic acid, 3,4-dihybenzaladehyde, 2,5-dihydroxyterephtalic acid, syringic acid and 3,4-dihydroxybenzalacetone were isolated from *Inonotus obliquus* and tested to have antioxidant and anticancer activities (Nakajima et al., 2007; Nakajima et al., 2009). 2,5-dihydroxybenzalac-etone and gallic acid were isolated and studied for the effects on the cancer cell, respectively (Kim et al., 2011; Kuriyama et al., 2013).

The *Inonotus obliquus* synthesized macromolecular polyphenolic pigments were classified as melanins, which were tested to contain strong antioxidant and genoprotective effects. (Shashkina et al. 2012). The melanins constituted the group of high-molecular-weight black and brown pigments formed as a result of the oxidative polymerization of phenols (Sava et al., 2001). In the previous reports (Babitskaya et al., 2000), it was shown that copper ions, pyrocatechol, and tyrosine stimulated melanogenesis and the synthesis of o- and p-diphenoloxidases had effects on the production of melanin. The compounds, pharmacological properties and corresponding references of the polyphenols in *Inonotus obliquus* are included in Table 2 and their structures are shown in Figure 2.

2.4. Steroids

In previous investigations on the steroids component of *Inonotus obliquus*, fungisterol (Kirsi et al., 1987), ergosterol (Yusoo et al., 2001), ergosterol peroxide (Yusoo et al., 2001; Kim et al., 2011), and β-Sitosterol (Kim et al., 2011) were reported to have antitumor and anti-inflammatory activities. The names, pharmacological properties and corresponding references are included in Table 3 and their structures are shown in Figure 3.

Table 1. Triterpenoids isolated from *Inonotus obliquus*

NO	Compound	Pharmacological Properties	Reference
1	Inotodiol	anticancer	Ludwiczak et al. (1962)
		hypoglycaemic	Lu et al. (2009)
2	3β-hydroxylanosta-8,24-dien-21-al	antitumor	Kahlos et al.(1984)
		hypoglycaemic	Lu et al. (2009)
3	Lanosterol	hypoglycaemic	Lu et al. (2009)
4	Trametenolic acid	anticancer	Yusoo et al. (2001)
		hypoglycaemic	Lu et al. (2009)
5	3β-Hydroxy-8,24-dien-lanosta-21,23-lactone		Yusoo et al. (2001)
6	21,24-Cyclopenta-3β,21,25-triol-8-ene		Yusoo et al. (2001)
7	3β,22,25-Trihydroxy-Lanosta-8-ene		Yusoo et al. (2001)
8	Inonotsulides A	antitumor	Taji et al. (2007)
9	Inonotsulides B	antitumor	Taji et al. (2007)
10	Inonotsulides C	antitumor	Taji et al. (2007)
11	Inonotsuoxides A	antitumor	Nakata et al. (2007)
12	Inonotsuoxides B		Nakata et al. (2007)
13	lanosta-8,23 E-diene-3β,22 R,25-triol	antitumor	Taji et al. (2008a)
14	lanosta-7:9(11),23 E-triene-3β,22 R,25-triol	antitumor	Taji et al. (2008a)
15	lanosta-8,24 -dien-3β,21-diol		Taji et al. (2008a)
16	Inonotsutriols A		Taji et al. (2008b)
17	Inonotsutriols B		Taji et al. (2008b)
18	Inonotsutriols C		Taji et al. (2008b)
19	Inonotsutriols D	anticancer	Tanaka et al. (2011)

NO	Compound	Pharmacological Properties	Reference
20	Inonotsutriols E	anticancer	Tanaka et al. (2011)
21	Inoterpenes A		Nakamura et al. (2009)
22	Inoterpenes B		Nakamura et al. (2009)
23	Inoterpenes C		Nakamura et al. (2009)
24	Inoterpenes D		Nakamura et al. (2009)
25	Inoterpenes E		Nakamura et al. (2009)
26	Inoterpenes F		Nakamura et al. (2009)
27	Spiroinonotsuoxodiol	anticancer	Handa et al. (2010)
28	Inonotsudiol A	anticancer	Handa et al. (2010)
29	Inonotsuoxodiol A	anticancer	Handa et al. (2010)
30	Inonotsuoxodiol B	anticancer	Handa et al. (2012)
31	Inonotsuoxodiol C		Handa et al. (2012)
32	Epoxyinonotsudiol	anticancer	Handa et al. (2012)
33	Methoxyinonotsutriol		Handa et al. (2012)
34	Betulin	anticancer	Kim et al. (2011)

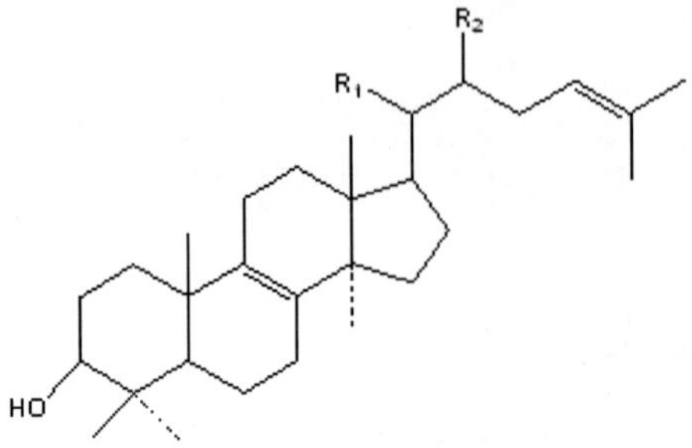

1: R_1=CH$_3$, R_2=OH 2: R_1=CHO, R_2=H

3: R_1=CH$_3$, R_2=H   4: R_1=COOH, R_2=H

15: R_1=CH$_2$OH, R_2=H

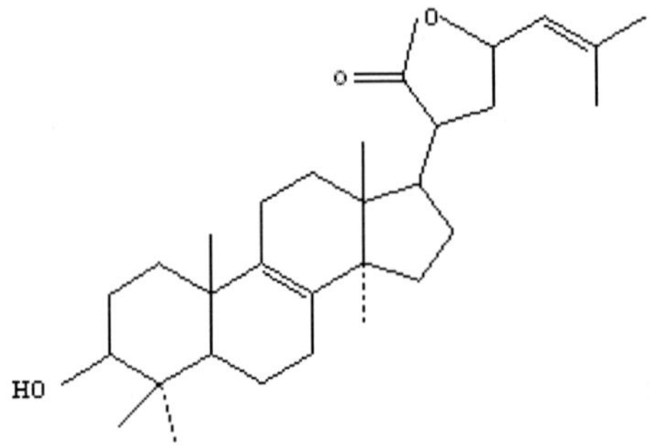

5

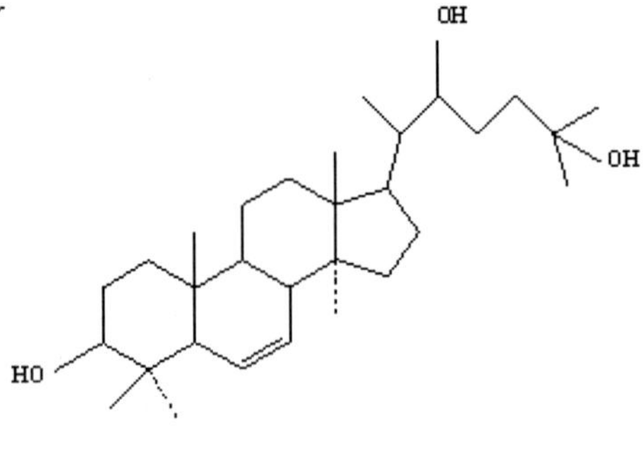

6

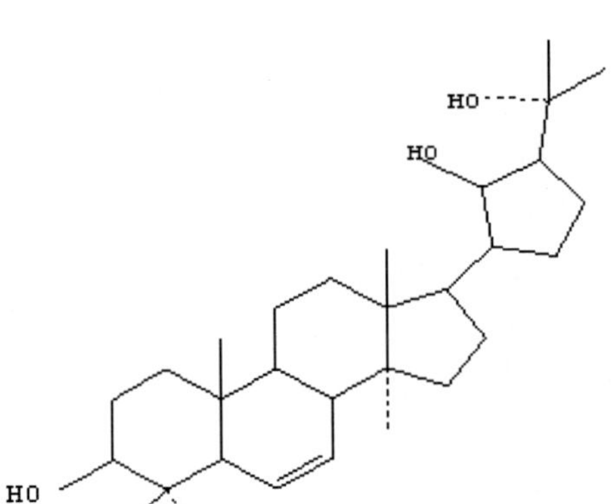

7

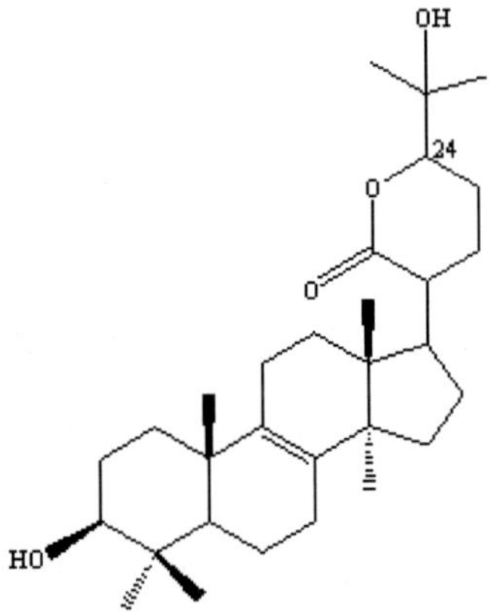

8:(24S)   9:(24R)

Figure 1. (Continued).

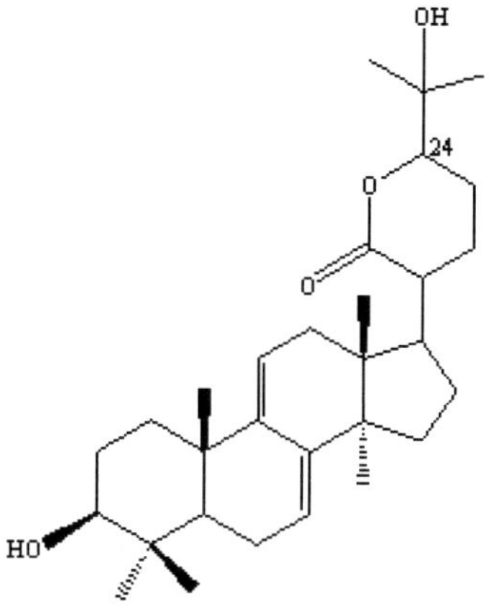

Phytochemistry, Traditional Uses and Health Benefits of the Mushroom ...   101

10

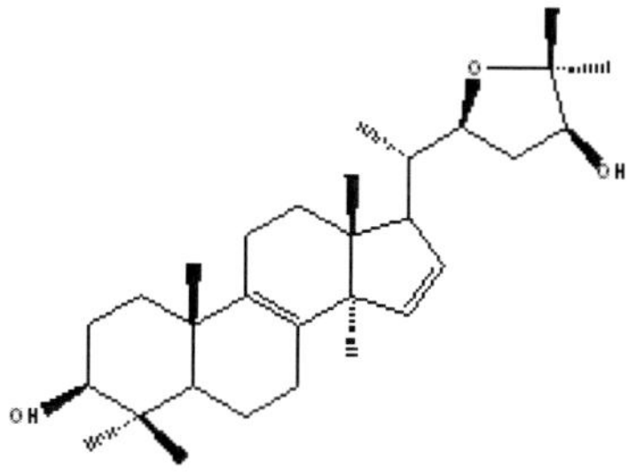

11

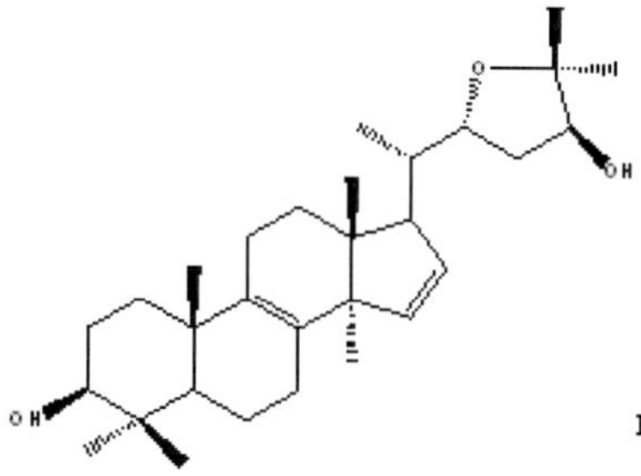

12

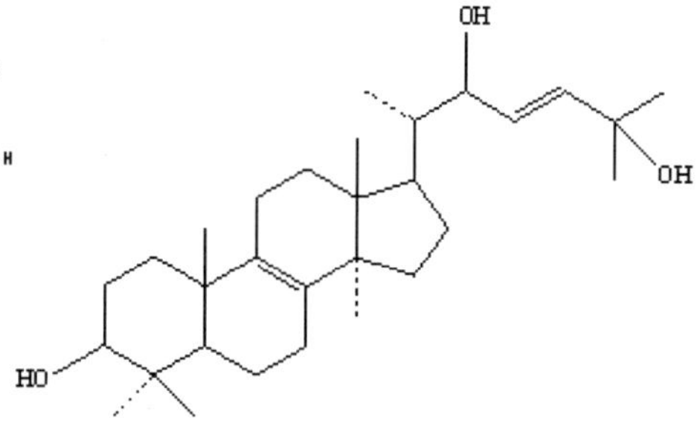

13

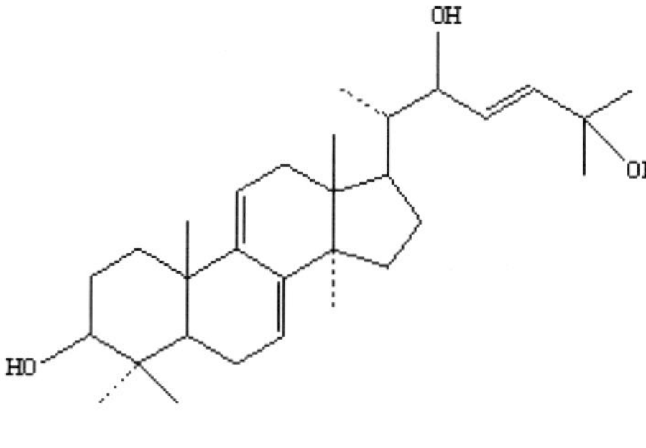

14

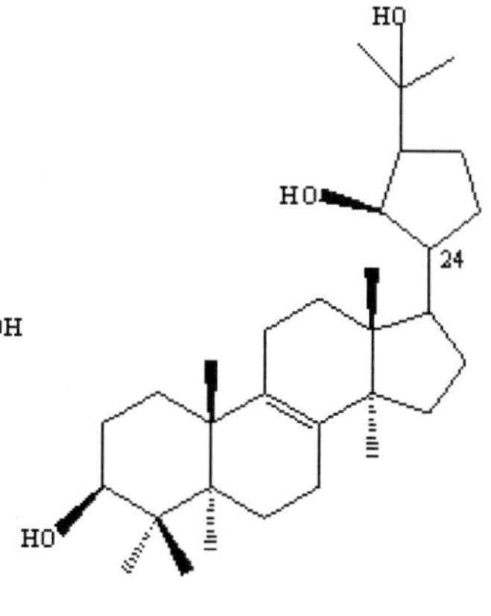

16:(24S) 17:(24R)

Figure 1. (Continued).

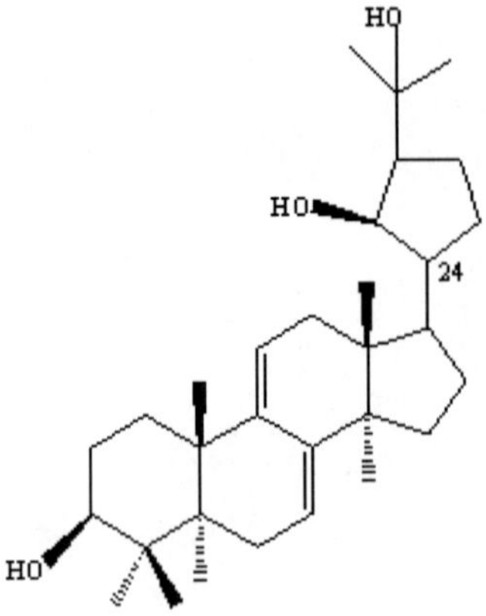

18

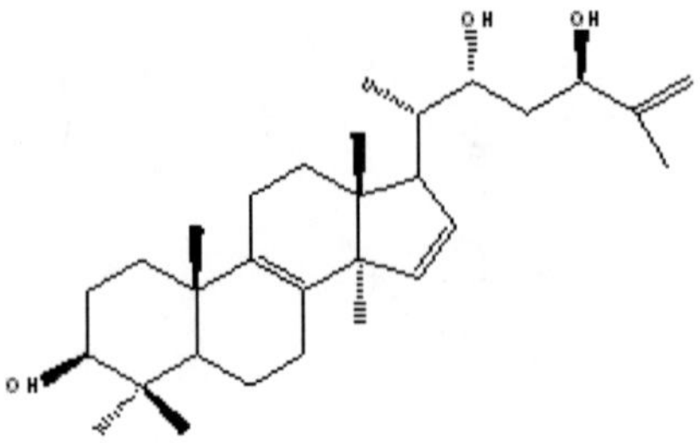

19

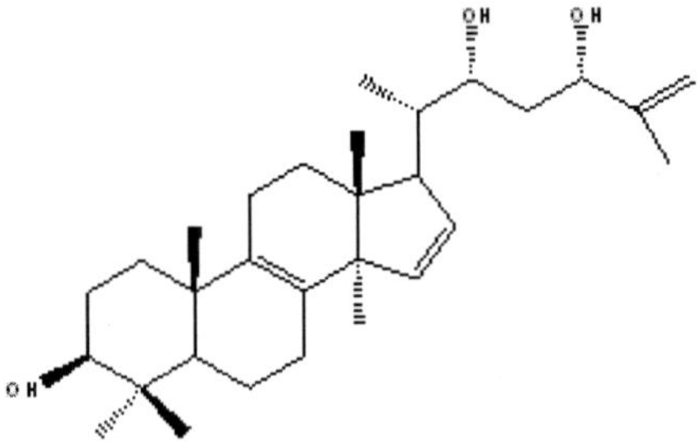

20

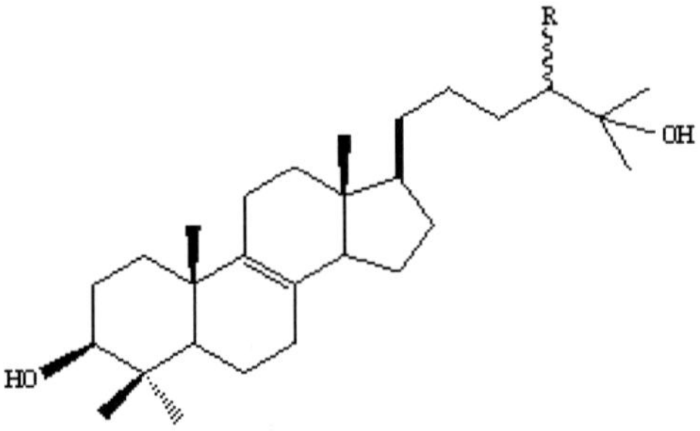

21 : R=α-OH   22 : R=β-OH

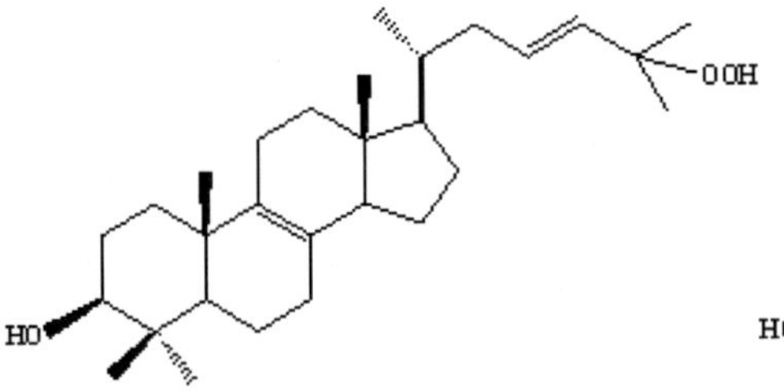

23

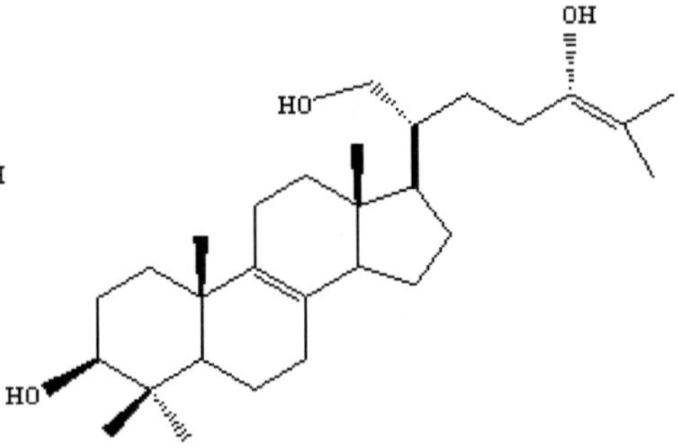

24

Figure 1. (Continued).

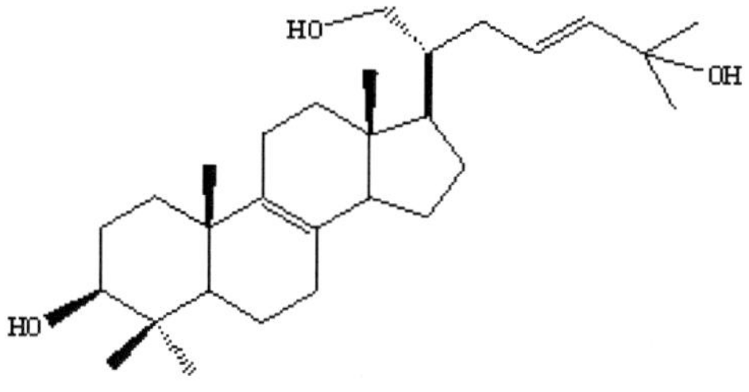

Figure 1. (Continued).

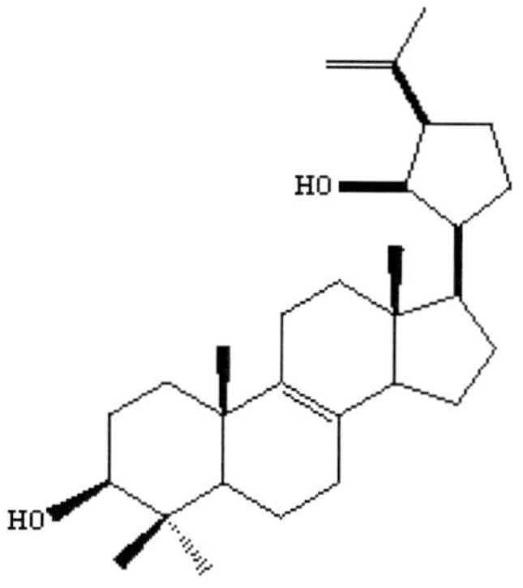

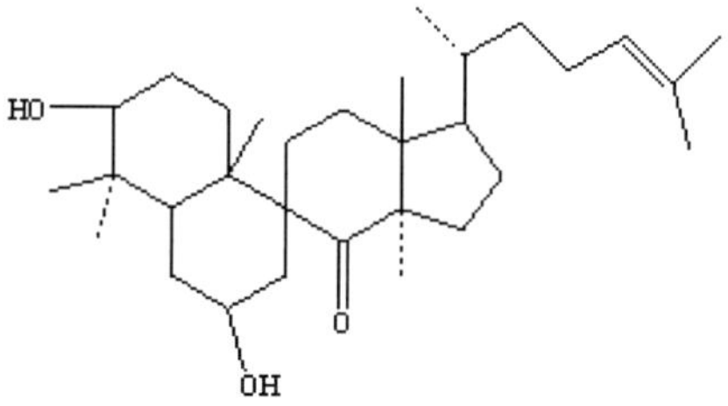

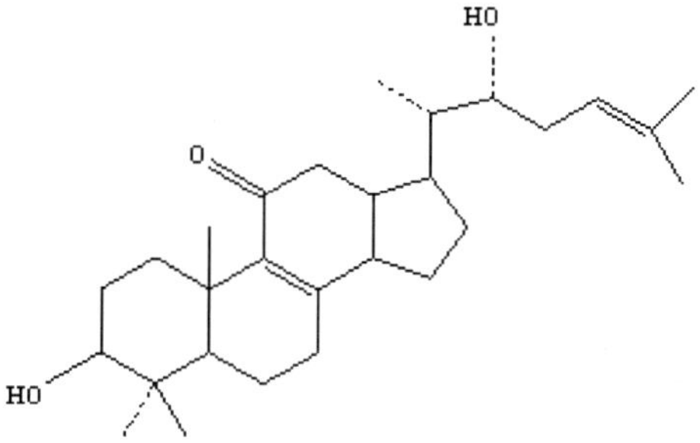

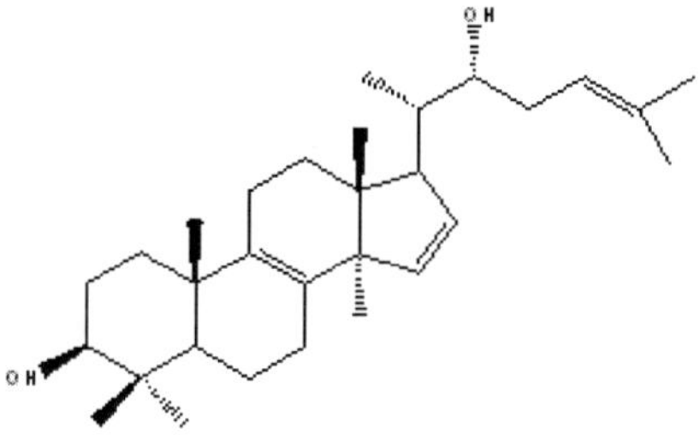

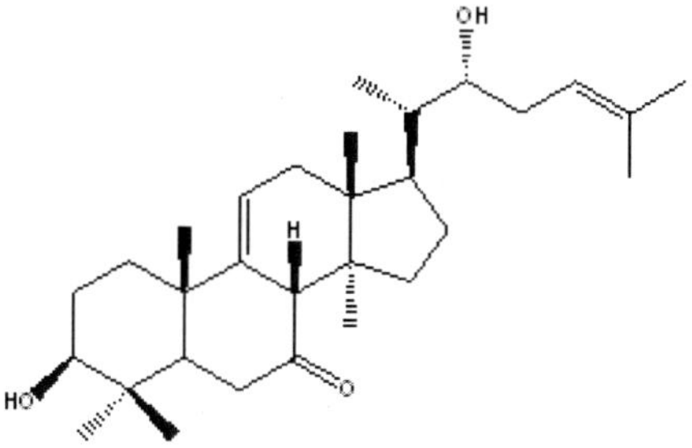

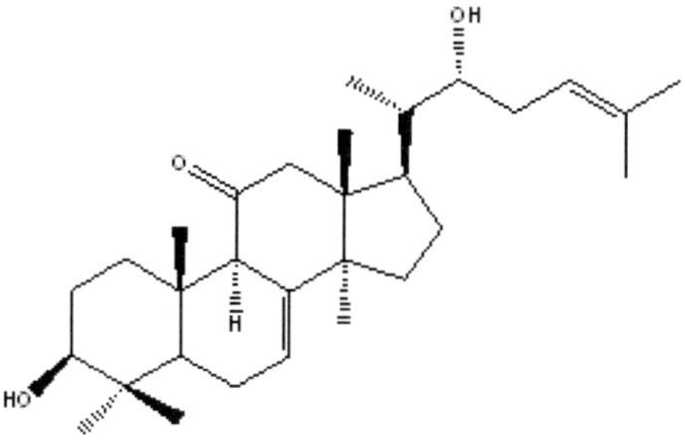

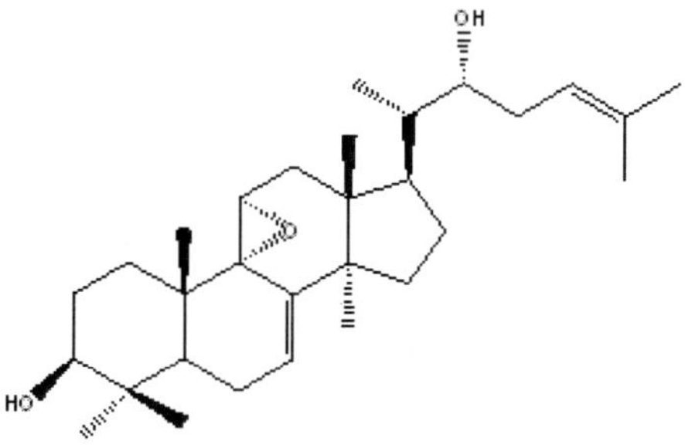

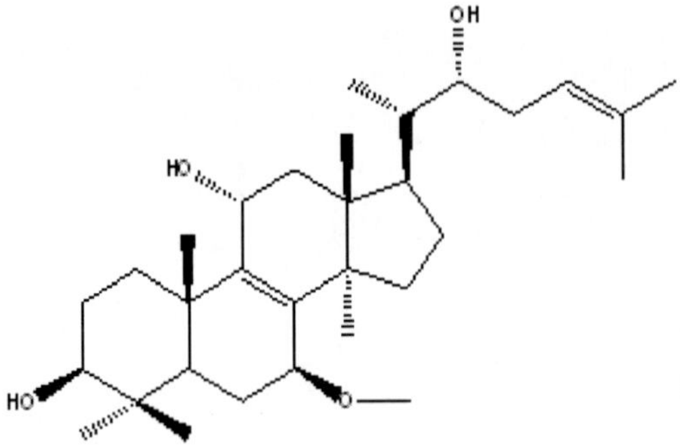

33

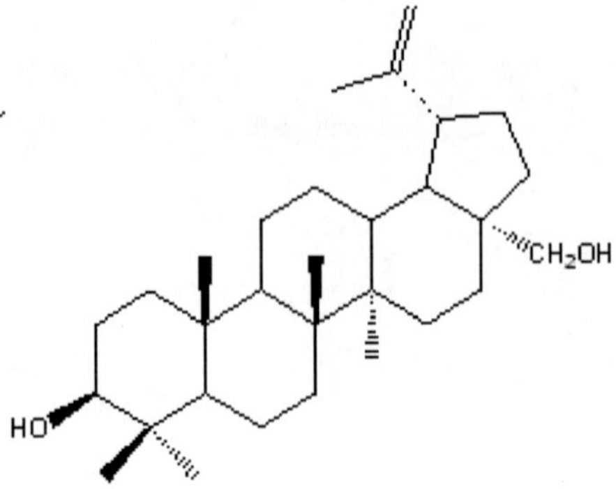

34

Figure 1. Structures of triterpenoids isolated from *Inonotus obliquus*. Structures of compounds 1-6 are missed here.

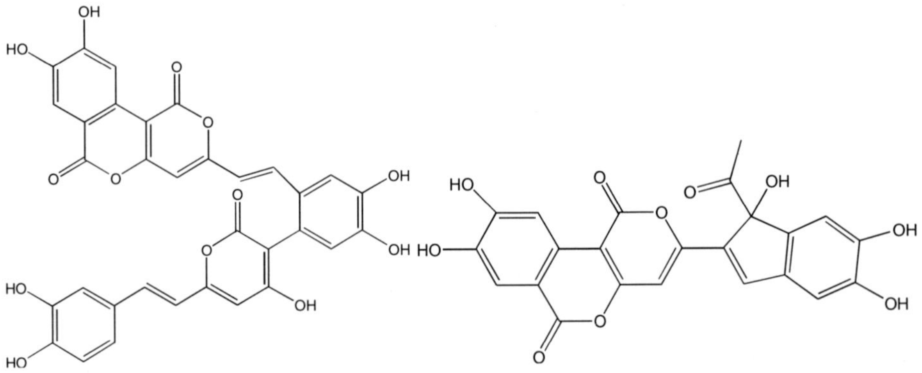

1 2

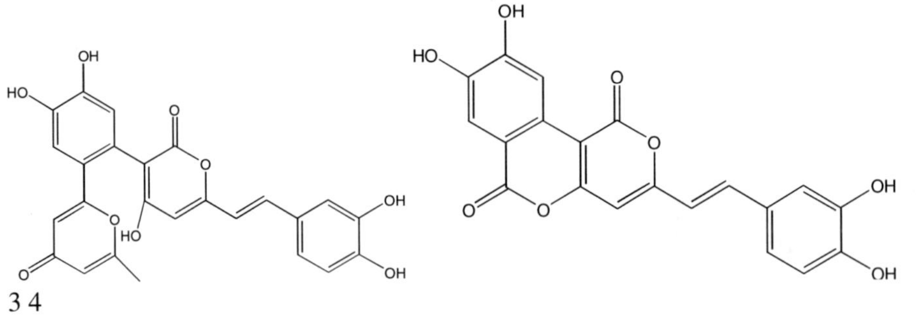

3 4

Figure 2. (Continued).

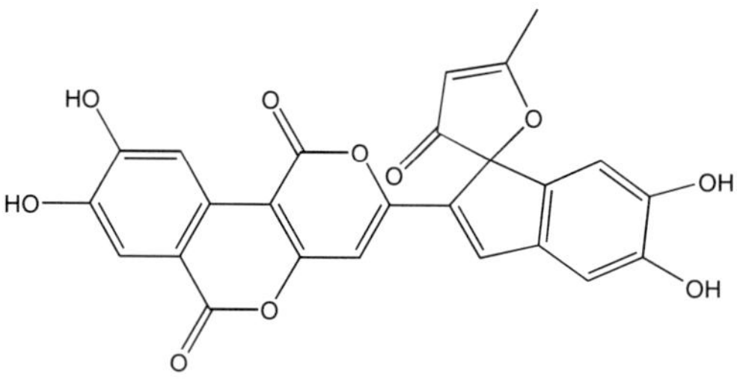

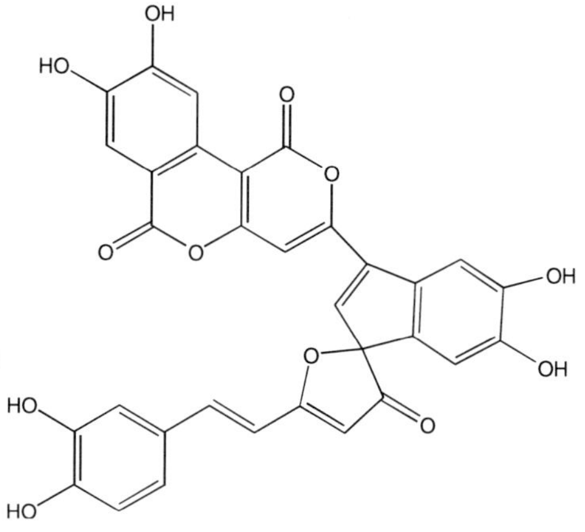

Phytochemistry, Traditional Uses and Health Benefits of the Mushroom ... 105

5 6

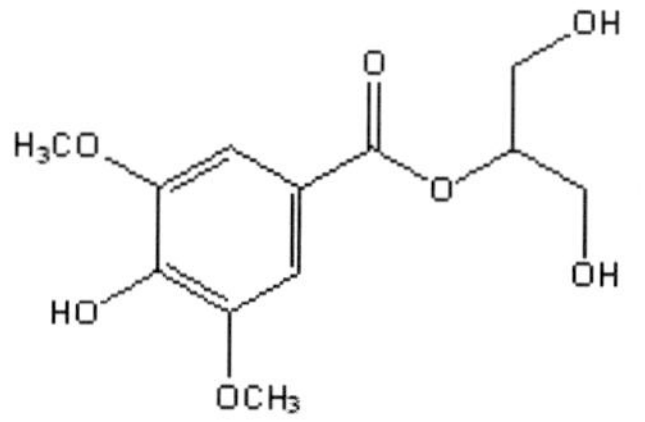

7

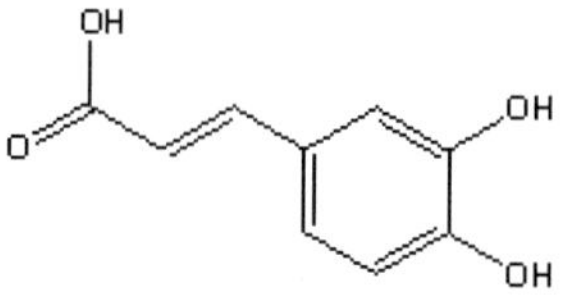

9

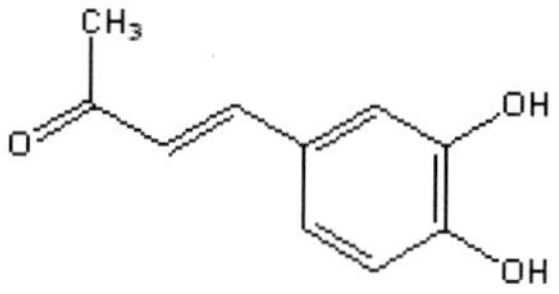

13

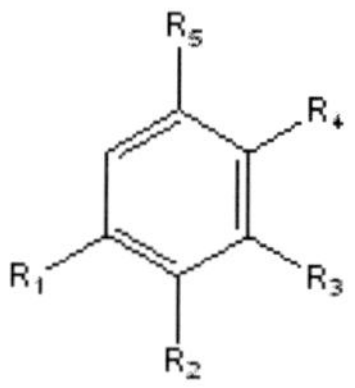

8: R₁=COOH R₂=H R₃=H R₄=OH R₅=OH 10:R₁=OH R₂=OH R₃=H R₄=H R₅=CHO

11: R₁=OH R₂=COOH R₃=H R₄=OH R₅=COOH 12: R₁=COOH R₂=H R₃=OCH₃ R₄=OH

R₅=OCH₃

14:R₁=OH R₂=H R₃=H R₄=OH R₅=CHO 15: R₁=COOH R₂=H R₃=OH R₄=OH R₅=OH

Figure 2. Structures of polyphenols isolated from *Inonotus obliquus*.

Table 2. Polyphenols isolated from *Inonotus obliquus*

NO	Compound	Pharmacological properties	Reference
1	Inonoblins A	antioxidant	Lee et al.(2007)
2	Inonoblins B	antioxidant	Lee et al.(2007)
3	Inonoblins C	antioxidant	Lee et al.(2007)
4	phelligridins D	antioxidant	Lee et al.(2007)
5	phelligridins E	antioxidant	Lee et al.(2007)
6	phelligridins G	antioxidant	Lee et al.(2007)
7	4-hydroxy-3,5-dimethoxy benzoic acid 2-hydroxy-l-hydroxymethyl ethyl ester	antioxidant	Nakajima et al. (2007)
8	protocatechic acid	antioxidant	Nakajima et al. (2007)
9	caffeic acid	antioxidant	Nakajima et al. (2007)
		anticancer	Nakajima et al. (2009)
10	3,4-dihybenzaladehyde	antioxidant	Nakajima et al. (2007)
11	2,5-dihydroxyterephtalic acid	antioxidant	Nakajima et al. (2007)
12	syringic acid	antioxidant	Nakajima et al. (2007)
13	3,4-dihydroxybenzalacetone	antioxidant	Nakajima et al. (2007)
		anticancer	Nakajima et al. (2009)
14	2,5-dihydroxybenzaldehyde	anticancer	Kim et al. (2011)
15	gallic acid	anticancer	Kuriyama et al. (2013)

Table 3. Steroids isolated from *Inonotus obliquus*

NO	Compound	Pharmacological properties	Reference
1	Fungisterol		Kirsi et al.(1987)
2	Ergosterol	anti-inflammatory	Yusoo et al. (2001)
3	Ergosterol peroxide	anti-inflammatory	Yusoo et al. (2001)
		anticancer	Kim et al. (2011)
4	β-Sitosterol		Kim et al. (2011)

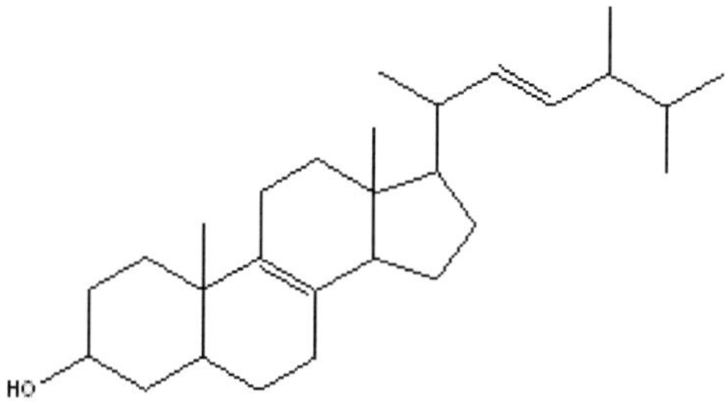

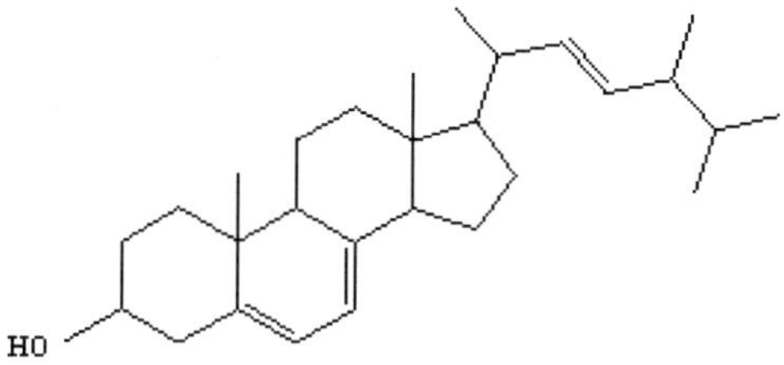

Figure 3. Structures of steroids isolated from *Inonotus obliquus*.

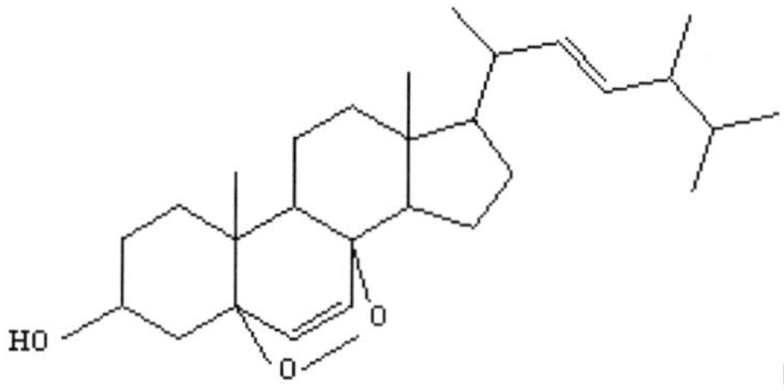

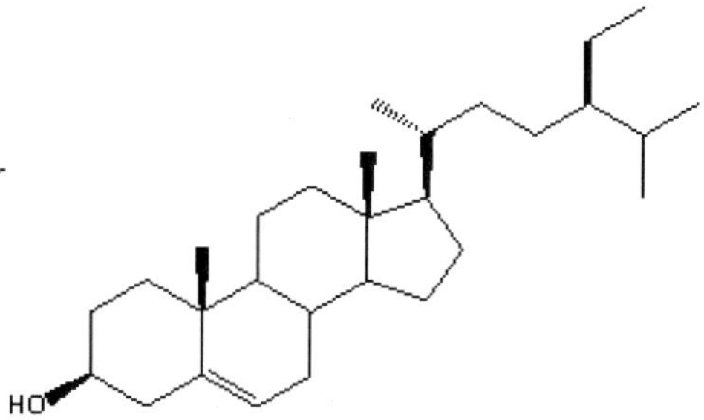

2.5. Protein

The products of hydrolysis of protein from *Inonotus obliquus* revealed 15 amino acids, predominantly glutamic acids (about 40% of total amino acids), glycine, aspartic, tyrosine, leucine, methionine, lysine,serine, threonine, and histidine (Shashkina et al., 2006). Hyun et al. (2006) found a novel platelet aggregation inhibitory peptide from *Inonotus obliquus*. The peptide was extracted with ethanol and further purified by systematic solvent fractionation, ultrafiltration, Sephadex G-10 column chromatography, and reverse-phase HPLC. Molecular mass of the peptide from *Inonotus obliquus* was estimated to be 365 Da by a LC/MS analysis, the amino acid composition was identified as Gly (50%), Cys (25%), and Typ (25%) and the sequence was found to be Trp-Gly-Cys.

2.6. Lignin

The boiling water extracts of *Inonotus obliquus* was repeatedly purified with ultrafiltration and Superdex 200 column. The fraction 23 was analyzed with IR, UV and ^{1}H NMR, and confirmed to be contained the most water-soluble lignin derivatives. The fraction 23 showed strongly inhibited HIV-1 protease activity, while the coniferyl alcohol and sinapyl alcohol, which are constituent units of lignin, had no inhibitory activity. It was infered that water-soluble lignin inhibits the effect of human immunodeficiency virus type 1 (HIV-1) might be due to the lignin derivative inhibits HIV reverse transcriptase (Ichimura et al., 1998).

2.7. Other Components

Inonotus obliquus had large content of ash elements, and the predominating ash components were potassium oxide (50%), sodium oxide (9-13%), and manganese oxide (1.2%). The elemental compositions of chaga and concentrated extract included calcium, silicon, iron, magnesium, zinc, copper, aluminum, phosphorus, and sulfur (Shashkina et al., 2006).

3. PHARMACOLOGICAL ACTIVITIES

3.1. Antioxidant Activities

It had been reported that the antioxidant activity of plants was associated with their therapeutic effect against cardiovascular disease, cancer and diabetes (Anderson et al., 2004; Stanner et al., 2004). So many studies are focused on the antioxidant constituents from natural resources.

Inonotus obliquus had been reported to contain high antioxidant activities. Because the main components of extracts obtained by various solvent extractions could be different, many studies had focused on the effects of difference solvent extraction on the antioxidant activities and tried to conclude the correlation relationship between chemical composition and antioxidant activities. The DPPH radical scavenging assay, superoxide scavenging assay, peroxyl radical scavenging assay, superoxide dismutase inhibition assay, liver lipid peroxidation inhibition assay and ferric reducing power were applied to test the antioxidant activities of *Inonotus obliquus*.

It had been reported that the polyphenolic components of *Inonotus obliquus* significantly contributed to the strong radical scavenging activity (Ju et al., 2010; Dewanto et al., 2002). Ju et al. (2010) had studied the effects of steam treatment on soluble phenolic content and antioxidant activity of the *Inonotus obliquus*. The IC_{50} values of extracts were decreased from

3.2 to 2.0 mg/mL after the steam treatment. Four phenolic acids, protocatechuic acid, vanillic acid, and syringic acid were identified in the extracts. The results of the DPPH assay, performed using the standard mixture including the quantified amount of the four phenolic acids, showed that the four phenolic acids contributed 41% of the total antioxidant activity in untreated sample, and 81% of the total antioxidant activity in the steamed sample. The results showed that the enhanced radical scavenging activities were correlated with the increased phenolic contents. Lee et al. (2007) had isolated the six polyphenols from *Inonotus obliquus*, which were inonoblins A–C and phelligridins D, E, and G. and Lee et al. also confirmed that these compounds exhibited significant scavenging activity against the ABTS radicals and DPPH radicals. Several small (poly) phenolic compounds were isolated from 80% methanol extract of *Inonotus obliquus* and investigated to be the major antioxidant components in the extracts (Nakajima et al., 2009).

In the study of Cui et al. (2005), the Fc extract, which contains polyphenolic components, showed highest antioxidant effect, the Fa extract, which contained triterpenoids and steroids had a relatively strong antioxidant activities. The Fb polysaccharide extract and the Fd extract, containing remnant polyphenolic compounds and low molecular weight polysaccharides, were almost inactive. And it also showed that the polyphenolic extract protected human keratinocyte cells against hydrogen peroxide-induced oxidative stress, while the three other extracts were showed a weakly protective effect at a concentration of 50 μg/mL. While in the investigation of Hu et al. (2009) the total phenolic content in the water crude extracts and ethanol crude extracts of *Inonotus obliquus* did not correlate with the difference in antioxidant activity, the ethanol crude extracts of *Inonotus obliquus* contained the highest content of total phenolic, but showed the lowest DPPH free radical-scavenging activity. However, the polysaccharide and protein contents of the water crude extracts were much higher than those of the ethanol crude extracts, and it had been found that the ratios of polysaccharide to protein of the water crude extracts were significantly correlated with their SOD-like activity ($r^2 = 0.99$, P < 0.05) and DPPH radical-scavenging activity ($r^2 = 0.81$, P < 0.05). The study of Liu et al. (1997) also indicated that the ratio of polysaccharide to protein appeared to contribute a direct effect on free radical scavenging activity and the ratio of bound protein in the polysaccharide-protein complexes was considered essential to the scavenging activity.

In the previous studies (Ma et al., 2012; Ma et al., 2013; Zhang et al., 2013), we had confirmed the IOPS which were further purified with DEAE-Cellulose and gel-filtration chromatography have high antioxidant abilities on DPPH radical scavenging, ferric-reducing power and lipid peroxidation inhibition activity. Furthermore, in order to study the effects of introduction of some fuctional groups with appropriate degree of substitution on the antioxidant properties of polysaccharide, the IOPS were modified by suflation, acetylation and carboxymethylation, and the results showed that the antioxidant activities of IOPS were differed each other after the chemical modification, in the assay of ferric-reducing power only the Ac-IOPS showed pronounced advantage compared with the native polysaccharide Un-IOPS and all the chemical modification derivatives including Ac-IOPS, Ca-IOPS and Su-IOPS showed stronger lipid peroxidation inhibition activity than the Un-IOPS. The antioxidant properties of IOPS modified by acid, alkali hydrolysis, thermal and ultrasonic treatment were tested, and the results showed that the thermal and ultrasonic treatment of IOPS exhibited desired antioxidant. Huang et al. (2012) had isolated and purified five polysaccharides IOP1b, IOP2a, IOP2c, IOP3a and IOP4 from *Inonotus obliquus*. The five polysaccharides have been demonstrated to have high antioxidant properties on hydroxyl radical assay, superoxide radical assay and ferric-reducing power and it has found that the content of uronic acid and proteinous substances were significantly correlated with the antioxidant activities, the higher content of uronic acid and proteinous substances, the stronger of polysaccharides of polysaccharide.

3.2. Antitumor Activities

The compounds lanosta-8,23E-diene-3β,22R,25-triol, lanosta-7:9(11),23E-triene-3β,22 R,25-triol, lanosta-8,24-dien-3β,21-diol, 3β-hydroxylanosta-8,24-dien-21-al (Taji et al., 2008) inonotsuoxides A, B, inotodiol, trametenolic acid and lanosterol (Nakata et al., 2007), were isolated and investigated for their anti-tumor-promoting activity using a short-term in vitro assay for Epstein–Barr virus early antigen (EBV-EA) activation induced by12-O-tetradecanoylphorbol-13-acetate (TPA). The most abundant 3β-hydroxylanosta-8,24-dien-21-al and inotodiol were tested for the inhibitory effect in a two-stage carcinogenesis test on mouse skin, using 7,12-dimethylben (a) anthracene (DMBA) as an initiator and TPA as a promoter, and both were found to exhibit the potent antitumor promoting activity in the in vivo carcinogenesis test. The compounds ergosterol peroxide and trametenolic acid which were isolated from the *Inonotus obliquus*, had been demonstrated to have obviously cytotoxicity on human prostatic carcinoma cell PC3 and breast carcinoma MDA-MB-231 cell (Ma et al., 2013).

In the report of Hu et al. (2009), the ethanol extract (EE) exhibited the strongest antiproliferative effect on DLD-1 cells in a time-dependent manner, and exposure to the EE resulted in the percentage of apoptotic cells reached 19.18% and 77.80% for the EE (400 μg/ml) treatment after 24 and 48 h, respectively, whereas no apoptosis was observed in DLD-1 cells exposed to the hot water extracts (HWEs). This might be due to the triterpenoids and steroids contained in the EE, but not in HWEs, contributed most to the antiproliferative effect of the EE.

The lanostane-type triterpenoids extracted from *Inonotus obliquus* using ethanol or hexane were to have the potential cytostatic properties against Walker 256 carcinosarcoma, MCF-7 human mammary adenocarcinoma, sarcoma 180, and carcinoma 755 (Shin et al., 2000; Mazurkiewicz et al., 2006). The cytotoxic effect of two aqueous extracts of *Inonotus obliquus* on human cervical uteri cancer cells (Hela S3) in vitro was evaluated. The results showed that the extracts at a concentration of 1 -2000 μg/ml inhibited cancer cells growth and the aqueous extracts of *Inonotus obliquus* were investigated not only effected mitoses but also the 8/G phase of the cell cycle (Burczyk et al., 1996).

Fan et al. (2012) reported that the purified polysaccharide ISP2a could significantly inhibited the growth of transplantable SGC-7901 in mice, the inhibitory rate was 39.02%, 48.24% and 57.45% at the ISP2a concentration of 50, 75 and 100 mg/kg, respectively, while ISP2a exhibited no significant antitumor activities of SGC-7901 cells in vitro. Simultaneously, the ISP2a significantly increased the concentration of TNF-α in serum of mice, which indicated that the ISP2a may indirectly play the role of antitumor activity through the releases of effective molecules TNF-α. Huang, et al. (2012) also found that the polysaccharides from *Inonotus obliquus* had the antitumor activities *in vivo*. The hot water extract of *Inonotus obliquus* exhibited a potential anticancer activity against human colon cancer cells (HT-29), and it had effects via the induction of apoptosis and inhibition of the growth of cancer cells through up-regulation of the expression of proapoptotic proteins and down-regulation of antiapoptotic proteins (Lee et al., 2009).

Mizuno et al. (1999) reported that the polysaccharides extracted and isolated from cultured mycelia of *Inonotus obliquus* had weak inhibitory effects against cdc25 phosphatase, which participates in regulation of cancer cell cycle. While Kim et al. (2006) observed that purified endo-polysaccharide from cultivated mycelia of *Inonotus obliquus* inhibited the growth of melanoma tumor cells and induced B cells and macrophages. The B16F10 murine melanoma cells which were intraperitoneally implanted into mice and were a highly metastatic-malignant neoplasm of melanocytes.

The results showed that the endo-polysaccharide suppressed the *in vivo* growth of melanoma cells in mice and significantly prolonged the survival rate of B16F10-implanted mice at a dose of 30 mg/kg/day (intraperitoneal) and 300 mg/kg/day (oral), respectively and intraperitoneal treatment (4.07-fold increase) was more effective in the survival rate than oral feeding (1.40-fold increase). After 60 days of feeding, approximately 67% of the initial number of mice survived with no tumor incidence based on macroscopic examination. The life-threatening toxic effect and body weight loss were not detected in any group of the mice administrated with endo-polysaccharide. The results were similar with the studies of Kim et al. (2005), in which it was indicated that the *in vivo* anti-tumor effects of endo-polysaccharide was probably related to activation of macrophages rather than to direct cytotoxicity against tumor cells.

3.3. Anti-Inflammatory Activities

Macrophages play an important role in the inflammatory response by releasing a variety of inflammatory mediators such as nitric oxide (NO), prostaglandin mediators and proinflammatory cytokines (TNF-α , IL-1 β, IL-6). *Inonotus obliquus* was a traditional medicinal mushroom and it had been reported to have anti-inflammatory potential on the extracts. Several studies on methanol extract and ethanol extract from *Inonotus obliquus* had shown to inhibit macrophage functions by decreasing the production of inflammatory mediators such as NO, prostaglandins (PGE_2) and some cytokines (Kim et al., 2007; Park et al., 2005; Van et al., 2009).

Mishra et al. (2012) had investigated that the aqueous extract from *Inonotus obliquus* could significantly suppressed edema, mucosal damage, the loss of crypts and mRNA expression of pro-inflammatory cytokines induced by dextran sulfate sodium and markedly attenuated DSS-induced iNOS levels and myeloperoxidase accumulation in colon tissues. The petroleum ether and ethyl acetate fractions were found to have significant inhibition effects on NO production and NF-κB luciferase activity in macrophage RAW 264.7 cells. Compounds ergosterol, ergosterol peroxide and trametenolic acid were isolated and confirmed to have potential anti-inflammatory activities (Ma et al., 2013).

3.4. Immunological Enhancement

The polysaccharide (ISP2a) had showed the ability to enhance splenocyte proliferation as well as ConA-induced splenocyte proliferation (p < 0.05) and ISP2a with ConA had stronger splenocytes proliferation activity than that without ConA. The lymphocytes proliferation activity seemed to be highly correlated with the dosage of ISP2a, however, proliferation activity of ISP2a to spleen cells did not respond to the dose-dependent manner. Compared with the control, ISP2a at the concentration of 100, 200 and 400 µg/ml significantly enhanced the proliferation of peritoneal macrophages, but no significant improvement was observed between the dosages of 200 and 400 µg/mL. Compared with the control group, ISP2a at the concentration of 50, 100, 200 and 400 µg/mL significantly enhanced the production of TNF-α. There existed a dose-dependent relationship with the highest concentration giving the strongest TNF-α production (R^2=0.932) (Fan et al., 2012).

Kim et al. (2005) had reported that the proliferation activity of endo-polysaccharide for splenic cells was much higher than the exo-polysaccharide from culture broths of *Inonotus obliquus*. The endo-polysaccharide showed the similar activities to lipopolysaccharide (LPS) for B cells and macrophages, but no proliferation of T cells. The action mechanisms of *Inonotus obliquus* polysaccharide and LPS were different, cellular activations induced by endo-polysaccharide were not affected by polymyxin B, a specific inhibitor of LPS, which might be due to the endo-polysaccharide does not have a lipid-A moiety of LPS and it seems to have other receptors that LPS does not have. In order to further investigate active composition, the composition of polysaccharides from mycelial cells was analyzed, the high-molecular-weight β-glucans appeared to be more active than low-molecular-weight varieties. The role of proteins complexed with the endo-polysaccharide fraction was examined, the immuno-stimulating activities were increased slightly after the complex was hydrolyzed by proteinase, which indicated that protein-polysaccharide complex did not affect the immuno-stimulating activities, while Liu et al. (1996) had found the Immunomodulation activity of polysaccharide-protein complex from the culture filtrates of a local edible mushroom.

3.5. Antithrombotic Effects

Platelet aggregation is a complex phenomenon that likely involves several biochemical pathways. The inhibition of platelet function is a promising approach for the prevention of thrombosis. In the report of Hyun et al. (2006), water and ethanol extract from 55 kinds of mushrooms mycelium or fruiting bodies were tested for platelet aggregation inhibitory activities, and the ethanol extracts of *Inonotus obliquus* ASI 74006 mycelium showed the highest platelet aggregation inhibitory activity (71.2%), while the extracts from its fruiting body was not determined or was very weak for the inhibitory activity. The purified peptide was found to have high inhibitory activity of 91.6% (IC_{50}= 0.16 mM) and low molecular mass of 365 Da. Therefore, this platelet aggregation inhibitory peptide from *Inonotus obliquus* might be considered to be easily absorbed in the intestine and widely used in the preparation of antithrombotic drugs and functional foods.

3.6. Hypoglycemic Effects

Polysaccharides in mycelia and sclerote of *Inonotus obliquus* were tested to show high hypoglycemic activity in mice with diabetes mellitus (Chen et al., 2006). It was reported that the hypoglycemic effect could maintained for 3-48 h after the mouse was injected with polysaccharides, and the active polysaccharides which were purified from mycelia and sclerote of *Inonotus obliquus*, mainly consisted of β-glucan, heteroglycan and proteinum complex (Mizuno et al., 1999). β-glucan was considered to be the prominent active biochemical compound and had attracted special research interest for its functions on reduction of blood cholesterol and blood glucose levels (Song et al., 2004). The *Inonotus obliquus* showed potential effects on endothelial dysfunction seen in patients with type 2 diabetes mellitus by decreasing the postprandial glucose excursion (Maenaka et al., 2008). The effects of ethyl acetate fraction of ethanol extract from *Inonotus obliquus* on hyperglycaemia in alloxan-induced diabetic mice were investigated and the main constituents, lanosterol, 3β-hydroxy-lanosta-8,24-diene-21-al, inotodiol, ergosterol peroxide and trametenolic acid were isolated and identified to have an inhibitory effect on α-amylase activity (Lu et al., 2009). Noh et al. (2003) found that a pharmaceutical composition containing water extract from Cordyceps militaris and *Inonotus obliquus* had a potentially beneficial effect against various types of diabetes, in particular types 1 and 2, without causing any adverse side effects.

The antihyperglycemic and antilipidperoxidative effects of the dry matter of culture broth (DMCB) of *Inonotus obliquus* were investigated (Sun et al., 2008). In alloxan-induced diabetic mice, the DMCB (500 and 1000 mg/kg body weight for 21 days) showed a significant decrease in blood glucose level (30.07 and 31.30%) and the serum contents of free fatty acid, total cholesterol, triglyceride and low density lipoprotein-cholesterol were significantly decreased after the DMCB treatment, whereas effectively increases were observed in high density lipoprotein-cholesterol, insulin level and hepatic glycogen contents in liver on diabetic mice. Histological morphology analysis showed that the DMCB restored the damage of pancreas tissues in mice with diabetes mellitus.

3.7. Anti-Virus Effects

The water-soluble lignin of *Inonotus obliquus* inhibited the effect of human immunodeficiency virus type 1 (HIV-1) via inhibited HIV reverse transcriptase (Ichimura et al., 1998). The black external surface of *Inonotus obliquus* had complete inhibition against influenza viruses including human influenza viruses A and B and horse influenza viruses A. The antiviral activity was thought to be mainly due to betulin, lupeol and mycosterols (Kahlos et al., 1996).

4. APPLICATION OF INONOTUS OBLIQUUS

In Russia, *Inonotus obliquus* was traditionally used to treat ulcer, gastritis, hyperplasia of the reproductive organs and various cancers such as lung cancer, breast cancer, skin cancer, rectal cancer and colon carcinoma. The Tartars of West Siberia used *Inonotus obliquus* to treat tuberculosis, liver diseases, heart diseases and ascariasis. There was increasing interest in *Inonotus obliquus* preparations, where *Inonotus obliquus* was both used alone and enters into numerous components preparations for internal (decoctions, infusions) and external (ointments) usage (Shashkina et al., 2006). *Inonotus obliquus* tincture was used to treat gastric disorders and even cancer. *Inonotus obliquus* tea was used as a means of increasing the general tone and the tea drink could assuages hunger, removes tiredness, refreshes. Patients were recommended to use *Inonotus obliquus* extracts when it was necessary to reduce the arterial or venous blood pressure. *Inonotus obliquus* infusions were also used for the treatment of periodontitis, eczema, dermatitis and psoriasis. Abrasions, scratches, and cuts could be treated with powdered *Inonotus obliquus* to arrest purulent wound development (Shashkina et al., 2006). *Inonotus obliquus* was nontoxic, well tolerated, and has virtually no counter indications for medicinal usage (Shashkina et al., 2006).

CONCLUSION

This review presents an attempt at systematizing available published data on the chemical components isolated from *Inonotus obliquus*, their pharmacological activity, and the mechanism action, but the mechanisms of actions need further investigation. Numerous attempts to elucidate the therapeutic potential of *Inonotus obliquus* preparations for the prophylaxis and treatment of cancer and other disorders gave rather ambiguous results, and most literature had only individually focused on the antioxidant, anti-cancer effects, anti-inflammatory and other biological activities of *Inonotus obliquus*, the synergistic and comprehensive studies in biochemistry, pharmacology, immunology, and clinical medicine should be given more attention.

REFERENCES

Anderson, R. A., Broadhurst, C. L., Polansky, M. M., Schmidt, W. F., Khan, A., Flanagan, V. P., Schoene, N. W., & Graves, D. J. (2004). Isolation and characterization of polyphenol type-A polymers from cinnamon with insulin-like biological activity. *Journal of Agricultural and Food Chemistry, 52,* 65-70.

Babitskaya, V. G., Shcherba, V. V., & Ikonnikova, N. V. (2000). Melanin Complex of the Fungus *Inonotus obliquus. Applied Biochemistry and Microbiology, 36,* 377-381.

Burczyk, J., Gawron, A., Slotwinska, M., Smietana, B., & Terminska, K. (1996). Antimitotic activity of aqueous extracts of *Inonotus obliquus. Bollettino Chimico Farmaceutico, 135,* 306-309.

Campbell, W. A., & Davidson, R. W. (1938). A *Poria* as the fruiting stage of the fungus causing the sterile conks on birch. *Mycologia, 30,* 553-560.

Chen, Y. Q., Zhou, L. J., & Li, Y. (2006). Study on experimental comparison of hypoglycemic effect of polysaccharides of cultured mycelia, sclerotia and wild sclerotia from *Inonotus obliquus. Edible Fungi (Chin), 28,* 52-54.

Chen, Y., Huang, S., Gu, X., Tang, J., & Li, J. (2010). Optimization of ultrasonic/microwave assisted extraction (UMAE) of polysaccharides from *Inonotus obliquus* and their antitumor activities. *International Journal of Biological Macromolecules, 46,* 429-435.

Cui, Y., Kim, D. S., & Park. K. C. (2005). Antioxidant effect of *Inonotus obliquus. Journal of Ethnopharmacology, 96,* 79-85.

Dewanto, V., Wu, X., & Liu, R. H. (2002). Processed sweet corn has higher antioxidant activity. *Journal of Agricultural and Food Chemistry, 50,* 4959-4964.

Fan, L. P., Ding, S. D., Ai, L. Z., & Deng, K. Q. (2012). Antitumor and immunomodulatory activity of water-soluble polysaccharide from *Inonotus obliquus. Carbohydrate Polymers, 90,* 870-874.

Gao, Q. P., Jiang, R. Z., Chen, H. Q., Jensen, E., & Seljelid, R. (1996). Characterization and cytokine stimulating activities of heteroglucans from *Tremella fusiformis. Planta Medica, 62,* 297 -302.

Handa, N., Yamada, T., & Tanaka, R. (2010). An unusual lanostane-type triterpenoid, spiroinonotsuoxodiol, and other triterpenoids from *Inonotus obliquus. Phytochemistry, 71,* 1774-1779.

Handa, N., Yamada, T., & Tanaka, R. (2012). Four new lanostane-type triterpenoids from *Inonotus obliquus. Phytochemistry Letters, 5,* 480-485.

Hawksworth, D. L., Kirk, P. M., Sutton, B. C., & Pegler, D. N. (1995). Ainsworth and Bisbi's Dictionary of the Fungi, (8th ed.). CAB International, University Press, Cambridge, p.616.

Hu, H. H., Zhang, Z. Y., Lei, Z. F., Yang, Y. N., & Sugiura, N. (2009). Comparative study of antioxidant activity and antiproliferative effect of hot water and ethanol extracts from the mushroom *Inonotus obliquus. Journal of Bioscience and Bioengineering, 107,* 42-48.

Huang, N. L. (2002). *Inonotus obliquus. Edible Fungi of China, 21,* 7-8.

Huang, S. Q., Ding, S. D., & Fan, L. P. (2012). Antioxidant activities of five polysaccharides from *Inonotus obliquus. International Journal of Biological Macromolecules, 50,* 1183-1187.

Hyun, K. W., Jeong, S. C., Lee, D. H., Park, J. S., & Lee, J. S. (2006). Isolation and characterization of a novel platelet aggregation inhibitory peptide from the medicinal mushroom, *Inonotus obliquus. Peptides, 27,* 1173-1178.

Ichimura, T., Watanabe, O., & Maruyama, S. (1998). Inhibition of HIV-1 protease by water-soluble lignin-like substance from an edible mushroom, *Fuscoporia obliqua. Bioscience, Biotechnology, Biochemistry, 62,* 575-577.

Jin, M. L., Lu, Z. Q., Huang, M., Wang, Y. M., & Wang, Y. Z. (2011). Sulfated modification and antioxidant activity of exopolysaccahrides produced by Enterobacter cloacae Z0206. *International Journal of Biological Macromolecules, 48,* 607-612.

Ju, H. K., Chung, H. W., Hong, S. S., Park, J. H., Lee, J., & Kwon, S. W. (2010). Effect of steam treatment on soluble phenolic content and antioxidant activity of the Chaga mushroom (*Inonotus obliquus*). *Food Chemistry, 119,* 619-625.

Kahlos, K., Lesnau, A., Lange, W., & Lindequist, U. (1996). Preliminary test of antiviral activity of two *Inonotus obliquus* strains. *Fitoterapia, 67,* 344-347.

Kim, Y. O., Han, S. B., Lee, H. W., Ahn, H. J., Yoon, Y. D., Jung, J. K., Kim, H. M., & Shin. C. S. (2005). Immuno-stimulating effect of the endo-polysaccharide produced by submerged culture of *Inonotus obliquus. Life Sciences, 77,* 2438-2456.

Kim, Y. O., Park, H. W., Kim, J. H., Lee, J. Y., Moon, S. H., & Shin, C. S. (2006). Anti-cancer effect and structural characterization of endo-polysaccharide from cultivated mycelia of *Inonotus obliquus*. *Life Sciences, 79,* 72-80.

Kim, H. G., Yoon, D. H., Kim, C. H., Shrestha, B., Chang, W. C., & Lim, S. Y. (2007). Ethanol extracts of *Inonotus obliquus* inhibits lipopolysaccharide-induced inflammation in RAW 264.7 macrophage cells. *Journal of Medicinal Food, 10,* 80-89.

Kirsi, K., & Raimo, H. (1987). Gas chromatographic-mass spectrometric study of some sterols and lupines from *Inonotus obliquus*. *Acta Pharmaceutica Fennnica, 96,* 1513-1524.

Kuriyama, I., Nakajima, Y., Nishida, H., Konishi, T., Takeuchi, T., Sugawara, F., Yoshida, H., & Mizushina, Y. (2013). Inhibitory effects of low molecular weight polyphenolics from *Inonotus obliquus* on human DNA topoisomerase activity and cancer cell proliferation. *Molecular Medicine Reports, 8,* 535-542.

Lee, I. K., Kim, Y. S., Jang, Y. W., Jung, J. Y., & Yun, B. S. (2007). New antioxidant polyphenols from the medicinal mushroom *Inonotus obliquus*. *Bioorganic and Medicinal Chemistry Letters, 17,* 6678-6681.

Lee, S. K., Hwang, H. S., & Yun, J. W. (2009). Antitumor Activity of Water Extract of a Mushroom, *Inonotus obliquus*, against HT-29 Human Colon Cancer Cells. *Phytotherapy Research, 23,* 1784-1789.

Liu, F., Ooi, V. E. C., Liu, W. K., & Chang, S. T., (1996). Immunomodulation and antitumor activity of polysaccharide–protein complex from the culture filtrates of a local edible mushroom, *Tricholoma lobayense*. *General Pharmacology, 27,* 621-624.

Liu, F., Ooi, V. E., & Chang, S. T. (1997). Free radical scavenging activities of mushroom polysaccharide extracts. *Life Science, 60,* 763-771.

Lu, X. M., Chen, H. X., Dong, P., Fu, L. L., & Zhang, X. (2010). Phytochemical characteristics and hypoglycaemic activity of fraction from mushroom *Inonotus obliquus*. *Journal of the science of* **food** *and agriculture, 90,* 276-280.

Ludwiczak, R. S., & Wrecino, U. (1962). Investigation of chemical components of *Inonotus obliquus*. *Polish Journal of Chemistry, 36,* 497-502.

Kahlos, K., Hiltunen, R., & Von Schantz, M. (1984). 3β-Hydroxylanosta-8,24-dien-21-al. *Planta Medica, 50,* 197-198.

Kim, Y. J., Park, J., Min, B. S., & Shim, S. H. (2011). Chemical Constituents from the Sclerotia of *Inonotus obliquus*. *Journal of the Korean Chemical Society, 54,* 287-294.

Ma, L. S., Chen, H. X., Zhang, Y., Zhang, N., & Fu. L. L. (2012). Chemical modification and antioxidant activities of polysaccharide from mushroom *Inonotus obliquus*. *Carbohydrate Polymers, 89,* 371-378.

Ma, L. S., Chen, H. X., Zhu, W. C., & Wang. Z. S. (2013). Effect of different drying methods on physicochemical properties and antioxidant activities of polysaccharides extracted from mushroom *Inonotus obliquus*. *Food Research International, 50,* 633-640.

Ma, L. S., Chen, H. X., Dong, P., & Lu, X. M. (2013). Anti-inflammatory and anticancer activities of extracts and compounds from the mushroom *Inonotus obliquus*. *Food Chemistry, 139,* 503–508.

Maenaka, T., Oshima, M., Itokawa, Y., Masubuchi, T., Takagi, Y., Choi, J. S., Ishida, T., & Gu. Y. (2008). Effects of *Fuscoporia oblique* on Postprandial Glucose Excursion and Endothelial Dysfunction in Type 2 Diabetic Patients. *Journal of traditional Chinese Medicine, 28,* 49-57.

Mazurkiewicz, W. (2006). Analysis of aqueous extract of *Inonotus obliquus*. *Acta Poloniae Pharmaceutica- Drug Research, 63,* 497-501.

Mishra, S. K., Kang, J. H., Kim, D. K., Oh, S. H., & Kim, M. K. (2012). Orally administered aqueous extract of *Inonotus obliquus* ameliorates acute inflammation in dextran sulfate sodium (DSS)-induced colitis in mice. *Journal of Ethnopharmacology, 143,* 524-532.

Mizuno, T., Zhuang, C., Abe, K., Okamoto, H., Kiho, T., Ukai, S., Leclerc, S., & Meijer, L. (1999). Antitumor and hypoglycemic activities of polysaccharides from the sclerotia and mycelia of *Inonotus obliquus* (Pers.:Fr.) Pil.(Aphyllophoromycetideae). *International Journal of Medical Mushrooms, 1,* 301-316.

Nakajima, Y., Sato, Y., & Konishi, T. (2007). Antioxidant small phenolic ingredients in *Inonotus obliquus* (persoon) pilat (chaga). *Chemical and Pharmaceutical Bulletin, 55,* 1222-1226.

Nakajima, Y., Hiroshi, N., Seiichi, M., & Tetsuya, K. (2009). Cancer cell cytotoxicity of extracts and small phenolic components from Chaga (*Inonotus obliquus* (persoon) Pilat). *Journal of medicinal food, 12,* 1-7.

Nakamura, S., Iwami, J., Matsuda, H., Mizuno, S., & Yoshikawa, M. (2009). Absolute stereostructures of inoterpenes A-F from sclerotia of *Inonotus obliquus*. *Tetrahedron, 65,* 2443-2450.

Nakata, T., Yamada, T., Taji, S., Ohishi, H., Wada, S. I., Tokuda, H., Sakuma, K., & Tanaka, R. (2007). Structure determination of inonotsuoxides A and B and in vivo anti-tumor promoting activity of inotodiol from the sclerotia of *Inonotus obliquus*. *Bioorganic and Medicinal Chemistry, 15,* 257-264.

Nie, S. P., & Xie, M. Y. (2011). A review on the isolation and structure of tea polysaccharides and their bioactivities. *Food Hydrocolloids, 25,* 144-149.

Noh, J. Y., Yoon, B. G., & Yoon, J. J. (2003). Composition for prevention and treatment of type 1 and type 2 diabetes, containing water extract of *Cordyceps militaris* and *Inonotus obliquus* as effective ingredient. Korean Patent, 2003-14648.

Olennikov, D. N., Tankhaeva, L., M.Rokhin, A. V., & Agafonova, S. V. (2012). Physicochemical properties and antioxidant activity of melanin fractions from *Inonotus obliquus* sclerotia. *Chemistry of Natural Compounds, 48,* 396-403.

Sava, V. M., Ming, S., Hong, M. Y., Yang, P. C., & Huang, G. S. (2001). Isolation and character of melanic pigments derived from tea and tea polyphenols. *Food Chemistry, 73,* 177-184.

Shashkina, M. Y., Shashkin, P. N., & Sergeev, A. V. (2006). Chemical and medicobiological properties of Chaga (review). *Pharmaceutical Chemistry Journal, 40,* 560-568.

Shin, Y., Tamai, Y., & Terazawa, M. (2000). Chemical constituents of *Inonotus obliquus*—A new triterpene, 3p-hydroxy-8,24-dien-lanos ta-21,23-lactone from sclerotium. *Eurasian Journal of Forest Research, 1,* 43-50.

Song, H. S., Lee, Y. J., Kim, S. K., Moon, W. K., Kim, D. W., Kim, Y. S., & Moon, K. Y. (2004). Down regulatory effect of AGI-1120 (β-glucosidase inhibitor) and Chaga mushroom (*Inonotus obliquus*) on cellular NF-κB activation and their antioxidant activity. *Korean Journal of Pharmacognosy, 35,* 92-97.

Stanner, S. A., Hughes, J., Kelly, C. N., & Buttriss, J. (2004). A review of the epidemiological evidence for the 'antioxidant hypothesis'. *Public Health Nutrition, 7,* 407–422.

Sun, J. E., Ao, Z. H., Lu, Z. M., Xu, H. Y., Zhang, X. M., Dou, W. F., & Xu. Z. H. (2008). Antihyperglycemic and antilipidperoxidative effects of dry matter of culture broth of *Inonotus obliquus* in submerged culture on normal and alloxan-diabetes mice. *Journal of Ethnopharmacology, 118,* 7-13.

Taji, S., & Yamada, T. (2007). Three New Lanostane Triterpenoids from *Inonotus obliquus. Helvetica Chimica Acta, 90,* 2047-2057.

Taji, S., Yamada, T., Wada, S. I., Tokuda, H., Sakuma, K., & Tanaka, R. (2008a). Lanostane-type triterpenoids from the sclerotia of *Inonotus obliquus* possessing anti-tumor promoting activity. *European Journal of Medicinal Chemistry, 43,* 2373-2379.

Taji, S., Yamada, T., & Tanaka, R. (2008b). Three new lanostane triterpenoids, inonotsutriols A, B, and C from *Inonotus obliquus. Helvetica Chimica Acta, 91,* 1513-1524.

Tanaka, R., Toyoshima, M., & Yamada, T. (2011). New lanostane-type triterpenoids, inonotsutriols D, and E, from *Inonotus obliquus. Phytochemistry Letters, 4,* 328-332.

Usui, T., Iwasaki, Y., Hayashi, K., Mizuno, T., Tanaka, M., Shinkai, K., & Arakawa , M. (1981). Antitumor activity of water-soluble β-D-glucan elaborated by *Ganoderma applanatum. Agricultural and Biological Chemistry, 45,* 323-326.

Van, Q., Nayak, B. N., Reimer, M., Jones, P. J. H., Fulcher, R. G., & Rempel, C. B. (2009). Anti-inflammatory effect of *Inonotus obliquus*, Polygala senega L., and Viburnum trilobum in a cell screening assay. *Journal of Ethnopharmacology, 125,* 487-493.

Vinogradov, E., Petersen, B. O., Duus, J. Ø., & Wassor, S. P. (2004). The isolation, structure, and applications of the exocellular heteropolysaccharide glucur-onoxylomannan produced by yellow brain mushroom *Tremella mesenterica* Ritz.: Fr. (Heterobasidiomycetes). *International Journal of Medicinal Mushrooms, 6,* 335–345.

Wasser, S. P. (2002). Medicinal mushrooms as a source of antitumor and immunomodulating polysaccharides. *Applied Microbiology and Biotechnology, 60,* 258-274.

Yusoo, S., Yutaka, T., & Minoru, T. (2001). Chemical constituents of *Inonotus obliquus* IV. *Eurasian Journal of Forest Research, 3,* 27-30.

Zhang, N., Chen, H. X., Ma, L. S., & Zhang, Y. (2013). Physical modifications of polysaccharide from *Inonotus obliquus* and the antioxidant properties. *International Journal of Biological Macromolecules, 54,* 209-215.

Zhong, X. H., Ren, K., Lu, S., J., Yang, S. Y., & Sun, D. Z. (2009). Progress of Research on *Inonotus obliquus. Chinese Journal of Integrative Medicine, 15,*156-160.

In: Mushrooms
Editor: Grégoire Pesti

ISBN: 978-1-63117-521-3
© 2014 Nova Science Publishers, Inc.

Chapter 5

IMMUNOMODULATORY EFFECTS OF MUSHROOM EXTRACTS AND COMPOUNDS

Tzi Bun Ng[*] *and Charlene Cheuk Wing Ng*
School of Biomedical Sciences, Faculty of Medicine,
The Chinese University of Hong Kong, Shatin, New Territories,
Hong Kong, China

ABSTRACT

The following is a list of mushrooms and mushroom products with immunostimulatory activity: *Agaricus bisporus* 2-amino-3H-phenoxazin-3-one, *Agaricus blazei,. Agaricus brasiliensis* β-glucans, *Antrodia camphorata* mycelial fraction and culture filtrate, *Antrodia camphorata* immunomodulatory protein, *Calocybe indica* polysaccharide, *Cordyceps taii* polysaccharide, protein-bound polysaccharide(PSK) and polysaccharopeptide (PSP) from *Coriolus versicolor, Calocybe indica* polysaccharide, *Cordyceps taii* polysaccharide, *Cryptosporus volvatus, Cordyceps militaris,* Der p 2-Fve fusion protein, *Flammulina velutipes* fungal immunomodulatory protein, *Flammulina velutipes* hemagglutinin, *Ganoderma capense* lectin, *Ganoderma lucidum* fungal immunomodulatory protein, *Ganoderma lucidum* immunomodulating substance, *Nectria haematococca* fungal immunomodulatory protein, *Grifola frondosa* ergosterol peroxide, extracts of mycelia and culture filtrate, *Pleurotus citrinopileatus, P. australis,* and *P. pulmonarius* polysaccharides, polysaccharide, *Hypsizigus marmoreus* water-soluble extracts, *Inonotus obliquus* polysaccharide, N-benzoylphenylisoserinates of Lactarius sesquiterpenoid alcohols, *Lentinula edodes* polysaccharide, *Lentinus squarrosulus* polysaccharide, *Lentinus polychrous* compounds, *Macrolepiota dolichaula* glucan, *Morchella conica* polysaccharide, *Pleurotus florida* polysaccharide, (1-->6)-beta-d-glucan from somatic hybrid between *Pleurotus florida* and *Volvariella volvace,* glucan from a hybrid mushroom (backcross mating between PfloVv12 and *Volvariella volvacea*), polysaccharide from somatic hybrid between *Pleurotus florida* and *Calocybe indica,* glucan from a hybrid mushroom of *Pleurotus florida* and *Lentinula edodes, Inonotus obliquus* water extract, hybrid of *Pleurotus florida* and *Lentinus squarrosulus*: water-soluble heteroglycan, *Pleurotus ostreatus* proteoglycan fractions, *Pleurotus ostreatus*

---

[*] Corresponding author: School of Biomedical Sciences, Faculty of Medicine, The Chinese University of Hong Kong, Shatin, New Territories, Hong Kong, China. Email: b021770@mailserv. cuhk. edu. hk.

pleuran-β-glucan, *Pleurotus ostreatus* protein fraction (Cibacron blue affinity purified protein), *Rubinoboletus ballouii* compounds, *Russula albonigra* glucan, *Trametes versicolor* glucan extracts, *Tricholoma crassum* polysaccharide, *Tricholoma matsutake* polysaccharides, *Tricholoma matsutake* alpha-D-glucan, *Tricholoma mongolicum* polysaccharide-peptide, *Volvariella volvacea* fungal immunomodulatory protein and *Volvariella volvacea* lectin

Keywords: Mushroom, extracts, compounds, immunomodulatory activity

INTRODUCTION

The human immune system enables us to combat cancer cells and pathogenic microorganisms. Immunodeficiency states such as acquired immune deficiency syndrome increase the susceptibility to infections and the proneness to develop cancer. Hence people rely on physical exercise, diet and dietary supplements to reinforce their immune system. Mushrooms represent an abundant source of biomolecules with immunostimulating activity. The purpose of this article is to review these molecules.

Agaricus bisporus 2-Amino-3h-Phenoxazin-3-One

2-amino-3H-phenoxazin-3-one from an extract of the brown mushroom *A. bisporus* inhibited lipopolysaccharide- and interferon-gamma- induced nitric oxide production and prostaglandin E(2) production by mouse peritoneal macrophages. It inhibited both cyclooxygenase-1 and -2. Secretion of nitric oxide and the pro-inflammatory cytokine interleukin-6 by interferon-gamma-activated mouse macrophage-like RAW264.7 cells was inhibited. 2-amino-3H-phenoxazin-3-one augmented the production of the anti-inflammatory cytokine interleukin-4 by antigen-stimulated T cells and increased polarization of CD4(+) Th cells to the anti-inflammatory Th2 phenotype at the same concentrations that suppressed nitric oxide production. 2-amino-3H-phenoxazin-3-one with immunomodulatory and anti-inflammatory activities may be used for treating chronic inflammatory diseases caused by bacteria and T cell-mediated inflammatory autoimmune diseases (Kohno et al., 2008).

Agaricus bisporus Lectin

The lectin up-regulated interleukin-1beta and tumor necrosis factor-alpha in splenocytes (Ooi et al., 2002).

Agaricus blazei

Serum levels of immunosuppressive acidic protein in mice receiving *A. blazei* fractions rose, suggesting possible granulocyte activation (Fujimiya et al., 1999).

Immunomodulatory Effects of Mushroom Extracts and Compounds 121

The mRNA expression of interleukin-6 and interleukin-1beta in spleen cells and peritoneal macrophages was augmented by *A. blazei* extract (Nakajima et al., 2002).

A fine particle of *A. blazei* fruiting bodies, prepared by mechanical disruption, reacted with human serum to form complement-opsonized powder, iC3b-ABP-F complexes, which bound to human peripheral blood monocytes. The resident human peripheral nucleated cells exposed to iC3b-ABP-F complexes exhibited antiproliferative activity toward TPC-1 tumor cells *in vitro* (Shimizu et al., 2002).

Boiling water extracts of *A. blazei* stimulated proliferation of T-cells, activated natural killer cells and promoted phagocytic activity of macrophages/monocytes, upregulated interleukin interleukin-1β, interleukin-6, and interferon-γ levels but downregulated interleukin -4 in leukemic mice. The levels of CD3 and CD19 elevated but those of Mac-3 and CD11b were depressed (Lin et al., 2012)

A. blazei protected against precancer colorectal lesions. Supplementation with *A. blazei* enhanced monocyte proliferation and phagocytic activity (Ishii et al., 2011).

Male Balb/cByJ mice that received an extract of the mushroom manifested higher splenocyte proliferation rate, spleen T-cell number, splenocyte tumor necrosis factor-alpha production, and delayed-type hypersensitivity.

Agaricus brasiliensis β-Glucans

Cytokine production from both murine splenocytes and bone marrow-derived dendritic cells was enhanced by the polysaccharides is mediated partly through dectin-1 together with granulocyte-macrophage colony-stimulating factor (Yamanaka et al., 2012).

Antrodia camphorata Mycelial Fraction and Culture Filtrate

The mycelial fraction, Fr. M II, and culture filtrate fractions, Fr. E II and Fr. E III, derived from *A. camphorata*, triggered production of interleukin-6 and tumor necrosis factor-alpha, and increased phagocytosis in human polymorphonuclear neutrophils and monocytes. Expression of CD11b, an early marker of PMN activation, was enhanced. The immunostimulatory effect of mycelia was due to adenosine and the 10-20kDa polysaccharides (Kuo et al., 2008).

Antrodia camphorata Immunomodulatory Protein

ACA, a 136-residue immunomodulatory glycoprotein showing homology to the fungal phytotoxic proteins, was purified from *A. camphorata* mycelial extract. Macrophage activation induced by ACA was dependent on TLR2/MyD88 but not on its glycosyl group(s). Recombinant ACA evoked a proinflammatory response from RAW 264.7 macrophage. It enhanced phagocytic activity and CD86 (B7-2) expression and elicited production of interleukin-1β and tumor necrosis factor-alpha in mouse peritoneal macrophages. mRNA expression of the cytokines TNF-α, interleukin -1β, -6, and -12, and the chemokines CCL3, 4,

5, and 10, but not interleukin -10, CCL17, 22, and 24, was upregulated after exposure of the macrophage to ACA (Sheu et al., 2009).

Armillaria mellea Polysaccharide

The water-soluble polysaccharide potentiated concanavalin A- or lipopolysaccharide-induced mouse lymphocyte proliferation (Sun et al., 2009).

Calocybe indica Polysaccharide

A water-soluble polysaccharide from *C. indica* var. APK2 possessing D-glucose, D-galactose, and L-fucose in a molar ratio of nearly 3: 1: 1 displayed immunoenhancing activity toward macrophages, splenocyte, thymocytes, and bone marrow cells and exerted a cytotoxic action toward HeLa cell lines (Mandai et al., 2011).

Cordyceps taii Polysaccharide

The antioxidant polysaccharide upregulated the antioxidant enzymes superoxide dismutase, catalase, and glutathione peroxidase. It curtailed malondialdehyde formation by lipid peroxidation and boosted immune function in a D-galactose-induced aging mouse model (Xiao et al., 2012).

Coriolus versicolor Protein-Bound Polysaccharide (PSK) and Polysaccharopeptide (PSP)

Protein-bound polysaccharide K (PSK) is a glycoprotein from *C. versicolor* used in Japan in conjunction with anticancer drugs after surgical removal of gastric cancer. Immunochemotherapy employing PSK as an adjuvant may have efficacy in MHC class I-negative gastric cancer patients exhibiting antitumor immunological tolerance, and patients with advanced lymph node metastasis of pN2 (Ito et al., 2012).

Coriolus versicolor Polysaccharopeptide (PSP)

Polysaccharide peptide (PSP) is a protein-bound polysaccharide extracted from *C. versicolor*. PSP (2g/kg/day) reversed immunosuppression brought about by cyclophosphamide(40 mg/kg/2 days) on lymphocyte proliferation, natural killer cell function, white blood cell production, and splenic and thymic growth in rats (Qian et al., 1997).

PSP provided in the drinking water for 14 days augmented the production of reactive oxygen intermediates, reactive nitrogen intermediates, and tumor necrosis factor and enhanced the transcription of tumor necrosis factor gene in mouse peritoneal macrophages (Liu et al., 1993).

Cryptosporus volvatus, Cordyceps militaris, Pleurotus citrinopileatus, P. australis, and *P. pulmonarius* Polysaccharides

Both exo- and endo polysaccharides of *C. volvatus* inhibited *in vitro* formation of the T lymphocyte Th1 cytokines interleukin-2 and interferon-ã, and the Th2 cytokines interleukin-4 and interleukin-5, as well as macrophage enzyme activity. Exo- and endo- polysaccharides from *C. militaris* also suppressed cytokine formation. However, the exopolysaccharides upregulated macrophage enzyme activity.

Exopolysaccharides from *P. australis, P. citrinopileatus, and P. pulmonarius* suppressed formation of interferon-ã and interleukin-5, but had varying effects on interleukin-2 and interleukin-4 formation. Three exopolysaccharides (from *Cordyceps sinensis, P. pulmonarius,* and *Tremella mesenterica,*) enhanced macrophage enzyme activity. All downregulated interleukin-5 formation, but those from *T. mesenterica* also suppressed formation of, interleukin-2, interleukin-4 and interferon-ã (Jeong et al., 2013).

Der P 2-Fve Fusion Protein

Der p 2 is a mite (*Dermatophagoides pteronyssinus*) allergen. FIP-fve protein (Fve) is a *Flammulina velutipes* immunomodulatory protein with potential Th1-skewed adjuvant properties. Recombinant Der p 2-Fve fusion protein (designated as OsDp2Fve) was expressed in rice cells. Mice treated with OsDp2Fve demonstrated augmented production of Der p 2-specific IgG antibodies without affecting formation of Der p 2-specific IgE and Th2 effector cytokines compared to mice treated concurrently with native Fve and Der p 2 proteins. The data indicate that the fusion protein is potentially useful for allergy immunotherapy (Su et al., 2011).

Flammulina velutipes Fungal Immunomodulatory Protein

FIP-fve triggered blast-forming activity of human peripheral blood lymphocytes and gene expression of interferon-gamma, interleukin-2, and tumor necrosis factor-alpha. On the other hand, it suppressed the Arthur and systemic anaphylaxis reactions in mice (Ko et al., 1997).

FIP-fve potently activated T-cells via regulation of p38 MAPK. The immunoprophylactic action of FIP-fve in Th2-mediated allergic anaphylaxis is related to the activation of interferon-gamma-releasing Th1 cells (Wang et al., 2004).

Mice (coimmunized mice) coimmunized with Fve and human papillomavirus oncoprotein HPV-16 E7 exhibited increased production of HPV-16 E7-specific antibodies and expansion of HPV-16 E7-specific interferon-gamma-producing CD4(+) and CD8(+) T cells compared with mice (immunized mice) imunized with HPV-16 E7 alone.

In comparison with immunized mice, coimmunized mice demonstrated a prolonged survival and a higher percentage of coimmunized mice remained tumor-free. Fve stimulated the splenic dendritic cells to mature *in vivo* and elicited antigen-specific CD8(+) T-cell immune responses. Fve manifested strong adjuvant properties that facilitated T helper type 1 antigen-specific humoral and cellular immune responses which contributed to anticancer activity (Ding et al., 2009).

W24, T28, D34, T90, I91, and W111 are the key residues of FIP-fve that are involved in binding to membrane polysaccharides of immune cells. Following removal of the carbohydrate moieties from human peripheral blood mononuclear cells using tunicamycin and deglycosylation enzymes, interferon-ã secretion from the cells was reduced. The ligand-binding CBM-34 on FIP-fve and ligand-like glycoproteins on the surface of human peripheral blood mononuclear cells are requisite for FIP-fve to exert its immunomodulatory action (Liu et al., 2012).

FIP-fve demonstrated anti-allergy, anti-tumor and immunomodulation activities. rFIP-fve could stimulate viability of murine splenocytes. The immunomodulatory and anti-tumor activities of rFIP-fve were evidenced by enhanced interleukin-2 secretion and interferon-ã release from mouse lymphocytes, similar to the biological FIP-fve (Lin et al., 2013).

The levels of expression of major histocompatibility complex class I and II molecules and costimulatory molecule CD80 on mouse peripheral blood mononuclear cells were elevated in response to Fve administration (10mg/kg by mouth). Interferon-gamma was involved in the anticancer activity of Fve (Chang et al., 2010)

FVE from *Flammulia velutipes* and LZ8 from *Ganoderma Lucidum*

The activity of FVE and LZ8 in stimulating splenocyte interferon-gamma secretion was stable to high temperatures exceeding 100 degrees C, to freezing at -80 degrees C and to 0. 6 M hydrochloric acid (pH 2) (Tong et al., 2008).

Flammulina velutipes Hemagglutinin

A 12-kDa hemagglutinin from the fruiting bodies enhanced incorporation of tritiated methylthymidine into murine spleen cells and exerted antiproliferative activity toward leukemia L1210 cells (Ng et al., 200r).

Ganoderma capense Lectin

An 18-kDa lectin from *G. capense* had higher mitogenic activity than concanavalin A toward murine spleen cells, and inhibited proliferation of leukemia cells and hepatoma cells (Ngai and Ng, 2004).

Ganoderma lucidum Mycelial Polysaccharides

The polysaccharides exerted a proliferative activity toward human peripheral blood mononuclear cells and stimulated phenotypic and functional maturation of human dendritic cells with production of interleukin-10 and interleukin-12 (Chan et al., 2007).

Ganoderma lucidum Fungal Immunomodulatory Protein LZ-8

Exposure of human monocyte-derived dendritic cells to recombinant LZ-8 ensued in an enhanced cell-surface expression of CD80, CD86, CD83, and HLA-DR, and at the same time, augmented production of interleukin-10, interleukin-12 p40, and interleukin-23, and attenuated endocytic activity of dendritic cells. Naïve T cell-stimulatory capacity and naïve T cell secretion of interferon-gamma and interleukin-10 were elevated. Interleukin-8rLZ-8 production by TLR4 or TLR4/MD2-transfected HEK293 cells was upregulated. A rise in IKK, NF-kappaB activity, and also IkappaBalpha and MAPK phosphorylation was observed (Lin et al., 2009).

The antitumor activity of *G. lucidum* can be ascribed to a diversity of mechanisms including (1) immunostimulatory/immunomodulatory effect on the host, (2) direct cytotoxic action on tumor cells, (3) antiangiogenic activity, (4) antiproliferative and antimetastatic activities and (5) carcinogen deactivating activity (Boh, 2013).

Ganoderma lucidum and Nectria haematococca FIPs (LZ-9 and FIP-Nha)

Compared with FIP-nha from the ascomycete *N. haematococca*, recombinant FIP-fve potently induced pro-inflammatory cytokine gene transcription in THP-1 macrophages (Bastiaan-Net et al., 2013).

Ganoderma lucidum Immunomodulating Substance

Subsequent to treatment with *G. lucidum* immunomodulating substance, bone marrow macrophages underwent hypertrophy, produced pseudopodia, and exhibited an elevated production of nitric oxide, enhancement of cellular respiratory burst activity, and heightened levels of interleukin -1â, -6, -12p35, -12p40, -18, and tumor necrosis factor-á gene expression, The levels of interleukin -1â, and -12 and tumor necrosis factor-á were increased (Ji et al., 2012).

Grifola frondosa Extracts of Mycelia and Culture Filtrate

Polysaccharide-enriched fractions of hot water mycelia extract stimulated phagocytic activity of human polymorphonuclear neutrophils, and the expression of CD11b, an early marker of PMN activation. The cytotoxic action of human peripheral blood natural killer cells was potentiated by the fractions (Wu et al., 2006).

Grifola frondosa **Ergosterol Peroxide**

Ergosterol peroxide protected human monocytic (THP-1) cells against lipopolysaccharide-induced cell toxicity. It attenuated MyD88 and VCAM-1 expression, and production of pro-inflammatory cytokine (interleukin-1â, interleukin-6 and tumor necrosis factor-á) in lipopolysaccharide-stimulated cells. NF-êB activation was suppressed (Wu et al., 2013).

Grifola frondosa **Polysaccharide**

GFPBW2 is a 26. 2-kDa water-soluble homogeneous polysaccharide from fruit bodies of *G. frondosa* with a backbone comprised of â-d-1, 3- and â-d-1, 4-linked glucopyranosyl residues and branches attached to O-6 of â-d-1, 3-linked glucopyranosyl residues. It induced tumor necrosis factor-á (TNF-á) and interleukin-6 (IL-6) secretion in murine resident peritoneal macrophages, and activated Syk and enhanced TNF-á production in RAW264.7 cells. Syk, NF-êB signaling, and cytokine release in resident peritoneal macrophages induced by GFPBW2 could be inhibited by a specific Dectin-1 blocking reagent, laminarin, signifying that GFPBW2 is a ligand of Dectin-1, and its activation of macrophages through enhancement of cytokine secretion might involve Dectin-1(Wang et al., 2013)

Hypsizigus marmoreus **Water-Soluble Extracts**

The crude and fractionated water-soluble *H. marmoreus* extracts (F(1), F(2) and F(3)), comprised primarily of carbohydrates (glucose and/or galactose bonded by 1, 6-glycosidic linkages) with varying protein content, were devoid of significant anticancer activity on cancer cell lines, but upregulated nitric oxide and prostaglandin E2 production by Raw 264.7 cells and mRNA expression of interleukin-1â, interleukin-6 and tumor necrosis factor-á (Bao andYou, 2011).

Inonotus obliquus **Water Extract**

Treatment of mice immunosuppressed by cyclophosphamide (400 mg/kg body weight) with *I. obliquus* water extract for 24 consecutive days restored the number of colony-forming unit granulocytes/macrophages and erythroid burst-forming unit, and elevated serum levels of interleukin-6 (Kim, 2005).

Inonotus obliquus Polysaccharide

A water-soluble polysaccharide (ISP2a) from *I. obliquus* stimulated the proliferation of lymphocytes and suppressed tumor growth in tumor-bearing mice (Fan et al., 2012).

N-Benzoylphenylisoserinates of *Lactarius* Sesquiterpenoid Alcohols

Six antiviral N-benzoylphenylisoserinates of *Lactarius* sesquiterpenoid alcohols significantly reduced the number of cell divisions which was probably related to its anti-HSV activity. One of them, isolactarorufin 8-epi-[N-benzoyl-(2' R, 3' S)-3'-phenylisoserinate] suppressed T lymphocyte proliferation and cytokine production (Krawczyk et al., 2005).

Lentinula edodes Polysaccharide

Polysaccharide fraction II (F-II) prepared from *L. edodes* liquid culture increased macrophage phagocytic uptake, cytokine expression, and reactive oxygen species/nitric oxide production, and induced morphological alterations. Nuclear translocation of NF-kappaB and its upstream signaling cascades such as PI3K/ Akt and mitogen-activated protein kinase pathways were stimulated, as judged by levels of phosphorylation. Antisera against dectin-1 and TLR-2 inhibited nitric oxide production induced by the polysaccharide fraction. Hence a variety of signaling pathways is involved(Lee et al., 2008).

Both mycelial and fruiting body extracts of *L. edodes* stimulated rat thymocyte proliferation in the absence as well as in the presence of phytohemagglutinin (Israilides et al., 2008).

Lentinus squarrosulus Polysaccharide

Mushroom immunomodulators are classified under four categories based on their chemical nature as: lectins, terpenoids, proteins, and polysaccharides (El Enshasy et al., 2013). A water-soluble polysaccharide from the hot water extract of the fruiting bodies of *L. squarrosulus* activated splenocytes, macrophages, and thymocytes (Bhunia et al., 2010).

A water-soluble glucan, isolated from the alkaline extract of the fruit bodies of *L. squarrosulus* containing (1→3, 6)-linked, (1→3)-linked, (1→6)-linked, and terminal β-d-glucopyranosyl moieties in a relative proportion of approximately 1: 2: 1: 1, and activated macrophages, splenocytes and thymocytes optimally at 10μg/mL(Bhunia et al., 2011).

Lentinus polychrous Compounds

6-methylheptane-1, 2, 3, 4, 5-pentaol isolated from of *L. polychrous* mycelia exerted weak cytotoxicity to murine splenocytes but did not adversely affect RAW264.7 cells or peripheral blood mononuclear cells. It reduced nitric oxide and intracellular O2 (-)formation in RAW264. 7 cells activated by lipopolysaccharide and phorbol-12-myristate-13-acetate. Messenger RNA expression of the-inflammatory mediators cyclooxygenase-1 and -2, inducible nitric oxide synthase, interleukin-1â and -6, and tumor necrosis factor–á were downregulated. Splenocyte proliferation under the stimulation of pokeweed mitogen and phytohemagglutinin was further enhanced (Fangkrathok et al., 2013).

Macrolepiota dolichaula Glucan

A 200-kDa water soluble branched glucan (PS-I) from aqueous extract of the fruit bodies activated RAW 264.7 macrophage cell line, splenocytes and thymocytes (Samanta et al., 2013).

Morchella conica Polysaccharide

A 81.2-kDa water-soluble polysaccharide enhanced splenocyte proliferation and modulated nitric oxide formation in macrophages (Su et al., 2013).

Morchella esculenta Extracellular Polysaccharides

M. esculenta extracellular polysaccharides enhanced macrophage phagocytosis and splenocyte proliferation in D-galactose induced mice (Fu et al., 2013).

Phellinus linteus Boiling Water Extract

The IgE-dependent mouse triphasic cutaneous reaction was induced in the ears of BALB/c mice passively sensitized with anti-dinitrophenol IgE by painting with 2, 4-dinitrofluorobenzene. Ear swelling occurred with a triphasic temporal pattern: maximal responses were attained one hour, then one day and finally eight days post-challenge. All three phases were suppressed following oral administration of the boiling water extract at 100 mg/kg. The extract reduced vascular permeability increase brought about by passive cutaneous anaphylaxis and histamine, and suppressed tumor necrosis factor alpha-elicited ear swelling. The boiling water extract augmented the production of interferon-gamma and interleukin-4 from anti-CD3-stimulated murine spleen cells (Inagaki et al., 2005).

Pleurotus ctrinopileatus Glycoprotein

A nonlectin glycoprotein from *P. citrinopileatus* boosted secretion of the cytokines interferon-γ, tumor interleukin-2, and necrosis factor-α from the stimulated human mononuclear cells and CD4(+) T lymphocytes(Chen et al., 2010).

Pleurotus florida **Aqueous Extract and Polysaccharide**

A decline in viability of spleen cells occurred after daily intraperitoneal injection of *P. florida* aqueous extract at 10, 20, and 50 mg/kg for14 days. On the other hand, when the extract was given orally at 1000 mg/kg it produced a rise in cell viability (Sedaghat and Ghazanfari, 2011).

An immunoenhancing polysaccharide from the hot water extract of the of *Pleurotus florida* fruiting bodies, cultivar Assam Florida, activated splenocytes, macrophages, and thymocytes (Roy et al., 2009).

An immunoenhancing polysaccharide isolated from the aqueous extract of the fruit bodies of the mushroom, *Pleurotus florida* blue variant, possessing D-glucose and D-galactose in a molar ratio of nearly 5: 1 and the structure of the repeating unit as →6)-β-D-Glcp-(1→3)-α-D-glcp-(1→[6)-β-D-Glcp-(1]3→α-D=Glcp, activated thymocytes, splenocytes, and macrophages (Dey et al., 2010)

(1-->6)-Beta-D-Glucan from Somatic Hybrid between *Pleurotus florida* and *Volvariella volvacea*

The polysaccharide from fruit bodies of the somatic hybrid (Pflo Vv5 FB) formed by protoplast fusion between *Pleurotus florida* and *Volvariella volvacea* strains activated splenocytes, macrophages, and thymocytes (Das et al., 2010).

A water soluble polysaccharide isolated from the hot aqueous extract of the fruit bodies of the somatic hybrid mushroom (PfloVv1aFB), produced by protoplast fusion between *P. florida* and *V. volvacea* strains, and containing d-glucose, d-galactose, and d-mannose in a molar ratio of nearly 4: 1: 1, activated macrophages, splenocytes and thymocytes(Patra et al., 2011).

Glucan from a Hybrid Mushroom (Backcross Mating between Pflovv12 and *Volvariella volvacea*)

A water-soluble glucan with (1→6)-linked β-D-glucopyranose from the alkaline extract of the fruit bodies of the hybrid mushroom activated macrophages, splenocytes, and thymocytes and demonstrated antioxidant activity (Sarkar et al., 2012).

Polysaccharide from Somatic Hybrid between *Pleurotus florida* and *Calocybe indica*

A water-soluble polysaccharide from the aqueous extract of the fruit bodies of somatic hybrid PCH9FB, produced by intergeneric protoplast fusion between the strains *P. florida* and *C. indica*, and exhibiting galactose, fucose, and glucose in a molar ratio of nearly 2: 1: 2 activated macrophages, splenocytes, as well as thymocytes, and displayed antioxidant property (Maity et al., 2011).

Glucan from a Hybrid Mushroom of *Pleurotus florida* and *Lentinula edodes*

A water soluble glucan rom hot aqueous extract of fruit bodies of an edible hybrid mushroom Pfle1r of *P. florida* and *L. edodes* activated macrophages, splenocytes, and thymocytes ion (Maji et al., 2012).

Hybrid of *Pleurotus florida* and *Lentinus squarrosulus*: Water-Soluble Heteroglycan

The heteroglycan (PS-II), composed of (1→6)- and (1→2, 4, 6)-α-D-galactopyranosyl, terminal β-D-mannopyranosyl and terminal β-D-glucopyranosyl residues in nearly equimolar ratio and produced by intergeneric protoplast fusion between *L. squarrosulu* and *P. florida*, activated macrophages, splenocytes, and thymocytes *in vitro* (Sen et al., 2013).

Pleurotus nebrodensis Crude Polysaccharides

Polysaccharides extracted from *P. nebrodensis* boosted interleukin-1β, interleukin-6 and tumor necrosis factor-α production (Cha et al., 2012).

Pleurotus ostreatus Proteoglycan Fractions

Three water-soluble proteoglycan fractions from P. ostreatus mycelia upregulated cytotoxicity of mouse natural killer cells and stimulated macrophage production of nitric oxide (Sarangi et al., 2006).

Pleurotus ostreatus Pleuran-β-Glucan

In a double-blind, placebo-controlled, randomised, multicentre investigation, Imunoglukan P4H® syrup (containing *Pleurotus ostreatus* pleuran-â-glucan and ascorbic acid) produced an immunomodulaory effect on cellular and humoral immunity and minimized recurrent respiratory tract infections in children(aged 5.65 ± 2.39 years) compared with the placebo group receiving ascorbic acid (Jesenak et al., 2013).

Pleurotus ostreatus Heteroglucan

A high-molecular-weight glucan, composed of glucose, mannose and fucose in a ratio of 3: 2: 1 and possessing both α and β linkages and folded into a triple helix, activated immune cells and exerted an anti-tumor action in tumor bearing mice (Devi et al., 2013).

Pleurotus ostreatus **Protein Fraction (Cibacron Blue Affinity Purified Protein)**

A protein fraction designated as Cibacron blue affinity purified protein (CBAEP) from *P. ostreatus* stimulated immune cells in the presence of Concanavalin A and lipopolysaccharide *ex vivo* and induced Th1 response with production of interleukin-2, interferon-γ, and tumor necrosis factor-α. Tumor-associated macrophages and natural killer cells were activated (Maiti et al., 2012).

Rubinoboletus ballouii **Compounds**

Pistillarin and 1-ribofuranosyl-s-triazin-2(1H)-one from *Rubinoboletus ballouii* demonstrated immunosuppressive activity on phytohemagglutinin-stimulated human peripheral blood mononuclear cells by reducing tritiated methyl-thymidine uptake and formation of inflammatory cytokines interferon–ã, interleukin-1â, interleukin-10, and tumor necrosis factor-á. They exhibited great potential in developing as anti-inflammatory reagents (Li et al., 2013).

Russula albonigra **Glucan**

A water-soluble glucan from the hot aqueous fruiting body extract activated macrophages, splenocytes and thymocytes *in vitro* (Nandi et al., 2012).

A water-soluble 145-kDa heteroglycan from the aqueous extract stimulated macrophage nitric oxide production and proliferation of splenocytes and thymocytes *in vitro* (Nandi et al., 2013).

Trametes versicolor **Glucan Extracts**

Trametes versicolor glucan extracts produced immunomodulatory effects in healthy adults and also in patients with canker sores and seasonal allergies (Ramberg et al., 2010)

Tricholoma crassum **Polysaccharide**

The water-soluble heteropolysaccharide isolated from an alkaline extract of the fruit bodies activated macrophages, splenocytes and thymocytes (Patra et al., 2012).

Tricholoma matsutake **Extracts**

The water extract and n-butyl alcohol extract of *T. matsutake,* which contained flavonoids, polysaccharides, and proteins, exhibited immunoenhancing effects in mice as evidenced by various parameters including delayed-type hypersensitivity, thymus and spleen index, splenocyte proliferation, macrophage phagocytic rate, and plaque-forming cells (Yin et al., 2012).

Tricholoma matsutake Polysaccharides

Polysaccharide fraction II (TMF-II) prepared from *T. matsutake* liquid culture upregulated macrophage production of nitric oxide and expression of the cytokines tumor necrosis factor-alpha, interleukin-1beta, interleukin-6, and interleukin-12. TMF-II induced Ikappa Balpha phosphorylation, vital for NF-kappaB activation and translocation. Src and Akt were the upstream signaling components implicated in induction of nitric oxide formation, although TMF-II upregulated phosphorylation of all of the mitogen-activated protein kinase pathway. TMF-II displayed an immunostimulating potency analogous to lipopolysaccharide through activation of a variety of pathways associated with NF-kappaB activation (Kim et al., 2008).

Tricholoma matsutake Alpha-D-Glucan

Alpha-D-glucan from *T. matsutake* exhibited a stimulatory action on the intestinal immune system through Peyer's patches It was found in the spleen, mesenteric lymph nodes, and Peyer's patches. It upregulated production of IL-12 p70 and activity of natural killer cells (Hoshi et al., 2008).

Tricholoma Sp. Polysaccharide-Peptide Complex

A 17- kDa polysaccharide-peptide complex from a submerged mycelial culture of *Tricholoma* sp. stimulated macrophages, enhanced T-cell proliferation, and exerted an antitumor action in sarcoma 180 bearing mice (Wang et al., 1995).

Tricholoma mongolicum Polysaccharide-Peptide

A 15.5-kDa, polysaccharide-peptide complex from *Tricholoma mongolicum* mycelial culture activated macrophages, stimulating macrophage antigen-presenting activity which promoted T-cell proliferation and exerted an antitumor action on sarcoma 180 bearing mice (Wang et al., 1996).

Volvariella volvacea Fungal Immunomodulatory Protein

A homodimeric 26-kDa fungal immunomodulatory nonglycoprotein from the straw mushroom enhanced proliferation of human peripheral blood lymphocytes, and suppressed the Arthus reaction induced in mice by bovine serum albumin. The transcriptional expression of interleukin-2, interleukin-4, lymphotoxin and interleukin-2 receptor, interferon-gamma, and tumour necrosis factor-alpha was upregulated (Hsu et al., 1997).

Volvariella volvacea Lectin

The homodimeric 32-kDa nonglycoprotein lectin augmented the transcriptional expression of interferon-gamma and interleukin-2 murine splenic lymphocytes (She et al., 1998).

CONCLUSION

A number of bioactive constituents have been isolated from mushrooms including antifungal proteins, ribosome inactivating proteins, ribonucleases, lectins, proteases, enzymes, polysaccharides, polysaccharopeptides, polysaccharide-protein complexes, immunomodulatory proteins (Singh et al., 2010) and small-molecular-weight compounds. It can be seen from the present account that out of the diversity of mushroom products, the following manifest immunoenhancing activities: proteins, polysaccharides, polysaccharide-peptide complexes, polysaccharide-protein complexes, and small-molecular-weight compounds.

Many people have resorted to use mushroom products as health supplements. Chang and Wasser (2012) have enumerated the advantages of using mushroom-based dietary supplements which comprise (1) commercial cultivation of mushrooms employed for dietary supplement production, (2) facile vegetative propagation of mushrooms, maintenance of a single clone, storage of mycelia over extended period of time, and feasibility of examining the genetic and biochemical consistency after a substantial duration has elapsed, and (3) submerged mycelial culture of mushrooms (Chang and Wasser, 2012). Besides immunoenhancing activity, mushrooms and their components display an array of other exploitable activities including anticancer, antidiabetic, antihyperlipidemic, antimicrobial and anti-pest activities. Thus mushrooms contribute substantially to the welfare of mankind.

REFERENCES

Bao, H; You, S. Molecular characteristics of water-soluble extracts from *Hypsizigus marmoreus* and their *in vitro* growth inhibition of various cancer cell lines and immunomodulatory function in Raw 264. 7 cells. *Biosci Biotechnol Biochem.*, 2011, 75(5), 891-8.

Bao, HH; Tarbasa, M; Chae, HM; You, SG. Molecular properties of water-unextractable proteoglycans from *Hypsizygus marmoreus* and their *in vitro* immunomodulatory activities. *Molecules.*, 2011 27, 17(1), 207-26.

Bastiaan-Net, S; Chanput, W; Hertz, A; Zwittink, RD; Mes, JJ; Wichers, HJ. Biochemical and functional characterization of recombinant fungal immunomodulatory proteins (rFIPs). *Int Immunopharmacol.*, 2013, 15(1), 167-75.

Bhunia, SK; Dey, B; Maity, KK; Patra, S; Mandal, S; Maiti, S; Maiti, TK; Sikdar, SR; Islam, SS. Structural characterization of an immunoenhancing heteroglycan isolated from an aqueous extract of an edible mushroom, *Lentinus squarrosulus* (Mont.) *Singer. Carbohydr Res.*, 2010, 345(17), 2542-9.

Bhunia, SK; Dey, B; Maity, KK; Patra, S; Mandal, S; Maiti, S; Maiti, TK; Sikdar, SR; Islam, SS. Isolation and characterization of an immunoenhancing glucan from alkaline extract of an edible mushroom, *Lentinus squarrosulus* (Mont.) *Singer. Carbohydr Res.*, 2011, 346(13), 2039-44.

Boh, B. Ganoderma lucidum: a potential for biotechnological production of anti-cancer and immunomodulatory drugs. *Recent Pat Anticancer Drug Discov.*, 2013, 8(3), 255-87.

Cha, YJ; Alam, N; Lee, JS; Lee, KR; Shim, MJ; Lee, MW; Kim, HY; Shin, PG; Cheong, JC; Yoo, YB; Lee, TS. Anticancer and immunopotentiating activities of crude polysaccharides from *Pleurotus nebrodensis* on mouse sarcoma 180. *Mycobiology.*, 2012, 40(4), 236-43.

Chang, HH; Hsieh, KY; Yeh, CH; Tu, YP; Sheu, F. Oral administration of an Enoki mushroom protein FVE activates innate and adaptive immunity and induces anti-tumor activity against murine hepatocellular carcinoma. *Int Immunopharmacol.*, 2010, 10(2), 239-46.

Chen, JN; Ma, CY; Tsai, PF; Wang, YT; Wu, JS. In vtro atitumor and imunomodulatory efects of the potein PCP-3A from mshroom *Pleurotus citrinopileatus. J Agric Food Chem.*, 2010 Nov 5. [Epub ahead of print]

Das, D; Mondal, S; Roy, SK; Maiti, D; Bhunia, B; Maiti, TK; Sikdar, SR; Islam, SS. A (1-->6)-beta-glucan from a somatic hybrid of, *Pleurotus florida* and *Volvariella volvacea*: isolation, characterization, and study of immunoenhancing properties. *Carbohydr Res.*, 2010, 345(7), 974-8.

Dey, B; Bhunia, SK; Maity, KK; Patra, S; Mandal, S; Maiti, S; Maiti, TK; Sikdar, SR; Islam, SS. Chemical analysis of an immunoenhancing water-soluble polysaccharide of an edible mushroom, *Pleurotus florida* blue variant. *Carbohydr Res.*, 2010, 345(18), 2736-41.

Ding, Y; Seow, SV; Huang, CH; Liew, LM; Lim, YC; Kuo, IC; Chua, KY. Coadministration of the fungal immunomodulatory protein FIP-Fve and a tumour-associated antigen enhanced antitumour immunity. *Immunology.*, 2009, 128(1 Suppl), e881-94.

El, Enshasy, HA; Hatti-Kaul, R. Mushroom immunomodulators: unique *molecules* with unlimited applications. *Trends Biotechnol.*, 2013, 31(12), 668-77.

Fan, L; Ding, S; Ai, L; Deng, K. Antitumor and immunomodulatory activity of water-soluble polysaccharide from *Inonotus obliquus. Carbohydr Polym.*, 2012 1, 90(2), 870-4.

Fangkrathok, N; Junlatat, J; Umehara, K; Noguchi, H; Sripanidkulchai, B. Cytotoxic and immunomodulatory effects of polyhydroxyoctane isolated from *Lentinus polychrous* mycelia. J Nat Med. 2013 Aug 15. [Epub ahead of print]

Fu, L; Wang, Y; Wang, J; Yang, Y; Hao, L. Evaluation of the antioxidant activity of extracellular polysaccharides from *Morchella esculenta. Food Funct.*, 2013, 4(6), 871-9.

Fujimiya, Y; Suzuki, Y; Katakura, R; Ebina, T. Tumor-specific cytocidal and immunopotentiating effects of relatively low molecular weight products derived from the basidiomycete, *Agaricus blazei* Murill. *Anticancer Res.*, 1999, 19(1A), 113-8.

Hoshi, H; Iijima, H; Ishihara, Y; Yasuhara, T; Matsunaga, K. Absorption and tissue distribution of an immunomodulatory alpha-D-glucan after oral administration of *Tricholoma matsutake*. *J Agric Food Chem.*, 2008, 56(17), 7715-20.

Hsu, HC; Hsu, CI; Lin, RH; Kao, CL; Lin, JY. Fip-vvo, a new fungal immunomodulatory protein isolated from *Volvariella volvacea*. *Biochem J.*, 1997, 323 (Pt 2), 557-65.

Inagaki, N; Shibata, T; Itoh, T; Suzuki, T; Tanaka, H; Nakamura, T; Akiyama, Y; Kawagishi, H; Nagai, H. Inhibition of IgE-dependent mouse triphasic cutaneous reaction by a boiling water fraction separated from mycelium of *Phellinus linteus*. *Evid Based Complement Alternat Med.*, 2005, 2(3), 369-74.

Ishii, PL; Prado, CK; Mauro, Mde, O; Carreira, CM; Mantovani, MS; Ribeiro, LR; Dichi, JB; Oliveira, RJ. Evaluation of *Agaricus blazei in vivo* for antigenotoxic, anticarcinogenic, phagocytic and immunomodulatory activities. *Regul Toxicol Pharmacol.*, 2011, 59(3), 412-22.

Israilides, C; Kletsas, D; Arapoglou, D; Philippoussis, A; Pratsinis, H; Ebringerová, A; Hríbalová, V; Harding, SE. In vitro cytostatic and immunomodulatory properties of the medicinal mushroom *Lentinula edodes*. *Phytomedicine.*, 2008, 15(6-7), 512-9.

Ito, G; Tanaka, H; Ohira, M; Yoshii, M; Muguruma, K; Kubo, N; Yashiro, M; Yamada, N, Maeda, K; Sawada, T; Hirakawa, K. Correlation between efficacy of PSK postoperative adjuvant immunochemotherapy for gastric cancer and expression of MHC class I. *Exp Ther Med.*, 2012, 3(6), 925-930.

Jeong, SC; Koyyalamudi, SR; Hughes, J; Khoo, C; Bailey, T; Marripudi, K; Park, JP; Kim JH; Song, CH. Antioxidant and immunomodulating activities of exo-and endopolysaccharide fractions from submerged mycelia cultures of culinary-medicinal mushrooms. *Int J Med Mushrooms.*, 2013, 15(3), 251-66.

Jesenak, M; Majtan, J; Rennerova, Z; Kyselovic, J; Banovcin, P; Hrubisko, M. Immunomodulatory effect of pleuran (â-glucan from *Pleurotus ostreatus*) in children with recurrent respiratory tract infections. *Int Immunopharmacol.*, 2013, 15(2), 395-9.

Ji, Z; Tang, Q; Zhang, J; Yang, Y; Liu, Y; Pan, YJ. Immunomodulation of bone marrow macrophages by GLIS, a proteoglycan fraction from Lingzhi or Reishi medicinal mushroom *Ganoderma lucidium* (W. Curt. :Fr.) P. Karst. *Int J Med Mushrooms.*, 2011, 13(5), 441-8.

Kim, JY; Byeon, SE; Lee, YG; Lee, JY; Park, J; Hong, EK; Cho, JY. Immunostimulatory activities of polysaccharides from liquid culture of pine-mushroom *Tricholoma matsutake*. *J Microbiol Biotechnol.*, 2008, 18:95-103.

Kim, YR. Immunomodulatory activity of the water extract from medicinal Mushroom *Inonotus obliquus*. *Mycobiology.*, 2005, 33(3), 158-62.

Ko, JL; Lin, SJ; Hsu, CI; Kao, CL; Lin, JY. Molecular cloning and expression of a fungal immunomodulatory protein, FIP-fve,from *Flammulina velutipes*. *J Formos Med Assoc.*, 1997, 96(7), 517-24.

Kohno, K; Miyake, M; Sano, O; Tanaka-Kataoka, M; Yamamoto, S; Koya-Miyata, S; Arai, N,Fujii, M; Watanabe, H; Ushio, S; Iwaki, K; Fukuda, S. Anti-inflammatory and immunomodulatory properties of 2-amino-3H-phenoxazin-3-one. *Biol Pharm Bull.*, 2008, 31(10), 1938-45.

Kuo, MC; Chang, CY; Cheng, TL; Wu, MJ. Immunomodulatory effect of *Antrodia camphorata* mycelia and culture filtrate. *J Ethnopharmacol.*, 2008, 120(2), 196-203.

Krawczyk, E; Luczak, M; Kniotek, M; Majewska, A; Kawecki, D; Nowaczyk M. Immunomodulatory activity and influence on mitotic divisions of N-benzoylphenylisoserinates of Lactarius sesquiterpenoid alcohols *in vitro. Planta Med.*, 2005, 71(9), 819-24.

Lee, JY; Kim, JY; Lee, YG; Rhee, MH; Hong, EK; Cho, JY. Molecular mechanism of macrophage activation by exopolysaccharides from liquid culture of *Lentinus edodes. J Microbiol Biotechnol.*, 2008, 18, 355-64.

Li, LF; Chan, BC; Yue, GG; Lau, CB; Han, QB; Leung, PC; Liu, JK; Fung, KP. Two immunosuppressive compounds from the mushroom *Rubinoboletus ballouii* using human peripheral blood mononuclear cells by bioactivity-guided fractionation. *Phytomedicine.*, 2013, 20(13), 1196-202.

Lin, JW; Jia, J; Shen, YH; Zhong, M; Chen, LJ; Li, HG; Ma, H; Guo, ZF; Qi, MF; Liu, LX; Li, TL. Functional expression of FIP-fve, a fungal immunomodulatory protein from the edible mushroom *Flammulina velutipes* in *Pichia pastoris* GS115. *J Biotechnol.*, 2013, 168(4), 527-33.

Lin, JG; Fan, MJ; Tang, NY; Yang, JS; Hsia, TC; Lin, JJ; Lai, KC; Wu, RS; Ma, CY; Wood, WG, Chung, JG. An extract of *Agaricus blazei* Murill administered orally promotes immune responses in murine leukemia BALB/c mice in vivo. *Integr Cancer Ther.*, 2012, 11(1), 29-36.

Lin, YL; Liang, YC; Tseng, YS; Huang, HY; Chou, SY; Hseu, RS; Huang, CT; Chiang, BL. An immunomodulatory protein, Ling Zhi-8, induced activation and maturation of human monocyte-derived dendritic cells by the NF-kappaB and MAPK pathways. *J Leukoc Biol.*, 2009, 86(4), 877-89.

Liu, WK; Ng, TB; Sze, SF; Tsui, KW. Activation of peritoneal macrophages by polysaccharopeptide from the mushroom, *Coriolus versicolor. Immunopharmacology.*, 1993, 26(2), 139-46.

Liu, YF; Chang, SH; Sun, HL; Chang, YC; Hsin, IL; Lue, KH; Ko, JL. IFN-ã induction on carbohydrate binding module of fungal immunomodulatory protein in human peripheral mononuclear cells. *J Agric Food Chem.*, 2012, 60(19), 4914-22

Maity, K; Kar, Mandal, E; Maity, S; Gantait, SK; Das, D; Maiti, S; Maiti, TK; Sikdar, SR; Islam, SS. Chemical analysis and study of immunoenhancing and antioxidant property of a glucan isolated from an alkaline extract of a somatic hybrid mushroom of *Pleurotus florida* and *Calocybe indica* variety APK2. *Int J Biol Macromol.*, 2011, 49(4), 555-60.

Maiti, S; Mallick, SK; Bhutia, SK; Behera, B; Mandal, M; Maiti, TK. Antitumor effect of culinary-medicinal oyster mushroom, *Pleurotus ostreatus* (Jacq. : Fr.) P. Kumm. , derived protein fraction on tumor-bearing mice models. *Int J Med Mushrooms.*, 2011, 13(5), 427-40.

Maji, PK; Sen, IK; Behera, B; Maiti, TK; Mallick, P; Sikdar, SR; Islam, SS. Structural characterization and study of immunoenhancing properties of a glucan isolated from a hybrid mushroom of *Pleurotus florida* and *Lentinula edodes. Carbohydr Res.*, 2012, 358:110-5.

Mandal, EK; Maity, K; Maity, S; Gantait, SK; Maiti, S; Maiti, TK; Sikdar, SR; Islam, SS. Structural characterization of an immunoenhancing cytotoxic heteroglycan isolated from an edible mushroom *Calocybe indica* var. APK2. *Carbohydr Res.*, 2011, 346(14), 2237-43

Nandi, AK; Samanta, S; Sen, IK; Devi, KS; Maiti, TK; Acharya, K; Islam, SS. Structural elucidation of an immunoenhancing heteroglycan isolated from *Russula albonigra* (Krombh.) Fr. *Carbohydr Polym.*, 2013, 94(2), 918-26.

Nandi, AK; Sen, IK; Samanta, S; Maity, K; Devi, KS; Mukherjee, S; Maiti, TK; Acharya, K; Islam, SS. Glucan from hot aqueous extract of an ectomycorrhizal edible mushroom, *Russula albonigra* (K rombh.) Fr.: structural characterization and study of immunoenhancing properties. *Carbohydr Res.*, 2012, 363, 43-50.

Ng, TB; Ngai, PH; Xia L. An agglutinin with mitogenic and antiproliferative activities from the mushroom Flammulina velutipes. *Mycologia.*, 2006, 98(2), 167-71.

Ngai, PH; Ng, TB. A mushroom (*Ganoderma capense*) lectin with spectacular thermostability, potent mitogenic activity on splenocytes, and antiproliferative activity toward tumor cells. *Biochem Biophys Res Commun.*, 2004, 314(4), 988-93.

Nakajima, A; Ishida, T; Koga, M; Takeuchi, T; Mazda, O; Takeuchi, M. Effect of hot water extract from *Agaricus blazei* Murill on antibody-producing cells in mice. *Int Immunopharmacol.*, 2002, 2(8), 1205-11.

Ooi, LS; Liu, F; Ooi, VE; Ng, TB; Fung, MC. Gene expression of immunomodulatory cytokines induced by *Narcissus tazetta* lectin in the mouse. *Biochem Cell Biol.*, 2002, 80(2), 271-7.

Patra, P; Bhanja, SK; Sen, IK; Nandi, AK; Samanta, S; Das, D; Devi, KS; Maiti, TK; Acharya, K; Islam, SS. Structural and immunological studies of hetero polysaccharide isolated from the alkaline extract of *Tricholoma crassum* (Berk.) Sacc. *Carbohydr Res.*, 2012, 362, 1-7.

Patra, S; Maity, KK; Bhunia, SK; Dey, B; Mandal, S; Maiti, TK; Sikdar, SR; Islam, SS. Structural characterization and study of immunoenhancing properties of heteroglycan isolated from a somatic hybrid mushroom (PfloVv1aFB) of *Pleurotus florida* and *Volvariella volvacea. Carbohydr Res.*, 2011, 346(13), 1967-72.

Qian, ZM; Xu, MF; Tang, PL. Polysaccharide peptide (PSP) restores immunosuppression induced by cyclophosphamide in rats. *Am J Chin Med.*, 1997, 25(1), 27-35.

Ramberg, JE; Nelson, ED; Sinnott, RA. Immunomodulatory dietary polysaccharides: a systematic review of the literature. *Nutr J.*, 2010, 9, 54.

Roy, SK; Das, D; Mondal, S; Maiti, D; Bhunia, B; Maiti, TK; Islam, SS. Structural studies of an immunoenhancing water-soluble glucan isolated from hot water extract of an edible mushroom, *Pleurotus florida*, cultivar Assam Florida. *Carbohydr Res.*, 2009, 344(18), 2596-601.

Samanta, S; Nandi, AK; Sen, IK; Maji, PK; Devi, KS; Maiti, TK; Islam, SS. Structural characterization of an immunoenhancing glucan isolated from a mushroom Macrolepiota dolichaula. *Int J Biol Macromol.*, 2013, 61, 89-96.

Sarangi, I; Ghosh, D; Bhutia, SK; Mallick, SK; Maiti, TK. Anti-tumor and immunomodulating effects of Pleurotus ostreatus mycelia-derived proteoglycans. *Int Immunopharmacol.*, 2006, 6(8), 1287-97.

Sarkar, R; Nandan, CK; Bhunia, SK; Maiti, S; Maiti, TK; Sikdar, SR; Islam, SS. Glucans from alkaline extract of a hybrid mushroom (backcross mating between PfloVv12 and *Volvariella volvacea*), structural characterization and study of immunoenhancing and antioxidant properties. *Carbohydr Res.*, 2012, 347(1), 107-13.

Sedaghat, R; Ghazanfari, T. The immunomodulatory effects of *Pleurotus florida* on cell-mediated immunity and secondary lymphoid tissues in Balb/c mice. *Immunopharmacol Immunotoxicol.*, 2011, 33(1), 28-33.

Sen, IK; Maji, PK; Behera, B; Mallick, P; Maiti, TK; Sikdar, SR; Islam, SS. Structural characterization of an immunoenhancing heteroglycan of a hybrid mushroo m (pfls1h) of *Pleurotus florida* and *Lentinus squarrosulus* (Mont.) *Singer. Carbohydr Res.*, 2013, 371, 45-51.

She, QB; Ng, TB; Liu, WK. A novel lectin with potent immunomodulatory activity isolated from both fruiting bodies and cultured mycelia of the edible mushroom *Volvariella volvacea. Biochem Biophys Res Commun.*, 1998, 247(1), 106-11.

Sheu, F; Chien, PJ; Hsieh, KY; Chin, KL; Huang, WT; Tsao, CY; Chen, YF; Cheng, HC; Chang, HH. Purification, cloning, and functional characterization of a novel immunomodulatory protein from *Antrodia camphorata* (bitter mushroom) that exhibits TLR2-dependent NF-êB activation and M1 polarization within murine macrophages. *J Agric Food Chem.*, 2009, 57(10), 4130-41.

Shimizu, S; Kitada, H; Yokota, H; Yamakawa, J; Murayama, T; Sugiyama, K; Izumi, H; Yamaguchi, N. Activation of the alternative complement pathway by *Agaricus blazei* Murill. *Phytomedicine.*, 2002, 9(6), 536-45.

Su, CF; Kuo, IC; Chen, PW; Huang, CH; Seow, SV; Chua, KY; Yu, SM. Characterization of an immunomodulatory Der p 2-FIP-fve fusion protein produced in transformed rice suspension cell culture. *Transgenic Res.*, 2012, 21(1), 177-92.

Sun, Y; Liang, H; Zhang, X; Tong, H; Liu, J. Structural elucidation and immunological activity of a polysaccharide from the fruiting body of *Armillaria mellea. Bioresour Technol.*, 2009, 100(5), 1860-3.

Tong, MH; Chien, PJ; Chang, HH; Tsai, MJ; Sheu, F. High processing tolerances of immunomodulatory proteins in Enoki and Reishi mushrooms. *J Agric Food Chem.*, 2008, 56(9), 3160-6.

Wang, HX; Liu, WK; Ng, TB; Ooi, VE; Chang, ST. Immunomodulatory and antitumor activities of a polysaccharide-peptide complex from a mycelial culture of *Tricholoma* sp. , a local edible mushroom. *Life Sci.*, 1995, 57(3), 269-81.

Wang, HX; Ng, TB; Ooi, VE; Liu, WK; Chang, ST. A polysaccharide-peptide complex from cultured mycelia of the mushroom *Tricholoma mongolicum* with immunoenhancing and antitumor activities. *Biochem Cell Biol.*, 1996, 74(1), 95-100.

Wang, PH; Hsu, CI; Tang, SC; Huang, YL; Lin, JY; Ko, JL. Fungal immunomodulatory protein from *Flammulina velutipes* induces interferon-gamma production through p38 mitogen-activated protein kinase signaling pathway. *J Agric Food Chem.*, 2004, 52(9), 2721-5.

Wang, Y; Fang, J; Ni, X; Li, J; Liu, Q; Dong, Q; Duan, J; Ding, K. Inducement of Cytokine Release by GFPBW2, a novel polysaccharide from fruit bodies of *Grifola frondosa* , through Dectin-1 in macrophages. *J Agric Food Chem.*, 2013, 61(47), 11400-9.

Wu, MJ; Cheng, TL; Cheng, SY; Lian, TW; Wang, L; Chiou, SY. Immunomodulatory properties of *Grifola frondosa* in submerged culture. *J Agric Food Chem.*, 2006, 54(8), 2906-14.

Xiao, JH; Xiao, DM; Chen, DX; Xiao, Y; Liang, ZQ; Zhong, JJ. Polysaccharides from the medicinal mushroom *Cordyceps taii* show antioxidant and immunoenhancing activities in a D-galactose-induced aging mouse model. *Evid Based Complement Alternat Med.*, 2012, 2012, 273435.

Yamanaka, D; Tada, R; Adachi, Y; Ishibashi, K; Motoi, M; Iwakura, Y; Ohno, N. *Agaricus brasiliensis*-derived β-glucans exert immunoenhancing effects via a dectin-1-dependent pathway. *Int Immunopharmacol.*, 2012, 14(3), 311-9.

Yin, X; You, Q; Jiang, Z. Immunomodulatory activities of different solvent extracts from *Tricholoma matsutake* (S. Ito et S. Imai) singer (higher basidiomycetes) on normal mice. *Int J Med Mushrooms.*, 2012, 14(6), 549-56.

In: Mushrooms
Editor: Grégoire Pesti

ISBN: 978-1-63117-521-3
© 2014 Nova Science Publishers, Inc.

Chapter 6

AN INSIGHT INTO ANTI-DIABETIC EFFECTS OF MUSHROOMS

Bin Du[1,2] and Baojun Xu[2,]*

[1]Hebei Normal University of Science and Technology, Qinhuangdao, Hebei, China
[2]Food Science and Technology Program, Beijing Normal University–Hong Kong Baptist University United International College, Zhuhai, Guangdong, China

ABSTRACT

Mushrooms have been valued as flavorful foods and as medicinal substances. Mushrooms are also recognized as functional foods for their bioactive compounds which offer multiple beneficial impacts on human health. Diabetes mellitus (DM) is a common metabolic disease characterized by high blood glucose levels. It is caused by insulin deficiency or functional disturbance of the receptors, which leads blood glucose to rise and induce metabolization disorders. Natural bioactive compounds, including polysaccharides, proteins, dietary fibres, and many other biomolecules isolated from mushrooms, have been shown to be effective in diabetes treatment as biological anti-hyperglycemic agents.

Over the past decade, numerous studies have demonstrated that mushrooms possess anti-diabetic effects, in particular, blood glucose lowering effect, glucose-stimulated insulin secretion, antioxidant, digestive enzymes (α-amylase and α-glycosidase) inhibitory effects and tyrosine kinase inhibitory effects. This chapter focuses on the anti-diabetic effects of mushrooms in both *in vitro* and *in vivo* studies and potential mechanisms of action. Future prospective for this field of research and the constraints that may affect the development of potential drug products from mushrooms are also reviewed.

---

[*] Author to whom correspondence should be addressed. Full postal address: 28, Jinfeng Road, Tangjiawan, Zhuhai, Guangdong 519085, China. Tel.:+86 756 3620636; fax: +86 756 3620882. E-mail: baojunxu@uic.edu.hk (B.J. Xu).

1. INTRODUCTION

Diabetes mellitus (DM) is a serious chronic disease and is known to relate to complications, such as cardiovascular diseases, hypertension and renal failure (Garduno-Diaz and Khokhar, 2012). It is characterized by an abnormal postprandial increase in blood glucose level, especially in the case of type-2-diabetes (T2D). T2D is a result of chronic insulin resistance (Gilbert and Liu, 2013). According to the WHO (2011), DM accounts for 2.2 % of deaths in the world and is one of the major causes of death among humans, it is estimated that around 300 million or more people will be affected by diabetes by the year 2025 in the world (Jung et al., 2006). The estimated number of diabetic patients in 2030 will be more than double that in 2005 (Gershell, 2005). The most recent data released by the Center for Disease Control and Prevention (CDC) of USA report that diabetes is the seventh leading cause of death in the United States; diabetes affects 25.8 million (8.3 %) of the US population (CDC, 2011). Moreover, DM imposes an increasing economic burden on national health care systems world-widely. According to the International Diabetes Federation, the global health expenditure on diabetes is expected to a total at least USD $490 billion in 2030. Finding cures for diabetes have been a great challenge for scientists throughout this and the previous century (De Silva et al., 2012). However, it has been recognized that T2D is a preventable disease and can be avoided or delayed by lifestyle intervention. Therefore, natural anti-diabetic products from natural produces have attracted a great deal of attention.

Mushrooms have been valued by humankind as an edible and medicinal resource for thousands of years. The number of mushrooms on earth is estimated around 140,000, yet maybe only 10% (approximately 14,000 named species) are known (Wasser, 2002). Mushrooms are believed to have various beneficial pharmacological activities, including anticancer, immuno-modulatory and anti-viral activities (Ren et al., 2012; Roupas et al., 2012).

Mushrooms have been used as an anti-diabetic medicine since ancient time. Of note, recent discoveries have opened up an exciting opportunity for developing new types of therapeutics from mushrooms to control DM and its complications. To date, more and more active components including polysaccharides and polysaccharides-protein complexes, dietary fibers, and other compounds extracted from fruiting bodies, submerged cultured mycelia, or cultured broth of mushrooms have been reported as to having anti-hyperglycemic activity (Lo and Wasser, 2011). Until recently, mushrooms are found to be extremely useful in the prevention of DM due to the presences of polysaccharides and their low glycemic index, and lack of sugar and starch. The polysaccharides (β-glucans) contained in mushrooms, in particular, can restore the functions of pancreatic tissues causing an increase in insulin output by the functional β-cells, thus lowering blood glucose levels. Mushroom polysaccharides have also been shown to have ability in improving the sensitivity of peripheral cells in circulating insulin (Misra et al., 2009; Qiang et al., 2009; Xiao et al., 2011).

On the other hand, some chemical and biochemical anti-diabetic agents are the mainstay in the treatment of DM. However, these anti-diabetic agents may have harmful side-effects, fail to significantly alter the course of diabetic complications and there is insufficient knowledge on the pharmacological management of the disease (Eurich et al., 2007; Anon, 2008; 2009; Liday, 2011; Seino et al., 2012). Expectedly, it is important to identify novel nutraceuticals or drugs for curing or preventing diabetes, which have fewer side-effects.

Table 1. Anti-diabetic effects of different mushrooms

Mushrooms	Activities	Models	References
Catathelasma ventricosum, *Clitocybe maxima*, *Stropharia rugoso-annulata*, *Raterellus cornucopioides*, *Laccaria amethystea*			Liu et al. (2012)
Ganoderma lucidum			Fatmawati et al. (2011)
Ganoderma lucidum			Fatmawati et al. (2013)
Grifola frondosa, *Hericium erinaceum*, *Agaricus blazei*, *Ganoderma lucidum*, *Coriolus versicolor*, *Phellinus linteus*	Anti-diabetic	*In vitro* α-glycosidase inhibition	Su et al. (2013a)
Ganoderma lucidum			Kim and Nho (2004)
Coriolus versicolor			Hsu et al. (2013)
Grifola frondosa			Matsuur et al. (2002) Su et al. (2013b)
Inonotus obliquus			Chen et al. (2010)
Phellinus merrillii			Huang et al. (2011)
Grifola frondosa, *Hericium erinaceum*, *Agaricus blazei*, *Ganoderma lucidum*, *Coriolus versicolor*, *Phellinus linteus*			Su et al. (2013a)
Catathelasma ventricosum, *Clitocybe maxima*, *Stropharia rugoso-annulata*, *Craterellus cornucopioides*, *Laccaria amethystea*	Anti-diabetic	*In vitro* α-amylase inhibition	Liu et al. (2012)
Grifola frondosa			Su et al. (2013b)
Inonotus obliquus			Lu et al. (2010)
Daedalea gibbosa	Anti-diabetic	*In vitro* tyrosine kinase inhibition	Yassin et al. (2008)
Phellinus linteus			Lee et al. (2008)
Phellinus merrillii			Huang et al. (2011)
Ganoderma applanatum	Anti-diabetic	*In vitro* aldose reductase inhibition	Lee et al. (2005)
Ganoderma lucidum			Fatmawati et al. (2010)

Table 1. (Continued)

Mushrooms	Activities	Models	References
Phellinus linteus			Lee et al. (2011)
			Jang et al. (2010)
Lentinus edodes	Anti-diabetic	*In vitro* cells	Yang et al. (2002)
Laetiporus sulphureus var. *miniatus*			Hwang et al. (2008)
Agaricus campestris	Anti-diabetic	Animal models	Gray and Flatt (1998)
			Yamac et al. (2010)
Agaricus bisporus			Jeong et al. (2010)
			Volman et al. (2010)
Agrocybe cylindracea			Kino et al. (1994)
Lentinus edodes			Yang et al. (2002)
Stropharia rugosoannulata			Zhai et al. (2013)
Laetiporus sulphureus var. *miniatus*			Hwang et al. (2010)
Sparassis crispa			Kwon et al. (2009)
Agaricus sylvaticus			Fortes et al. (2008)
Cordyceps sinensis			Guo and Zhang (1995)
Agaricus blazei Murill			Hsu et al. (2007)
Agaricus sylvaticus	Anti-diabetic	Human models	Fortes and Novaes (2011)
Ganoderma lucidum			Gao et al. (2004)
Oyster mushroom			Agrawal et al. (2010)

Most of mushroom extracts that have potential to treat T2D have unfortunately not been studied in depth. In terms of the ongoing active research for novel solutions to the diabetes prevention and treatment, large number of active compounds from mushrooms can potentially provide better glycemic control with no or relatively fewer side-effects. Therefore, an attempt has been made to summarize *in vitro* and *in vivo* studies of anti-diabetic effects of mushrooms. The anti-diabetic effects of different mushrooms were summarized in Table 1.

2. IN VITRO STUDIES IN ANTI-DIABETIC EFFECTS OF MUSHROOMS

2.1. Effects of Mushrooms on Enzymes

Hydrolysis of dietary carbohydrates is the major source of glucose in the blood. This hydrolysis is carried out by a group of hydrolytic enzymes, namely α-amylase and α-glycosidase (Su et al., 2013a).

2.1.1. Effects of Mushrooms on α-Glycosidase
α-Glycosidase, which locates in the brush-border surface membrane of intestinal cells, activates the final step of the digestive process (Lordan et al., 2013). This exo-type

carbohydrase enzyme catalyzes hydrolyses of complex carbohydrates and disaccharides to absorbable monosaccharides (Kim et al., 2010). Any compound that inhibits the activity of α-glycosidase can be proposed as a potential treatment agent for T2D, since it works by preventing the digestion of carbohydrates. Although previous anti-diabetic bio-screening studies have been mainly focused on medicinal plants, recent research on certain fungi have shown promising results on α-glycosidase inhibitory activity. For example, aqueous extracts of wild edible mushrooms such as *Catathelasma ventricosum*, *Clitocybe maxima*, *Stropharia rugoso-annulata*, *Craterellus cornucopioides* and *Laccaria amethystea* revealed potent inhibition of α-glycosidase activity (Liu et al., 2012).

The search for the constituents reducing α-glycosidase activity led to the finding of active compounds in the fruiting body of mushroom *Ganoderma lucidum*. The chloroform extract of the fruiting body of *G. lucidum* was found to show inhibitory activity on α-glycosidase *in vitro*. Lanostane triterpenoid from *G. lucidum*, namely ganoderol B, had high α-glycosidase inhibition with an IC_{50} of 48.5 μg mL^{-1} (119.8 μM) (Fatmawati et al., 2011). A series of lanostane-type triterpenoids, identified as ganoderma alcohols and ganoderma acids, were isolated from the fruiting body of *Ganoderma* lingzhi. This study aimed to explain the structural requirement for α-glycosidase inhibition. The structure-activity studies of ganoderma alcohols showed that the hydroxyl substituent at C-3 and the double-bond moiety at C-24 and C-25 are necessary to increase α-glycosidase inhibitory activity. The structure-activity relationships of ganoderma acids revealed that the hydroxyl substituent at C-11 is an important feature and that the carboxylic group in the side chain is essential for the recognition of α-glycosidase inhibitory activity (Fatmawati et al., 2013).

Su et al. (2013a) examined the inhibitory effects of six medicinal mushrooms (*Grifola frondosa*, *Hericium erinaceum*, *Agaricus blazei*, *G. lucidum*, *Coriolus versicolor* and *Phellinus linteus*) on α-glycosidase related to hyperglycemia. The results showed that the *n*-hexane extract of *G. frondosa* showed the most potent anti-α-glycosidase activity. In addition, this study suggested that oleic acid and linoleic acid could have contribution to the potent anti-α-glycosidase activity of selected medicinal mushrooms. Kim and Nho (2004) found the active compound, designated SKG-3, in a methanol extract of the fruiting body of mushroom *G. lucidum*. It showed very potent inhibitory activity against α-glycosidase with an IC_{50} value of 4.6 μg mL^{-1}.

Three intracellular polysaccharides fractions were extracted, separated, and purified from mycelia of submerged liquid cultured *Coriolus versicolor* LH1. The α-glycosidase inhibitory activity, IC_{50} values, of the three fractions were 1.7, 1.8, and 0.8 mg mL^{-1}, respectively (Hsu et al., 2013). They also found that the α-glycosidase inhibitory properties were related to the presence of α-(1, 4) glycosidic linkages in the polysaccharide structure and the total relative percentages of *D*-glucose and *D*-galactose in the structure of polysaccharides, other than small molecular triterpenoids. Furthermore, α-glycosidase inhibitory activities were found in methanol aqueous extracts of the fruit bodies of *G. frondosa*. The structure of the isolated compound was identified as *D*-(+)-trehalose by field desorption mass spectrometry, and ^{1}H-, ^{13}C-NMR. Trehalose showed 45% inhibitory activity at the concentration of 2×10^{-3} M (Matsuur et al., 2002). Another study examined the inhibitory effects of *G. frondosa* on α-glycosidase related to type-2-diabetes. Results showed that all *G. frondosa* extracts showed strong anti-α-glycosidase activity, in which *n*-hexane (GF-H) extract from *G. frondosa* was noted. The inhibitory kinetics of GF-H on α-glycosidase was a competitive inhibition. GF-H was as good as acarbose (a positive anti-diabetic drug) in inhibiting the starch digestion *in vitro* (Su et al., 2013b). A water-soluble polysaccharide from *Inonotus obliquus* (IOPS) was isolated from mushroom *Inonotus obliquus* (*Fr.*) *Pilat*. The polysaccharide IOPS exhibited an inhibitory activity against α-glycosidase with an IC_{50} value of 93.3 μg mL^{-1} (Chen et al., 2010).

The inhibitory activity of an ethanol extract from fruiting body of mushroom *Phellinus merrillii* was evaluated against α-glycosidase and compared to acarbose as a positive α-glycosidase inhibitor. The ethanol extract of *P. merrillii* showed a strong α-glycosidase inhibitory activity. These findings demonstrated that *P. merrillii* may be a good source for leading compounds as alternatives for anti-diabetic agents currently used (Huang et al., 2011). The importance of finding effective anti-diabetic therapeutics led us to further investigate natural compounds from mushrooms.

2.1.2. Effects of Mushrooms on α-Amylase

Human α-amylase is one of the major secretory products of human pancreas and salivary glands, playing a role in digestion of starch and glycogen (Kandra, 2003). The *in vitro* inhibitory effects of six selected medicinal mushrooms, namely *Grifola frondosa*, *Hericium erinaceum*, *Agaricus blazei*, *Ganoderma lucidum*, *Coriolus versicolor* and *Phellinus linteus* on α-amylase related to hyperglycemia was investigated (Su et al., 2013a). The results showed that the *n*-hexane extract of *Coriolus versicolor* had the strongest anti-α-amylase activity (IC_{50}: 1.20 mg mL^{-1}). The chemical composition and anti-hyperglycemic activity of five wild edible mushrooms (*Clitocybe maxima*, *Catathelasma ventricosum*, *Stropharia rugoso-annulata*, *Craterellus cornucopioides* and *Laccaria amethystea*) from Southwest China were evaluated. The aqueous extract of *L. amethystea* showed the highest α-amylase inhibitory activity (IC_{50} value 4.37 μg mL^{-1}) (Liu et al., 2012). Su et al., (2013b) examined the inhibitory effects of *Grifola frondosa* on α-amylase related to T2D. Results showed that all *G. frondosa* extracts exhibited weak anti-α-amylase activity. In addition, Lu et al. (2010) investigated the effects of ethyl acetate fraction from *Inonotus obliquus* (EAIO) on hyperglycemia. Five compounds were isolated from EAIO and identified as lanosterol (1), 3-beta-hydroxy-lanosta -8,24-diene-21-al (2), inotodiol (3), ergosterol peroxide (4) and trametenolic acid (5) by spectral methods. Inotodiol and trametenolic acid were found to have inhibitory effects on α-amylase activity.

2.1.3. Effects of Mushrooms on Tyrosine Kinase

Signaling through receptor tyrosine kinase is a major mechanism for intercellular communication during development and in the adult organism, as well as in disease-associated processes.

Metabolic insulin signal transduction occurs through activation of insulin receptor, including auto-phosphorylation of tyrosine residues in the insulin-receptor activation loop (Saltiel and Pessin, 2002). This leads to recruitment of insulin-receptor substrate proteins, followed by activation of phosphatidylinositol 3-kinase and downstream protein kinase B, and activation and subsequent translocation of the glucose transporter (Bryant et al., 2002; Smith et al., 2002).

This process is negatively regulated by protein tyrosine phosphatases, and is a general mechanism for down-regulation of receptor tyrosine kinase activity (Ostman et al., 2001). Yassin et al. (2008) isolated an active fraction from mycelium organic extracts of *Daedalea gibbosa*, which inhibited *in vitro* kinase activity of recombinant Abl.

2.1.4. Effects of Mushrooms on Aldose Reductase

Aldose reductase (AR) (E.C.1.1.1.21) is the first enzyme in the polyol pathway; it catalyzes the reduction of the aldehyde functionality of D-glucose to form D-sorbitol with concomitant conversion of NADPH to $NADP^+$ (Lee, 2002). Some complications of diabetes, such as the elevated blood glucose levels, characteristic of diabetes mellitus, cause a significant flux of glucose through the polyol pathway in tissues such as nerves, retina, lens, and kidney, where glucose uptake is independent of insulin (Kato et al., 2008). Thus, AR inhibitor is an attractive pharmacological target for the treatment of diabetic complications.

In an effort to characterize active principles for diabetic complication from medicinal mushroom, aldose reductase inhibitors were isolated from the fruiting body of *Phellinus linteus*. The findings indicated that davallialactone, hypholomine B and ellagic acid exhibited potent rat lens aldose reductase and human recombinant aldose reductase inhibitory activity with IC_{50} values of 0.33, 0.82, 0.63 μM and 0.56, 1.28, 1.37 μM, respectively (Lee et al., 2008). Moreover, the inhibitory activity from the isolated component from the fruiting body of mushroom *P. merrillii* was evaluated against lens aldose reductase from Sprague-Dawley male rats and compared to quercetin as an aldose reductase positive inhibitor. The ethanol extracts of *P. merrillii* (EPM) showed the strong aldose reductase activities. Aldose reductase inhibitors were isolated from ethyl acetate-soluble fractions of EPM and identified as hispidin, hispolon, and inotilone. Among them, hispidin, hispolon, and inotilone exhibited potent aldose reductase inhibitory activity with IC_{50} values of 48.26, 9.47, and 15.37 μg mL^{-1}, respectively (Huang et al., 2011). Lee et al. (2005) isolated rat lens aldose reductase (RLAR) inhibitors from the fruiting bodies of mushroom *Ganoderma applanatum*. The methanol extract and ethyl acetate fraction were found to own potent RLAR inhibitory effect *in vitro*, their IC_{50} were 1.7 and 0.8 μg mL^{-1}, respectively. From the active ethyl acetate fraction, protocatechualdehyde was found to be the most potent RLAR inhibitor ($IC_{50} = 0.7$ μg mL^{-1}), and may be useful for prevention and treatment of diabetic complications.

Ganoderic acid Df, a new lanostane-type triterpenoid, was isolated from the fruiting body of *G. lucidum*. This compound exhibited potent human aldose reductase inhibitory activity, with an IC_{50} of 22.8 μM *in vitro* (Fatmawati et al., 2010).

2.2. Effects of Mushrooms on Cultured Animal Cells

T2D is a result of loss of pancreatic islet β-cell mass and function. Strategies to preserve β-cell mass and a greater understanding of the mechanisms underlying β-cell turnover are needed to prevent and treat this devastating disease.

Reactive oxygen species (ROS) are associated with tissue damage and are considered to be prime contributing factors in inflammation, diabetes, aging, and cancer. In a study, Lee et al. (2011) investigated whether or not hispidin protects pancreatic MIN6N β-cells from oxidative stress caused by hydrogen peroxide. Pretreatment of MIN6N β-cells with hispidin for 24 hours reduced the loss of cell viability and decreased the number of apoptotic cells. The results suggested that hispidin might be effective for protecting MIN6N β-cells from ROS toxicity in diabetes. Jang et al. (2010) examined the anti-diabetic efficacy of *Phellinus linteus*. Hispidin from *P. linteus* was shown to inhibit hydrogen peroxide-induced apoptosis and increased insulin secretion in hydrogen peroxide-induced cells. These results showed that hispidin might act as an anti-diabetic agent and that this property occurred through preventing β-cells from the toxic action of ROS in diabetes.

The hypoglycemic effect of an exo-polymer (a kind of glycoprotein containing 83.5% carbohydrate and 16.5% protein) produced from a submerged mycelial culture of *Lentinus edodes* was investigated (Yang et al., 2002). It concluded that exo-polymer of *L. edodes* could probably repair the damage of pancreatic β-cells to some extent, promoted insulin synthesis and thus lowered the level of plasma glucose.

Hwang et al. (2008) found the optimum culture conditions for the production of extracellular polysaccharides (EPS) in submerged culture of an edible mushroom *Laetiporus sulphureus* var. *miniatus* and their stimulatory effects on insulinoma cell (RINm5F) proliferation and insulin secretion. The EPS were proved to be glucose-rich polysaccharides and were able to increase proliferation and insulin secretory function of rat insulinoma RINm5F cells in a dose-dependent manner. In addition, EPS also strikingly reduced the streptozotocin (STZ)-induced apoptosis in RINm5F cells indicating the mode of the cytoprotective role of EPS on RINm5F cells.

3. Animal Studies in Anti-Diabetic Effects of Mushrooms

A large number of animal studies, in both normal and diabetic animal models, have confirmed the hypoglycaemic effects of mushrooms and mushroom components. The hypoglycaemic effects appear to be mediated via mushroom polysaccharides (possibly both α- and β-glucans) via a direct interaction with insulin receptors on target tissues.

3.1. The Blood Glucose Control

Diabetes is a condition frequently controlled by proper dietary management. Studies have indicated that increased dairy intake may reduce risk of T2D, overweight and insulin resistance syndrome (Liu et al., 2006). Recent studies have indicated that a low glycemic index of food has a significant influence on blood glucose levels. The incidence of DM and its chronic complications have been on the increase for decades. Recently, many evidences have supported that chronic diabetic complications can be prevented through controlling blood glucose strictly (Kwon et al., 2004). The administration of mushroom *Agaricus campestris* in the diet (62.5 g kg^{-1}) and drinking water (2.5 g L^{-1}) countered the hyperglycaemia of STZ-induced diabetic mice. An aqueous extract from this mushroom (1 mg mL^{-1}) stimulated 2-deoxyglucose transport (2.0-fold), glucose oxidation (1.5-fold) and incorporation of glucose into glycogen (1.8-fold) in mouse abdominal muscle. The results demonstrated the presence of anti-hyperglycemic, insulin-releasing and insulin-like activity of *A. campestris* (Gray and Flatt, 1998). Another study indicated that extracts from *Agaricus bisporus* might result in decreased severity of STZ-induced diabetes in rats with considerable protective effects on the pancreas and apparent repopulation of β-cells (Yamac et al., 2010). The serum glucose levels significantly decreased by 29.7% after oral administration with *A. bisporus* extract at the dose of 400 mg kg^{-1} body weight per day. Furthermore, the serum insulin levels in the STZ-induced diabetic rats were increased to 78.5% at the administration dose of 400 mg kg^{-1} body weight per day. Moreover, diabetic rats fed with of fruiting bodies *Agaricus bisporus* exhibited significant anti-glycemic and anti-hypercholesterolemic effects (Jeong et al., 2010; Volman et al., 2010).

Cholesterol directly effects β-cells metabolism and opens a novel set of mechanisms that may contribute to β-cells dysfunction and the onset of diabetes (Hao et al., 2007). A glucan isolated from a hot-water extract of the fruiting bodies of *Agrocybe cylindracea* showed a remarkable hypoglycemic activity in both normal and STZ-induced diabetic mice (Kino et al., 1994). Yang et al. (2002) found the hypoglycemic effect of an exo-polymer produced from a submerged mycelial culture of *Lentinus edodes* in STZ-induced diabetic rats. The administration of the exo-polymer (200 mg kg^{-1} body weight) reduced the plasma glucose level by as much as 21.5% as compared to the control group. This exo-polymer also lowered the total cholesterol and triglyceride levels in plasma by 25.1% and 44.5%. The hypoglycemic effect of extracellular polysaccharide produced by *Stropharia rugosoannulata* was investigated in STZ-induced diabetic rats, the polysaccharide decreased in the plasma concentrations of glucose (37%), total cholesterol (26%), and triacylglycerol (24%) (Zhai et al., 2013).

Hypoglycemic effect of crude EPS extracted from submerged mycelial culture of an edible mushroom *Laetiporus sulphureus* var. *miniatus* was evaluated in streptozptocin-induced diabetic rats and its possible mechanism was suggested by western blot analysis and immuno-histchemical staining. The results revealed that orally administrated EPS, when given 48 hr after STZ treatment, lowered the average plasma glucose level in EPS-fed rats to 43.5% of STZ-treated rats (Hwang et al., 2010).

3.2. The Impaired Wound Healing

The impaired wound healing in DM is a major clinical problem. Kwon et al. (2009) investigated whether oral administration of mushroom *Sparassis crispa* (SC) could improve the impaired wound healing in diabetic rats. The results indicated that SC could improve the impaired healing of diabetic wounds. Wound closure was significantly accelerated by oral administration of SC. Furthermore, there were significant increases in macrophage and fibroblast migration, collagen regeneration, and epithelialization in SC-treated wounds compared with the control group.

4. HUMAN STUDIES IN ANTI-DIABETIC EFFECTS OF MUSHROOMS

A new area of research focused on the prevalence of depression in diabetic patients. A small human trial has suggested a positive effect of mushrooms on insulin resistance and therefore potentially a positive effect in the treatment of T2D. Fortes et al. (2008) evaluated the effects of dietary supplementation with medicinal fungus *Agaricus sylvaticus* in fasting glycemia of post-surgery patients with colorectal cancer. The results suggested that the dietary supplementation with medicinal fungus *A. sylvaticus* could significantly reduce fasting glycemia levels of colorectal cancer patients in post-surgery phase. In a randomized controlled trial, 95% patients treated with 3 g per day of *Cordyceps sinensis* (caterpillar fungus) showed a decrease in their blood glucose levels, while the control group showed only 54% improvement with treatment by other methods (Guo and Zhang, 1995).

Moreover, a randomized, double-blind, placebo-controlled clinical trial to *Agaricus blazei* Murill (ABM) showed that supplement of ABM extract improved insulin resistance among subjects with T2D (Hsu et al., 2007). The increase in adiponectin concentration after taking ABM extract for 12 weeks might be the mechanism that brought the beneficial effect. Opposite results were found in another study, where a significant reduction of fasting glycemia was observed in the *Agaricus sylvaticus* group after six months of supplementation for patients with colorectal cancer (Fortes and Novaes, 2011). Since animal studies have demonstrated that the polysaccharide fractions of *Ganoderma lucidum* (lingzhi, reishi mushroom) have potential hypoglycemic and hypolipidemic activities, Gao et al. (2004) further evaluated the efficacy and safety of ganopoly (polysaccharide fractions extracted from *G. lucidum* by patented technique) in 71 patients with confirmed T2D. The results concluded that the treatment of ganopoly significantly decreased the mean glycosylated hemoglobin (HbA1c) from 8.4% at baseline to 7.6% at 12 weeks. Significant changes in mean fasting plasma glucose and post-challenge plasma glucose levels at the last visit paralleled the changes in mean HbA1c levels. A randomized double blind study with history and clinical examinations was carried out for suitable inclusion criteria. In this study, a total of 150 newly onset type 2 diabetic patients were recruited. Agrawal et al. (2010) demonstrated a significant association between oyster mushroom supplementation and gradual reduction in hyperglycemia in T2D subjects.

CONCLUSION AND FUTURE PROSPECTIVES

Despite the increasing number of studies on the anti-diabetic activities of mushrooms, studies on their active components and mechanisms of action remain limited. Furthermore, specific recommendations and standards for the use of mushrooms in treating diabetes are lacking, which is mainly due to insufficient data concerning the efficacy of individual mushroom species and their products on diabetes. Therefore, much research is needed on mushrooms, particularly in the topics which are proving to support numerous undescribed and un-tapped mushroom species.

On the other hand, in order to achieve a good control in diabetic patients, intimate doctor–patient relationship and individualized care and education are essential. And this relationship and care system for the patients with diabetes should be lifelong and consistent. To maintain normal range of blood glucose and prevent diabetic complications, patients ought to contact more frequently with their health care providers, but this will in turn increase health care expenditure.

Overall, as scientific technologies have been developed and the pathological pathways of DM discovered. Specific research can be done to identify the active constitutions from mushrooms for the anti-diabetic activity and explore the possible mechanisms of action. These studies will significantly facilitate research to discover novel anti-diabetic drugs from medicinal and edible mushrooms leads by using medicinal chemistry approaches and to develop their mechanistic functions through pharmacological studies.

REFERENCES

Agrawal, R. P., Chopra, A., Lavekar, G. S., Padhi, M. M., Srikanth, N., Ota, S., & Jain, S. (2010). Effect of oyster mushroom on glycemia, lipid profile and quality of life in type 2 diabetic patients. *Australian Journal of Medical Herbalism*, *22*, 50-54.

Anon. (2008). Canadian Diabetes Association 2008 clinical practice guidelines for the prevention and management of diabetes in Canada. *Canadian Journal of Diabetes*, *32*, S1-S201.

Anon. (2009). A randomized trial of therapies for type 2 diabetes and coronary artery disease. *New England Journal of Medicine*, *360*, 2503-2515.

Bryant, N. J., Govers, R. & James, D. E. (2002). Regulated transport of the glucose transporter GLUT4. *Nature Reviews Molecular Cell Biology*, *3*, 267-277.

Chen, H. X., Lu, X. M., Qu, Z. S., Wang, Z. S., & Zhang, L. P. (2010). Glycosidase inhibitory activity and antioxidant properties of a polysaccharide from mushroom *Inonotus obliquus*. *Journal of Food Biochemistry*, *34*, 178-191.

CDC Centers for Disease Control and Prevention. (2011). *Diabetes successes and opportunities for population-based prevention and control; at a glance 2011.* http://www.cdc.gov/chronicdisease/resources/publications/aag/ddt.htm.

De Silva, D. D., Rapior, S., Hyde, D. K., & Bahkali, A. H. (2012). Medicinal mushrooms in prevention and control of diabetes mellitus. *Fungal Diversity*. *56*, 1-29.

Eurich, D. T., McAlister, F. A., Blackburn, D. F., Majumdar, S. R., Tsuyuki, R. T., Varney, J., & Johnson, J. A. (2007). Benefits and harms of antidiabetic agents in patients with diabetes and heart failure: systematic review. *British Medical Journal*, *335*, 497.

Fatmawati, S., Shimizu, K., & Kondo, R. (2011). Ganoderol B: A potent α-glycosidase inhibitor isolated from the fruiting body of *Ganoderma lucidum*. *Phytomedicine*, *18*, 1053-1055.

Fatmawati, S., Kondo, R., & Shimizu, K. (2013). Structure-activity relationships of lanostane-type triterpenoids from Ganoderma lingzhi as α-glycosidase inhibitors. *Bioorganis & Medicinal Chemistry Letters*, *23*, 5900-5903.

Fatmawati, S., Shimizu, K., & Kondo, R. (2010). Ganoderic acid Df, a new triterpenoid with aldose reductase inhibitory activity from the fruiting body of *Ganoderma lucidum*, *Fitoterapia*, *81*, 1033-1036.

Fortes, R. C., Recôva, V. L., Melo, A. L., & Novaes, M. R. C. G. (2008). Effects of dietary supplementation with medicinal fungus in fasting glycemia levels of patients with colorectal cancer: A randomized, double-blind, placebo-controlled clinical study. *Nutricion Hospitalaria*, *23*, 591-598.

Fortes, R. C., & Novaes, M. R. C. G. (2011). The effects of *Agaricus sylvaticus* fungi dietary supplementation on the metabolism and blood pressure of patients with colorectal cancer during post surgical phase. *Nutricion Hospitalaria*, *26*, 176-186.

Gao, Y., Lan, J., Dai, X., Ye, J., & Zhou, S. (2004). A phase I/II study of Ling Zhi mushroom *Ganoderma lucidum* (W. Curt.: Fr.) Lloyd (*Aphyllophoromyceticeae*) extract in patients with type II diabetes mellitus. *International Journal of Medicinal Mushrooms*, *6*, 33-39.

Garduno-Diaz, S. D., & Khokhar, S. (2012). Prevalence, risk factors and complications associated with type 2 diabetes in migrant South Asians. *Diabetes/Metabolism Research and Reviews*, *28*, 6-24.

Gershell, L. (2005).Type 2 diabetes market. *Nature Reviews Drug Discovery, 4*, 367-368.

Gilbert, E. R., & Liu, D. M. (2013). Anti-diabetic functions of soy isoflavone genistein: Mechanisms underlying its effects on pancreatic β-cell function. *Food & Function, 4*, 200-212.

Gray, A. M., & Flatt, P. R. (1998). Insulin-releasing and insulin-like activity of *Agaricus campestris* (mushroom). *Journal of Endocrinology, 157*, 259-266.

Guo, Q. C., & Zhang, C. (1995). Clinical observations of adjunctive treatment of 20 diabetic patients with JinShuiBao capsule. *Journal of Administration Traditional Chinese Medicine, 5*, 22.

Hao, M., Head, W. S., Gunawardana, S. C., Hasty, A. H., & Piston, D. W. (2007). Direct effect of cholesterol on insulin secretion; a novel mechanism for pancreatic β-cell dysfunction. *Diabetes, 56*, 2328-2338.

Hsu, C. H., Liao, Y. L., Lin, S. C., Hwang, K. C., & Chou, P. (2007). The mushroom *Agaricus blazei* Murill in combination with metformin and gliclazide improves insulin resistance in type 2 diabetes: A randomized, double-blinded, and placebo-controlled clinical trial. *The Journal of Alternative and Complementary Medicine, 13*, 97-102.

Hsu, W. K., Hsu, T. H., Lin, F. Y., Cheng, Y. K., & Yang, J. P. W. (2013). Separation, purification, and α-glycosidase inhibition of polysaccharides from *Coriolus versicolor* LH1 mycelia. *Carbohydrate Polymers, 92*, 297-306.

Huang, G. J., Hsieh, W. T., Chang, H. Y., Huang, S. S., Lin, Y. C., & Kuo, Y. H. (2011). α-Glycosidase and aldose reductase inhibitory activities from the fruiting body of *Phellinus merrillii. Journal of Agricultural and Food Chemistry, 59*, 5702-5706.

Hwang, H. S., Lee, S. H., Baek, Y. M., Kim, S. W., Jeong, Y. K., & Yun, J. W. (2008). Production of extracellular polysaccharides by submerged mycelial culture of *Laetiporus sulphureus* var. *miniatus* and their insulinotropic properties. *Applied Microbiology and Biotechnology, 78*, 419-429.

Hwang, H. S., & Yun, J. W. (2010). Hypoglycemic effect of polysaccharides produced by submerged mycelial culture of *laetiporus sulphureus* on streptozotocin-induced diabetic rats. *Biotechnology and Bioprocess Engineering, 15*, 173-181.

Jang, J. S., Lee, J. S., Lee, J. H., Kwon, D. S., Lee, K. E., Lee, S. Y., & Hong, E. K. (2010). Hispidin produced from *Phellinus linteus* protects pancreatic β-cells from damage by hydrogen peroxide. *Archives of Pharmacal Research, 33*, 853-861.

Jung, M., Park, M., Lee, H. C., Kang, Y. H., Kang, E. S., & Kim, S. K. (2006). Antidiabetic agents from medicinal plants. *Current Medicinal Chemistry, 13*, 1203-1218.

Jeong, S. C., Jeong, Y. T., Yang, B. K., Islam, R., Koyyalamudi, S. R., Pang, G., Cho, K. Y., & Song, C. H. (2010). White button mushroom (*Agaricus bisporus*) lowers blood glucose and cholesterol levels in diabetic and hypercholesterolemic rats. *Nutrition Research, 30*, 49-56.

Kandra, L. (2003). α-Amylase of medical and industrial importance. *Journal of Molecular Structure: THEOCHEM, 666-667*, 487-498.

Kato, A., Minoshima, Y., Yamamoto, J., Adachi, I., Watson, A. A., & Nash, R. J. (2008). Protective effects of dietary chamomile tea on diabetic complications. *Journal of Agricultural and Food Chemistry, 56*, 8206-8211.

Kim, K. Y., Nguyen, T. H., Kurihara, H., & Kim, S. M. (2010). α-Glycosidase inhibitory activity of bromophenol purified from the red algae *Polyopes lancifolia. Journal of Food Science, 75*, H145-H150.

Kim, S. D., & Nho, H. J. (2004). Isolation and characterization of α-glycosidase inhibitor from the fungus *Ganoderma lucidum*. *The Journal of Microbiology, 42*, 223-227.

Kiho, T., Sobue, S., & Ukai, S. (1994). Structural features and hypoglycemic activities of two polysaccharides from a hot-water extract of *Agrocybe cylindracea*. *Carbohydrate Research, 251*, 81-87.

Kwon, A. H., Qiu, Z., Hashimoto, M., Yamamoto, K., & Kimura, T. (2008). Effects of medicinal mushroom (*Sparassis crispa*) on wound healing in streptozotocin- induced diabetic rats. *American Journal of Surgery, 197*, 503-509.

Kwon, H. S., Cho, J. H., Kim, H. S., Lee, J. H., Song, B. R., Oh, J. A., Han, J. H., Kim, H. S., Cha, B. Y., Lee, K. W., Son, H. Y., Kang, S. K., Lee, W. C., & Yoon, K. H. (2004). Development of web-based diabetic patient management system using short message service (SMS). *Diabetes Research and Clinical Practice, 66S*, S133-S137.

Lee, H. S. (2002). Rat lens aldose reductase inhibitory activities of *Coptis japonica* root-derived isoquinoline alkaloids. *Journal of Agricultural and Food Chemistry, 50*, 7013-7016.

Lee, J. H., Lee, J. S., Kim, Y. R, Jung, W. C., Lee, K. E., Lee, S. Y., & Hong, E. K. (2011). Hispidin isolated from *Phellinus linteus* protects against hydrogen peroxide-induced oxidative stress in pancreatic MIN6N *β*-cells. *Journal of Medicinal Food, 14*, 1431-1438.

Lee, S., Shim, S. H., Kim, J. S., Shin, K. H., & Kang, S. S. (2005). Aldose reductase inhibitors from the fruiting bodies of *Ganoderma applanatum*. *Biological & Pharmaceutical Bulletin, 28*, 1103-1105.

Lee, Y. S., Kang, Y. H., Jung, J. Y., Kang, I. J., Han, S. N., Chung, J. S., Shin, H. K., & Lim, S. S. (2008). Inhibitory constituents of aldose reductase in the fruiting body of *Phellinus linteus*. *Biological & Pharmaceutical Bulletin, 31*, 765-768.

Liday, C. (2011). Overview of the guidelines and evidence for the pharmacologic management of type 2 diabetes mellitus. *Pharmacotherapy, 31*, 37S-43S.

Liu, S., Choi, H. K., Ford, E., Song, Y., Klevak, A., Buring, J. E., & Manson, J. E. (2006). A prospective study of dairy intake and the risk of type 2 diabetes in women. *Diabetes Care, 29*, 1579-1584.

Liu, Y. T., Sun, J., Luo, Z. Y., Rao, S. Q., Su, Y. J., Xu R. R., & Yang, Y. J. (2012) Chemical composition of five wild edible mushrooms collected from Southwest China and their antihyperglycemic and antioxidant activity. *Food and Chemical Toxicology, 50*, 1238-1244.

Lo, H. C., & Wasser, S. P. (2011). Medicinal mushrooms for glycemic control in diabetes mellitus: History, current status, future perspectives, and unsolved problems (review). *International Journal of Medicinal Mushrooms, 13*, 401-426.

Lordan, S., Smyth, T. J., Soler-vila, A., Stanton, C., & Ross, R. P. (2013). The α-amylase and α-glycosidase inhibitory effects of Irish seaweed extracts. *Food Chemistry, 141*, 2170-2176.

Lu, X., Chen, H., Dong, P., Fu, L., & Zhang, X. (2010). Phytochemical characteristics and hypoglycaemic activity of fraction from mushroom *Inonotus obliquus*. *Journal of the Science of Food and Agriculture, 90*, 276-80.

Matsuur, H., Asakawa, C., Kurimoto, M., & Mizutani, J. (2002). Alpha-glycosidase inhibitor from the seeds of balsam pear (*Momordica charantia*) and the fruit bodies of *Grifola frondosa*. *Bioscience, Biotechnology, and Biochemistry, 66*, 1576-1578.

Misra, A., Lalan, M. S., Singh, V. K., & Govil, J. N. (2009). Role of natural polysaccharides in treatment and control of diabetes. Chemistry and medicinal value book series. *Recent Progress in Medicinal Plants 25*, 347-373.

Ostman, A., & Bohmer, F. D. (2001). Regulation of receptor tyrosine kinase signaling by protein tyrosine phosphatases. *Trends in Cell Biology, 11*, 258-266

Ren, L., Perera, C., & Hemar, Y. (2012). Antitumor activity of mushroom polysaccharides: A review. *Food & Function, 3*, 1118-1130.

Roupas, P., Keogh, J., Noakes, M., Margetts, C., & Taylor, P. (2012). The role of edible mushrooms in health: Evaluation of the evidence. *Journal of Functional Foods, 4*, 687-709.

Saltiel, A. R., & Pessin, J. E. (2002). Insulin signaling pathways in time and space. *Trends in Cell Biology, 12*, 65-71

Seino, S., Takahashi, H., Takahashi, T., & Shibasaki, T. (2012). Treating diabetes today: A matter of selectivity of sulphonylureas. *Diabetes, Obesity and Metabolism, 14*, 9-13.

Smith, U. (2002). Impaired ('diabetic') insulin signaling and action occur in fat cells long before glucose intolerance — is insulin resistance initiated in the adipose tissue? *International Journal of Obesity and Related Metabolic Disorders, 26*, 897-904

Su, C. H., Lai, M. N., & Ng, L. T. (2013a). Inhibitory effects of medicinal mushrooms on α-amylase and α-glycosidase – enzymes related to hyperglycemia. *Food & Function, 4*, 644-649.

Su, C. H., Lu, T. M., Lai, M. N., & Ng, L. T. (2013b). Inhibitory potential of *Grifola frondosa* bioactive fractions on α-amylase and α-glycosidase for management of hyperglycemia. *Biotechnology and Applied Biochemistry, 60*, 446-452.

Volman, J. J., Mensink, R. P., & van Griensven, L. J. (2010). Effects of alpha-glucans from *Agaricus bisporus*) on ex vivo cytokine production by LPS and PHA- stimulated PBMCs; a placebo-controlled study in slightly hypercholesterotemic subjects. *European Journal of Clinical Nutrition, 64*, 720-726.

Wasser, S. P. (2002). Medicinal mushrooms as a source of antitumor and immunomodulating polysaccharides. *Applied Microbiology and Biotechnology, 60*, 258-274.

WHO. (2011). World Health Organization. Diabetes program http://www.who.int/mediacentre/factsheets/fs312/en/.

Xiao, C., Wu, Q. P., Tan, J. B., Cai, W., Yang, X. B., & Zhang, J. M. (2011). Inhibitory effects on alpha-glycosidase and hypoglycemic effects of the crude polysaccharides isolated from 11 edible fungi. *Journal of Medicinal Plants Research, 5*, 6963-6967.

Xu, Q., Chao, Y. L., & Wang, Q. B. (2009) Health benefit application of functional oligosaccharides. *Carbohydrate Polymers, 77*, 435-441.

Yamac, M., Kanbak, G., Zeytinoglu, M., Senturk, H., Bayramoglu, G., Dokumacioglu, A., & van Griensven, L. J. L. D. (2010). Pancreas protective effect of button mushroom *Agaricus bisporus* (J.E. Lange) Imbach (*Agaricomycetidae*) extract on rats with streptozotocin-induced diabetes. *International Journal of Medicinal Mushrooms, 124*, 379-389.

Yang, B. K., Kim, D. H., Jeong, S. C., Das, S., Choi, Y. S., Shin, J. S., Lee, S. C., & Song, C. H. (2002). Hypoglycemic effect of a *Lentinus edodes* exo-polymer produced from a submerged mycelial culture. *Bioscience, Biotechnology, and Biochemistry, 66*, 937-942.

Yassin, M., Wasser, S. P., & Mahajna, J. (2008). Substances from the medicinal mushroom *Daedalea gibbosa* inhibit kinase activity of native and T315I mutated Bcr-Abl. *International Journal of Oncology, 32*, 1197-204.

Zhai, X. H., Zhao, A. J., Geng, L. J., & Xu, C. P. (2013). Fermentation characteristics and hypoglycemic activity of an exopolysaccharide produced by submerged culture of *Stropharia rugosoannulata #2. Annals of Microbiology, 63*, 1013-1020.

In: Mushrooms
Editor: Grégoire Pesti

ISBN: 978-1-63117-521-3
© 2014 Nova Science Publishers, Inc.

Chapter 7

PROTECTIVE EFFECTS OF MUSHROOMS AGAINST TISSUE DAMAGE WITH EMPHASIS ON NEUROPROTECTIVE, HEPATOPROTECTIVE AND RADIOPROTECTIVE ACTIVITIES

Tzi Bun Ng[*] and Charlene Cheuk Wing Ng
School of Biomedical Sciences, Faculty of Medicine,
The Chinese University of Hong Kong, Shatin, New Territories,
Hong Kong, China

ABSTRACT

Many mushrooms protect against damage induced by noxious chemicals and organisms. *Agaricus bisporus, Agaricus blazei, Antrodia cinnamomea, Coprinus comatus, Ganoderma. lucidum, Ganoderma tsugae, Inonotus xeranticus, Lentinus edodes, Morchella esculenta, Panellus serotinus, Panus giganteus, Pholiota dinghuensis, Pleurotus cornucopiae, Pleurotus florida, Pleurotus ostreatus* and *Tremella mesenterica* had hepatoprotective effects. *Pleurotus porrigens* offered protection against gentamicin-induced nephrotoxicity. *Antrodia camphorata, Cordyceps sinensis Cordyceps militaris Dictyophora indusiata, Ganoderma. lucidum, Grifola frondosa, Inonotus obliquus, Paxillus curtisii, Paxillus panuoides, Phellinus linteus* and *Phellinus rimosus* exhibited neuroprotective effects. *Hericium erinaceus* has neurotrophic effect. *Ganoderma. lucidum* exhibited cardioprotective effect. *Agaricus brasiliensis* protected against pulmonary inflammation. *Grifola frondosa Lactarius deterrimus* and *Castanea sativa*: demonstrated protective effects on pancreatic β-cells. *Hericium erinaceus* protected against *Salmonella typhimurium. Ganoderma lucidum* had protective effects against malaria. *Pleurotus ostreatus laccase* manifested protection against hepatitis C virus. *Phellinus baumii* offers protection against bovine collagen type II induced arthritis. *Hohenbuehelia serotina, Phellinus rimosus* and *Tremella mesenterica* displayed radioprotective effects.

---

[*] Corresponding author: School of Biomedical Sciences, Faculty of Medicine, The Chinese University of Hong Kong, Shatin, New Territories, Hong Kong, China. Email: b021770@mailserv.cuhk.edu.hk.

INTRODUCTION

Mushrooms have a repertoire of health promoting activities encompassing antioxidant, free radical scavenging, anti-inflammatory, antibacterial, antifungal, antiviral, anti-parasitic, antihypercholesterolemic, antiatherogenic, antiallergic, antidiabetic, anticancer, immunomodulatory, hepatoprotective, and detoxifying actions (Lindequist et al., 2005; Wasser, 2011; Chang and Wasser, 2012; Petrova, 2012). Some mushroom polysaccharides have gone through phases 1 to 3 required of clinical trials and are used in the Orient as therapeutic agents for cancer and other ailments as well as health supplements (Chang and Wasser, 2012). Low-molecular-weight substances derived from mushrooms have been demonstrated to interact with intracellular signaling pathways involved in cell differentiation and survival, apoptosis, cancer progression, angiogenesis, metastasis, and inflammation etc. (Petrova, 2012).The literature on health-promoting biomolecules present in mushrooms is voluminous. The present review aims to cover mushroom extracts and biomolecules with protective actions on various organs in the body. The bulk of the investigations was conducted on laboratory animals but it is highly likely that the results can be extrapolated to humans.

Agaricus Bisporus: Protective against Hepatic Steatosis

Dietary intake of *A. bisporus* protected against hepatic steatosis, lowered liver weight, fat accumulation and markers of liver damage, improved glucose clearance ability, and down-regulated genes encoding fatty acid synthetase and fatty acid elongase 6 in ovariectomized mice (a model of postmenopausal women). In HepG2 cells, *A. bisporus* extract down-regulated the expression of FAS and ELOVL6 through inhibition of Liver X receptor (LXR) signaling and its downstream transcriptional factor SREBP1c (Kanaya et al., 2011).

Agaricus Blazei Aqueous Extract: Hepatoprotective Effect

After diethylnitrosamine treatment, alanine transaminase levels, proliferating cell nuclear antigen labeling index, and the number of glutathione S-transferase placental form positive hepatocytes were lower in rats that received *A. blazei* treatment for 2 weeks and were exposed to a single intraperitoneal injection of 100 mg diethylnitrosamine/kg body weight., indicating a hepatoprotective effect of *A. blazei* (Barbisan et al., 2002). Both a low oral dose (0.2g per kg body weight) and a high oral dose (2g per kg body eight) of *A. blazei* extract reduced activities of aspartate and alanine aminotransferases, hepatic necrosis and fibrosis caused by intraperitoneal injections of carbon tetrachloride twice weekly in mice (Chang et al., 2011).

The activities of various enzymes (aspartate and alanine aminotransferases, glutathione reductase, lactate dehydrogenase), and concentrations of non-enzymatic antioxidants (vitamin C, vitamin E, reduced glutathione) underwent a decline and level of lipid peroxidation (indicated by malondialdehyde) was elevated subsequent to carbon tetrachloride administration in male rats. The changes were reversed by treatment with *A. blazei* extract (Al-Dbass et al., 2012).

Agaricus Blazei Extract: Protective against Diet-Induced Obesity and Insulin Resistance

Rats fed a high-fat diet demonstrated hyperleptinemia, hyperinsulinemia, insulin resistance and glucose intolerance. The visceral fat tissue expressed inflammation biomarkers. Dietary supplementation with *Agaricus blazei* extract for 20 weeks inhibited gain in body weight and the accompanying disorders. This was not caused by reduced food intake or alteration in composition of intestinal microorganisms but rather, at least in part, to an increase in locomotor activity and energy expenditure and a decline in pancreatic lipase activity in jejunum indicating reduced fat absorption (Vincent et al., 2013).

Agaricus Brasiliensis: Protective against Pulmonary Inflammation

Orally administered aqueous *A.brasiliensis* extract (14.3- and 42.9-mg) was effective in attenuating parenchymal lung damage induced by 4-(methylnitrosamino)-1-(3-pyridyl)-1-butanone as revealed by histopathological data and computed tomography scans (Croccia et al., 2013).

Antrodia Cinnamomea Antroquinonol: Hepatoprotective Effect

Traditionally, *A.cinnamomea* is used for the treatment of alcoholic liver diseases Antroquinonol (1-20µM) pretreatment inhibited ethanol(100mM)-induced changes in aminotransferases, reactive oxygen species, nitric oxide, malondialehyde, and reduced glutathione in HepG2 cells. Antroquinonol activated Nrf-2 and its downstream antioxidant gene HO-1 via the mitogen activated protein kinase pathway. Ethanolic mycelial extracts yielded similar results (Kumar et al., 2011).

Antrodia cinnamomea demonstrated hepatoprotective effects against hepatic disorders including hepatitis, hepatocarcinoma, and alcohol-induced liver diseases such as fibrosis and fatty liver. In addition, it had a variety of other effects (Lu et al., 2013; Yue et al., 2013).

Antrodia Camphorata: Neuroprotective Effect

The fruiting body extract suppressed neurocytotoxicity in PC-12 cells exposed to amyloid β-protein Aβ40, inhibited Aβ40 accumulation in Aβ40-infused brain, attenuated hyperphosphorylated tau protein expression, and alleviated memory deterioration in an animal model of Alzheimers disease (Wang et al., 2012a).

Coprinus Comatus Crude Exopolysaccharides: Hepatoprotective Effect

Crude exopolysaccharides from *Coprinus comatus* OBCC 1014 given to rats following the onset of alcohol-induced liver damage at 100 mg per kg body weight daily for one week led to a decline in serum alanine aminotransferase activity and preserved outer membrane integrity of liver cells (Uyanoglu et al., 2013).

Cordyceps Sinensis Cordymin: Neuroprotective Effect

It was found that using the right middle cerebral artery occlusion rat model, orally administered cordymin exerted a protective action against cerebral ischemia by augmenting the activities of the antioxidant enzymes comprising catalase, glutathione peroxidase, and glutathione reductase. Cordymin suppressed polymorphonuclear cell infiltration and up-regulation of the brain production of C3 protein, tumor necrosis factor-α, and interleukin-1β induced by focal cerebral ischemic/reperfusion. Neurobehavioral function after cerebral ischemia and reperfusion was improved (Wang et al., 2012b).

Cordyceps Militaris: Neuroprotective Effect

The neuroprotective activity in addition to a host of other activities of *C. militaris* has been reported (Das et al., 2010).

Dictyophora Indusiata Dictyoquinazols: Neuroprotective Effect

Dictyoquinazols exerted a protective action on murine cortical neurons in primary culture from excitotoxicity induced by NMDA and glutamate (Lee et al., 2002).

Polysaccharides from *Flammulina Velutipes* Base, *Lentinula Edodes* Stipe, and *Pleurotus Eryngii* Base: Protective Effects on Probiotic Bacteria

Polysaccharides from low-economic value mushroom stipe and base enhanced survival of the probiotic bacteria *Bifidobacterium longum* subsp. Longum, *Lactobacillus acidophilus,* and *Lactobacillus casei* in cold storage. The polysaccharides displayed synergism with amino acids and peptides from a yogurt culture in the maintenance of probiotics (Chou et al., 2013).

Ganoderma Lucidum: Protective Effect against Malaria

An ethanolic *G. lucidum* extract demonstrated antimalarial activity against the rodent malaria parasite, *Plasmodium berghei* and reduced the Plasmodium-induced hepatic injury as seen in the reduced serom activities of alkaline phosphatase, aminotransferases, and gamma glutamine transpeptidase (Oluba et al., 2012).

Ganoderma Lucidum **Ganodermanondiol and Ganodermanontriol: Hepatoprotective Effect**

G. lucidum had hepatoprotective activity (Soares et al., 2013). Ganodermanontriol, a sterol isolated from *G. lucidum*, induced heme oxidase-1expression via the activation of the nuclear translocation of NF-E2-related factor-2 and the subsequent transcription of the heme oxidase-1gene *in vitro* and *in vivo*, regulated by phosphatidylinositol 3-kinase/protein kinase B (Akt) and p38 signaling pathways. Ganodermanontriol exhibited *in vitro* and *in vivo* hepatoprotective activity as determined by the reduced activities of hepatic enzymes and level of malondialdehyde and the heightened levels of reduced glutathione. Ganodermanontriol exhibited anti-inflammatory activity in liver cells damaged by tert-butyl hydroperoxide via the expression of heme oxidase-1. PI3K/Akt and p38 kinases were involved. (Ha et al., 2013).

The mushroom toxin α-amanitin from *Amanita exitialis* induced in mice enhanced activities of aminotransferases in serum, and decreased activities of antioxidant enzymes and elevated malondialdehyde concentration in the liver. *G.lucidum* extract reversed the changes probably due to its antioxidant activity (Wu et al., 2013).

Ganodermanondiol protected human HepG2 cells through nuclear factor-E2-related factor 2 (Nrf2) pathway-dependent heme oxygenase-1 expression. It elevated cellular reduced glutathione levels and the expression of the glutamine-cysteine ligase gene, increased phosphorylation of adenosine monophosphate-activated protein kinase and its upstream kinase activators, LKB1 and Ca(2+)/calmodulin-dependent protein kinase-II (CaMKII). Ganodermanondiol exhibited potent cytoprotective effects on t-BHP-induced hepatotoxicity in human liver-derived HepG2 cells, presumably through Nrf2-mediated antioxidant enzymes and AMPK (Li et al., 2013).

*Ganoderma. Lucidum:***Oligosaccharide: Neuroprotective Effect**

An oligosaccharide fraction from *G. lucidum* mycelia suppressed convulsions in rats and the expression of tumor necrosis factor-α and interleukin-1β induced by kainic acid. The degeneration pattern in the CA3 region, and astrocytic reactivity, were reduced (Tello et al., 2013).

Ganoderma. Lucidum: **Cardioprotective Effect**

The hot water extract of *G. lucidum* orally administered at 10, 25 and 50 mg/kg inhibited lipid peroxidation and malondialdehyde formation, and displayed superoxide scavenging activity level in murine heart homogenate. Hence the cardioprotective effect of *G. lucidum* is associated with its antioxidative activity (Wong et al., 2004).

Ganoderma Tsugae: **Hepatoprotective Effect**

The mushroom extract administered at 0.9375 and 1.875 g/kg/day for one month manifested anti-apoptotic and hepatoprotective activities after exhaustive exercise on a motorized treadmill in rats (Huang et al., 2013).

Grifola Frondosa **Lysophosphatidylethanolamine***:* **Neuroprotective Effect**

Lysophosphatidylethanolamine activated mitogen-activated protein kinase, upregulated neurofilament M expression, exerted antiapoptotic effects, and induced neuronal differentiation in cultured rat pheochromocytoma PC12 cells (Nishina et al., 2006)

Grifola Frondosa: **Protective Effect on Pancreatic Beta-Cells**

The α-glucan from the mushroom reduced nitric oxide synthesis and hepatic malondialdehyde formation, inhibited nitric oxide synthase and inducible nitric oxide synthase, and hence reduced oxidative stress to pancreatic β-cells and minimized histopathological changes caused by streptozotocin (Lei et al., 2013).

Grifola Gargal: **Protective Effect against DMBA Toxicity**

The addition of *G. gargal* fruit bodies or mycelia from liquid culture or from solid culture lowered mortality of heterozygous (white/white+) fruitfly larvae induced by 7-12-dimethyl-benz(α)anthracene (25 µmol/vial). Mutations，enumerated as number of light spots per 100 eyes and as percentage of eyes exhibiting light spots, rose with escalating doses of DMBA and were reduced in the presence of the aforementioned *G. gargal* extracts (Postemsky et al., 2011).

Hericium Erinaceus **Extract: Neurotrophic Effect**

The extract promoted development of cultured cerebellar cells and regulated myelinogenesis *in vitro* (Kolotushkina et al., 2003).

Hericenones and erinacines from *H. erinaceus* promoted synthesis of nerve growth factor in neurons. The combination of *H. erinaceus* extract (1 µg/mL) and nerve growth factor (10 ng/mL) was optimal for neurite outgrowth. The extract possessed neuroactive compounds which stimulated NG108-15 neuroblastoma-glioma cells to produce extracellular nerve growth factor, thus enhancing neurite outgrowth (neurotrophic) activity. However, the extract lacked neuroprotective activity on NG108-15 cells exposed to oxidative stress (Lai et al., 2013).

Hericium Erinaceus: Protective Effects against Salmonella Typhimurium

Hot water extract and microwave/50% ethanol extract of the mushroom enriched in β-glucan, administered daily by intraperitoneal injection to mice infected with a sublethal dose (ten thousand CFU) of *Salmonella typhimurium,* protected the mice against hepatic necrosis, a salmonellosis biomarker, and prolonged the lifespan of mice infected with a lethal dose (0.1 million CFU) of *S. typhimurium.* The mushroom extract combatted bacterial infection by activating macrophages and enhancing mRNA expression of inducible nitric oxide synthase (Kim et al., 2012).

Hohenbuehelia Serotina Polysaccharides: Radioprotective Effect

Mice exposed to 6Gy irradiation with Co60 and treated with the polysaccharides manifested elevated superoxide dismutase and catalase activities, and lowered malondialdehyde concentrations, compared to untreated irradiated mice. Treatment with the polysaccharides (200mg/kg BW) stimulated spleen cell proliferation, and inhibited spleen cell arrest in G0/G1 phase, and decline in leukocyte count and hematopoietic function brought about by irradiation (Li et al., 2012).

Inonotus Obliquus Crude Polysaccharides: Neuroprotective Effect

Carbohydrate-rich fractions IOW-1 and IOA-1 derived respectively from the water-soluble and alkali-soluble crude polysaccharide fractions (IOW and IOA) following removal of proteins and pigments exhibited scavenging activity against superoxide anion radical, hydroxyl radical, and 1,1'-diphenyl-2-picrylhydrazyl radical. All four fractions were capable of increasing the viability of PC12 cells exposed to hydrogen peroxide probably due to their antioxidant activities (Mu et al., 2012).

Inonotus Xeranticus Davallialactone: Hepatoprotective Effects

Administration of davallialactone (10 mg/kg), a hispidin analog from *I. xeranticus*, before treatment of mice with a hepatotoxic dose of acetaminophen (600 mg/kg) elevated survival rate compared to acetaminophen treatment alone. Mice receiving acetaminophen (400 mg/kg) half an hour following davallialactone treatment and killed 0.5, 1, 3, and 6 hours later exhibited attenuation of the changes elicited by acetaminophen which encompassed hepatic damage, elevated activities of alanine and aspartate aminotransferases in the plasma, increased hepatic reactive oxygen species level, lowered reduced glutathione concentration, lowered reduced glutathione/oxidized glutathione ratio and formation of peroxynitrite and 4-HNE, and activation of ERK and JNK (Noh et al., 2013).

Lactarius Deterrimus and Castanea Sativa: **Protective Effects against Streptozotocin-Induced Pancreatic Beta-Cell Death**

The chestnut extract and the mushroom-chestnut combination suppressed the streptozotocin-induced increases in activities of the antioxidant enzymes catalase and superoxide dismutase, although the mushroom extract did not produce a similar effect. The mushroom extract exhibited good nitric oxide-scavenging activity. Both *L. deterrimus* and *C. sativa* (chestnut) extracts, and especially the *L. deterrimus-C. sativa* combination enhanced viability of pancreatic β-cells following administration of streptozotocin, owing to decrease of damage to DNA and a better redox status (Grdović et al., 2012).

Lentinus Edodes: **Hepatoprotective Effects**

Injection of concanavalin A into the caudal vein elicited a sharp rise in the serum activities of aminotransferases. Intraperitoneal injection of hot-water mycelial extract,or syringic acid and vanillic acid, the predominant phenolic components of hot-water mycelial extract, suppressed the activities of the transaminases and serum levels of interferon-gamma, interleukin-6 and tumor necrosis factor-alpha, and inhibited the disorganization of the hepatic sinusoids. Thus the phenolic constituents exerted their hepatoprotective activity by repressing hepatic inflammation (Itoh et al., 2009).

Both hot-water mycelial extract and ethanolic mycelial extract purified on Sephadex lowered the activities of circulating aminotransferases in dimethylnitrosamine-treated mice, partially prevented collagen fibril overaccumulation, and downregulated the overexpression of genes encoding heat-shock protein 47 and/or alpha-smooth muscle actin in the animals. Both fractions, which contained polyphenols as the possible hepatoprotective principles, suppressed the morphological alterations and proliferation of isolated rat hepatic stellate cells important in the development of liver fibrosis (Akamatsu et al., 2004).

The phenolic compounds syringic acid and vanillic acid produced by *L. edodes* mycelia maintained the viability of liver cells, lowered activities of circulating aminotransferases, prevented hepatic collagen accumulation and suppressed the fibrosis marker, hepatic hydroxyproline content. The activation of hepatic stellate cells, pivotal to hepatic fibrogenesis, was repressed (Itoh et al., 2010).

Mice given paracetamol (1 g/kg) and treated with *L. edodes* methanolic extract (200 mg/kg) for one week displayed lower activities of aminotransferases and alkaline phosphatase and decreased bilirubin concentration in the serum (Sasidharan et al., 2010).

The alcohol extract of cultured *L. edodes* mycelia contained low-molecular-weight lignin with hepatoprotective effects due to its antioxidant activity (Yoshioka et al., 2011).

The hot-water extracts of *L. edodes* mycelia and syringic acid and vanillic acid isolated from the mycelial extract exerted a hepatoprotective action due to antioxidative and anti-inflammation activities in animals with. hepatic damage induced by carbon tetrachloride, concanavalin A or D-galactosamine (Yagi, 2012).

Morchella Esculenta Cultured *Mycelia:* **Hepatoprotective Effects**

Treatment with both ethanol (36%, v/v, 6 ml/animal, 35 oral doses) and carbon tetrachloride (1:5, v/v, 3.75 ml/kg body weight, 30 intraperitoneal doses) led to a pronounced rise in activities of alkaline phosphatase, alanine aminotransferase and aspartate aminotransferase. Administration of the mycelial extract (250 and 500 mg/kg body weight) lowered the heightened serum enyme activities and raised the depressed levels of hepatic antioxidants (Nitha et al., 2013).

Panellus Serotinus: **Protection against Nonalcoholic Fatty Liver Disease**

Feeding of either a water extract or an ethanol extract of *P. serotinus* to obese, diabetic db/db mice mitigated the severity of nonalcoholic fatty liver disease as witnessed in the decline in hepatic triglyceride content, number of macrovesicular hepatocytes and activities of key enzymes in the fatty acid biosynthetic pathway. The water extract brought about a reduction in the serum concentration of monocyte chemoattractant protein-1 which aggravates insulin resistance. On the other hand, the ethanol extract raised the serum concentration of adiponectin which prevents the metabolic syndrome (Inafuku et al., 2012)

Panus Giganteus: **Hepatoprotective Effects**

Rats that received intraperitoneal injections of thioacetamide thrice weekly and oral treatment with freeze-dried *P. giganteus* fruiting bodies (0.5 or 1 g/kg) daily for two months, exhibited reduced a liver to body weight ratio, serum biomarkers of hepatic function and oxidative stress parameters and liver histopathological results similar to those obtained after administration of the drug silymarin (Wong et al., 2012).

Paxillus Curtisii: **p-Terphenyl Curtisians: Neuroprotective Effect**

The curtisians protected cortical neurons from glutamate-induced toxicity, and prevented cell death mediated by NMDA receptor but not that mediated by AMPA/kainate. Curtisians suppressed iron-mediated oxidative damage produced by hydrogen peroxide neurotoxocity and lipid peroxidation, and protected N18-RE-105 cells with a decline of reduced glutathione induced by glutamate. The curtisians, through their iron chelation ability similar to that of the iron chelator desferrioxamine, prevented DNA single strand breakage induced by iron and hydrogen peroxide (Lee et al., 2003b).

Paxillus Panuoides **p-Terphenyl Leucomentins: Neuroprotective Effect**

Leucomentins suppress hydrogen peroxide-induced neurotoxicity and lipid peroxidation. Iron-mediated oxidative damage is involved in these processes, supplying reactive oxygen species through iron. When iron and hydrogen peroxide are present, chelation of iron by leucomentins prevents DNA single-strand breakage (Lee et al., 2003a).

Phellinus Baumii Ethyl Acetate Extract: Protection against Bovine Collagen Type II Induced Arthritis

P. baumii ethyl acetate extract (50 and 150 mg/kg) protected against arthritis induced in DBA/1 mice by bovine collagen type II. It decreased the CIA score and the number of leukocytes in draining lymph nodes and inflamed joints. The expression of $CD3^+$ (T cells), $CD4^+$ (T-helper), $CD8^+$(T-cytotoxic), $CD19^+$ (B cells), MHC class II/$CD11c^+$ (antigen-presenting cells), double positives ($B220^+$/$CD23^+$ and $CD3^+$/$CD69^+$: early lymphocyte activation markers) and $CD4^+$/$CD25^+$ (activated T-helper) leukocyte subpopulations in draining lymph nodes was reduced. $CD3^+$ and $Gr-1^+CD11b^+$ (neutrophil) counts in inflamed joints were reduced. Circulatory levels of interleukin-1β and interleukin-6, tumor necrosis factor-α an anti-collagen type immunoglobulin G underwent a decline. Hence the extract may be useful in the treatment of rheumatoid arthritis (Yayeh et al., 2013).

Phellinus Linteus Culture Filtrate: Neuroprotective Effect

The fraction of the culture filtrate, with a molecular weight of at least 12000, exhibited higher activity than fraction with a lower molecular weight in reducing volumes of cortical and caudoputaminal infarcts in a rat model of focal cerebral ischemia caused by occlusion of the right middle cerebral artery (Suzuki et al., 2011).

Phellinus Linteus: Protects against Tacrine-Induced Mitochondrial Impairment and Oxidative Stress

P. linteus suppressed tacrine-induced reactive oxygen species formation, 8-OHdG formation in mitochondrial DNA, disruption of mitochondrial membrane potential, and cytotoxicity in HepG2 cells (Gao et al., 2013).

Phellinus Rimosus Polysaccharide- Protein Complex: Radioprotective Effects

Polysaccharide-protein complex from aqueous extracts of *P. rimosus*, given intraperitoneally to mice at 5 and 10 mg/kg body weight for 5 successive days and exposed to 4 Gy of gamma irradiation, elevated the the survival rate and the suppressed levels of nonenzymatic and enzymatic antioxidants such as reduced glutathione, catalase, glutathione peroxidase, glutathione reductase, superoxide dismutase, and comet parameters, signifying its antioxidant and DNA protecting activities. The results were analogous to those obtained by employing the radioprotective drug amifostine (Joseph et al., 2012).

Pholiota Adiposa Adenosine: Protection against Oxidative Stress

Mice treated intraperitoneally with *Pholiota adiposa* adenosine displayed, 7 days after injection, an elevated interleukin-10 mRNA level, a reduced expression of interleukin-2, interleukin-6 and interferon-γ in spleen, and augmented superoxide dismutase expression level. *Pholiota adiposa* adenosine showed anti-inflammatory activity (Wang et al., 2011).

Pholiota Dinghuensis Crude Mycelial Polysaccharide: Hepatoprotective Effects

The polysaccharide minimized carbon tetrachloride-induced liver damage by inhibiting the rise in activities of serum aminotransferases and malondialdehyde formation and augmented the activities of antioxidative enymes (Gan et al., 2012)

Pleurotus Cornucopiae Aqueous Extracts: Hepatoprotective Effects

Oral administration of aqueous extracts of *Pleurotus cornucopiae* (0, 100, 200, and 400 mg/kg) for 8 days before an intraperitoneal dose of carbon tetrachloride (0.5 ml/kg) reduced hepatic damage as evidenced by the suppressed serum activities of alanine aminotransferase and aspartate aminotransferase, attenuated expression of CYP2E1, and the histological and ultrastructural appearance of the hepatocytes (El et al., 2009)

Pleurotus Florida Lectin: Protection against Arsenic-Induced Hepatotoxicity

Arsenic brought about apoptosis in rat hepatocytes and changes in lipid peroxidation, protein carbonyl, and activities of antioxidant enzymes in rat erythrocytes. These changes were reverted by *P. florida* lectin. The lectin may be useful for treatment of people exposed to arsenic such as many of the Indians (Rana et al., 2011).

Pleurotus Ostreatus: Hepatoprotective Effects

Intraperitoneally administered carbon tetrachloride (2ml/kg) to rats for 4 days raised serum activities of alanine aminotransferase, aspartate aminotransferase and alkaline phosphatase. In the liver, malondialdehyde level was elevated, and reduced glutathione concentrations and catalase, superoxide dismutase and glutathione peroxidase activities were suppressed. *P. ostreatus* extract reversed the abovementioned changes supported by histopathological evidence (Jayakumar et al., 2006).

Pleurotus Ostreatus Laccase: **Protection against Hepatitis C Virus**

The laccase suppressed HCV replication at 1.25 and 1.5 mg/ml after the first dose of treatment for four days and at 0.75, 1.0, 1.25 and 1.5 mg/ml after the second dose of treatment for another four days (El-Fakharany et al., 2010).

Pleurotus Porrigens: **Protection against Gentamicin- Induced Nephrotoxicity**

The methanolic fraction of *Pleurotus porrigens* (200 and 400 mg/kg) reduced gentamicin (100 mg/kg)–induced increase in levels of serum creatinine, urea, and blood urea nitrogen (Moghaddam et al., 2010).

Termitomyces Titanicus: **Protection against Endoplasmic Reticulum Stress-Dependent Cell Death**

The fatty acid amides termitomycamides B and E protected against endoplasmic reticulum stress-dependent cell death (Choi et al., 2010).

Tremella Mesenterica: **Hepatoprotective and Radioprotective**

T. mesenterica and its polysaccharide possess a wide spectrum of medicinal properties, including hepatoprotective, radioprotective, antiallergic, and anti-inflammatory effects. (Vinogradov et al., 2004).

CONCLUSION

Many organs in the human body come into contact with toxins. In type 1 diabetes, the pancreatic β cells may be destroyed by viruses or cytotoxins. The liver is exposed to toxins and employs the cytochrome P 450 enzymes for detoxification and converts them into more water-soluble forms for excretion by the kidneys. The blood-brain barrier prevents entry of toxins into the brain. It is imperative to protect the organs since severe intoxication may be life-threatening. For instance, liver failure may ensue from an overdose of acetaminophen.

The aforementioned review discloses that mushroom extracts can protect a variety of cells such as liver cells, kidney cells and neurons from the deleterious effects of noxious chemicals such as hepatotoxins (carbon tetrachloride and acetaminophen), nephrotoxin (gentamycin) and neurotoxins (amyloid β protein) and oxidative damage produced by radiation. In fact, the extracts of *Ganoderma lucidum* and *Coriolus versicolor* are sold as health supplements over the counter in many pharmacies in the Orient. Generally speaking, a diet with mushrooms is a health-promoting diet.

REFERENCES

Akamatsu, S; Watanabe, A; Tamesada, M; Nakamura, R; Hayashi, S; Kodama, D; Kawase, M; Yagi, K. Hepatoprotective effect of extracts from *Lentinus edodes* mycelia on dimethylnitrosamine-induced liver injury. *Biol Pharm Bull.*, 2004, 27(12), 1957-60.

Al-Dbass, AM; Al-Daihan, SK; Bhat, RS. *Agaricus blazei* Murill as an efficient hepatoprotective and antioxidant agent against CCl4-induced liver injury in rats. *Saudi J Biol Sci.*, 2012, 19(3), 303-9.

Barbisan, LF; Miyamoto, M; Scolastici, C; Salvadori, DM; Ribeiro, LR; Eira, AF; de Camargo, JL. Influence of aqueous extract of *Agaricus blazei* on rat liver toxicity induced by different doses of diethylnitrosamine. *J Ethnopharmacol.*, 2002, 83(1-2), 25-32.

Bennett, L; Sheean, P; Zabaras, D; Head, R. Heat-stable components of wood ear mushroom, *Auricularia polytricha* (higher Basidiomycetes), inhibit *in vitro* activity of beta secretase (BACE1). *Int J Med Mushrooms.*, 2013, 15(3), 233-49.

Chang, JB; Wu, MF; Yang, YY; Leu, SJ; Chen, YL; Yu, CS; Yu, CC; Chang, SJ; Lu, HF, Chung, JG. Carbon tetrachloride-induced hepatotoxicity and its amelioration by *Agaricus blazei* Murrill extract in a mouse model. *In Vivo.*, 2011, 25(6), 971-6.

Chang, ST; Wasser, SP. The role of culinary-medicinal mushrooms on human welfare with a pyramid model for human health. *Int J Med Mushrooms.*, 2012, 14(2), 95-134

Choi, JH; Maeda, K; Nagai, K; Harada, E; Kawade, M; Hirai, H; Kawagishi, H. Termitomycamides A to E, fatty acid amides isolated from the mushroom *Termitomyces titanicus*, suppress endoplasmic reticulum stress. *Org Lett.*, 2010, 12(21), 5012-5.

Chou, WT; Sheih, IC; Fang, TJ. The applications of polysaccharides from various mushroom wastes as prebiotics in different systems. *J Food Sci.*, 2013, 78(7), M1041-8.

Croccia, C; Lopes, AJ; Pinto, LF; Sabaa-Srur, AU; Vaz, LC; Trotte, MN; Tessarollo, B; Silva, AC; de, Matos, HJ; Nunes, RA. Royal sun medicinal mushroom *Agaricus brasiliensis* (higher Basidiomycetes) and the attenuation of pulmonary inflammation induced by 4-(methylnitrosamino)-1-(3-pyridyl)-1-butanone (NNK). *Int J Med Mushrooms.*, 2013, 15(4), 345-55.

Das, SK; Masuda, M; Sakurai, A; Sakakibara, M. Medicinal uses of the mushroom *Cordyceps militaris*: current state and prospects. *Fitoterapia.*, 2010 Dec, 81(8), 961-8.

El-Fakharany, EM; Haroun, BM; Ng, TB; Redwan, ER. Oyster mushroom laccase inhibits hepatitis C virus entry into peripheral blood cells and hepatoma cells. *Protein Pept Lett.*, 2010, 17(8), 1031-9.

El, BK; Hashimoto, Y; Muzandu, K; Ikenaka, Y; Ibrahim, ZS; Kazusaka, A; Fujita, S; Ishizuka, M. Protective effect of *Pleurotus cornucopiae* mushroom extract on carbon tetrachloride-induced hepatotoxicity. *Jpn J Vet Res.*, 2009, 57(2), 109-18.

Gan, D; Ma, L; Jiang, C; Wang, M; Zeng, X. Medium optimization and potential hepatoprotective effect of mycelial polysaccharides from *Pholiota dinghuensis* Bi against carbon tetrachloride-induced acute liver injury in mice. *Food Chem Toxicol.*, 2012, 50(8), 2681-8.

Gao, C; Zhong, L; Jiang, L; Geng, C; Yao, X; Cao, J. *Phellinus linteus* mushroom protects against tacrine-induced mitochondrial impairment and oxidative stress in HepG2 cells. *Phytomedicine.*, 2013, 20(8-9), 705-9.

Grdović, N; Dinić, S; Arambašić, J; Mihailović, M; Uskoković, A; Marković, J; Poznanović, G; Vidović, S; Zeković, Z; Mujić, A; Mujić, I; Vidaković, M. The protective effect of a mix of *Lactarius deterrimus* and *Castanea sativa* extracts on streptozotocin-induced oxidative stress and pancreatic β-cell death. *Br J Nutr.*, 2012, 108(7), 1163-76.

Ha, do, T; Oh, J; Minh, Khoi, N; Dao, TT; Dung, le, V; Do, TN; Lee, SM; Jang, TS; Jeong, GS; Na, M. *In vitro* and *in vivo* hepatoprotective effect of ganodermanontriol against t-BHP-induced oxidative stress. *J Ethnopharmacol.*, 2013, 150(3), 875-85.

Huang, CC; Huang, WC; Yang, SC; Chan, CC; Lin, WT. *Ganoderma tsugae*hepatoprotection against exhaustive exercise-induced liver injury in rats. *Molecules.*, 2013, 18(2), 1741-54.

Inafuku, M; Nagao, K; Nomura, S; Shirouchi, B; Inoue, N; Nagamori, N; Nakayama, H; Toda, T; Yanagita, T. Protective effects of fractional extracts from *Panellus serotinus* on non-alcoholic fatty liver disease in obese, diabetic db/db mice. *Br J Nutr.*, 2012, 107(5), 639-46.

Itoh, A; Isoda, K; Kondoh, M; Kawase, M; Kobayashi, M; Tamesada, M; Yagi, K. Hepatoprotective effect of syringic acid and vanillic acid on concanavalin a-induced liver injury. *Biol Pharm Bull.*, 2009, 32(7), 1215-9.

Itoh, A; Isoda, K; Kondoh, M; Kawase, M; Watari, A; Kobayashi, M; Tamesada, M; Yagi, K. Hepatoprotective effect of syringic acid and vanillic acid on CCl4-induced liver injury. *Biol Pharm Bull.*, 2010, 33(6), 983-7.

Jayakumar, T; Ramesh, E; Geraldine, P. Antioxidant activity of the oyster mushroom, *Pleurotus ostreatus*, on CCl(4)-induced liver injury in rats. *Food Chem Toxicol.*, 2006, 44(12), 1989-96.

Joseph, J; Panicker, SN; Janardhanan, KK. Protective effect of polysaccharide-protein complex from a polypore mushroom, *Phellinus rimosus* against radiation-induced oxidative stress. *Redox Rep.*, 2012, 17(1), 22-7.

Kanaya, N; Kubo, M; Liu, Z; Chu, P; Wang, C; Yuan, YC; Chen, S. Protective effects of white button mushroom (*Agaricus bisporus*) against hepatic steatosis in ovariectomized mice as a model of postmenopausal women. *PLoS One.*, 2011, 6(10), e26654.

Kim, SP; Moon, E; Nam, SH; Friedman, M. *Hericium erinaceus* mushroom extracts protect infected mice against *Salmonella Typhimurium*-Induced liver damage and mortality by stimulation of innate immune cells. *J Agric Food Chem.*, 2012, 60(22), 5590-6.

Kolotushkina, EV; Moldavan, MG; Voronin, KY; Skibo, GG. The influence of *Hericium erinaceus* extract on myelination process in vitro. *Fiziol Zh.*, 2003, 49(1), 38-45.

Kumar, KJ; Chu, FH; Hsieh, HW; Liao, JW; Li, WH; Lin, JC; Shaw, JF; Wang, SY. Antroquinonol from ethanolic extract of mycelium of *Antrodia cinnamomea* protects hepatic cells from ethanol-induced oxidative stress through Nrf-2 activation. *J Ethnopharmacol.*, 2011, 136(1), 168-77.

Lai, PL; Naidu, M; Sabaratnam, V; Wong, KH; David, RP; Kuppusamy, UR; Abdullah, N; Malek, SN. Neurotrophic properties of the lion's mane medicinal mushroom, *Hericium erinaceus* (Higher Basidiomycetes) from Malaysia. *Int J Med Mushrooms.*, 2013, 15(6), 539-54.

Lee, IK; Yun, BS; Han, G; Cho, DH; Kim, YH; Yoo, ID. Dictyoquinazols A, B, and C, new neuroprotective compounds from the mushroom *Dictyophora indusiata. J Nat Prod.*, 2002, 65(12), 1769-72.

Lee, IK; Yun, BS; Kim, JP; Kim, WG; Ryoo, IJ; Oh, S; Kim, YH; Yoo, ID. p-Terphenyl curtisians protect cultured neuronal cells against glutamate neurotoxicity via iron chelation. *Planta Med.*, 2003b, 69(6), 513-7.

Lee, IK; Yun, BS; Kim, JP; Ryoo, IJ; Kim, YH; Yoo, ID. Neuroprotective activity of p-terphenyl leucomentins from the mushroom *Paxillus panuoides*. *Biosci Biotechnol Biochem.*, 2003a, 67(8), 1813-6.

Lei, H; Zhang, M; Wang, Q; Guo, S; Han, J; Sun, H; Wu, W. MT-α-glucan from the fruit body of the maitake medicinal mushroom *Grifola frondosa* (higher Basidiomyetes) shows protective effects for hypoglycemic pancreatic β-cells. *Int J Med Mushrooms.*, 2013, 15(4), 373-81.

Li, B; Lee, DS; Kang, Y; Yao, NQ; An, RB; Kim, YC. Protective effect of ganodermanondiol isolated from the Lingzhi mushroom against tert-butyl hydroperoxide-induced hepatotoxicity through Nrf2-mediated antioxidant enzymes. *Food Chem Toxicol.*, 2013, 53, 317-24.

Li, X; Wang, Z; Wang, L. Polysaccharide of *Hohenbuehelia serotina* as a defense against damage by whole-body gamma irradiation of mice. *Carbohydr Polym.*, 2013, 94(2), 829-35.

Lindequist, U; Niedermeyer, TH; Jülich, WD. The pharmacological potential of mushrooms. *Evid Based Complement Alternat Med.*, 2005, 2(3), 285-99.

Lu, MC; El-Shazly, M; Wu, TY; Du, YC; Chang, TT; Chen, CF; Hsu, YM; Lai, KH; Chiu, CP; Chang, FR; Wu, YC. Recent research and development of *Antrodia cinnamomea*. *Pharmacol Ther.*, 2013, 139(2), 124-56.

Moghaddam, AH; Javaheri, M; Nabavi, SF; Mahdavi, MR; Nabavi, SM; Ebrahimzadeh, MA. Protective role of *Pleurotus porrigens* (Angel's wings) against gentamicin-induced nephrotoxicty in mice. *Eur Rev Med Pharmacol Sci.*, 2010, 14(12), 1011-4.

Mu, H; Zhang, A; Zhang, W; Cui, G; Wang, S; Duan, J. Antioxidative Properties of Crude Polysaccharides from *Inonotus obliquus*. *Int J Mol Sci.*, 2012, 13(7), 9194-206.

Nishina, A; Kimura, H; Sekiguchi, A; Fukumoto, RH; Nakajima, S; Furukawa, S. Lysophosphatidylethanolamine in *Grifola frondosa* as a neurotrophic activator via activation of MAPK. J Lipid Res. 2006, 47(7), 1434-43. Nitha B, Fijesh PV, Janardhanan KK. Hepatoprotective activity of cultured mycelium of Morel mushroom, *Morchella esculenta*. *Exp Toxicol Pathol.*, 2013, 65(1-2), 105-12.

Noh, JR; Kim, YH; Hwang, JH; Gang, GT; Kim, KS; Lee, IK; Yun, BS; Lee, CH. Davallialactone protects against acetaminophen overdose-induced liver injuries in mice. *Food Chem Toxicol.*, 2013, 58,14-21.

Oluba, OM; Olusola, AO; Fagbohunka, BS; Onyeneke, E. Antimalarial and hepatoprotective effects of crude ethanolic extract of Lingzhi or Reishi medicinal mushroom, *Ganoderma lucidum* (W.Curt.:Fr.)P. Karst. (higher Basidiomycetes), in *Plasmodium berghei*-infected mice. *Int J Med Mushrooms.*, 2012, 14(5), 459-66.

Petrova, RD. New scientific approaches to cancer treatment: can medicinal mushrooms defeat the curse of the century? *Int J Med Mushrooms.*, 2012, 14(1), 1-20.

Postemsky, PD; Palermo, AM; Curvetto, NR. Protective effects of new medicinal mushroom, *Grifola gargal* singer (higher Basidiomycetes), on induced DNA damage in somatic cells of *Drosophila melanogaster*. *Int J Med Mushrooms.*, 2011, 13(6), 583-94.

Qi, W; Zhang, Y; Yan, YB; Lei, W; Wu, ZX; Liu, N; Liu, S; Shi, L; Fan, Y. The Protective effect of cordymin, a peptide purified from the medicinal mushroom *Cordyceps sinensis*, on diabetic osteopenia in alloxan-induced diabetic rats. *Evid Based Complement Alternat Med.* 2013, 2013, 985636. ites. *Curr Top Med Chem.*, 2013, 13(21), 2660-76.

Rana, T; Bera, AK; Bhattacharya, D; Das, S; Pan, D; Das, SK. Characterization of arsenic induced cytotoxicity in liver with stress in erythrocytes and its reversibility with *Pleurotus florida* lectin. *Toxicol Ind Health.*, 2013 Jan 2. Epub ahead of print

Sasidharan, S; Aravindran, S; Latha, LY; Vijenthi, R; Saravanan, D; Amutha, S. In vitro antioxidant activity and hepatoprotective effects of *Lentinula edodes* against paracetamol-induced hepatotoxicity. *Molecules.*, 2010, 15(6), 4478-89.

Shi, Y; Sun, J; He, H; Guo, H; Zhang, S. Hepatoprotective effects of *Ganoderma lucidum* peptides against D-galactosamine-induced liver injury in mice. *J Ethnopharmacol.*, 2008, 117(3), 415-9.

Soares, AA; de, Sá-Nakanishi, AB; Bracht, A; da, Costa, SM; Koehnlein, EA; de Souza CG; Peralta, RM. Hepatoprotective effects of mushrooms. *Molecules.*, 2013, 18(7), 7609-30.

Suzuki, S; Kawamata, T; Okada, Y; Kobayashi, T; Nakamura, T; Hori, T. Filtrate of *Phellinus linteus* broth culture reduces infarct size significantly in a rat model of permanent focal cerebral ischemia. *Evid Based Complement Alternat Med.*, 2011, 2011:326319.

Tello, I; Campos-Pena, V; Montiel, E; Rodriguez, V; Aguirre-Moreno, A; Leon-Rivera, I; Del, Rio-Portilla, F; Herrera-Ruiz, M; Villeda-Hernandez, J. Anticonvulsant and Neuroprotective effects of oligosaccharides from Lingzhi or Reishi medicinal mushroom, *Ganoderma lucidum* (Higher Basidiomycetes). *Int J Med Mushrooms.*, 2013, 15(6), 555-68.

Uyanoglu, M; Yamac, M; Canbek, M; Senturk, H; Kartkaya, K; Oglakci, A; Turgak, O; Kanbak, G. Curative effect of crude exopolysaccharides of some macrofungi on alcohol-induced liver damage. *Ultrastruct Pathol.*, 2013, 37(3), 218-26.

Vincent, M; Philippe, E; Everard, A; Kassis, N; Rouch, C; Denom, J; Takeda, Y; Uchiyama, S; Delzenne, NM; Cani, PD; Migrenne, S; Magnan, C. Dietary supplementation with *Agaricus blazei* murill extract prevents diet-induced obesity and insulin resistance in rats. *Obesity* (Silver Spring). 2013, 21(3), 553-61.

Vinogradov, E; Petersen, BO; Duus, JØ; Wasser, S. The structure of the glucuronoxylomannan produced by culinary-medicinal yellow brain mushroom (*Tremella mesenterica* Ritz.: Fr., Heterobasidiomycetes) grown as one cell biomass in submerged culture. *Carbohydr Res.*, 2004, 339(8), 1483-9.

Wang, LC; Wang, SE; Wang, JJ; Tsai, TY; Lin, CH; Pan, TM; Lee, CL. *In vitro* and *in vivo* comparisons of the effects of the fruiting body and mycelium of *Antrodia camphorata* against amyloid β-protein-induced neurotoxicity and memory impairment. *Appl Microbiol Biotechnol.*, 2012a, 94(6), 1505-19.

Wang, J; Liu, YM; Cao, W; Yao, KW; Liu, ZQ; Guo, JY. Anti-inflammation and antioxidant effect of Cordymin, a peptide purified from the medicinal mushroom *Cordyceps sinensis*, in middle cerebral artery occlusion-induced focal cerebral ischemia in rats. *Metab Brain Dis.*, 2012b, 27(2), 159-65.

Wang, CR; Qiao, WT; Zhang, YN; Liu, F. Effects of adenosine extract from *Pholiota adiposa* (Fr.) quel on mRNA expressions of superoxide dismutase and immunomodulatory cytokines. *Molecules.*, 2013, 18(2), 1775-82.

Wasser, SP. Current findings, future trends, and unsolved problems in studies of medicinal mushrooms. *Appl Microbiol Biotechnol.*, 2011, 89(5), 1323-32.

Wong, KL; Chao, HH; Chan, P; Chang, LP; Liu, CF. Antioxidant activity of *Ganoderma lucidum* in acute ethanol-induced heart toxicity. *Phytother Res.*, 2004, 18(12), 1024-6.

Wong, WL; Abdulla, MA; Chua, KH; Kuppusamy, UR; Tan, YS; Sabaratnam, V. Hepatoprotective effects of *Panus giganteus* (Berk.) Corner against thioacetamide- (TAA-) induced liver injury in rats. *Evid Based Complement Alternat Med.*, 2012, 2012, 170303.

Wu, X; Zeng, J; Hu, J; Liao, Q; Zhou, R; Zhang, P; Chen, Z. Hepatoprotective effects of aqueous extract from Lingzhi or Reishi medicinal mushroom *Ganoderma lucidum* (higher basidiomycetes) on α-amanitin-induced liver injury in mice. *Int J Med Mushrooms.*, 2013, 15(4), 383-91.

Yagi, K. Liver protective effect of *Lentinula edodes* mycelia(LEM). *Gan To Kagaku Ryoho.*, 2012, 39(7), 1099-102.

Yayeh, T; Lee, WM; Ko, D; Park, SC; Cho, JY; Park, HJ; Lee, IK; Kim, SH; Hong, SB; Kim, S; Yun, BS; Rhee, MH. *Phellinus baumii* ethyl acetate extract alleviated collagen type II induced arthritis in DBA/1 mice. *J Nat Med.*, 2013, 67(4), 807-13.

Yoshioka, Y; Kojima, H; Tamura, A; Tsuji, K; Tamesada, M; Yagi, K; Murakami, N. Low-molecular-weight lignin-rich fraction in the extract of cultured *Lentinula edodes* mycelia attenuates carbon tetrachloride-induced toxicity in primary cultures of rat hepatocytes. *J Nat Med.*, 2012, 66(1), 185-91.

Yue, PY; Wong, YY; Wong, KY; Tsoi, YK; Leung KS. Current evidence for the hepatoprotective activities of the medicinal mushroom *Antrodia cinnamomea. Chin Med.*, 2013, 8(1), 21.

Zhang, C; Han, C; Zhao, B; Yu, H. The protective effects of aqueous extracts of wild-growing and fermented Royal Sun mushroom, *Agaricus brasiliensis* S. Wasser et al. (higher basidiomycetes), in CCl4-induced oxidative damage in rats. *Int J Med Mushrooms.*, 2012, 14(6), 557-61.

In: Mushrooms
Editor: Grégoire Pesti

ISBN: 978-1-63117-521-3
© 2014 Nova Science Publishers, Inc.

Chapter 8

EFFECTS OF MUSHROOM EXTRACTS AND COMPOUNDS ON EXPERIMENTAL DIABETES

Tzi Bun Ng[*] and Charlene Cheuk Wing Ng

School of Biomedical Sciences, Faculty of Medicine, The Chinese
University of Hong Kong, Shatin, New Territories, Hong Kong, China

ABSTRACT

Diabetes mellitus is a disease that afflicts an innumerable number of people worldwide. There has been much effort dedicated to ascertain natural products with antidiabetic potential. Mushroom species with antihyperglycemic activity comprise Agaricus bisporus, Agaricus blazei, Agaricus brasiliensis, Coriolus versicolor, Ganoderma applanatum, Grifola frondosa, Hericium erinaceus, Inonotus obliquus, Lentinus edodes, Lentinus strigosus, Mycoleptodonoides aitchisonii, Panellus serotinus, Phellinus baumii, Phellinus linteus, Phellinus rimosus, Pleurotus ostreatus, Pleurotus cystidiosus, Tremella aurantialba, Tremella fuciformis and Tremella mesenterica. In some cases the active principles have been identified to be polysaccharides. Aldose reductase inhibitors have been identified in some mushrooms.

Keywords: Mushroom, glucose, diabetes

INTRODUCTION

Impaired glucose tolerance or hyperglycemia may lead to diabetes mellitus. Type 1 diabetes is characterized by insulin deficiency while Type 2 diabetes is caused by insulin receptor unresponsiveness. Previously type 1 diabetes was known as juvenile onset diabetes and insulin dependent diabetes mellitus whereas type 2 diabetes was referred to as maturity onset diabetes and noninsulin dependent diabetes mellitus. The old terms have been

---

[*] Corresponding author. School of Biomedical Sciences, Faculty of Medicine, The Chinese University of Hong Kong, Shatin, New Territories, Hong Kong, China. Email: b021770@mailserv.cuhk.edu.hk.

discontinued because some of them do not reflect the whole scenario and are at best partially correct. Type 1 diabetes requires insulin injections for treatment. Type 2 diabetes may not require insulin initially and instead rely on orally administered hypoglycemic drugs such as metformin, sulfonylurea, acarbose and thiazolidenedione. However, sooner or later insulin is required. New drugs like dipeptidyl peptidase IV inhibitors and incretins have been discovered. Mushrooms are a source of antidiabetic compounds. In the following, mushroom extracts and compounds with antihyperglycemic activity are reviewed.

AGARICUS BISPORUS

Agaricus bisporus powder (200 mg/kg body weight) fed to streptozotocin-induced diabetic rats for 3 weeks produced hypoglycemic and hypotriglyceridemic effects (Jeong et al., 2010).

AGARICUS BISPORUS EXOPOLYSACCHARIDES

The exopolysaccharides scavenged hydroxyl and superoxide radicals *in vitro*, and exerted anti-diabetic actions in alloxan-induced diabetic mice (Mao et al., 2013).

AGARICUS BLAZEI BETA-GLUCANS

Agaricus blazei beta-glucans lowered blood levels of glucose, triglyceride, and cholesterol, and exerted an anti-arteriosclerotic action in diabetic rats (Kim et al., 2005).

AGARICUS BLAZEI BETA-GLUCANS

Beta-glucans from *Agaricus blazei* and oligosaccharides derived from beta-glucan hydrolysis showed anti-hyperglycemic, anti-hypertriglyceridemic, anti-hypercholesterolemic, and anti-arteriosclerotic activity indicating overall anti-diabetic activity in diabetic rats (Kim et al., 2005).

AGARICUS BLAZEI

A randomized, double-blind, placebo-controlled clinical trial was performed on 536 registered Chinese patients diagnosed with type 2 diabetes for over a year and taking the antidiabetic drugs gliclazide and metformin for over half a year. Administration of *A. blazei* extract, 1500 mg daily for four months, brought about a reduced homeostasis model assessment for insulin resistance index and an elevated circulating adiponectin level compared with the placebo (cellulose) (Hsu et al., 2007).

The aqueous extract manifested antioxidant activity in the hipoxanthine/xanthine oxidase and DPPH-scavenging assays, and suppressed the increase in pulmonary lipoperoxidation and inducible nitric oxide synthase in diabetic animals (Di Naso et al., 2010).

Oh et al. (2010) conducted a study on the hot-water extract of the submerged culture broth of *Agaricus blazei* enriched in isoflavonoids including daidzein, daidzin, genistein, and genistin. Ethanol was used to eliminate beta-glucans and glycoproteins from the extract, which was then lyophilized, and fractionated into hexane, chloroform, ethyl acetate, and butanol fractions. The ethyl acetate fraction at a dosage of 200 mg/kg body weight suppressed the blood glucose level in the oral glucose tolerance test, when compared with the control and other aforementioned fractions.

Administration of the ethyl acetate fraction to streptozotocin-induced diabetic rats for 2 weeks lowered plasma levels of glucose, triglyceride and cholesterol and activities of glutamate-oxaloacetate transaminase and glutamate-pyruvate transaminase, raised plasma insulin level, and increased glucose transporter-4. and reduced renal and hepatic levels of thiobarbituric acid reactive substance. The hypoglycemic efficacy of the ethyl acetate fraction (400 mg/kg body weight) was similar to that of metformin (500 mg/kg body weight) (Oh et al., 2010).

AGARICUS BRASILIENSIS GARICOGLYCERIDE

Agaricoglyceride, a new fungal secondary metabolite, alleviated glycemic metabolism dysfunction, inflammation, and oxidative stress in mice through suppressing the nuclear factor-êB pathway and decreasing the levels of inflammatory cytokines and total antioxidant activities (Yu et al., 2013).

AGARICUS CAMPESTRIS

Dietary administration of *Agaricus campestris* (62.5 g/kg) and addition of *Agaricus campestris* in the drinking water (2.5 g/l) suppressed blood glucose concentrations in streptozotocin-diabetic mice. 2-deoxyglucose transport, glucose oxidation and glucose incorporation into glycogen in mouse abdominal muscle, and insulin secretion from the BRIN-BD11 pancreatic B-cell line were upregulated by an aqueous extract of the mushroom. Activity of the mushroom extract was < 2000 Da in molecular mass, acetone-soluble, thermostable, alkali- stable, and acid-labile (Gray and Flatt, 1998).

AGROCYBE CHAXINGU POLYSACCHARIDE

Agrocybe chaxingu polysaccharide suppressed nitric oxide generation and level of expression of iNOS in RINm5F cells. It lowered blood glucose levels and iNOS expression and augmented the resistance of pancreatic beta-cells to the damaging effects of streptozotocin in streptozotocin-induced diabetic mice (Lee et al., 2010).

AURICULARIA AURICULA-JUDAE POLYSACCHARIDES

Dietary supplementation of mice with crude *Auricularia auricula-judae* polysaccharides suppressed nonfasting and fasting blood glucose concentrations, blood HbA1c level, urinary glucose level, water intake, and. food intake, and improved glucose tolerance although there was no effect on nonfasting blood insulin level. Dietary supplementation with neutral polysaccharide fractions had similar effects except for the lack of an effect on glucose tolerance.

Fraction FA-A administration showed no beneficial effects in KK-Ay mice (Yuan et al., 1998a). Fraction FA had a hypoglycemic effect on KK-Ay mice, and the reduced food consumption was not a major factor which contributed to the hypoglycemic action of fraction FA (Yuan et al., 1998b).

CATATHELASMA VENTRICOSUM SELENIUM-POLYSACCHARIDE SPC-2

Following administration of SPC-2 to streptozotocin-induced diabetic mice for one month, the concentrations of low-density lipoprotein cholesterol and malondialdehyde were lowered, whereas the concentration of high -density lipoprotein cholesterol was elevated.

The activities of hepatic and renal antioxidant enzymes were restored. Histopathologic studies disclosed that SPC-2 exerted a protective action on the kidneys, liver and pancreas against peroxidation damage (Liu et al., 2013).

COLLYBIA CONFLUENS MYCELIAL POWDER

Collybia confluens mycelial powder produced by a submerged culture, CCMP, lowered in streptozotocin-induced diabetic rats, plasma concentrations of glucose, total cholesterol, triglyceride, and low density lipoprotein cholesterol, hepatic cholesterol and triglyceride, and the activity of alanine and aspartate transaminases. The aforementioned effects were evident after oral administration of the mycelial powder for 3 weeks (Yang et al., 2006).

CORDYCEPS MILITARIS, CORDYCEPS SINENSIS, TRICHOLOMA MONGOLICUM, AND OMPHALIA LAPIDESCENS POLYSACCHARIDE-ENRICHED FRACTIONS

Polysaccharide-enriched fractions from *Tricholoma mongolicum*, *Cordyceps sinensis*, and *Omphalia lapidescens* lowered blood glucose level in adult rats when orally administered one day prior to an intraperitoneal streptozotocin injection, and then daily for the following four days. The ranking of antihyperglycemic potencies was in the order *C. militaris* polysaccharide-enriched fraction > *C. sinensis* polysaccharide-enriched fraction >*O. lapidescens* and *T. mongolicum* polysaccharide-enriched fractions (Zhang et al., 2006).

CORDYCEPS SINENSIS

Daily injections of cordymin (20, 50, and 100 mg/kg/day) into alloxan-induced diabetic rats for 5 weeks normalized the circulatory levels of insulin, glucose, Hba1c, alkaline phosphatase, and tartrate-resistant acid phosphatase. The death of pancreatic beta cells and reduction in the total antioxidant status were partly reversed. The bone mineral density and content were elevated indicating an anti-osteoporotic effect (Qi et al., 2013).

FERMENTED MUSHROOM COPRINUS COMATUS RICH IN VANADIUM (CCRV)

After CCRV administration into alloxan-induced diabetic mice, the blood glucose fell to a concentration resembling that of control mice (Zhang et al., 2012).

CORIOLUS VERSICOLOR HEPTAPEPTIDE (TERNATIN)

Administration of (-)-ternatin, a highly methylated cyclic heptapeptide, to KK-A(y) mice at a dosage of 8.5 or 17 nmol/day and its derivative [D-Leu(7)]ternatin at a dosage of 68 nmol/day using a subcutaneous osmotic pump, lowered the blood glucose level and hepatic SREBP-1c mRNA level (Kobayashi et al., 2012).

GANODERMA APPLANATUM EXO-POLYMER AND COLLYBIA CONFLUENS EXO-POLYMER

Exo-polymers from *Ganoderma applanatum* and *Collybia confluens* produced by submerged mycelial cultures lowered plasma levels of glucose, total cholesterol and triglyceride, as well as the activities of alanine transaminase and aspartate transaminase when administered to streptozotocin -induced diabetic rats at 100 mg/kg body weight /day for 21 days (Yang et al. 2007).

GRIFOLA FRONDOSA ALPHA-GLUCAN

Treatment of the genetic type 2 diabetes animal model KK-Ay mice with the alpha-glucan (450 or 150 mg/ kg) brought about a reduction in body weight, plasma level of glucose, insulin, cholesterol, free fatty acid, triglycerides, and hepatic malondialdehyde content,and upregulated hepatic glycogen content, level of reduced glutathione, and activities of glutathione peroxidase and superoxide dismutase. Insulin binding to crude hepatic plasma membranes was elevated and pathological alterations in the pancreas were reduced (Hong et al., 2007).

GRIFOLA FRONDOSA (MAITAKE MUSHROOM) FRACTION SX

The fraction elevated insulin sensitivity, lowered systolic blood pressure and activity of the renin-angiotensin system and increased activity of the nitric oxide system in male diabetic rats (Preuss et al., 2012).

GRIFOLA FRONDOSA

In male rats with diabetes induced by nicotinamide and streptozotocin, *Grifola frondosa* cultured mycelia lowered postprandial serum glucose level; and *G.frondosa* cultured mycelia and culture broth reduced serum glucose, fructosamine, and triglyceride (Lo et al., 2008).

HERICIUM ERINACEUS

H. erinaceus has anti-diabetic, wound healing, and anti-hypertensive activities (Khan et al., 2013).

INONOTUS OBLIQUUS

Bioactivity-guided fractionation led to the identification of nineteen compounds with DPP-4 inhibitory activity from the chloroform extract of *I. obliquus* mycelium using UPLC-Q-TOF-MS.

Molecular docking between the compounds and DPP-4 revealed that compounds 5, 8, 9, 14, 15 were mot probably the active principles (Geng et al., 2013).

The ethyl acetate fraction from *I. obliquus* exerted an antihyperglycemic action in alloxan induced diabetic mice, and suppressed the serum levels of total cholesterol, triglyceride and malondialdehyde, augmented serum levels of high-density lipoprotein cholesterol level, glutathione peroxidase activity, and the hepatic glycogen content in liver of diabetic mice. Five terpenoid and sterol compounds including lanosterol, inotodiol, ergosterol peroxide, beta-hydroxy-lanosta-8,24-diene-21-al, and trametenolic acid were identified. Inotodiol and trametenolic acid exhibited alpha-amylase inhibitory and 1,1-diphenyl-2-picrylhydrazyl radical scavenging activities (Luet al., 2010).

LENTINUS EDODES EXO-POLYMER

A 52-kDa glycoprotein exo-polymer produced from a submerged mycelial culture of *Lentinus edodes* (200 mg/kg BW) reduced the plasma glucose level, increased plasma insulin, and lowered plasma total cholesterol and triglyceride levels in streptozotocin-induced diabetic rats (Yang et al., 2002).

LENTINUS STRIGOSUS EXOPOLYSACCHARIDE

Crude exopolysaccharide produced from submerged mycelial culture of *Lentinus strigosus,* at 50-150 mg/kg of body weight for 7 days, reduced the serum glucose levels and plasma insulin levels in streptozotocin-induced diabetic rats. Results of histological studies of the pancreatic islets were in keeping with the hypoglycemic activity (Yamac et al., 2008).

MYCOLEPTODONOIDES AITCHISONII

The antidiabetic and other activities of this mushroom have been reviewed (Chandrasekaran et al., 2012)

PANELLUS SEROTINUS EXTRACTS

The extract lowered the triglyceride content and activities of key enzymes involved in fatty acid synthesis in the liver. The serum level of monocyte chemoattractant protein-1, which aggravates insulin resistance, underwent a decline after treatment with the water-soluble extract. The serum adiponectin level rose and visceral fat accumulation was inhibited (Inafuku et al., 2012).

PANELLUS SEROTINUS

Inclusion of powdered *Panellus serotinus* fruiting body extracts in the diet inhibited dyslipidemia in obese, diabetic ob/ob mice and non-alcoholic fatty liver disease in leptin-resistant db/db mice (Inoue et al., 2013)

PHELLINUS BAUMII EXOPOLYSACCHARIDES

Phellinus baumii crude exopolysaccharides produced from submerged mycelial culture comprised two heteropolysaccharides and two proteoglycans.The mixture reduced plasma glucose level and activities of alanine aminotransferase and asparate aminotransferase in streptozotocin –induced diabetic rats (Hwang et al., 2005).

PHELLINUS LINTEUS ALDOSE REDUCTASE INHIBITORS

Davallialactone, ellagic acid, and hypholomine B, were isolated as aldose reductase inhibitors from *Phellinus linteu*s fruiting bodies.They inhibited human recombinant aldose reductase and rat lens aldose reductase with IC50 values of 0.56, 1.37, 1.28, microM, and 0.33, 0.63, 0.82, microM respectively. Caffeic acid, hispidin, inoscavin A, interfungins A, methyldavallialactone, phelligridimer A, protocatechualdehyde,and protocatechuic acid were identified as less potent aldose reductase inhibitors from the same source(Lee et al., 2008).

PHELLINUS RIMOSUS EXTRACT

Daily oral administration of the mushroom extract at 50 and 250 mg/kg body weight for 10 days to alloxan-induced diabetic rats reduced hyperglycemia. The glutathione content and activities of the antioxidant enzymes copper/zinc catalase, glutathione peroxidase, and superoxide dismutase were elevated but the level of lipid peroxidation was reduced in kidneys, liver, and pancreas (Rony et al., 2013).

PLEUROTUS ABALONUS POLYSACCHARIDE-PEPTIDE

A novel antioxidant polysaccharide-peptide complex from abalone mushroom fruiting bodies lowered blood glucose level in drug-induced diabetic mice, inhibited proliferation of breast cancer MCF7 cells and hepatoma HepG2 cells, activity of HIV-1reverse transcriptase, and haemolysis *in vitro* (Li et al., 2012).

PLEUROTUS ABALONES, PLEUROTUS CITRINOPILEATUS AND *SPARASSIS CRISPA*

Pleurotus Abalones Polysaccharide

The 120-kDa polysaccharide exhibited 1,1- diphenyl-2-picryl-hydrazyl radicals and hydroxyl radical scavenging activities, antiproliferative activity towards breast cancer MCF7 cells and HepG2 cells. It manifested a hypoglycemic action on diabetic mice and inhibited HIV-1 reverse transcriptase (Wang et al., 2011).

Pleurotus Citrinopileatus Polysaccharides

The streptozotocin-induced diabetic rats fed with water-soluble polysaccharide of *P. citrinopileatus* lost less body weight and had lower serum total cholesterol and triglyceride levels and a lesser extent of damage to the islets of Langerhans than diabetic rats given a diet without the polysaccharide (Hu et al.,2006).

Pleurotus Ostreatus

The ethanolic extract of fruiting bodies of *P. ostreatus* brought about decreased serum levels of glucose, cholesterol, triglyceride and LDL-cholesterol, creatinine, urea, and increased serum HDL cholesterol level (Ravi et al., 2013).

The ethanolic extract of *P. ostreatus* suppressed the circulatory glucose, cholesterol, triglyceride, LDL-cholesterol, creatinine, and urea levels, elevated HDL- cholesterol level, and prevented body weight loss in alloxan-induced BALB/C diabetic mice (Ravi et al., 2013).

Pleurotus Ostreatus and *P. Cystidiosus*

A single dose of *Pleurotus ostreatus* and *P. cystidiosus* reduced the serum glucose concentrations in male diabetic rats. The hypoglycemic activity in female rats, similar to those of glibenclamide and metformin, was highest in the proestrous stage (Jayasuriya et al., 2012).

Sparassis Crispa Beta-Glucan

Daily oral administration of 1g *Sparassis crispa* /kg body weight for one month expedited the impaired healing of full-thickness skin wounds on the back, macrophage and fibroblast migration, collagen regeneration, and epithelialization in streptozotocin-induced diabetic rats (Kwon et al., 2009).

Tremella Aurantialba Broth Extract and Polysaccharides

Both *Tremella aurantialba* broth extract which contained saponins, and mycelial polysaccharides which contained polysaccharides, lowered the serum glucose concentration in alloxan-induced diabetic rats. The broth extract was more potent in curtailing the serum concentrations of total cholesterol, triglyceride and malondialdehyde, and augmenting the activities of the antioxidant enzymes glutathione reductase and superoxide dismutase in various organs. Both broth extract and mycelial polysaccharides increased the tissue activities of the antioxidant enzymes glutathione peroxidase and catalase (Zhang et al., 2009).

Tremella Fuciformis and *Phellinus Baumii* Exopolysaccharides

Exopolysaccharides, produced by submerged mycelial culture of the mushrooms, *Tremella fuciformis* and *Phellinus baumii*, when administered orally at the daily dosage of 200 mg/kg body weight for 52 days, exerted a hypoglycemic action in ob/ob mice, and improved glucose disposal in the oral glucose tolerance test. PPAR-gamma was activated indicating enhanced insulin sensitivity (Cho et al., 2007).

TREMELLA MESENTERICA FRUITING BODY EXTRACT

Tremella mesenterica fruiting bodies have hypoglycemic and immunomodulatory activities. Its fruiting bodies augmented peripheral cell-mediated immunity while submerged culture yeast-like cells suppressed pro-inflammatory and Th1 cytokine production in diabetic rats.In normal rats both reduced peripheral cell-mediated immunity (Lo et al., 2012).

CONCLUSION

Diabetes mellitus is a disease with acute and chronic complications if the blood glucose control is poor. Chronic complications may affect the nervous system, cardiovascular system, the kidneys, and the eyes, sometimes with disastrous consequences such as blindness, kidney failure and limb amputations. Enormous sums of money have been spent on the treatment and care of diabetic patients.The currently available drugs may have some drawbacks. Hence, there is a search for alternative and complementary medicine for antidiabetic therapy.

Mushrooms are delicious and nutritious and well-liked by many people. It can be seen from the foregoing account that many mushrooms and polysaccharides have antihyperglycemic activity in the streptozotocin-induced diabetic animal model. More clinical studies using mushrooms and their products on diabetic patients should be encouraged.

REFERENCES

Chandrasekaran G, Oh DS, Shin HJ. Versatile applications of the culinary-medicinal mushroom *Mycoleptodonoides aitchisonii* (Berk.) Maas G. (Higher Basidiomycetes): a review. *Int. J. Med. Mushrooms*. 2012; 14(4):395-401.

Cheng PG(1), Phan CW(1), Sabaratnam V(1), Abdullah N(1), Abdulla MA(2), KuppusamyUR. Polysaccharides-rich extract of *Ganoderma lucidum* (M.A. Curtis:Fr.) P. Karst accelerates wound healing in streptozotocin-induced Diabetic rats. *Evid. Based Complement Alternat. Med.* 2013; 2013:671252.

Cho EJ, Hwang HJ, Kim SW, Oh JY, Baek YM, Choi JW, Bae SH, Yun JW. Hypoglycemic effects of exopolysaccharides produced by mycelial cultures of two different mushrooms *Tremella fuciformis* and *Phellinus baumii* in ob/ob mice. *Appl. Microbiol. Biotechnol.* 2007 Jul; 75(6):1257-65.

Di Naso FC, de Mello RN, Bona S, Dias AS, Porawski M, Ferraz Ade B, Richter MF, Marroni NP. Effect of *Agaricus blazei* Murill on the pulmonary tissue of animals with streptozotocin-induced diabetes. *Exp. Diabetes Res.* 2010; 2010:543926.

Geng Y, Lu ZM, Huang W, Xu HY, Shi JS, Xu ZH. Bioassay-guided isolation of DPP-4 inhibitory fractions from extracts of submerged cultured of *Inonotus obliquus*. *Molecules*. 2013; 18(1):1150-61.

Gray AM, Flatt PR. Insulin-releasing and insulin-like activity of *Agaricus campestris* (mushroom). *J. Endocrinol.* 1998; 157(2): 259-66.

Hong L, Xun M, Wutong W (2007)Anti-diabetic effect of an alpha-glucan from fruit body of maitake (*Grifola frondosa*) on KK-Ay mice. *J. Pharm. Phar.* 59(4): 575-82.

Hsu CH, Liao YL, Lin SC, Hwang KC, Chou P. The mushroom *Agaricus Blazei* Murill in combination with metformin and gliclazide improves insulin resistance in type 2 diabetes: a randomized, double-blinded, and placebo-controlled clinical trial. *J. Altern. Complement. Med.* 2007; 13:97-102.

Hu SH, Wang JC, Lien JL, Liaw ET, Lee MY. Antihyperglycemic effect of polysaccharide from fermented broth of *Pleurotus citrinopileatus*. *Appl. Microbiol. Biotechnol.* 2006; 70(1): 107-13.

Hwang HJ, Kim SW, Lim JM, Joo JH, Kim HO, Kim HM, Yun JW. Hypoglycemic effect of crude exopolysaccharides produced by a medicinal mushroom *Phellinus baumii* in streptozotocin-induced diabetic rats. *Life Sci.* 2005; 76(26): 3069-80.

Inafuku M, Nagao K, Nomura S, Shirouchi B, Inoue N, Nagamori N, Nakayama H, Toda T, Yanagita T. Protective effects of fractional extracts from *Panellus serotinus* on non-alcoholic fatty liver disease in obese, diabetic db/db mice. *Br. J. Nutr.* 2012; 107(5): 639-46.

Inoue N, Inafuku M, Shirouchi B, Nagao K, Yanagita T. Effect of Mukitake mushroom (*Panellus serotinus*) on the pathogenesis of lipid abnormalities in obese, diabetic ob/ob mice. *Lipids Health Dis.* 2013; 12:18.

Jayasuriya WJ, Suresh TS, Abeytunga D, Fernando GH, Wanigatunga CA. Oral hypoglycemic activity of culinary-medicinal mushrooms *Pleurotus ostreatus* and *P. cystidiosus* (higher basidiomycetes) in normal and alloxan-induced diabetic Wistar rats. *Int. J. Med. Mushrooms.* 2012; 14(4): 347-55.

Jeong SC, Jeong YT, Yang BK, Islam R, Koyyalamudi SR, Pang G, Cho KY, Song CH. White button mushroom (*Agaricus bisporus*) lowers blood glucose and cholesterol levels in diabetic and hypercholesterolemic rats. *Nutr. Res.* 2010; 30(1):49-56.

Khan MA, Tania M, Liu R, Rahman MM. *Hericium erinaceus*: an edible mushroom with medicinal values. *J. Complement. Integr. Med.* 2013; 24;10.

Kim YW, Kim KH, Choi HJ, Lee DS. Anti-diabetic activity of beta-glucans and their enzymatically hydrolyzed oligosaccharides from *Agaricus blazei*. *Biotechnol. Lett.* 2005; 27(7): 483-7.

Kobayashi M, Kawashima H, Takemori K, Ito H, Murai A, Masuda S, Yamada K, Uemura D, Horio F. Ternatin, a cyclic peptide isolated from mushroom, and its derivative suppress hyperglycemia and hepatic fatty acid synthesis in spontaneously diabetic KK-A(y) mice. *Biochem. Biophys. Res. Commun.* 2012; 427(2):299-30.

Konno S, Tortorelis DG, Fullerton SA, Samadi AA, Hettiarachchi J, Tazaki H. A possible hypoglycaemic effect of maitake mushroom on Type 2 diabetic patients. *Diabet. Med.* 2001; 18(12):1010.

Kwon AH, Qiu Z, Hashimoto M, Yamamoto K, Kimura T. Effects of medicinal mushroom (*Sparassis crispa*) on wound healing in streptozotocin-induced diabetic rats. *Am. J. Surg.* 2009; 197(4):503-9.

Lee YS, Kang YH, Jung JY, Kang IJ, Han SN, Chung JS, Shin HK, Lim SS. Inhibitory constituents of aldose reductase in the fruiting body of *Phellinus linteus*. *Biol. Pharm. Bull.* 2008; 31(4):765-8.

Li N, Li L, Fang JC, Wong JH, Ng TB, Jiang Y, Wang CR, Zhang NY, Wen TY, Qu LY, Lv PY, Zhao R, Shi B, Wang YP, Wang XY, Liu F. Isolation and identification of a novel polysaccharide-peptide complex with antioxidant, anti-proliferative and hypoglycaemic activities from the abalone mushroom. *Biosci. Rep.* 2012; 32(3):221-8.

Lee BR, Lee YP, Kim DW, Song HY, Yoo KY, Won MH, Kang TC, Lee KJ, Kim KH, Joo JH, Ham HJ, Hur JH, Cho SW, Han KH, Lee KS, Park J, Eum WS, Choi SY. Amelioration of strept ozotocin-induced diabetes by *Agrocybe chaxingu* polysaccharide. *Mol. Cells.* 2010; 29(4):349-54.

Lin H, De Stanchina E, Zhou XK, She Y, Hoang D, Cheung SW, Cassileth B, Cunningham-Rundles S. Maitake beta-glucan enhances umbilical cord blood stem cell transplantation in the NOD/SCID mouse. *Exp. Biol. Med.* (Maywood). 2009; 234(3):342-53.

Liu Y, Sun J, Rao S, Su Y, Li J, Li C, Xu S, Yang Y. Antidiabetic activity of mycelia selenium-polysaccharide from *Catathelasma ventricosum* in STZ-induced diabetic mice. *Food Chem. Toxicol.* 2013; 62:285-91.

Lo HC, Hsu TH, Chen CY. Submerged culture mycelium and broth of *Grifola frondosa* improve glycemic responses in diabetic rats. *Am. J. Chin. Med.* 2008; 36(2):265-85.

Lo HC, Hsu TH, Lin FY, Wasser SP, Chen YH, Lee CH. Effects of yellow brain culinary-medicinal mushroom, *Tremella mesenterica* Ritz.:Fr. (higher Basidiomycetes), on immune function in normal and type 1 diabetic rats. *Int. J. Med. Mushrooms.* 2012; 14(5):447-57.

Lu X, Chen H, Dong P, Fu L, Zhang X. Phytochemical characteristics and hypoglycaemic activity of fraction from mushroom *Inonotus obliquus*. *J. Sci. Food Agric.* 2010; 90(2): 276-80.

Mao Y, Mao J, Meng X. Extraction optimization and bioactivity of exopolysaccharides from *Agaricus bisporus*. *Carbohydr. Polym.* 2013; 92(2):1602-7.

Oh TW, Kim YA, Jang WJ, Byeon JI, Ryu CH, Kim JO, Ha YL. Semipurified fractions from the submerged-culture broth of *Agaricus blazei* Murill reduce blood glucose levels in streptozotocin-induced diabetic rats. *J. Agric. Food Chem.* 2010; 58(7):4113-9.

Preuss HG, Echard B, Fu J, Perricone NV, Bagchi D, Kaylor M, Zhuang C. Fraction SX of maitake mushroom favorably influences blood glucose levels and blood pressure in streptozotocin-induced diabetic rats. *J. Med. Food.* 2012; 15(10):901-8.

Qi W, Zhang Y, Yan YB, Lei W, Wu ZX, Liu N, Liu S, Shi L, Fan Y. The Protective Effect of cordymin, a peptide purified from the medicinal mushroom *Cordyceps sinensis*, on diabetic osteopenia in alloxan-induced diabetic rats. *Evid. Based Complement. Alternat. Med.* 2013; 2013: 985636.

Ravi B, Renitta RE, Prabha ML, Issac R, Naidu S. Evaluation of antidiabetic potential of oyster mushroom (*Pleurotus ostreatus*) in alloxan-induced diabetic mice. *Immunopharmacol. Immunotoxicol.* 2013; 35(1):101-9.

Rony KA, Ajith TA, Mathew J, Janardhanan KK. The medicinal cracked-cap polypore mushroom *Phellinus rimosus* (higher Basidiomycetes) attenuates alloxan-induced hyperglycemia and oxidative stress in rats. *Int. J. Med. Mushrooms.* 2013; 15(3):287-300.

Wang CR, Ng TB, Li L, Fang JC, Jiang Y, Wen TY, Qiao WT, Li N, Liu F. Isolation of a polysaccharide with antiproliferative, hypoglycemic, antioxidant and HIV-1 reverse transcriptase inhibitory activities from the fruiting bodies of the abalone mushroom *Pleurotus abalonus*. *J. Pharm. Pharmacol.* 2011; 63(6):825-32.

Yamac M, Kanbak G, Zeytinoglu M, Bayramoglu G, Senturk H, Uyanoglu M. Hypoglycemic effect of *Lentinus strigosus* (Schwein.) Fr. crude exopolysaccharide in streptozotocin-induced diabetic rats. *J. Med. Food*. 2008; 11(3):513-7.

Yang BK, Jung YS, Song CH. Hypoglycemic effects of *Ganoderma applanatum* and Collybia confluens exo-polymers in streptozotocin-induced diabetic rats. *Phytother. Res.* 2007; 21(11):1066-9.

Yang BK, Kim DH, Jeong SC, Das S, Choi YS, Shin JS, Lee SC, Song CH. Hypoglycemic effect of a *Lentinus edodes* exo-polymer produced from a submerged mycelial culture. *Biosci. Biotechnol. Biochem.* 2002; 66(5):937-42.

Yang UK, Jeong SC, Lee HJ, Sohn DH, Song CH. Antidiabetic and hypolipidemic effects of *Collybia confluens* mycelia produced by submerged culture in streptozotocin-diabetic rats. *Arch. Pharm. Res.* 2006 Jan; 29(1):73-9.

Yu H, Han C, Sun Y, Qi X, Shi Y, Gao X, Zhang C. The agaricoglyceride of royal sun medicinal mushroom, *Agaricus brasiliensis* (higher basidiomycetes) is anti-inflammatory and reverses diabetic glycemia in the liver of mice. *Int. J. Med. Mushrooms.* 2013; 15(4): 357-64.

Yuan Z, He P, Cui J, Takeuchi H. Hypoglycemic effect of water-soluble polysaccharide from Auricularia auricula-judae Quel. on genetically diabetic KK-Ay mice. *Biosci. Biotechnol. Biochem.* 1998b Oct; 62(10):1898-903.

Yuan Z, He P, Takeuchi H. Ameliorating effects of water-soluble polysaccharides from woody ear (*Auricularia auricula-judae* Quel.) in genetically diabetic KK-Ay mice. *J. Nutr. Sci. Vitaminol.* (Tokyo). 1998a Dec; 44(6):829-40.

Zhang C, Qi X, Shi Y, Sun Y, Li S, Gao X, Yu H. Optimization of cultivation conditions of fermented shaggy ink cap culinary-medicinal mushroom, *Coprinus comatus* (O.Mull.:Fr.) Pers. (higher Basidiomycetes) rich in Vanadium. *Int. J. Med. Mushrooms.* 2012; 14(2): 189-95.

Zhang G, Huang Y, Bian Y, Wong JH, Ng TB, Wang H. Hypoglycemic activity of the fungi *Cordyceps militaris, Cordyceps sinensis,Tricholoma mongolicum*, and *Omphalia lapidescens* in streptozotocin-induced diabetic rats. *Appl. Microbiol. Biotechnol.* 2006 Oct; 72(6): 1152-6.

Zhang Y, Zhao Y, Cui H, Cao C, Guo J, Liu S. Comparison of hypoglycemic activity of fermented mushroom of *Inonotus obliquus* rich in vanadium and wild-growing I. obliquus. *Biol. Trace Elem. Res.* 2011; 144(1-3): 1351-7.

Zhang ZC, Lian B, Huang DM, Cui FJ. Compare activities on regulating lipid-metabolism and reducing oxidative stress of diabetic rats of *Tremella aurantialba* broth's extract (TBE) with its mycelia polysaccharides (TMP). *J. Food Sci.* 2009; 74(1):H15-21.

In: Mushrooms
Editor: Grégoire Pesti

ISBN: 978-1-63117-521-3
© 2014 Nova Science Publishers, Inc.

Chapter 9

ANTIHYPERLIPIDEMIC EFFECTS OF MUSHROOM EXTRACTS AND COMPOUNDS

Tzi Bun Ng[*] and Charlene Cheuk Wing Ng
School of Biomedical Sciences, Faculty of Medicine,
The Chinese University of Hong Kong, Shatin,
New Territories, Hong Kong, China

ABSTRACT

A diversity of mushroom species including *Agaricus bisporus, A. blazei, Ganoderma lucidum, Grifola frondosa, Hericium erinaceus, Lentinus edodes, Pholiota nameko, Pleurotus citrinopileatus P. eryngii, P. florida, P.ostreatus, P. sajor-caju sajor-caju* and *P. confluens* are able to lower blood levels of cholesterol and/or triglyceride. In an investigation, *Omphalotus olearius* OBCC 2002 and *Pleurotus ostreatus* OBCC 1031were found to produce the largest amount of the hydroxymethylglutaryl coenzyme A reductase inhibitor lovastatin which competitively inhibits the key enzyme on the cholesterol biosynthetic pathway. Chitosan and fiber of mushroom origin can reduce blood lipid levels.

Keywords: Mushroom, cholesterol, triglyceride

INTRODUCTION

Hyperlipidemia refers to an elevation of cholesterol and triglyceride in the blood circulation. The bulk of cholesterol is transported by low density lipoprotein (LDL), high density lipoprotein (HDL), very low density lipoprotein (VLDL), and. the bulk of triglyceride is transported by chylomicron and very low density lipoprotein. Hypertriglyceridemia can be caused by abnormal metabolism of chylomicron and very low density lipoprotein.

---

[*] Corresponding author. School of Biomedical Sciences, Faculty of Medicine, The Chinese University of Hong Kong, Shatin, New Territories, Hong Kong,China. Email : b021770@mailserv.cuhk.edu.hk.

Hypercholesterolemia can be caused by defects in the receptor for low density lipoprotein. All of the aforementioned plasma lipoproteins and their remnants except high density lipoprotein are atherogenic. High density lipoprotein has anti-inflammatory and antithrombotic activities. Hence efforts are directed to lower the low density lipoprotein-cholesterol and elevate high density lipoprotein-cholesterol. Dyslipidemia refers to a low level of high density lipoprotein-cholesterol and high levels of the other plasma lipoproteins. It increases the risk of heart attacks and stroke. The aim of this review is to review the mushroom compounds and extracts with the ability to lower blood cholesterol and triglyceride.

MUSHROOM CHITOSAN

Dietary supplementation with 5% mushroom chitosan for two-and-a-half months mitigated lipid accumulation in white adipose tissue, liver, and muscle, hypertriglyceridemia, and fasting hyperinsulinemia induced by a high fat diet in mice. At the same time, hepatic and muscle fat deposition, feed efficiency, fat mass, adipocytokine secretion and serum interleukin-6, leptin and resistin levels were reduced. Probably lipid absorption was decreased as evidenced by an increased cecal fat content and the attenuated expression of fasting-induced adipose factor in visceral adipose tissue led to a reduced serum triglyceride level (Neyrinck et al., 2009).

Grifola Frondosa Fiber, and *Flammulina Velutipes* Fiber

In rats, *Grifola frondosa* fiber (50 g/kg) and *Flammulina velutipes* fiber (50 g/kg) suppressed serum level of total cholesterol by promoting fecal cholesterol excretion, and *F.velutipes* fiber increased hepatic LDL receptor mRNA (Fukushima et al., 2001).

Fermented Mushroom Milk-Supplemented Dietary Fibre

Fermented milk product containing edible mushroom water extracts (mushroom yogurt) exhibited a hypotriglyceridemic action in Zucker diabetic fatty rats. Jeon et al. (2005) demonstrated in 10-weeks-old Otsuka Long-Evans Tokushima fatty rats, that dietary administration of mushroom yogurt-supplemented dietary fibre (10 and 20%, v/w) for 6 weeks reduced the body weight, perirenal fat, and serum levels of non-esterified fatty acid and triglyceride, without affecting the serum cholesterol levels (Jeon et al., 2005).

Mushroom Lovastatin

Atli and Yamac (2012) conducted a screening of 136 basidiomycetes mushroom isolates from the Basidiomycetes Culture Collection of Eskisehir Osmangazi University in Turkey and found six isolates that produced lovastatin. *Omphalotus olearius* OBCC 2002 and *Pleurotus ostreatus* OBCC 1031produced the largest amount of lovastatin, 5.8 mg/L and 4 mg/L, respectively. The commercial strains *Aspergillus terreus* NRRL 255 (7.0 mg/L) and *Penicillium citrinum* NRRL 1841 produced 7.0 mg lovastatin /L.

Agaricus Bisporus

The white button mushroom has an abundance of fiber, ascorbic acid, cobalamin, folic acid, vitamin D, and polyphenols with beneficial actions on the cardiovascular system. Oral administration of *A. bisporus* fruiting bodies to hypercholesterolemic rats fed a high-cholesterol diet (0.5% cholesterol; 14% fat) for one month suppressed plasma total cholesterol, plasma low-density lipoprotein cholesterol, hepatic cholesterol and triglyceride, but elevated plasma high-density lipoprotein cholesterol (Jeong et al., 2010).

Agaricus Blazei

Female rats were allocated into four groups which received, respectively,(i) the standard AIN-93 M diet, (ii) the standard AIN-93 M diet + 1 % *A. blazei*, (iii) a high-cholesterol diet with 25 % soybean oil and 1 % cholesterol or (iv) the high-cholesterol diet + 1 % *A. blazei* for 6 weeks. In group (ii), supplementing the high-cholesterol diet with *A. blazei* resulted in a decline in weight gain, abdominal fat weight, serum total cholesterol and non-high density lipoprotein cholesterol, as well as in the atherogenic index, compared with group (iii). No hepatotoxic effects due to the mushroom was observed (de Miranda et al., 2013).

Ganoderma Lucidum

In minipigs, 5% *Ganoderma lucidum* suppressed total cholesterol, LDL- cholesterol and HDL cholesterol 20%, 27%, and 18%, respectively; increased fecal cholestanol and coprostanol; and decreased cholate hamsters, 5% *Ganoderma lucidum* had no effect on LDL-cholesterol; but suppressed total cholesterol by 9.8%, and HDL- cholesterol by 11.2% whereas in (Berger et al., 2004).

Grifola Frondosa

The MD-fraction, a Japanese proprietary *Grifola frondosa* extract regarded to be an improvement over the preceding D-fraction, and D-fraction, and other extracts, often in conjunction with whole maitake powder, may be useful in the treatment of hyperlipidemia, hypertension, and hepatitis, and adjunct to treatment of cancer and AIDS (Mayel, 2001).

Hericium Erinaceus

This mushroom has a variety of activities including hypolipidemic, anti-hypertensive, and other health promoting activities (Khan et al., 2013).

Hericium Erinaceus Exo-Biopolymer

The exo-biopolymer from a submerged mycelial culture of *Hericium erinaceus* had a molecular mass under 40 kDa, 91.2% total sugar content and 8.8% protein content. At the dosage of 200 mg/kg body weight, it elevated plasma HDL-cholesterol concentration, lowered plasma triglyceride, LDL-cholesterol, total cholesterol, and phospholipid levels, atherogenic index, and hepatic HMG-CoA reductase activity in dietary-induced hyperlipidemic rats (Yang et al., 2003).

Lentinus Edodes

Krasnopol'skaia et al. (2012) isolated a *Lentinus edodes* strain producing lentinomycin B, a hypolipidemic erythadenin metabolite and developed the optimum medium composition for the submerged cultivation of the strain.

A diet containing 5% *Lentinus edodes* fruiting bodies given to hypercholesterolemic six-week old female rats reduced body weight, plasma total lipid, phospholipids, triglyceride, total cholesterol, low-density lipoprotein, very low-density lipoprotein, and the low-density lipoprotein/high-density lipoprotein ratio but increased fecal excretion of total lipid and cholesterol. Plasma glucose, albumin, total protein, direct bilirubin, total bilirubin, blood urea nitrogen, creatinine, uric acid, potassium, sodium, calcium, magnesium, chloride, inorganic phosphate, or enzyme activities were not affected. Liver cells had a normal histological appearance (Yoon et al., 2001b, 2013). Similar effects were seen when 5% *Lentinus lepideus* (Yoon et al., 2001a). 5% *Pleurotus eryngii* (Alam et al., 2011b), 5% *Pleurotus ferulae* (Alam et al., 2011a), 5% *Pleurotus salmoneostramineus* (Yoon et al., 2012) and 5% *Pleurotus ostreatus* (Alam et al., 2011c) fruiting bodies were used.

Lentinus edodes mycelia had anti-atherogenic properties as seen in the decrease of the number of foam cells in the intima of the rabbit aorta (Yamada et al., 2002).

Lentinus Edodes Fruiting Bodies and Eritadenine

In mice (5 weeks old) treated with *L. edodes* (5, 10 or 20%), elevations on serum levels of total cholesterol, low-density lipoprotein cholesterol and triglyceride brought about by a high-fat diet were reduced. Eritadenine (also referred to as lentysine, lentinacin) with the molecular formula C9H11N5O4 is a hypolipidemic agent produced by *L. edodes*. The reduced mRNA expression of cholesterol 7-α-hydroxylase 1 (CYP7A1) in hypercholesterolemic mice was elevated by dietary treatment with eritadenine (10 mg/kg body weight) and *L. edodes* (5, 10 and 20%) for one month. Production of atherosclerotic plaques and hepatic lipid accumulation caused by the high-fat diet was also mitigated by eritadenine and *L. edodes* (Yang et al., 2013). (Rokujo et al., 1970).

Pholiota Nameko Polysaccharide

Treatment of hyperlipidemic rats with the polysaccharide reduced serum concentrations of triacylglyceride, phospholipids, very low-density lipoprotein cholesterol /low-density lipoprotein cholesterol, and the atherogenic index and increased serum high-density lipoprotein cholesterol. The concentrations of total lipids, total cholesterol, triacylglyceride, and phospholipids in the liver underwent a decline. Lipid peroxidation decreased. The activities of the antioxidant enzymes in serum and in the liver were elevated. Body weight and weights of the heart, liver, and kidneys were reduced. The pathologic changes in coronary arteries were attenuated (Li et al., 2010).

Pleurotus Citrinopileatus Extracts

Dietary supplementation of ethyl acetate extract and methanolic extract to hyperlipidemic rats on a high-fat diet resulted in a reduction of serum concentrations of cholesterol and triglycerides and an increase in high density lipoprotein-cholesterol. Both treatment with ethyl acetate extract and treatment with methanolic extract enhanced ferric-reducing and DPPH free radical scavenging activities. The largest elevation of serum superoxide dismutase and glutathione peroxidase activities were found in rats fed with the ethyl acetate extract. Nicotinic acid and ergosterol were respectively the major components of ethyl acetate extract and methanolic extract (Hu et al., 2006).

Pleurotus Eryngii Water Extract

Pleurotus eryngii water extract demonstrated pancreatic lipase inhibitory activity but did not affect lipoprotein lipase activity. It suppressed fat absorption in fat-loaded mice, and attenuated the rise in plasma and chylomicron triglyceride concentrations after oral treatment with corn oil (Mizutani et al., 2010).

Pleurotus Eryngii, Grifola Frondosa, and Hypsizygus Marmoreus

Dietary administration of 3% dried *Hypsizygus marmoreus, Pleurotus eryngii,* and *Grifola frondosa* powder for 10 weeks to male atherosclerosis-susceptible C57BL/6J, apolipoprotein E-deficient (apoE(-/-)) mice (at 6 weeks of age)lowered serum total cholesterol concentrations in the *Hypsizygus marmoreus* group and reduced atherosclerotic lesions in all three treated groups with the *Hypsizygus marmoreus* powder exhibiting the most potent effect (Mori et al., 2008).

Pleurotus Florida

Dietary administration of *Pleurotus florida* to hypercholesterolemic rabbits brought about a decline of hepatic and of total lipids, and plasma concentrations of total cholesterol and triglyceride without affecting cardiac lipids. On the other hand, the ratios of HDL-cholesterol/LDL-cholesterol and HDL-cholesterol/total cholesterol were elevated. Tissue damage was minimized as revealed by histopathological results. The reduction in plasma cholesterol concentration was probably a result of an increase in bile acid excretion (Bajaj et al., 1997).

Pleurotus Ostreatus

In female rats exhibiting hereditary sensitivity to dietary cholesterol, addition of 4% *Pleurotus ostreatus* mushroom to a 1% cholesterol diet brought about a reduction in serum levels of very-low-density lipoprotein cholesterol and low-density lipoprotein cholesterol (Bobek et al., 1991).

In male rats fed a 0.3% cholesterol diet soon after weaning for two to two-and-a-half months, dietary supplementation with 5% of dried oyster mushroom suppressed cholesterol absorption, serum and hepatic cholesterol levels, hepatic HMG-CoA activity and production of low-density lipoprotein and very-low-density lipoprotein. Cholesterol was redistributed in favor of high-density lipoprotein. 7 alfa-hydroxylase activity in liver and bile acid excretion were elevated (Bobek et al., 1997).

Freeze-dried *P. ostreatus* (15 gm/day) administered to HIV patients, with a mean of 13.7 years of HIV infection and exhibiting hypercholesterolemia caused by treatment with antiretroviral drugs, failed to suppress non-HDL cholesterol and the minor alterations in HDL and triglycerides were considered to be not worthy of further pursuit(Abrams et al.,2011).

Pleurotus Ostreatus **Ethanolic Extract and Major Component Chrysin**

Oral administration of the mushroom extract (500 mg/kg b.wt.) and chrysin (200 mg/kg b.wt.) to rats with hypercholesterolemia induced by a single intraperitoneal injection of Triton WR-1339 (300 mg/kg body weight for 7 days) reduced mean blood/serum levels of glucose, lipid profile parameters, and hepatic marker enzymes and a concomitant increase in hepatic antioxidant enzymes (catalase, superoxide dismutase, and glutathione peroxidase) and nonenzymatic antioxidants (reduced glutathione, vitamin C, and vitamin E). The hypercholesterolemia-ameliorating effect was more pronounced in chrysin-treated animals than the mushroom extract-treated animals, with the potency close to that of the lipid-lowering drug, lovastatin (10 mg/kg b.wt.). These results suggest that chrysin, a major component of the oyster mushroom extract, may protect against the hypercholesterolemia and elevated serum hepatic marker enzyme (alanine aminotransferase, aspartate aminotransferase, alkaline phosphatase, and lactate dehydrogenase) levels induced in rats injected with Triton WR-1339 (Anandhi et al., 2013).

A clinical investigation on diabetic subjects lasting for 24 days was conducted in BIRDEM hospital from July 2005 to January 2006. The age of the participants was 46.3 +/- 10 years old (mean +/- standard deviation).The diet administered comprised one week treatment with oyster mushroom, one week treatment without mushroom and then oyster mushroom for one week again. It was found that oyster mushroom lowered plasma glucose level following fasting and also 2 hours after breakfast. Systolic and diastolic blood pressure, and plasma levels of total cholesterol and triglyceride fell, but body weight and plasma high density lipoprotein-cholesterol concentration were not affected. When mushroom treatment was discontinued, essentially all except systolic blood pressure that had previously undergone a decline in level now bounced back. Blood glucose, triglyceride and cholesterol levels fell again when mushroom treatment was resumed. There was no adverse effect on the kidneys and the liver (Khatun et al., 2007).

Pleurotus Sajor-Caju β -Glucan-Rich Extract

Administration of β-glucan-rich extract of *P. sajor-caju* to C57BL/6J mice fed on a high-fat diet brought about a decline in body weight, serum lipid, and hepatic enzyme activities, and lowered protein carbonyl and lipid hydroperoxide levels by upregulating the activities of antioxidant enzymes including glutathione peroxidase, superoxide dismutase, and catalase. The expression of hormone-sensitive lipase and adipose triglyceride lipase was upregulated whereas the expression of peroxisome proliferator-activated receptor gamma, sterol regulatory binding protein-1c, and lipoprotein lipase was downregulated (Kanagasabapathy et al., 2013).

Polyporus Confluens

The ethyl acetate-soluble fraction derived from an 80% ethanol extract of *Polyporus confluens* powder, when administered in a diet containing 1% cholesterol and 0.25% sodium cholate, reduced plasma cholesterol level. Fractionation of the fraction on silica gel yielded neogrifolin (4-trans, trans-farnesyl-5-methylresorcinol) and grifolin (2-trans, trans-farnesyl-5-methylresorcinol). Dietary administration of neogrifolin and grifolin to the aforementioned high cholesterol diet suppressed plasma cholesterol concentration (Sugiyama et al., 1992).

Conclusion

The extracts of many mushroom species can suppress the elevation of blood lipids resulting from a high-fat diet. However, in some cases the chemical identity of the active principle has not been elucidated and the underlying mechanism of lipid lowering awaits clarification. Lovastatin found in some fungi and mushrooms belongs to the class of lipid lowering drugs known as hydroxymethylglutaryl coenzyme A reductase inhibitors which can lower low density lipoprotein cholesterol and triglyceride and raise high density lipoprotein cholesterol. Thus a diet rich in these mushrooms may help lower the risk of cardiovascular diseases and cerebrovascular accidents.

References

Abrams DI, Couey P, Shade SB, Kelly ME, Kamanu-Elias N, Stamets P. Antihyperlipidemic effects of *Pleurotus ostreatus* (oyster mushrooms) in HIV-infected individuals taking antiretroviral therapy. *BMC Complement Altern Med.* 2011;11:60.

Alam N, Yoon KN, Lee TS. Antihyperlipidemic activities of *Pleurotus ferulae* on biochemical and histological function in hypercholesterolemic rats. *J. Res. Med. Sci.* 2011a;16:776-86.

Alam N, Yoon KN, Lee JS, Cho HJ, Shim MJ, Lee TS. Dietary effect of *Pleurotus eryngii* on biochemical function and histology in hypercholesterolemic rats. *Saudi J. Biol. Sci.* 2011b;18:403-9.

Alam N, Yoon KN, Lee TS, Lee UY. Hypolipidemic activities of dietary *Pleurotus ostreatus* in hypercholesterolemic rats. *Mycobiology.* 2011c;39:45-51.

Anandhi R, Annadurai T, Anitha TS, Muralidharan AR, Najmunnisha K, Nachiappan V, Thomas PA, Geraldine P. Antihypercholesterolemic and antioxidative effects of an extract of the oyster mushroom, *Pleurotus ostreatus*, and its major constituent, chrysin, in Triton WR-1339-induced hypercholesterolemic rats. *J. Physiol. Biochem.* 2013 Jun;69(2):313-23.

Atli B, Yamac M. Screening of medicinal higher Basidiomycetes mushrooms from Turkey for lovastatin production. *Int. J. Med. Mushrooms.* 2012;14:149-59.

Bajaj M, Vadhera S, Brar AP, Soni GL. Role of oyster mushroom (*Pleurotus florida*) as hypocholesterolemic/antiatherogenic agent. *Indian J. Exp. Biol.* 1997;35:1070-5.

Berger A, Rein D, Kratky E, Monnard I, Hajjaj H, Meirim I, Piguet-Welsch C, Hauser J, Mace K, Niederberger P. Cholesterol-lowering properties of *Ganoderma lucidum in vitro, ex vivo*, and in hamsters and minipigs. *Lipids Health Dis.* 2004 ;3:2.

Bobek P, Ozdín L, Kuniak L, Hromadová M. Regulation of cholesterol metabolism with dietary addition of oyster mushrooms (*Pleurotus ostreatus*) in rats with hypercholesterolemia. *Cas Lek Cesk.* 1997;136:186-90.

Bobek P, Ginter E, Jurcovicová M, Kuniak L. Cholesterol-lowering effect of the mushroom *Pleurotus ostreatus* in hereditary hypercholesterolemic rats. *Ann. Nutr. Metab.* 1991;35:191-5.

de Miranda AM, Ribeiro GM, Cunha AC, Silva LS, Dos Santos RC, Pedrosa ML,Silva ME. Hypolipidemic effect of the edible mushroom *Agaricus blazei* in rats subjected to a hypercholesterolemic diet. *J. Physiol. Biochem.* 2013 Nov 8. [Epub ahead of print].

Fukushima M, Ohashi T, Fujiwara Y, Sonoyama K, Nakano M. Cholesterol-lowering effects of maitake (*Grifola frondosa*) fiber, shiitake (*Lentinus edodes*) fiber, and enokitake (*Flammulina velutipes*) fiber in rats. *Exp. Biol. Med.* (Maywood). 2001;226:758-65.

Hu SH, Liang ZC, Chia YC, Lien JL, Chen KS, Lee MY, Wang JC. Antihyperlipidemic and antioxidant effects of extracts from *Pleurotus citrinopileatus*. *J. Agric. Food Chem.* 2006;54:2103-10.

Jeon BS, Park JW, Kim BK, Kim HK, Jung TS, Hahm JR, Kim DR, Cho YS, Cha JY. Fermented mushroom milk-supplemented dietary fibre prevents the onset of obesity and hypertriglyceridaemia in Otsuka Long-Evans Tokushima fatty rats. *Diabetes Obes Metab.* 2005;7:709-15.

Jeong SC, Jeong YT, Yang BK, Islam R, Koyyalamudi SR, Pang G, Cho KY, Song CH. White button mushroom (*Agaricus bisporus*) lowers blood glucose and cholesterol levels in diabetic and hypercholesterolemic rats. *Nutr. Res.* 2010 ;30(1):49-56.

Kanagasabapathy G, Malek SN, Mahmood AA, Chua KH, Vikineswary S, Kuppusamy UR.Beta-glucan-rich extract from *Pleurotus sajor-caju* (Fr.) Singer prevents obesity and oxidative stress in C57BL/6J mice fed on a high-fat diet. *Evid Based Complement Alternat Med.* 2013;2013:185259.

Khanna PK, Bhandari R, Soni GL, Singh CK, Garcha HS, Mittar D. Role of mushroom (*Pleurotus florida*) as hypocholesterolemic/hypolipidemic agent. *Indian J. Exp. Biol.* 1993;31:567-8.

Khan MA, Tania M, Liu R, Rahman MM. *Hericium erinaceus*: an edible mushroom with medicinal values. *J. Complement Integr. Med.* 2013 May 24;10.

Khatun K, Mahtab H, Khanam PA, Sayeed MA, Khan KA. Oyster mushroom reduced blood glucose and cholesterol in diabetic subjects. *Mymensingh. Med. J.* 2007;16:94-9.

Krasnopol'skaia LM, Kats NIu, Usov AI, Barkov AV, Vinokurov VA. Submerged cultivation of *Lentinus edodes* strain with broad spectrum biological activity. *Antibiot Khimioter.* 2012;57(9-10):3-7.

Li H, Zhang M, Ma G. Hypolipidemic effect of the polysaccharide from *Pholiota nameko*. *Nutrition.* 2010;26:556-62.

Mizutani T, Inatomi S, Inazu A, Kawahara E. Hypolipidemic effect of *Pleurotus eryngii* extract in fat-loaded mice. *J. Nutr. Sci. Vitaminol.* (Tokyo).2010;56:48-53.

Mayell M. Maitake extracts and their therapeutic potential. *Altern Med. Rev.*2001;6:48-60.

Mori K, Kobayashi C, Tomita T, Inatomi S, Ikeda M. Antiatherosclerotic effect of the edible mushrooms *Pleurotus eryngii* (Eringi), *Grifola frondosa* (Maitake), and *Hypsizygus marmoreus* (Bunashimeji) in apolipoprotein E-deficient mice. *Nutr. Res.* 2008;28:335-42.

Neyrinck AM, Bindels LB, De Backer F, Pachikian BD, Cani PD, Delzenne NM. Dietary supplementation with chitosan derived from mushrooms changes adipocytokine profile in diet-induced obese mice, a phenomenon linked to its lipid-lowering action. *Int. Immunopharmacol.* 2009;9:767-73.

Rokujo T, Kikuchi H, Tensho A, Tsukitani Y, Takenawa T, Yoshida K, Kamiya T. Lentysine: a new hypolipidemic agent from a mushroom. *Life Sci.* 1970;9:379-85.

Sugiyama K, Kawagishi H, Tanaka A, Saeki S, Yoshida S, Sakamoto H, Ishiguro Y. Isolation of plasma cholesterol-lowering components from ningyotake (*Polyporus confluens*) mushroom. *J. Nutr. Sci. Vitaminol.* (Tokyo). 1992;38:335-42.

Yamada T, Oinuma T, Niihashi M, Mitsumata M, Fujioka T, Hasegawa K, Nagaoka H, Itakura H. Effects of *Lentinus edodes* mycelia on dietary-induced atherosclerotic involvement in rabbit aorta. *J. Atheroscler Thromb.* 2002;9:149-56.

Yang BK, Park JB, Song CH. Hypolipidemic effect of an exo-biopolymer produced from a submerged mycelial culture of *Hericium erinaceus. Biosci. Biotechnol. Biochem.* 2003;67:1292-8.

Yang H, Hwang I, Kim S, Hong EJ, Jeung EB. *Lentinus edodes* promotes fat removal in hypercholesterolemic mice. *Exp. Ther. Med.* 2013;6:1409-1413.

Yang uK, Jeong SC, Lee HJ, Sohn DH, Song CH. Antidiabetic and hypolipidemic effects of *Collybia confluens* mycelia produced by submerged culture instreptozotocin-diabetic rats. *Arch. Pharm. Res.* 2006;29:73-9.

Yoon KN, Alam N, Lee JS, Cho HJ, Kim HY, Shim MJ, Lee MW, Lee TS. Antihyperlipidemic Effect of dietary *Lentinus edodes* on plasma, feces and hepatic tissues in hypercholesterolemic rats. *Mycobiology.* 2011b;39:96-102.

Yoon KN, Alam N, Shim MJ, Lee TS. Hypolipidemic and antiatherogenesis effect of culinary-medicinal pink oyster mushroom, *Pleurotus salmoneostramineus* L. Vass. (higher Basidiomycetes), in hypercholesterolemic rats. *Int. J. Med. Mushrooms.* 2012;14(1):27-36.

Yoon KN, Lee JS, Kim HY, Lee KR, Shin PG, Cheong JC, Yoo YB, Alam N, Ha TM, Lee TS. Appraisal of antihyperlipidemic activities of *Lentinus lepideus* in hypercholesterolemic rats. *Mycobiology.* 2011a;39:283-9.

In: Mushrooms
Editor: Grégoire Pesti

ISBN: 978-1-63117-521-3
© 2014 Nova Science Publishers, Inc.

Chapter 10

MUSHROOM PROTEINS WITH ANTIBACTERIAL, ANTIFUNGAL, ANTIVIRAL, ANTI-PARASITE AND ANTI-INSECT ACTIVITIES

Jack Ho Wong and Tzi Bun Ng[†]

School of Biomedical Sciences, Faculty of Medicine, The Chinese
University of Hong Kong, Shatin, New Territories, Hong Kong, China

ABSTRACT

Mushrooms are a rich source of potentially exploitable proteins. Antibacterial proteins are produced by *Clitocybe sinopica, Pseudoplectanus nigrella,* and *Pleurotus eryngii.* Antifungal proteins are produced by *Agrocybe cylindracea, Armillaria mellea, Cordyceps militaris Pleurotus eryngii, Ganoderma lucidum, Hypsizygus marmoreus, Lentinus edodes, Lyophyllum shimeji, Pleurotus ostreatus, Polyporus alveolaris,* and *Tricholoma giganteum.* Antiviral proteins are produced by *Rozites caperata* and *Pseudoplctanus nigrella.* Anti-insect proteins are produced by *Clitocybe nebularis* and *Xerocomus chrysenteron.* Anti-parasite proteins are produced by *Lentinus edodes, Agaricus blazei, Agrocybe cylindracea, Boletus edulis, Ganoderma lucidum, Tricholoma mongolicum* and *Xylaria hypoxylon.*

Keywords: Mushroom, antibacterial proteins, antifungal proteins, antiviral proteins, anti-insect proteins, anti-parasite proteins

INTRODUCTION

Due to the emergence of drug-resistant strains, there is a need to search for new agents for the treatment of bacterial, fungal and viral diseases. Mushrooms furnish a rich source of molecules with a diversity of activities. The intent of this article is to summarize proteins with

---

[*] Corresponding author. Email : jack1993@yahoo.com.
[†] Corresponding author. Email : b021770@mailserv.cuhk.edu.hk.

antibacterial, antifungal, antiviral, anti-insect, and anti-parasite activities. Mushrooms produce these proteins to protect themselves from pathogens, parasites and predators.

MUSHROOM ANTIBACTERIAL PROTEINS

Clitocybe sinopica Antibacterial Protein

The 44-kDa antibacterial protein displayed a prominent antibacterial action against *Xanthomonas oryzae, X. malvacearum, Agrobacterium rhizogenes, A. tumefaciens,* and *A.vitis,* with a minimum inhibitory concentration under 0.6 microM in most of the cases. However, it was devoid of activity toward the bacterial species *Erwinia herbicola, Escherichia coli Staphylococcus aureus,* and *Pseudomonas batatae,* and lacked activity against the fungal species *Bipolaris maydis, B. sativum, Setosphaeria turcica, Fusarium oxysporum,* and *Verticillium dahliae.* The antibacterial antivity against A. *tumefaciens* was preserved following exposure to 20-60 degrees C for half an hour and to pH 4-9 for 1 h (Zheng et al., 2010).

Pseudoplctanus nigrella Antibacterial Proteín (Plectasin)

Plectasin, the first defensin isolated from *Pseudoplectania nigrella,* is endowed with primary, secondary and tertiary structures highly homologous to defensins found in invertebrates encompassing dragonflies, mussels, scorpions, and spiders. Recombinant plectasin was highly efficacious against *Streptococcus pneumoniae,* including antibiotic-resistant strains to *Staphyloccocus aureus.* Plectasin was as potent as penicillin and vancomycin for treatment of *S. pneumoniae*-induced experimental peritonitis and pneumonia, and demonstrated negligible toxicity in mice (Mygind et al., 2005).

In a rabbit model of experimental meningitis, plectasin was found to penetrate into the cerebrospinal fluid and exerted bactericidal activity in cerebrospinal fluid against a penicillin-resistant *Streptococcus pneumoniae* strain (Ostergaard et al., 2009).

Plectasin directly binds to the bacterial cell-wall precursor Lipid II, resulting in the production of an equimolar stoichiometric complex. The amino acids in plectasin important to formation of the complex have been elucidated by employing nuclear magnetic resonance spectroscopy and computational modeling (Schneider et al., 2010).

At a concentration of 2560 μg/ml, plectasin showed activity against *Streptococcus pneumoniae, Staphyloccocus aureus, Streptococcus suis,* and *Staphylococcus epidermidis,* comparable to those of 160 μg/ml vancomycin, 320 μg/ml vancomycin, 320 μg/ml vancomycin and 640 μg/ml penicillin, respectively. The anti-*S. aureus* activity was highly pH stable and thermostable (Zhang et al., 2011).

The antimicrobial peptide Agplectasin, with remarkable thermostability, minimal hemolytic activity and potent activity against *S. aureus* and methicillin-resistant *S. aureus*(MRSA) but not *S. epidermidis* or other bacteria species, was produced by fusing the AgrD1 pheromone to the N-terminal end of plectasin (Mao et al., 2013).

NZ2114, a plectasin variant with remarkable thermostability and minimal hemolytic activity has been overexpressed in *Pichia pastoris* X-33 via pPICZαA. When tested at 4 × MIC it wiped out virtually all of tested *Staphylococcus aureus* (ATCC 25923 and ATCC 43300) in 6 h. It synergized with the antibiotics vancomycin, kanamycin, and streptomycin against *S. aureus* ATCC 25923. It exhibited additivity with the antibiotics spectinomycin and.ampicillin. It synergized with vancomycin, kanamycin, streptomycin and ampicillin against methicillin-resistant *S. aureus* ATCC 43300 (Zhang et al., 2014).

Xiong et al. (2011) compared the efficacy of NZ2114 with those of vancomycin and daptomycin, in an experimental rabbit model of infective endocarditis caused by methicillin-resistant *Staphylococcus aureus*. At the dosage of 20 mg/kg body weight, twice daily for 3 days, NZ2114 was more potent than vancomycin and equipotent with daptomycin in reducing MRSA densities in cardiac vegetations, kidneys, and spleen. Only NZ2114 (at 10 and 20 mg/kg regimens) but neither antibiotic was able to inhibit posttherapy relapse in cardiac vegetations, kidneys, and spleen. The tissue bacterial counts continued to escalate in antibiotic-treated animals (Xiong et al., 2011).

Pleurotus eryngii **Hemolysin (Eryngeolysin)**

The monomeric 17-kDa hemolysin manifested pronounced N-terminal sequence resemblance to the mushroom hemolysins *Agrocybe cylindracea* aegerolysin and *Pleurotus ostreatus* ostreolysin. It demonstrated antibacterial activity against *Bacillus* sp. but not against other bacterial species, and toxicity toward leukemia (L1210) cells but not toward fungi. It suppressed basal as well as Con A-stimulated mitogenic response of murine splenocytes. Polyethylene glycol 10000 protected eryngeolysin-induced hemolysis but had no effect on the antiproliferative and antimitogenic activities of eryngeolysin (Ngai and Ng, 2006).

MUSHROOM ANTIFUNGAL PROTEINS

Agrocybin (*Agrocybe cylindracea* **Antifungal Peptide)**

The 9-kDa antifungal peptide inhibited growth in several fungal species but was devoid of antibacterial activity even at 300 microM and antiproliferative activity on Hep G2 (hepatoma) cells when tested at 110 microM. The activity of HIV-1 reverse transcriptase was reduced when the enzyme was exposed to agrocybin. It demonstrated a less potent mitogenic activity than Con A on mouse splenocytes (Ngai et al., 2005).

Armillaria mellea **Antifungal Protein**

Grapevine root rot brought about by *Armillaria mellea* is a devastating disease in some grape-growing countries. The grapevine homolog of the *Quercus spp.* phase-change -related protein exerted a growth-retarding action on *A. mellea* mycelia *in vitro* (Perazzolli et al., 2010).

Cordyceps militaris Antifungal Peptide

Cordymin, a 11-kDa thermostable antifungal peptide suppressed mycelial growth in *Mycosphaerella arachidicola, Bipolaris maydis, Rhizoctonia solani* and *Candida albicans* with an IC(50) value of 10 μM, 50 μM, 80 μM, and 0.75 mM, respectively. To the contrary, it was inactive on *Aspergillus fumigatus, Fusarium oxysporum* and *Valsa mali* even up to 2 mM. The antifungal activity of the peptide was unaffected by 10 mM Zn(2+) and 10 mM Mg(2+) ions. Cordymin inhibited HIV-1 reverse transcriptase with an IC(50) of 55 μM. Cordymin displayed antiproliferative activity toward MCF-7 breast cancer cells. There was no inhibitory effect on HT-29 colon cancer cells, and no effect on splenocyte mitogenesis and macrophage nitric oxide production (Wong et al., 2011).

The 12-kDa *Cordyceps militaris* antifungal protease expressed a highly potent growth inhibitory action on the fungus *Fusarium oxysporum*, and demonstrated cytotoxicity against human breast cancer cells and bladder cancer cells (Park et al., 2009).

Ganoderma lucidum Antifungal Protein (Ganodermin)

The 15-kDa antifungal protein inhibited the mycelial growth of *Fusarium oxysporum, Botrytis cinerea,* and *Physalospora piricola* with an IC50 value of 12.4 microM, 15.2 microM and 18.1 microM, respectively (Wang and Ng, 2009).

Hypsizygus marmoreus Antifungal Protein

The 9.5-kDa antifungal protein, which resembled *Clostridium thermocellum* ribonuclease H in N-terminal amino acid sequence, exerted an antifungal action on *Flammulina velutipes* (Suzuki et al., 2011).

Hypsizigus marmoreus Ribosome-Inactivating Protein (Hypsin)

The 20-kDa ribosome-inactivating protein hindered growth in *Botrytis cinerea, Physalospora piricola, Mycosphaerella arachidicola,* and *Fusarium oxysporum,* with an IC50 of 0.06, 2.5, 2.7, and 14.2 microM, respectively. It exhibited HIV-1 reverse transcriptase inhibitory activity (IC50 =8 microM) and translation inhibitory activity in the rabbit reticulocyte lysate system (IC50= 7 nM). It suppressed proliferation of murine leukemia cells and human leukemia and hepatoma cells (Lam and Ng, 2001).

Lentinus edodes Antifungal Protein (Lentin)

The 27.5-kDa antifungal protein impeded growth in *Physalospora piricola, Botrytis cinerea* and *Mycosphaerella arachidicola*. It inhibited leukemia cell proliferation and HIV-1 reverse transcriptase activity (Ngai and Ng, 2003).

Lyophyllum shimeji Ribosome Inactivating Protein

The 20-kDa ribosome inactivating protein exhibiting antifungal activity against *Physalospora piricola* (IC(50) = 2.5 microM) and *Coprinus comatus* It inhibited tritiated thymidine incorporation by mouse splenocytes with an IC(50) of 1 microM, translation in the cell-free rabbit reticulocyte lysate system with an IC(50) of 1 nM, and HIV-1 reverse transcriptase activity with an IC(50) of 7.9 nM (Lam and Ng, 2001).

Lyophyllum shimeji Antifungal Protein

The14-kDa antifungal protein, with an N-terminal amino acid sequence showing some extent of similarity to those of angiosperm thaumatin-like proteins and thaumatins and an inactive variant of the ubiquitin-conjugating enzyme, demonstrated an antifungal action against *P. piricola* (IC(50) = 70 nM) and *Mycosphaerella arachidicola*. It did not inhibit *Colletotrichum gossypii, Rhizoctonia solani* and *Coprinus comatus*.

It inhibited HIV-1 reverse transcriptase with an IC(50) of about 5.2 nM. It synergized with the homologous ribosome-inactivating protein in antifungal activity against *P. piricola* (Lam and Ng, 2001).

Pleurotus eryngii Antifungal Peptide (Eryngin)

The 10-kDa antifungal peptide repressed growth in *Fusarium oxysporum and Mycosphaerella arachidicola* (Wang and Ng, 2004).

Pleurotus ostreatus Antifungal Protein (Pleurostrin)

The 7-kDa peptide suppressed mycelial growth in *Fusaerium oxysporum, Mycosphaerella arachidicola* and *Physalospora piricola* (Chu et al., 2005).

Polyporus alveolaris Antifungal Protein (Alveolarin)

The 28-kDa dimeric antifungal polypeptide inhibited a diversity of fungi including *Botrytis cinerea, Fusarium oxysporum, Mycosphaerella arachidicola* and *Physalospora piricola* (Wang et al., 2004).

Tricholoma giganteum Antifungal Protein (Trichogin)

The antifungal protein inhibited fungal growth in *Fusarium oxysporum, Physalospora piricola* and *Mycosphaerella arachidicola*. It manifested HIV-1 reverse transcriptase inhibitory activity (IC50= 83 nM) (Guo et al., 2005).

MUSHROOM ANTIVIRAL PROTEINS

Rozites caperata Antiviral Protein

The 10-kDa protein inhibited herpes simplex virus types 1 and 2 replication with an IC50 value below or equal to 5 microM. It mitigated the severity of HSV-1 induced ocular disease in a murine model of keratitis. HSV mutants devoid of thymidine kinase and ribonucleotide reductase were also inhibited, excluding the possibility of involvement of these viral enzymes in its mechanism. It also manifested inhibitory activity against influenza A virus, respiratory syncytial virus, and varicella zoster virus. However, there was no activity against other viruses such as coxsackie viruses A9 and B5 human immunodeficiency virus, or adenovirus type VI (Piraino and Brandt., 1999).

Pseudoplctanus nigrella Antibacterial Proteína (Plectasin)

Antiviral activity of recombinant plectasin inhibited dengue serotype-2 NS2B-NS3 protease (DENV2 NS2B-NS3pro) and viral replication in Vero cells (Rothan et al., 2013).

MUSHROOM ANTI-PARASITE PROTEINS

Lectins from *Agrocybe cylindracea, Tricholoma mongolicum* (TML-1) and *Xylaria hypoxylon* displayed highly potent anti-nematode activity against *Ditylenchus dipsaci*, with EC(50) values of 9, 20 and 4.7mg/ml, respectively. They were also highly active against another nematode species *Heterodera glycines*. Lectins from *Boletus edulis Ganoderma lucidum,* and *T. mongolicum* (TML-2) were potent against *H.glycines* but not *D. dipsaci*. The anti-nematode activity of the proteins was dose- and time-dependent. The anti-nematode activity was partially destroyed by addition of their competing sugars i.e., the sugar toward which the lectin exhibited specificity (Zhao et al., 2009)

The *Agaricus blazei* extract can potentially be used as an alternative therapeutic agent on its own, or in association with other drugs, to treat cutaneous and visceral leishmaniasis caused by *Leishmania amazonensis, L. chagasi,* and *L. major* (Valadares et al.,2011).

Lentinan, a (1-3)-beta glucan from *Lentinus edodes* can induce protective Th1 immune responses to control the proliferation of malaria parasites during the blood-stage of *Plasmodium yoelii* 17XL infection by stimulating maturation of spleen dendritic cells to inhibit negative regulation of the Th1 immune response by Tregs. Taken together, the findings suggest that lentinan has prophylactic potential for the treatment of malaria (Zhou et al., 2009).

MUSHROOM ANTI-INSECT PROTEINS

Many mushrooms entomotoxic. Mushroom lectins and hemolysins were regarded as good insecticidal proteins since the toxicities were unaffected by protease (Wang et al.,

2002).The 15-kDa *Xerocomus chrysenteron* lectin was more toxic to the fruitfly *Drosophila melanogaster* and the hemipteran insect *Acyrthosiphon pisum* than G*alanthus nivalis* (snowdrop) and *Lathyrus ochrus* (bean) lectins (Trigueros et al., 2003).

Clitocybe nebularis lectin had activity against the fruit fly (*Drosophila melanogaster*), and Colorado potato beetle (*Leptinotarsa decemlineata*) (Pohleven et al., 2011).

CONCLUSION

Mushrooms produce antimicrobial biomolecules with different molecular sizes. The low-molecular-weight antimicrobial compounds include anthraquinones, benzoic acid derivatives, oxalic acid, quinolines, steroids, and terpenes. 2-aminoquinoline from *Leucopaxillus albissimus* has potent antimicrobial activity against gram-negative bacteria (Alves et al., 2012). Plectasin from *Pseudoplectania nigrella* is the isolated compound with the highest antimicrobial activity against gram-positive bacteria. High-molecular-weight antimicrobial molecules comprise the proteins and peptides referred to in the foregoing account. Recombinant plectasin can be produced in bulk quantities. It has tremendous therapeutic potential regarding Streptococcus and Staphyloccocus infections, in particular in drug-resistant cases when most traditional antibiotics show no effect on them.Thus plectasin is a promising candidate for the prevention and therapy of Staphyloccocus and Streptococcus infections (Zhang et al., 2011). The high efficacy of the plectasin derivatives NZ2114 and Agplectasin in treating MRSA is also a very important observation. The proteins mentioned in the review above await development into useful therapeutic drugs (Xiong et al., 2011).

ACKNOWLEDGMENTS

The award of a research grant (number 81201270) from National Science Foundation of China and a direct grant (4054049) from Medicine Panel, Research Committee, the Chinese University of Hong Kong, is gratefully acknowledged.

REFERENCES

Alves MJ, Ferreira IC, Dias J, Teixeira V, Martins A, Pintado M. A review on antimicrobial activity of mushroom (Basidiomycetes) extracts and isolated compounds. *Planta Med.* 2012; 78(16):1707-18.

Carrizo ME, Capaldi S, Perduca M, Irazoqui FJ, Nores GA, Monaco HL. The antineoplastic lectin of the common edible mushroom (*Agaricus bisporus*) has two binding sites, each specific for a different configuration at a single epimeric hydroxyl. *J. Biol. Chem.* 2005; 280(11):10614-23.

Chu KT, Xia L, Ng TB. Pleurostrin, an antifungal peptide from the oyster mushroom. *Peptides*. 2005; 26(11):2098-103.

Guo Y, Wang H, Ng TB. Isolation of trichogin, an antifungal protein from fresh fruiting bodies of the edible mushroom *Tricholoma giganteum. Peptides.* 2005 ; 26(4):575-80.

Han CH, Liu QH, Ng TB, Wang HX. A novel homodimeric lactose-binding lectin from the edible split gill medicinal mushroom *Schizophyllum commune. Biochem. Biophys. Res Commun.* 2005; 336(1):252-7.

Lam SK, Ng TB. First simultaneous isolation of a ribosome inactivating protein and an antifungal protein from a mushroom (*Lyophyllum shimeji*) together with evidence for synergism of their antifungal effects. *Arch. Biochem. Biophys.* 2001; 393(2):271-80.

Lam SK, Ng TB. Hypsin, a novel thermostable ribosome-inactivating protein with antifungal and antiproliferative activities from fruiting bodies of the edible mushroom *Hypsizigus marmoreus. Biochem. Biophys. Res. Commun.* 2001; 285(4):1071-5.

Lam YW, Ng TB, Wang HX. Antiproliferative and antimitogenic activities in a peptide from puffball mushroom *Calvatia caelata. Biochem. Biophys. Res. Commun.* 2001; 289(3): 744-9.

Mahajan RG, Patil SI, Mohan DR, Shastry P. *Pleurotus Eous* mushroom lectin (PEL) with mixed carbohydrate inhibition and antiproliferative activity on tumor cell lines. *J. Biochem. Mol. Biol. Biophys.* 2002; 6(5):341-5.

Mao R, Teng D, Wang X, Xi D, Zhang Y, Hu X, Yang Y, Wang J. Design, expression, and characterization of a novel targeted plectasin against methicillin-resistant *Staphylococcus aureus. Appl. Microbiol. Biotechnol.* 2013; 97(9):3991-4002.

Marty-Detraves C, Francis F, Baricault L, Fournier D, Paquereau L. Inhibitory action of a new lectin from *Xerocomus chrysenteron* on cell-substrate adhesion. *Mol. Cell Biochem.* 2004; 258(1-2):49-55.

Mygind PH, Fischer RL, Schnorr KM, Hansen MT, Sönksen CP, Ludvigsen S, Raventós D, Buskov S, Christensen B, De Maria L, Taboureau O, Yaver D, Elvig-Jørgensen SG, Sørensen MV, Christensen BE, Kjaerulff S, Frimodt-Moller N, Lehrer RI, Zasloff M, Kristensen HH. Plectasin is a peptide antibiotic with therapeutic potential from a saprophytic fungus. *Nature.* 2005 437(7061):975-80.

Ngai PH, Ng TB. Lentin, a novel and potent antifungal protein from shitake mushroom with inhibitory effects on activity of human immunodeficiency virus-1 reverse transcriptase and proliferation of leukemia cells. *Life Sci.* 2003;73(26):3363-74.

Ngai PH, Ng TB. A ribonuclease with antimicrobial, antimitogenic and antiproliferative activities from the edible mushroom *Pleurotus sajor-caju. Peptides.* 2004; 25(1):11-7.

Ngai PH, Ng TB. A mushroom (*Ganoderma capense*) lectin with spectacular thermostability, potent mitogenic activity on splenocytes, and antiproliferative activity toward tumor cells. *Biochem. Biophys. Res. Commun.* 2004; 314(4):988-93.

Ngai PH, Ng TB. A hemolysin from the mushroom *Pleurotus eryngii. Appl. Microbiol. Biotechnol.* 2006;72(6):1185-91.

Ngai PH, Wang HX, Ng TB. Purification and characterization of a ubiquitin-like peptide with macrophage stimulating, antiproliferative and ribonucleases activities from the mushroom *Agrocybe cylindracea. Peptides.* 2003 ;24(5):639-45.

Ngai PH, Zhao Z, Ng TB. Agrocybin, an antifungal peptide from the edible mushroom *Agrocybe cylindracea. Peptides.* 2005; 26(2):191-6.

Ostergaard C, Sandvang D, Frimodt-Møller N, Kristensen HH. High cerebrospinal fluid (CSF) penetration and potent bactericidal activity in CSF of NZ2114, a novel plectasin variant, during experimental pneumococcal meningitis. *Antimicrob. Agents Chemother.* 2009; 53(4):1581-5.

Park BT, Na KH, Jung EC, Park JW, Kim HH. Antifungal and anticancer activities of a protein from the mushroom *Cordyceps militaris*. *Korean J. Physiol. Pharmacol.* 2009; 13(1):49-54.

Parret AH, Temmerman K, De Mot R. Novel lectin-like bacteriocins of biocontrol strain *Pseudomonas fluorescens* Pf-5. *Appl. Environ. Microbiol.* 2005; 71(9):5197-207.

Perazzolli M, Bampi F, Faccin S, Moser M, De Luca F, Ciccotti AM, Velasco R, Gessler C, Pertot I, Moser C. *Armillaria mellea* induces a set of defense genes in grapevine roots and one of them codifies a protein with antifungal activity. *Mol. Plant. Microbe Interact.* 2010; 23(4):485-96.

Pohleven J, Brzin J, Vrabec L, Leonardi A, Cokl A, Strukelj B, Kos J, Sabotič J. Basidiomycete *Clitocybe nebularis* is rich in lectins with insecticidal activities. *Appl. Microbiol. Biotechnol.* 2011; 91(4):1141-8.

Piraino F, Brandt CR. Isolation and partial characterization of an antiviral, RC-183, from the edible mushroom *Rozites caperata*. *Antiviral. Res.* 1999 ;43(2):67-78.

Piraino F, Brandt CR. Isolation and partial characterization of an antiviral, RC-183, from the edible mushroom *Rozites caperata*. *Antiviral. Res.* 1999; 43(2):67-78.

Rothan HA, Mohamed Z, Suhaeb AM, Rahman NA, Yusof R. Antiviral cationic peptides as a strategy for innovation in global health therapeutics for dengue virus: high yield production of the biologically active recombinant plectasin peptide. *OMICS.* 2013; 17(11):560-7.

Schneider T, Kruse T, Wimmer R, Wiedemann I, Sass V, Pag U, Jansen A, Nielsen AK, Mygind PH, Raventós DS, Neve S, Ravn B, Bonvin AM, De Maria L, Andersen AS, Gammelgaard LK, Sahl HG, Kristensen HH. Plectasin, a fungal defensin, targets the bacterial cell wall precursor Lipid II. *Science.* 2010;328(5982):1168-72.

Suzuki T, Umehara K, Tashiro A, Kobayashi Y, Dohra H, Hirai H, Kawagishi H. An antifungal protein from the culinary-medicinal beech mushroom, *Hypsizygus marmoreus* (Peck) Bigel. (Agaricomycetideae). *Int. J. Med. Mushrooms.* 2011;13(1):27-31.

Pohleven J, Brzin J, Vrabec L, Leonardi A, Cokl A, Strukelj B, Kos J, Sabotič J. Basidiomycete *Clitocybe nebularis* is rich in lectins with insecticidal activities. *Appl. Microbiol. Biotechnol.* 2011; 91(4):1141-8.

Trigueros V, Lougarre A, Ali-Ahmed D, Rahbé Y, Guillot J, Chavant L, Fournier D, Paquereau L. *Xerocomus chrysenteron* lectin: identification of a new pesticidal protein. *Biochim. Biophys. Acta.* 2003; 1621(3):292-8.

Valadares DG, Duarte MC, Oliveira JS, Chávez-Fumagalli MA, Martins VT, Costa LE, Leite JP, Santoro MM, Régis WC, Tavares CA, Coelho EA. Leishmanicidal activity of the *Agaricus blazei* Murill in different *Leishmania* species. *Parasitol. Int.* 2011; 60(4): 357-63.

Wang H, Ng TB. Eryngin, a novel antifungal peptide from fruiting bodies of the edible mushroom *Pleurotus eryngii*. *Peptides.* 2004;25(1):1-5.

Wang H, Ng TB, Liu Q. Alveolarin, a novel antifungal polypeptide from the wild mushroom *Polyporus alveolaris*. *Peptides.* 2004;25(4):693-6.

Wang H, Ng TB. Ganodermin, an antifungal protein from fruiting bodies of the medicinal mushroom *Ganoderma lucidum*. *Peptides.* 2006;27(1):27-30.

Wang H, Ng TB, Liu Q. A novel lectin from the wild mushroom *Polyporus adusta*. *Biochem. Biophys. Res. Commun.* 2003;307(3):535-9.

Wang M, Triguéros V, Paquereau L, Chavant L, Fournier D. Proteins as active compounds involved in insecticidal activity of mushroom fruitbodies. *J. Econ. Entomol.* 2002; 95(3): 603-7.

Wong JH, Ng TB, Wang H, Sze SC, Zhang KY, Li Q, Lu X. Cordymin, an antifungal peptide from the medicinal fungus *Cordyceps militaris. Phytomedicine.* 2011; 18(5):387-92.

Xia L, Chu KT, Ng TB. A low-molecular mass ribonuclease from the brown oyster mushroom. *J. Pept. Res.* 2005; 66(1):1-8.

Xiong YQ, Hady WA, Deslandes A, Rey A, Fraisse L, Kristensen HH, Yeaman MR, Bayer AS. Efficacy of NZ2114, a novel plectasin-derived cationic antimicrobial peptide antibiotic, in experimental endocarditis due to methicillin-resistant *Staphylococcus aureus. Antimicrob. Agents Chemother.* 2011; 55(11):5325-30.

Zhang J, Yang Y, Teng D, Tian Z, Wang S, Wang J. Expression of plectasin in *Pichia pastoris* and its characterization as a new antimicrobial peptide against Staphyloccocus and Streptococcus. *Protein Expr. Purif.* 2011; 78(2):189-96.

Zhang Y, Teng D, Mao R, Wang X, Xi D, Hu X, Wang J. High expression of a plectasin-derived peptide NZ2114 in Pichia pastoris and its pharmacodynamics, postantibiotic and synergy against *Staphylococcus aureus. Appl. Microbiol. Biotechnol.* 2014; 98(2):681-94.

Zhao S, Guo YX, Liu QH, Wang HX, Ng TB. Lectins but not antifungal proteins exhibit anti-nematode activity. *Environ. Toxicol. Pharmacol.* 2009; 28(2):265-8.

Zheng S, Liu Q, Zhang G, Wang H, Ng TB. Purification and characterization of an antibacterial protein from dried fruiting bodies of the wild mushroom *Clitocybe sinopica. Acta Biochim. Pol.* 2010; 57(1):43-8.

Zhou LD, Zhang QH, Zhang Y, Liu J, Cao YM. The shiitake mushroom-derived imuno-stimulant lentinan protects against murine malaria blood-stage infection by evoking adaptive immune-responses. *Int. Immunopharmacol.* 2009;9(4):455-62.

In: Mushrooms
Editor: Grégoire Pesti

ISBN: 978-1-63117-521-3
© 2014 Nova Science Publishers, Inc.

Chapter 11

MICRONUTRIENTS BENEFITS OF CONSUMPTION OF THE SCLEROTIUM (TUBER) OF *PLEUROTUS TUBER-REGIUM* (ÓSŪ) MUSHROOM IN SOUTHEASTERN NIGERIA

Innocent C. Nnorom[*]
Department of Pure and Industrial Chemistry, Abia State University,
Uturu, Abia State, Nigeria

ABSTRACT

In Nigeria and around the world, edible mushrooms are valued for their nutritional value, aroma and unique taste. Many edible mushroom species are also used in traditional medicines. For instance, in Nigeria, P. tuber-regium is commonly used in alleviating headache, stomach pain fever, cold, and constipation. Mushrooms of the genus *Pleurotus* are among the very popular edible varieties. They have rapid growth and are easy to cultivate. The mushroom species, *Pleurotus tuber-regium,* also known as the 'king tuber oyster' or 'tiger milk,' is a saprotroph, found on dead woods, and native to the tropical and subtropical regions of the world. The fungus infects dry wood, producing the sclerotium or storage tuber, which is usually buried within the decaying wood tissues or in the underlying soil. Both the sclerotia and the fruiting bodies that emerge from it are edible. The sclerotia are mostly spherical or ovoid in shape, and from dark brown to black on the surface, with a white underneath. The tuber of *Pleurotus tuber-regium* is a rich source of food nutrients, and is used in preparing foods considered delicacies in Nigeria. This chapter discusses the micronutrient benefits of the consumption of the tuber of *Pleurotus tuber-regium.* From the nutritional point of view, the sclerotia of *P. tuber-regium* would serve as a good dietary source of many essential elements to humans. The estimated elements intakes are compared with regulatory limits for the elements such as the provisional tolerable weekly intake (PTWI).

Keywords: Mushroom, *Pleurotus tuber-regium*, micronutrient, sclerotia, Nigeria

---

[*] Corresponding author e-mail: chidiabsu@yahoo.co.uk.

1. Introduction

Out of the vast number of mushroom species available worldwide estimated at 10,000 during early 1990's, only 2000 from about 30 genera are edible (Chang, 1990), and they are valued in gourmet traditions around the world for their unique taste, aroma, nutritional value, and medicinal potentials (Jonathan and Fasidi, 2003; Falandysz and Gucia, 2008; Nnorom et al., 2013). Many mushroom species are also used in traditional medicines in many countries around the world, including China, Japan, Nigeria, Tibet, etc. (Alonso et al., 2003; Adejumo and Awosanya, 2005; Bernas et al., 2006; Zhang et al., 2010 ; Nnorom, 2011).

Summarily, mushrooms are highly appreciated by many in most communities, because:

- They are considered as valuable health foods;
- They have acceptable texture and flavor;
- They have low energy content, high proportion of indigestible fiber, and antioxidant constituents;
- They have good medicinal values; and,
- They contain significant amounts of vitamins, and minerals (Falandysz and Borovička, 2013; Elmastas et al., 2007; Aloupi et al., 2012).

The picking and consumption of wild-growing mushrooms are very popular in many countries in Africa, Asia and Europe. For instance, Sisak (1996) reported that in the Czech Republic, 72% of families collected mushrooms, with a mean yearly level of 7 kg per household in the first half of the 1990s. However, yearly consumption exceeds 10 kg in some individuals (Svoboda et al., 2006). Akpaja et al. (2003) in a survey in southeastern Nigeria reported that over 95% of the respondents consumed edible mushrooms because of the taste.

In Nigeria and in many countries, they are considered as food supplements and are consumed for their delicacy and medicinal values (Adejumo and Awosanya, 2005; Ude et al., 2001; Gregori et al., 2007; Nnorom, 2011). Many Nigerians still depend largely on organic food sources, including mushrooms, which are collected from the wild. Mushrooms are considered as source of rich food because they contain proteins, sugars, glycogen, lipids, vitamins, amino acids, crude fibres, and many beneficial minerals (Ude et al., 2001; Adejumo and Awosanya 2005; Ikewuchi and Ikewuchi, 2008; Agomuo, 2011; Adedayo, 2011). They could, in some cases, also contain elevated concentrations of some toxic heavy metals such as Pb, Cd and Hg (Falandysz et al., 2001; 2008; 2012a-c; Chojnacka et al., 2012; Dryżałowska et al., 2012; Kojta et al., 2011; Branco, 2010; Aloupi et al., 2012; Gadd, 1993).

Mushrooms of the genus *Pleurotus* are among the very popular edible varieties not only due to these properties, but also for their rapid growth and ease of cultivation (Gregori et al., 2007). This chapter discusses the sclerotia of *P. tuber-regium* with respect to its consumption in Nigeria and estimates the micronutrients intakes and the health benefits therein.

2. Mushroom Consumption in Nigeria

In recent times, there has been an increase in the consumption of mushrooms both in the rural and urban areas of Nigeria. Studies into the cultivation, composition, and other possible uses of edible mushrooms have also been on the increase in Nigeria (Okhuoya and Okogbo, 1990; Isikhuemhen and LeBauer, 2004; Isikhuemhen and Okhuoya, 1996). They grow naturally in Nigeria during the early and late rainy seasons (Ijeh et al., 2009). For example, the genus Pleurotus comprises some of the very popular edible mushrooms due to their nutritional value, favourable organoleptic and medicinal properties, vigorous growth and undemanding cultivation conditions (Ude et al., 2001; Gregori et al., 2007).

Akpaja and co-workers studied the uses of mushrooms by the Igbo people of southeast Nigeria and reported that on the average, each respondent consumed 8.64±3.70 species of mushrooms. While over 95% of the respondents consumed edible mushrooms because of the taste, 86% used them as substitutes for meat and fish, while 36.36% used some mushroom species for medicinal purposes (Akpaja et al., 2003).

3. *PLEUROTUS TUBER-REGIUM* MUSHROOM

The mushroom species, *Pleurotus tuber-regium,* also known as the 'king tuber oyster' or 'tiger milk,' is a saprotroph, an edible basidiomycete, found on dead woods, and native to the tropical and subtropical regions of the world (Okhuoya and Okogbo, 1991; Adejumo and Awosanya, 2005; Ijeh et al., 2009). It is a common mushroom in the southern part of Nigeria and forms large spherical to ovoid, subterranean sclerotia, which sometimes measure up to 30 cm in diameter (Okhuoya and Okogbo, 1991; Iwuagwu and Onyekweli, 2002; Nnorom, 2011). Being sclerotial, the fungus produces a sclerotium, or underground tuber, as well as fruiting body (mushroom). The fungus infects dry wood, producing the sclerotium or storage tuber, which is usually buried within the decaying wood tissues or in the underlying soil. Both the sclerotia and the fruiting bodies that emerge from it are consumed in Nigeria. Sclerotia are used in various soup and medicinal preparations both for human consumption and in traditional medical practices in Nigeria. The sclerotium of *P. tuber-regium* is known as *Ósū* in Isuikwuato community and the other *Igbo* speaking communities of Southeastern Nigeria. The sclerotia are mostly dark brown to black on the surface, with a white underneath. Sometimes, sclerotia could be quite large in size and could weigh as much as 5 kg (Iwuagwu and Onyekweli, 2002). They are usually found in forests, grasslands, damp rotten logs, etc. (Ijeh et al., 2009). Ude et al. (2001) reported the sclerotium to be richer source of food nutrients compared to the fruiting body. Prior to use, the dark brown/black exterior of the sclerotia is removed using a knife to reveal the white compact mycelial tissue.

3.1. Cultivation of *Pleurotus tuber-regium*

Mushroom cultivation is still in its infancy in Nigeria, and many species that might be cultivated for food are known only in the wild state (Okhuoya and Okogbo, 1991). Several studies have investigated *P. tuber-regium* mushroom cultivation in Nigeria (Ogunlana, 1992; Fasidi et al., 1993; Fasidi and Olorunmaiye, 1994). *P. tuber-regium* mushroom is similar to the commonly cultivated oyster (*Pleurotus ostreatus*) mushroom except that the caps are cup-like shaped when mature (Aloha, 2013). In addition, this mushroom forms dark-brown sclerotia and naturally occurs in both subtropical and tropical climates. It requires a high temperature (warm strain): 82-90 °F (28-32 °C) for sclerotia formation which happens within 3-5 months. Ideally, this species is grown on straw and some agricultural wastes, which are low in lignin content. The recommended substrate include straw (wheat, rice, etc), hardwood sawdust and agricultural wastes such as banana leaves, corn cobs, cotton waste, oil palm fruit fiber, etc (Aloha, 2013).

P. tuber-regium fungus grows with relative ease in the laboratory and is noted for rapid growth and for causing extensive wood decay (Okhuoya and Okogbo, 1991). The cultivation of *P. tuber-regium* has been investigated by Okhuoya and Okogbo (1990; 1991). Okhuoya and Okogbo (1990) found that the sclerotia of *Pleurotus tuber-regium* grow well on dead trees and fallen logs of *Daniella oliveri* in the forests. They further reported that the sclerotia of *P. tuber-regium* were produced in the laboratory when the fungus was cultured in moist drill dusts of D oliveri and Elaeis guineensis, and the resulting sclerotia were viable and had features similar to those found in the natural habitat. In a related study, Okhuoya and Okogbo (1991) investigated the use of various farm wastes as substrates in the cultivation of *Pleurotus tuber-regium* and reported that the highest mushroom harvest (fresh weight) was obtained from oil palm fruit fiber substrate and the lowest yield was from yam (*Dioscorea* sp.) peelings.

Fasidi et al. (1993) conducted studies on the growth and cultivation of *Pleurotus tuber-regium* on local cellulosic wastes and reported that *Andropogon tectorum* straw supported the greatest mycelial growth, while cotton and oil palm pericarp wastes supported the least. For cultivation of edible sclerotia, cotton waste and rice straw gave the highest yield and banana leaves gave the lowest. The protein, lipid, ethanol-soluble sugar, crude fibre, calcium and magnesium contents of cultivated sclerotia have been observed to be dependent on the substrate on which the mushroom grows (Fasidi et al., 1993). The sclerotia grown on banana leaves were the richest while that cultivated on corn cob were the poorest in sodium, potassium, calcium, magnesium and phosphorus contents. In all the sclerotia cultivated on banana leaves, corn cob, cotton waste and rice straw, protein and potassium were the most abundant nutrients (Fasidi et al., 1993). Several studies have shown that *P. tuber-regium* can also be cultivated on other organic wastes such as corn, sawdust, cardboard, etc. (Okhuoya and Okogbo, 1990; Isikhuemhen and Okhuoya, 1996; Isikhuemhen and LeBauer, 2004).

Cultivation of mushrooms have certain drawback; the consumption of wild grown mushrooms is mostly preferred to that of cultivated ones in many countries of Central and Eastern Europe, China, and this is considered to be increasing, even in the developed world (Agrahar-Murugkar and Subbulakshmi, 2005).

3.2. Proximate Composition of *Pleurotus tuber-regium*

It has been observed that on the average, mushrooms on a dry-weight basis contain 63% carbohydrates, 25% protein, 4% fat, and the remaining 8% is accounted by minerals represented by ash (Rajarathnam and Shashirekha, 2003). Agomuo (2011) studied the sclerotia of *P. tuber-regium* and the results obtained for the proximate analysis were: lipid (2.20%), protein (7.88%), ash (1.20%), moisture (41.60%), fiber (10.69%), and carbohydrate (36.43%). Results of the proximate analysis of fresh samples and dried samples of the sclerotia of *P. tuber-regium* are presented in Figure 1 (Ikewuchi and Ikewuchi, 2008). The results (%) showed total ash of 2.2 and 2.4; crude protein of 64.31 and 71.21; crude lipid of

0.9 and 1.0; total carbohydrate of 20 and 22.15 and crude fibre of 2.89 and 3.2 for wet samples and dry samples respectively (Figure 1). Similarly, Adedayo (2011) studied the fruiting bodies of the *P. tuber-regium* and reported 3.48mg/g of total soluble carbohydrate, 3.61mg/g of protein, 0.85% ash and 89% moisture. Agomuo (2011) reported an energy value of 197.04±1.40, while Ikewuchi and Ikewuchi (2008) reported a total metabolizable energy (kcal/100g) of 345.34 for wet samples and 382.44 for dried samples of *P. tuber-regium*. Species of Pleurotus are reported to be predominantly rich in vitamins of B-complex and folic acid (Rajarathnam and Shashirekha, 2003). The tuber of *Pleurotus tuber-regium* is a rich source of food nutrients, and has been shown to be richer than the fruiting bodies (Ude et al., 2001).

Rajarathnam and Shashirekha (2003) estimated vitamins intake from the consumption of 100 g fresh Pleurotus mushrooms as a percentage of the amounts recommended by the Food and Agriculture Organization/World Health organization (FAO/WHO) per person per day (allowing for differences in moisture contents) and observed that Pleurotus mushrooms are good sources for meeting the human requirements for riboflavin and folic acid in particular. Vitamins contributed by 100g fresh Pleurotus mushrooms as a percentage of the daily requirement recommended by the Food and Agriculture Organization/World Health Organisation (FAO/WHO) per person ranges from 53-60% for male adult and 53-60% for female adult for folic acid; 33-39% for male adult and 46-54% for female adult for riboflavin; 26-33% for male adult and 36-46% for female adult for niacin; and 24-43% for male adult and 24-43% for female adult for ascorbic acid, and, 10-15% for male adult and 13-19% for female adult for thiamine (Rajarathnam and Shashirekha, 2003)

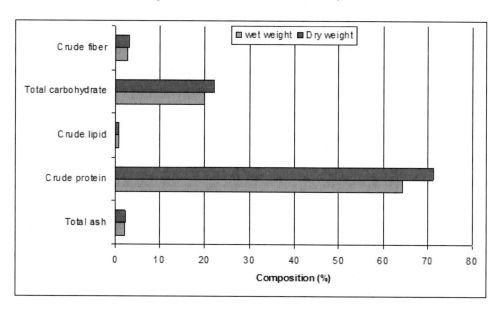

Figure 1. Proximate composition of the sclerotia of *P. tuber-regium* (Data from Ikewuchi and Ikewuchi, 2008).

3.3. *Pleurotus tuber-regium* Consumption in Nigeria

In Nigeria, the commercial cultivation of mushrooms is not common (Jonathan and Fasidi, 2003); however, most residents of rural communities enjoy mushrooms from the wild (Ude *et al.*, 2001; Gregori *et al.*, 2007; Nnorom, 2011). During the mushrooming season, most communities that are within the highways pick mushrooms fresh and display same for sale to motorists along major highways and this results in more earnings for the pickers and subsequent export of the mushrooms to the urban areas. This appears to be the same in many communities within the West African sub-region and elsewhere around the world (Barcan *et al.*, 1998; Falandysz, *et al.*, 2003; Zhang *et al.*, 2010; Gucia *et al.*, 2011). Foods prepared with the sclerotium of *P. tuber-regium* are perceived as delicacies in the South-eastern Nigeria.

Inhabitants of Isuikwuato and nearby communities in southeastern Nigeria consider foods and local snacks prepared with the sclerotia as a delicacy especially when rolled into dumplings after mixing with melon (*Colocynthis citrullus* L.; *egwusi* in *Igbo*) and seasoning. The dumpling popularly called *ahu* in Igbo Language are eaten as the 'ahu cake' or added to soups such as the "*egwusi*", "*óhà*" and "*ónugbú*" soups (Nnorom, 2011; Nnorom *et al.*, 2012; 2013). In some cases, the dumplings act as meat substitute in the diet (especially in soups) of some inhabitants (Nwokolo and Sim, 1987). This kind of food is sometimes used in achieving weight gain in malnourished babies (Alobo, 2003). One of the most common dietary applications of *P. tuber-regium* in Nigeria is as soup thickener because of its good swelling property.

3.4. Medicinal Applications of *P. tuber-regium* and other Nigerian Mushrooms

The chemical composition of mushrooms is the main cause for their therapeutic properties in preventing diseases such as hypertension (Talpur et al., 2002), hypercholesterolemia (Jeong et al., 2010) and several types of cancer (Lavi et al., 2006; Sullivan et al., 2006). Various wild edible mushroom species exhibit significant antioxidant activity, and therefore, can be used as an easily accessible source of natural antioxidants, as a potential food supplement, or in the pharmaceutical industry (Elmastas et al., 2007).

Edible fungi are reported to possess anti-allergic, anti-cholesterol, anti-tumour, and anticancer properties. They are also regarded as therapeutic foods having anti-cholesterolaemic and anti-viral properties, and also prophylactic properties with regard to coronary heart disease and hypertension (Bernas et al., 2006). In fact, various Pleurotus species have been shown to possess a number of medicinal properties, such as antitumor, immunomodulatory, antigenotoxic, antioxidant, anti-inflammatory, hypocholesterolaemic, antihypertensive, antiplatelet-aggregating, antihyperglycaemic, antimicrobial, and antiviral activities (Gregori et al., 2007).

The medicinal uses of mushrooms from Nigeria have been documented (Oso, 1975; Akpaja et al., 2003) and this includes the use of *P. tuber-regium* in alleviating headache, stomach pain, fever, cold, and constipation; *L. squarullosus* for mumps, and heart diseases; *T. microcarpus* for gonorrhea; *C. cyathiformis* for leucorrhea, and barreness; *Ganoderma lucidum* for treating arthritis, and neoplasia; *G. resinaceum* is used for treating hyperglycemia, and liver diseases (hepatoprotector); *G. applanatum* used as antioxidant and for diabetes. In fact, worldwide, mushrooms have been recognized as food and are grown on commercial scale in many countries.

3.5. Other Uses of *Pleurotus tuber-regium*

Researchers have also been investigating other applications of the sclerotia of *P. tuber-regium*, including its use in remediation (mycoremediation) of crude oil contaminated soils (Anoliefo et al., 2002; Ogbo and Okhuoya, 2008; 2011; Ogbo et al., 2010). P. tuber-regium has also been investigated as a local pharmaceutical excipient in drug manufacturing (Iwuagwu and Onyekweli, 2002) as well as considerations for other medical applications (Ezeronye et al., 2005). Iwuagwu and Onyekweli (2002) reported that the Pleurotus tuber-regium powder can be used as an alternative to maize starch BP as a disintegrant in tableting. The sclerotia's swelling property necessitated investigation into its possible use as a tablet disintegrant by Iwuagwu and Onyekweli (2002).

4. MACRO AND MICRONUTRIENT CONTENTS OF *P. TUBER-REGIUM*: INTAKE BENEFITS AND RISKS

Many metals are essential for fungal growth and metabolism (e.g., Ca, Cu, Fe, Mg, K, Na and Zn). Both essential and non-essential metals (such as Hg, Cd and Pb) can cause toxic effects to living organisms, including fungi, when present above certain threshold concentrations (Gadd, 1993; Aloupi et al., 2012). Metals exert toxic effects in many ways, e.g., by blocking operational groups of significant biological molecules such as enzymes or interacting with systems, which normally protect against harmful effects of free radicals generated during normal metabolism (Gadd, 2007; Aloupi et al., 2012). Nevertheless many fungi have developed a variety of mechanisms, both active and incidental, which allow them to survive, grow and flourish on substrates with high metal levels (Branco, 2010; Aloupi *et al.*, 2012).

Several studies have investigated the trace elements concentrations of wild edible mushrooms of diverse species (Ogundana and Fagade, 1982; Falandysz et al., 2001; 2008; 2012d; Kojta et al., 2011; Nnorom et al. 2013). Data are, however, scanty on the trace elements concentrations of both fruiting bodies and sclerotia of the *P. tuber-regium*. Available literature prior to the detailed studies of Nnorom et al., (2012; 2013) showed the determination of only a limited number of elements, especially heavy metals, in both the sclerotia and fruiting bodies of the mushroom of *P. tuber-regium* (Ude et al., 2001; Adejumo and Awosanya, 2005; Akindahunsi and Oyetayo, 2006; Gregori et al., 2007; Ijeh et al., 2009; Nnorom, 2011; Agomuo, 2011).

The results of major and trace elements concentrations of *P. tuber-regium* (on dry weight basis) as reported by Nnorom et al. (2013) are presented in Figures 2-4. Presented in Figures 2-4 are the mean values (dry weight) for the two locations investigated (standard deviation as error bars).

4.1. K, Mg, Ca, and Na Concentrations and Intake Levels

Several studies have reported varying element concentrations for the sclerotia of *P. tuber-regium* while a recent report by Nnorom et al. (2013) showed a detailed metal profile of *P. tuber-regium* collected form south-eastern Nigeria. The results of the study by Nnorom et al. (2013) are the basis of the estimations of the micronutrients benefits from consumption of the sclerotia of *P. Tuber-regium* (as well as the potential risks of intake of toxic elements, Pb, Hg, and Cd) in this chapter.

The detailed study by Nnorom et al. (2013) showed the sclerotia of the mushroom *P. tuber-regium* to be very rich in K, Mg, Ca, and Na (Figure 2; Table 1). Ijeh et al., (2009), who had worked on the fruiting bodies of *P. tuber-regium,* reported 4000±3000 for K, 3600±600 for Mg, 2000±500 for Na and 80 µg/g dw for Ca. Agomuo (2011) studied the sclerotia of *P. tuber-regium* and the results obtained for mineral element compositions were sodium, 192.6 ±0.70mg/kg; calcium, 37.2 ±0.92 mg/kg; and magnesium, 26.35±0.85 mg/kg.

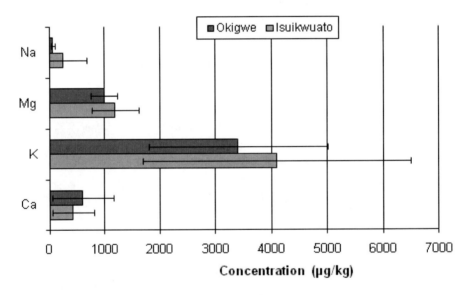

Figure 2. Na, Mg, K and Ca concentrations of the sclerotia of *P. tuber-regium* (Data from: Nnorom et al., 2013).

The estimated intakes of micronutrients and toxic metals from the consumption of 300g of sclerotia of *P. tuber-regium* collected from two towns (Okigwe and Isuikwuato both in southeast Nigeria) are presented in Table 1. The Table shows that food prepared with the sclerotia of *P. tuber-regium* would serve as a good dietary source of many essential elements, including K, Mg, Ca, and Na, to humans. A meal containing 300 g portion of the sclerotia will provide very good amounts of Na, Mg, K and Ca. The estimated intakes from a meal containing 300 g of *P. tuber-regium* are presented in Table 1.

Literature shows that for Na, the minimum daily requirement is 1500 mg and the maximum recommended Na intake is 2400 mg per day (USDA, 1995; Anderson et al., 2012). Thus the consumption of food prepared with sclerotia of *P. tuber-regium* does not increase the risk of hypertension and cardiovascular disease (assuming no other sources of Na intake) and a consumer will need to consume between 0.6 – 2.2 kg of sclerotia to exceed the maximum intake value of 2400 mg. The recommended dietary allowance for calcium is between 800 - 1200 mg daily (Chan, 1991).

Table 1. Estimated human exposure to micronutrients and toxic metals from consumption of 300g of sclerotia of *P. tuber-regium*

Element	Ag	Al	Ba	Ca	Cd	Co	Cr	Cu	Fe	Hg
Mean (wet weight, μg)	0.025[*] 0.041[†]	11.13 8.48	2.28 1.33	233 323	0.021 0.030	0.025 0.027	0.095 0.175	3.657 2.915	25.44 29.68	0.013 0.021
Exposure concentration (mg)[‡]	0.008 0.012	3.34 2.54	0.68 0.40	70.0 97.0	0.006 0.009	0.008 0.008	0.003 0.053	1.10 0.88	7.63 8.90	0.004 0.006

Estimates were made with data from Nnorom et al. (2013) which were converted to wet weight. [*]Data for Isuikwuato town; [†]data for Okigwe town. [‡]Exposure concentration on consumption of 300g sclerotia.

Element	K	Mg	Mn	Na	Ni	P	Pb	Rb	Sr	Zn
Mean (wet weight, μg)	2173[*] 1802[†]	636 530	9.01 10.6	133 36.0	0.074 0.376	1.325 1.007	0.138 0.636	9.54 6.89	3.498 2.173	10.07 14.84
Exposure concentration (mg)[‡]	652 541	191 159	2.70 3.18	39.8 10.81	0.022 0.11	0.40 0.30	0.04 0.19	2.86 2.07	1.05 0.65	3.02 4.45

Estimates were made with data from Nnorom et al. (2013) which were converted to wet weight. [*]Data for Isuikwuato town; [†]data for Okigwe town. [‡]Exposure concentration on consumption of 300g sclerotia.

4.2. Al, Ba, Cu, Fe, Mn, P, Rb, Sr and Zn Concentrations and Intake Levels

The concentrations of Rb, Cu, Sr, Ba, and P as well as for Al, Fe, Mn and Zn are presented in Figure 3. The estimated intake of these elements on the consumption of 300g of the sclerotia of *P. tuber-regium* for the two towns, using the mean contents as reported by Nnorom et al. (2013) are presented in Table 1.

In an earlier study, the concentrations of Cu were reported to be between 0.5±0.2 mg/kg and 1.2±0.6 mg/kg with 78% of the results below 1 mg/kg (Nnorom, 2011). Agomuo (2011) studied the sclerotia of *P. tuber-regium* and the results obtained for mineral element compositions are manganese, 3.5±1.02 mg/kg; copper, 84.25±0.53mg/kg; and iron, 122.0±0.70 mg/kg. Ijeh *et al.* (2009) reported a mean concentration of 0.135 mg/kg of Zn and 0.502 mg/kg of Fe in the fruiting bodies of *P. tuber-regium*. Ijeh et al. (2009) also reported a mean Cu concentration of 0.083 mg/kg in the fruiting bodies of *P. tuber-regium*, while Ayodele and Odogbili (2010) reported a mean Cu concentration of 0.055 mg/kg in the pileus (cap) and 0.049 mg/kg in the stipe (stem or stalk) of *P. tuber-regium*.

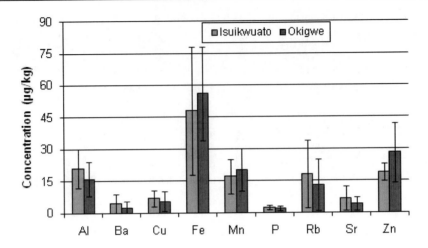

Figure 3. Al, Ba, Cu, Fe, Mn, P, Rb, Sr and Zn concentrations of the sclerotia of *P. tuber-regium* (Data from: Nnorom et al., 2013).

Literature indicates that an adequate intake of Cu and Zn in adults is estimated at 1.5-4 mg and 10 mg per day respectively (Kabata-Pendias and Pendias, 1999). Consequently, a meal containing 300 g sclerotia portion (assuming no other sources of the elements considered) will provide 0.88-1.10 mg of Cu, and these intakes will be 59-73 % of the lower recommended Cu intake limit of 1.5 mg per day; and 22-28 % of the upper limit of 4 mg per day. Similarly, a meal containing 300 g sclerotia will provide 3.02-4.45 mg of Zn and this will amount to 30-45 % of the recommended Zn intake per day. Therefore, the consumption of sclerotia will be a good source of Cu and Zn.

The UK Expert Group on Vitamins and Minerals (Rose et al., 2010) observed that a daily intake of Mn of up to 200 µg per kg bw (14 mg for 70 kg bw man) is not likely to give rise to adverse health effects. Consumption of 300 g of sclerotia will provide 2.7 – 3.2 mg of Mn. Similarly, the consumption of 300g sclerotia from a meal will provide 7.6 – 8.9 mg Fe.

Considering the Cobalt content of sclerotia, a meal containing 300 g sclerotia will provide approximately 7.6 µg at Isuikwuato and 8.0 µg of Co at Okigwe and these will amount to approximately 20% of the lower recommended daily dietary intake of Co for an adult which is 40-50 µg (Seiler et al., 1988 cited in NLM, 2013; Nnorom et al., 2013).

4.3. Ag, Cd, Co, Cr, Hg, Ni and Pb Concentrations and Intake Levels

Evaluation of the levels of toxic elements such as Pb, Cd and Hg in foodstuff is necessary since the safety of consumption of such food materials is very important. The results of Nnorom et al. (2013) showed the median concentrations of Cr, Ni, Ag, Co, Hg, and Cd in the sclerotia of *P. tuber-regium* to be generally low and <1 µg/g.

The concentrations of Ag, Co, and Cr were also reported by Nnorom et al., (2013) that also varied widely. Literature shows that the recommended adequate Cr intake is 25 µg per day for adults and between 0.1 and 1.0 µg for children and adolescents (Rose et al., 2010). A related report recommended a higher Cr dose of 50 - 200 µg for children (> 6 years), adolescents, and adults (Krejpcio, 2001). Considering the Cr content of sclerotia (Table 1), a meal of 300 g will provide 28.5-52.5 µg (0.03 – 0.053 mg) of Cr which shows that sclerotia will be a good source of Cr intake.

The Ni, Hg, Cd and Pb concentrations though low also varied widely (Nnorom et al., 2013).

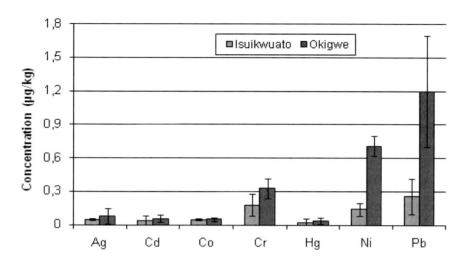

Figure 4. Ag, Cd, Co, Cr, Hg, Ni and Pb concentrations of the sclerotia of *P. tuber-regium* (Data from: Nnorom et al., 2013).

An earlier study of the sclerotia of *P. tuber-regium* reported a Pb concentration that ranged from 0.2±0.1 mg/kg to 0.8±0.5 mg/kg with approximately 91% of the results below 1 mg/kg (Nnorom, 2011). The overall mean of the study by Nnorom (2011) is 0.5±0.4 µg/g and this is comparable to the results of Nnorom et al. (2013). In a similar study, Nnorom et al. (2012) investigated the Hg content of the sclerotia from five towns in southeastern Nigeria and reported a mean Hg values of 48±30 (range, 16-120 ng g^{-1}) for samples from Abakpa Okigwe; 46±21 (17-97 ng g^{-1}) for Ahonta, Eluama; 41±51 (7.6-180 ng g^{-1}) for Ekeama, Umuobiala; 39±28 (3.3-100 ng g^{-1}) for Eke-Okigwe and 24±36 (7.6-150 ng g^{-1}) for Ukwunwangwu, Uturu.

Regulatory agencies around the world set concentration limits for toxic elements (and compounds) in foods. For mushrooms, the European Union established a maximum concentration limit of 0.2 µg/g wet weight for Cd for three cultivated species of fungi (Champignon Mushroom, Oyster Mushroom and Shi-take); while for other fungi species, the limit is 1.0 µg/g wet weight (10 µg/g dw; assuming 90 % moisture) (EU, 2008). The established maximum concentration limit for Pb in the above listed cultivated fungi is 0.3 µg/g ww (3.0 µg/g dw) (EU, 2008). Nnorom et al. (2013) reported the Cd concentrations of the sclerotia to be below the EU regulatory limit of 10 µg/g dw for other fungi while the Pb concentrations were below the EU threshold limit of 3.0 µg/g dw.

The Joint FAO/WHO Expert Committee on Food Additives (JECFA) established a provisional tolerable weekly intake (PTWI) of 7 µg/kg body weight (equivalent to 1 µg/kg bw per day) for Cd (WHO, 1989; JECFA, 2010). Similarly, the European Food Safety Authority (EFSA) set a tolerable weekly intake (TWI) of 2.5 µg/kg bw (equivalent to 0.36 µg/kg bw per day) for cadmium (EFSA, 2009). Nnorom et al. (2013) observed that a meal consisting of 300 g of fresh sclerotia would expose a consumer to 0.089 µg Cd in Isuikwuato, and 0.13 µg in Okigwe (using the mean Cd contents of the sclerotia) and these exposure values are 8.9 and 13 % of the PTWI, respectively. Likewise, for the EFSA TWI value, it was reported that a 300 g meal of sclerotia would expose a 70 kg consumer to 25 % of the EFSA value in Isuikwuato and 36 % in Okigwe (Nnorom et al., 2013).

According the World Health Organisation, the acceptable daily intake of Pb for adults is between 0.21 and 0.25 mg per day, and between 1.5 and 1.75 mg per week (WHO, 1993). Nnorom et al. (2013) observed that a meal of 300 g of the sclerotia of *Pleurotus tuber-regium* will contribute between 17 and 20 % of the daily Pb intake in Isuikwuato, and between 76 and 91 % of daily intake in Okigwe (Nnorom et al., 2013).

The study of mercury in sclerotia of *P. tuber-regium* by Nnorom et al., (2012) showed that approximately 7% of samples investigated exceeded the EU recommended Hg limit of 100 ng g^{-1} for food supplements (EC, 2006; 2008). In the assessment of possible risks from Hg intake from meals prepared with the sclerotia of *P. tuber-regium*, a reference dose (RfD) of 0.0003 mg/kg body mass daily, and the Provisionally Tolerable Weekly Intake (PTWI) of 0.004 mg/kg (body mass, bm) as established were applied (US EPA, 1987; JECFA, 2010). Based on these established references, the consumption of 300 g of sclerotia for the sites investigated by Nnorom et al. (2012), would expose a consumer to between 0.72 and 1.4 µg of Hg and (assuming 90 % water content in the sclerotia samples and an adult individual of 70 kg body mass) these exposure levels would be from 3.4 to 6.9% of the recommended reference dose for Hg (Nnorom et al., 2012). This indicates that the consumption of sclerotia does not pose health risk. The Hg intake from consumption of 300g sclerotia would be between 5.0 and 10 µg of Hg amounting to between 1.0 and 2.8% of the PTWI. Fanciers of sclerotia would consume very large amounts to exceed the PTWI for Hg. For instance, an adult (70 kg body weight) would need to consume in excess of 4.4 to 8.7 kg of fresh sclerotia (depending on the site investigated) to exceed the Hg PTWI limit (Nnorom et al., 2012).

There is therefore no health risk from the ingestion of toxic metals such as Cd, Hg, Pb and Ni from the consumption of sclerotia of *P. tuber-regium* and the reported low concentrations may indicate that these metals are of natural sources only. However, Agomuo (2011) studied the sclerotia of *P. tuber-regium* and reported a mean nickel concentration of 26.35±0.65 which is rather too high.

CONCLUSION

The discussion presented here shows the benefits of consuming *P. tuber-regium* and this will contribute to available data on benefits of consuming natural foods such as mushrooms. Estimates of micronutrients intake indicate that the consumption of *P. tuber-regium* will act as a rich source of micronutrients to the consuming population. Visitors to southeastern Nigeria may not be able to differentiate soups prepared with *egwusi* only from those cooked with a combination of *egwusi* and the sclerotia of *P tuber-regium* which is often added because it is cheaper and enhances thickening of the soup. The sclerotia are very rich in minerals and would serve as a dietary source of Zn, K, Mn, Mg, Ca, and Na among other micronutrients. The Hg concentrations are very low and would not pose any risk to consumers. Similarly, the Cd and Pb contents of the sclerotia of *P. tuber-regium* have been reported to be low and below the European Union limits for these metals in fungi (10 μg/g dw and 3 μg/g dw respectively), indicating that the sclerotia are safe for human consumption and that there is no health risk on the consumption of delicacies prepared with the sclerotia of *P. tuber-regium*. To reduce exogenous contamination, it is recommended that the outer layers of the sclerotia be properly scrapped before use (Nnorom, 2011).

ACKNOWLEDGMENTS

The author appreciates the invaluable contributions of Mr Ugochukwu Ewuzie and Uka Ugwu Imo of Abia State University Uturu, Nigeria, and Prof Jerzy Falandysz of Research Group of Environmental Chemistry, Ecotoxicology & Food Toxicology, Institute of Environmental Sciences & Public Health, University of Gdańsk, Poland.

REFERENCES

Adedayo, M.R. (2011). Proximate analysis on four edible mushrooms. *Journal of Applied Science and Environmental Management*, 15 (1), 9 – 11.

Adejumo, T.O., Awosanya, O.B., (2005). Proximate and mineral composition of four edible mushrooms species from southwestern Nigeria. *African Journal of Biotechnology*, 4, 1084-1088.

Agomuo, E. N. (2011). Proximate, phytochemical, and mineral element analysis of the sclerotium of *pleurotus tuber-regium*. *International Science Research Journal*, 3: 104 – 107.

Agrahar-Murugkar, D., Subbulakshmi, G., (2005). Nutritional value of edible wild mushrooms collected from the Khasi hills of Meghalaya. *Food Chemistry*, 89, 599–603.

Akindahunsi, A.A., Oyetayo, F.L. (2006). Nutrient and anti-nutrient distribution of edible mushroom, *Pleurotus tuber-regium* (fries) singer. *LWT Food Science and Technology (Lebensmittel-Wissenschaft and Technologie)*, 39, 548-553.

Akpaja EO, Isikhuemhen OS, Okhuoya JA. (2003). Ethnomycology and uses of edible and medicinal mushrooms among the Igbo people of Nigeria. *International Journal of Medicinal. Mushrooms*, 5, 313–319.

Alobo A.P (2003). Proximate Composition and Functional Properties of *Pleurotus tuberregium* sclerotia Flour and Protein Concentrate. *Plant Foods for Human Nutrition*, 58, 1-9.

Aloha. (2013) *Pleurotus tuber-regium*. Aloha Medicinals. Aloha Medicinal inc. http://www.alohaculturebank.com/Pleurotustuber-regiumMS.html Accessed on November, 2013.

Alonso J., García MÁ., Pérez-López M., Melgar M.J. (2003). The concentrations and bioconcentration factors of copper and zinc in edible mushrooms. *Archives of Environmental Contamination Toxicology*, 4, 44,180–188.

Aloupi, M., Koutrotsios, G., Koulousaris, M., Kalogeropoulos, N. (2012). Trace metal contents in wild edible mushrooms growing on serpentine and volcanic soils on the island of Lesvos, Greece. *Ecotoxicology and Environmental Safety*, 78, 184–194.

Anderson, J., Young, L., Long, E., Prior, S. (2012). Sodium in the Diet. Colorado State University Extension. Fact Sheet No. 9.354 http://www.ext.colostate.edu/pubs/foodnut/09354.html

Anoliefo, G.O., Isikhuemhen, O.S., Ohimain, E., (2002). Phytoassessment of soil polluted with Forcados blend crude oil exposed to a white rot fungus, *Pleurotus tuberregium* (Fr.) Sing. *Proceedings of National Conference on Environmental Science and Technology,* 2002; 43-59, 8-10 September 2002, Greensboro, North Carolina.

Ayodele, S.M., Odogbili, O.D., (2010). Metal impurities in three edible mushrooms collected in Abraka, Delta State, Nigeria. *Micología Aplicada Internacional,* 22, 27–30.

Barcan. V., Kovnatsky, E.F., Smetannikova, M.S., (1998). Absorption of heavy metals in wild berries and edible mushrooms in areas affected by smelter emissions. *Water Air Soil Pollution,* 103, 173-195.

Bernas, E., Jaworska, G., Lisiewska, Z. (2006). Edible mushroom as a source of valuable nutritive constituents. *Acta Scientiarum Polonorum, Technologia Alimentaria,* 5, 5–20.

Branco, S., (2010). Serpentine soils promote ectomycorrhizal fungal diversity. *Molecular Ecology,* 19, 5566–5576.

Chan, G.M. (1991). Dietary calcium and bone mineral status of children and adolescents. *Archives of Pediatric and Adolescent Medicine,* 145, 631-634.

Chang, S.T. 1990. Composition of foods. Mushrooms as food. Food Laboratory

Chojnacka, A., Drewnowska, M., Jarzynska, G., Nnorom, I.C., Falandysz, J (2012) Mercury in Yellow-cracking Boletes *Xerocomus subtomentosus* mushrooms and soils from spatially diverse sites: Assessment of bioconcentration potential by species and human intake. *Journal of Environmental Science and Health, Part A,* 47 (13), 2094-2100.

Dryżałowska M., Sąpór, A., Jarzyńska G., Nnorom I.C., Sajwan K.S., Falandysz J. (2012) Mercury in Russula mushrooms: Bioconcentration by Yellow-ocher Brittle Gills *Russula ochroleuca.* J*ournal of Environmental Science and Health, Part A,* 47 (11), 1577-1591.

EFSA., 2009. European Food Safety Authority (EFSA). Cadmium in food. *EFSA Journal,* 980, 1–139; [cited 2009 Dec 12]. Available from: http://www.efsa.europa.eu/cs/Blob Server/Scientific_Opinion/contam_op_ej980_cadmium_en_rev.1.pdf?ssbinary=true/

Elmastas-, M., Isildak, O., Turkekul, I., Temur, N., (2007). Determination of antiox- idant activity and antioxidant compounds in wild edible mushrooms. *Journal of Food Composition and Analysi*s, 20, 337–345.

EU., (2006). Commission Regulation (EC) No 1881/2006 of 19 December 2006. *Setting maximum levels for certain contaminants in foodstuffs.* Off J Eur Un L 364/5. 20.12.2006.

EU., (2008). Commission Regulation (EC) No 629/2008 of 2 July 2008 amending Regulation (EC) No 1881/2006 setting maximum levels for certain contaminants in foodstuffs. Official Journal of the European Union. 3.7.2008, L.173/6-9.

Ezeronye, O.U. , Daba A.S. Okwujiako and I.A.Onumajuru, I.C. (2005). Antibacterial Effect of Crude Polysaccharide Extracts from Sclerotium and Fruitbody (Sporophore) of *Pleurotus tuber-regium* (Fried) Singer on Some Clinical Isolates. *International Journal of Molecular Medicine and Advance Sciences, 1: 202-205.*

Falandysz J, Mazur A, Kojta A.K, Drewnowska M, Dryżałowska A, Nnorom I.C (2012b) Mercury in fruiting bodies of dark honey fungus *(Armillaria solidipes)* and beneath substratum soils collected from spatially distant areas. *Journal of Science Food and Agriculture,* 93 (4) 853-858 :doi.:10.1002/jsfa.5807. PMID: 22836787.

Falandysz, J. and Borovička, J. 2013. Macro and trace mineral constituents and radionuclides in mushrooms: health benefits and risks. *Applied Microbiology and Biotechnology*, 97: 477–501.

Falandysz, J. Gucia, M. (2008). Bioconcentration factors of mercury by Parasol mushroom (*Macrolepiota procera*). *Environmental Geochemistry and Health*, 30, 121-125.

Falandysz, J., Kawano, M., Świeczkowski, A., Brzostowski, A. Dadej, M. (2003). Total mercury in wild-grown higher mushrooms and underlying soil from Wdzydze Landscape Park, Northern Poland. *Food Chemistry*, 81, 21-26.

Falandysz, J., Kojta, A.K., Jarzyńska, G., Drewnowska, A., Dryżałowska, A., Wydmańska, D., Kowalewska, I., Wacko, A., Szlosowska, M., Kannan, K., Szefer, P. (2012d). Mercury in Bay Bolete *Xerocomus badius*: bioconcentration by fungus and assessment of element intake by humans eating fruiting bodies. *Food Additives and Contaminants Part A*, 29, 951-961.

Falandysz, J., Kowalewska, I., Nnorom, I.C., Drewnowska, M., Jarzyńska, G., (2012a). Mercury in Red Aspen Boletes (*Leccinum aurantiacum*) mushrooms and the soils. *Journal of Environmental Science and Health, Part A*, 47 (11), 1695-1700.

Falandysz, J., Kunito, T., Kubota, R., Bielawski, L., Frankowska, A., Falandysz, J., Tanabe, S. 2008. Multivariate characterization of elements accumulated in King Bolete, *Boletus edulis*, mushroom at lowland and high mountain regions. *Journal of Environmental Science and Health Part A* 43, 1692-1699.

Falandysz, J., Szymczyk, K., Ichihashi, H., Bielawski, L., Gucia, M., Frankowska, A., (2001). Yamasaki S, ICP/MS and ICP/AES elemental analysis (38 elements) of edible wild mushrooms growing in Poland. *Food Additives and Contamination* 18, 503-513.

Falandysz, J., Widzicka, E., Kojta, A.K., Jarzyńska, G., Drewnowska, M., Danisiewicz-Czupryńska, D., Dryżałowska, A., Lenz, E., Nnorom, I.C. (2012c). Mercury in Common Chanterelles mushrooms: *Cantharellus* spp. update. *Food Chemistry* 133, 842-850.

Fasidi I.A., Olorunmaiye K.S. (1994). Studies on the Requirements for Vegetative Growth of *Pleurotus tuber-regium* (Fr.) Singer, a Nigerian Mushroom. *Food Chemistry* 50, 397-401.

Fasidi I.O., Ekuere, F., Usukama, U. (1993) Studies on *Pleurotus tuber regium* (Fries) singer: Cultivation, proximate composition and mineral content of sclerotia. *Food Chemistry* 48, 255 – 258.

Gadd, G.M. (1993). Interactions of fungi with toxic metals. *New Phytologist*, 124, 25–60.

Gadd, G.M. (2007). Geomycology, biogeochemical transformations of rocks, miner- als, metals and radionuclides by fungi, bioweathering and bioremediation. *Mycology Research*, 111, 3–49.

Gregori, A., Svagelj, M. Pohleven. J. (2007). Cultivation techniques and medicinal properties of Pleurotus spp. *Food Technology and Biotechnology* 45, 238–429.

Gucia, M., Kojta, A.K., Jarzyńska, G., Rafał, E., Roszak, M., Osiej, I., Falandysz, J. (2011). Multivariate analysis of mineral constituents of edible Parasol Mushroom (*Macrolepiota procera*) and soils beneath fruiting bodies collected from Northern Poland. *Environmental Science and Pollution Research*, 19, 416-431.

Ijeh, I., Okwujiako, I.A., Nwosu, P.C., Nnodim, H.I., (2009). Phytochemical composition of *Pleurotus tuber regium* and effect of its dietary incorporation on body/organ weights and serum triacylglycerols in albino mice. *Journal of Medicinal Plants Research*, 3, 939-943.

Ikewuchi, C.C., Ikewuchi, J.C (2008) Chemical Profile *of Pleurotus tuberregium* (Fr) Sing's Sclerotia. *The Pacific Journal of Science and Technology*, 10 (1), 295- 299.

Isikhuemhen, O.S., LeBauer, D.S. (2004). Growing *Pleurotus tuber-regium. Oyster Mushroom Cultivation*. Seoul (Korea): Mushworld. pp. 270–281. ISBN 1-883956-01-3.

Isikhuemhen, O.S., Okhuoya, J.A. (1996). "Cultivation of *Pleurotus tuber-regium* (Fr.) Sing. for production of edible sclerotia on agricultural wastes". In Royse, D.J. (Ed.) *Mushroom biology and mushroom products: proceedings of the 2nd International Conference, June 9-12, 1996*. University Park, PA (USA): Pennsylvania State University: World Society for Mushroom Biology and Mushroom Products. pp. 429–436. ISBN 1-883956-01-3.

Iwuagwu, M.A., Onyekweli, A.O. (2002). Preliminary investigation into the use of *Pleurotus tuber-regium* powder as a tablet disintegrant. *Tropical Journal of Pharmaceutical Research* 1, 29-37.

JECFA. (2010). Joint FAO/WHO Expert Committee on Food Additives. Seventy-second meeting. Rome, 16–25 February 2010. Summary and Conclusions. JECFA/72/SC. Food and Agriculture Organization of the United Nations World Health Organization. Issued 16th March 2010.

Jeong, S.C., Jeong, Y.T., Yang, B.K., Islam, R., Koyyalamudi, S.R., Pang, G.,Cho, K.Y., Song, C.H. (2010). White button mushroom (*Agaricus bisporus*) lowers blood glucose and cholesterol levels in diabetic and hypercholesterolemic rats. *Nutrition Research,* 30,49–56.

Jonathan, S.G., Fasidi, I. O. (2003). Studies on *Psathyrella atroumbonata* (Pegler), a Nigerian edible fungus. *Food Chemistry,* 81, 481–484.

Kabata-Pendias, A.K., Pendias, H. (1999). Biogeochemia pierwiastków śladowych. Warszawa: Wydawnictwo Naukowe PWN.

Kojta, A.K., Gucia, M., Jarzyńska, G., Lewandowska, M, Zakrzewska, A., Falandysz, J., Zhang, D. (2011). Phosphorous and metallic elements in Parasol Mushroom (*Macrolepiota procera*) and soil from the Augustowska Forest and Ełk regions in north-eastern Poland. *Fresenius Environmental Bulletin,* 20, 3044-3052.

Krejpcio, Z., 2001. Essentiality of chromium for human nutrition and health. *Polish Journal of Environmental Studies,* 10, 399–404.

Lavi, I., Friesem, D., Geresh, S., Hadar, Y., Schwart, B. (2006). An aqueous poly- saccharide extract from the edible mushroom *Pleurotus ostreatus* induces anti- proliferative and pro-apoptotic effects on HT-29 colon cancer cells. *Cancer Letters*. 244, 61–70. News, August No. *21,* 7–8.

NLM (2013) Cobalt compounds. National Library of Mdicine. TOXNET. Toxicological Data Network. http://toxnet.nlm.nih.gov/cgi-bin/sis/search/a?dbs+hsdb:@term+@ DOCNO+ 7141 accessed on December 31, 2013.

Nnorom, I.C. (2011). Lead and copper contents of the sclerotium of the mushroom *Pleurotus tuber-regium* (Osu): assessment of contribution to dietary intake in southeastern Nigeria. *Toxicological and Environmental Chemistry,* 93, 1359–1367.

Nnorom, I.C., Jarzyńska, G., Drewnowska, M., Drewnwska, A., Kojta, A., Pankavec, S., Falandysz, J. (2013) Major and trace elements in sclerotium of *Pleurotus tuber-regium* (Ósū) mushroom - dietary intake and risk in Southeastern Nigeria. *Journal of Food Composition and Analysis*, 29, 73-81.

Nnorom, I.C., Jarzyńska, G., Falandysz, J., Drewnowska, M., Okoye I., Oji-Nnorom, C.G. (2012). Occurrence and accumulation of mercury in two species of wild grown *Pleurotus* mushrooms from Southeastern Nigeria. *Ecotoxicology and Environmental Safety,* 84, 78-83 .

Nwokolo, E., Sim J.S. (1987). Nutritional assessment of defatted seed meal of melon (*Colocynthis citrullus* L.) and fluted pumpkin (*Telfaria occidentales* Hook) by chick assay. *Journal of Science, Food and Agriculture*, 38, 237–246.

Ogbo E.M., Okhuoya, J.A. (2011). Bio-Absorption of Some Heavy Metals by *Pleurotus tuber-regium* Fr. Singer (An Edible Mushroom) from Crude Oil Polluted Soils Amended with Fertilizers and Cellulosic Wastes. *International Journal of Soil Science, 6: 34-48.*

Ogbo, E.M., Okhuoya, J.A. (2008). Bioremediation of aliphatic, aromatic, resinic and asphaltic fractions of crude oil contaminated soils by *Pleurotus tuber-regium* Fr. Singer-a white rot fungus. *African Journal of Biotechnology*, 7, 4291-4297.

Ogbo, E.M., Tabuanu, A., Ubebe, R. (2010). Phytotoxicity assay of diesel fuel-spiked substrates remediated with *Pleurotus tuberregium* using Zea mays. *International Journal of Applied Research in Natural Products*, 3 (2), 12-16.

Ogundana, S. K., Fagade, O. E. (1982). Nutritive value of some Nigerian edible mushrooms. *Food Chemistry*, 8(4), 263–268.

Ogunlana, S.K. (1992). Studies on the cultivation of the edible mushroom *Pleurotus tuber regium* (Fr) Singer. *Tropical Journal of Applied Sciences* 2, 56 – 60.

Okhuoya J.A., Okogbo, F.O. (1990). Induction of edible sclerotia of Pleurotus tuber-regium (FR) Sing, in the laboratory. *Annals of Applied Biology* 117 (2), 295–298.

Okhuoya, J.A., Okogbo, F.O. (1991). Cultivation of *Pleurotus tuber-regium* (Fr) Sing on various farm wastes. *Proceedings of the Oklahoma Academy of Science*, 71, 1- 3.

Oso, B.A., 1975. Mushrooms and Yoruba people of Nigeria. *Mycologia*. 67:311–319.

Rajarathnam, S., Shashirekha, M. N. (2003) "Mushrooms and truffles: use of wild mushrooms," in Encyclopedia of Food. Science and Nutrition, pp. 4048–4054. Academic Press, London, UK.

Rose, M., Baxter, M., Brereton, N., Baskaran, C. (2010). Dietary exposure to metals and other elements in the 2006 UK Total Diet Study and some trends over the last 30 years. *Food Additives and Contaminants A* 27, 1380 - 1404.

Seiler, H.G; Sigel, H; Sigel, A (Eds) (1988) Handbook of inorganic compounds. New York, NY: Marcel Dekker Inc. p 254.

Sisak, L. (1996). The importance of forests as a source of mushrooms and berries in the Czech Republic. *Mykologicky´ Sbornı´k*, 73, 98–101 (in Czech).

Sullivan, R., Smith, J.E., Rowan, N.J. (2006). Medicinal mushrooms and cancer therapy. Translating a traditional practice into western medicine. *Perspective in Biology and Medicine, 49*, 159–170.

Svoboda, L., Havličkova, B., Kalač, P. (2006). Contents of cadmium, mercury and lead in edible mushrooms growing in a historical silver-mining area. *Food Chemistry*, 96, 580-585.

Talpur, N.A., Echard, B.W., Fan, A.Y., Jaffari, O., Bagchi, D., Preuss, H.G. (2002). Antihypertensive and metabolic effects of whole Maitake mushroom powder and its fractions in two rat strains. *Molecular and Cellular Biochemistry*, 237, 129–136.

Ude, C.M., Ezenwugo, A.E.N., Agu, R.C. (2001). Composition and food value of sclerotium (Osu) and edible mushroom (*Pleurotus tuber-regium*). *Journal of Food Science and Technology, 38*, 612–614.

US EPA. (1987). Peer review workshop on mercury issues. Environmental criteria and assessments office. Summary report. US Environment Protection Agency. Cincinnati, 1987.

USDA. (1995). US Department of Agriculture, US Department of Health and Human Services, Nutrition and your Health: Dietary Guidelines for Americans. 4th ed. Washington, DC US Dept of Agriculture: Home and Garden Bulletin 232.

WHO. (1989). Toxicological evaluation of certain food additives and contaminants, 33rd Report of the Joint FAO/WHO Expert Committee on Food Additives. Food Additives Series No. 24. Geneva (Switzerland): World Health Organization.

WHO. (1993). Evaluation of certain food additives and contaminants, 41st Report of the Joint FAO/WHO Expert Committee on Food Additives. Technical Report Series No. 837. Geneva (Switzerland): World Health Organization.

Zhang, D., Frankowska, A., Jarzyńska, G., Kojta, A.K., Drewnowska, M., Wydmańska, D., Bielawski, L., Wang, J., Falandysz, J. (2010). Metals of King Bolete (*Boletus edulis*) collected at the same site over two years. *African Journal of Agricultural Research,* 5, 3050-3055.

In: Mushrooms
Editor: Grégoire Pesti

ISBN: 978-1-63117-521-3
© 2014 Nova Science Publishers, Inc.

Chapter 12

VALORIZATION OF COFFEE-GROUNDS SUPPLEMENTED WITH WHEAT STRAW BY CULTIVATION OF A *PLEUROTUS OSTREATUS* LOCAL STRAIN

Malika Mansour-Benamar[*], *Souhila Aoudia and Nadia Ammar-Khodja*

Laboratoire de Production, Amélioration et Protection des Végétaux.
Faculté des Sciences Biologiques et des Sciences Agronomiques.
Université Mouloud MAMMERI de Tizi-Ouzou. Algérie

ABSTRACT

Valorization of both local agro-wastes and local biological resources by edible mushroom cultivation is a stake for many countries. Coffee-grounds has previously been shown to be a cultivation substrate for a local Algerian strain of *Pleurotus ostreatus* but the yields were low. In order to improve the process, the addition of wheat straw in mixture with coffee-grounds was studied in the present chapter. The pH of the substrates was optimized by the addition of 2 % calcium carbonate. By using a low-tech and inexpensive cultivation process at an experimental scale, improved yields were measured in mixture of coffee-grounds and wheat straw reaching biological efficiency to 102% and 153% with a local strain and a commercial strain of *P. ostreatus* respectively, when they were measured in a mixture of 50% coffee-grounds and 50% wheat straw supplemented with calcium carbonate. Analysis of physic-chemical parameter in cultivation substrates revealed that the two strains had the same behavior for substrate transformation. Coffee grounds is a waste having a good potential as component of cultivation substrates for the production of *Pleurotus* mushrooms.

Keywords: Coffee-grounds, wheat straw, supplementation, *Pleurotus ostreatus*, valorization

---

[*] Corresponding author: Malika Mansour – Benamar. Tél. /fax: 0021326216819, Tel: 00213775052680, E-mail: mansour_benamar@yahoo.fr.

INTRODUCTION

All researchers working on wild or cultivated mushrooms agree that edible mushrooms are gourmet cuisine and are nutritionally valuable food with subtle flavor and taste and a fragrance appreciated by all consumers across the world. Indeed, fruiting bodies contain an important amount of proteins well balanced with essential amino acids, vitamins (vitamin C and B complex) and minerals and have low sugar and fat contents and high content of fiber (Delmas, 1989, Olivier et al., 1991, Ayodele and Okhuoya, 2007, Ahmed et al., 2009, Akyüz and Kirbað, 2010, Bano and Rajarathnam, 2010, Upadhyay and Singh, 2010, Patel and Goyal, 2012, Yehia, 2012, Manimozhi and Kaviyarasan, 2013). In addition, mushrooms can be used as drug and neutraceutical and have numerous pharmacological potentials (Wasser and Weis, 1999, Lindequist et al., 2005, Aida et al., 2009, De Silva et al., 2012, El Enshasy, 2013).

Mushroom cultivation is an opportunity for developing countries dependent on cereal since edible mushrooms are recommended by the FAO as food (Islam et al., 2009). Besides solving problem of protein shortage, mushroom cultivation can help solving others problems like resources recovery and environmental management since mushroom cultivation is based on the bioconversion of wastes or by products to food. The most cultivated and commercialized mushrooms in the world are *Agaricus bisporus* (Lange) Imbach (button mushroom), *Lentinula edodes* (Berk.) Pegler (Shiitake) and *Pleurotus* species (Oyster Mushrooms) (Zied et al., 2011, Savoie et al., 2013). However cultivation of edible mushroom in Africa seems to be limited. Publications of research on wild edible and mushroom cultivation are relatively recent and come mostly from two countries: Nigeria and Kenya (Gbolagade, et al., 2006, Kariaga, 2005, Shimelis, 2011, Kariaga et al., 2012). In recent years, a lot of works has been achieved both on wild edible mushrooms and cultivated edible mushrooms, specially *Pleurotus tuber-regium* and *P. ostreatus* (Isikhuemhen and Okhuoya, 1996, Ayodele and Okhuoya, 2007, Shimelis, 2011). In Algeria mushroom cultivation is still poorly known. Precisely in Kabylia, harvesting of wild edible fungi is mainly held during olive harvest period. It would be very interesting to promote oyster mushrooms cultivation and introduce a new culture in Algeria. Oyster mushrooms or *Pleurotus* spp. are the most cultivated mushrooms worldwide (Zied et al., 2011). They belong to the group of Basidiomycetes and have favorable organoleptic and medicinal properties and vigorous growth (Gregori et al., 2007). The interesting aspects of the cultivation of *Pleurotus* spp. are that it is relatively simple and needs a low cost technology with promising high yielding and it does not require a composted substrate (Philippoussis et al., 2001, Velăzquez Cedeňo, 2005, Philippoussis, 2009). Most agricultural residues and agro-industrial by-products can be used (Zied et al., 2011). Among the many agro-residues to value in Algeria, after the olive pomace (Mansour-Benamar et al., 2013), there are coffee-grounds (Mansour-Benamar et al., 2007). Coffee-grounds are the residual wastes obtained during the treatment of roasted and milled green coffee bean with hot water or steam to prepare coffee beverage told simply coffee. Coffee is one of the most popular beverages or drinks worldwide. In Algeria, particularly in Kabylia, it is an everyday beverage. It is consumed at breakfast in the morning and afternoon snack generally by 16 hours mixed with milk. Coffee is also consumed all day long, after lunch, at home, in restaurant and in cafeteria. Coffee is always served at every opportunity. Coffee enhance alertness because of stimulant action of caffeine (Gokulakrishnan et al., 2013).

Green coffee beans traded are seeds of coffee plant recovered after dry or wet processing of the coffee cherries (Mussatto et al., 2011). Coffee plant belongs to the family of Rubiaceae and the genus *Coffea*. Among the numerous species existing, only two species are cultivated and world traded, *Coffea arabica* L. commonly known as Arabica coffee or Arabica and which is mainly cultivated in Latin America and in some African countries and *Coffea canephora* (Pierre ex Froehner) variety *robusta* known as Robusta coffee or Robusta cultivated mainly in African countries like Ethiopia, and Asia countries like Indonesia (Coste, 1989, Daviron and Lerin, 1990, Shimelis, 2011). Arabica coffee is more acid and aromatic but Robusta coffee is more foaming and has a better yielding. Coffee is native to Ethiopia (Daviron, and Lerin, 1990). Today, it is widely grown throughout the tropics (Fairtrade Foundation, 2012).

Algeria is a consumer country and imports, according to UGCAA (Union Générale des Commerçants et Artisans Algériens: Algerian Tradesmen and Craftmen Association), mainly green bean coffee from Viet Nam, Indonesia and Cote d'Ivoire (personal communication). Algeria imports more Robusta coffee (about 95 %) than Arabica coffee (less than 5%). In 2010, Algerian import of coffee and tea ranked at the fifth place of consumer food product after cereals and in 2011, Robusta and Arabica coffee had cost respectively 2539.65 and 6006.01 US dollars per ton (Directorate General of Algerian Customs, 2010, Algerian Ministry of Commerce, 2011). Algerian coffee imports are estimated to an average of 125,000 tons/year (UGCAA). In Algerian market coffee price follows the world trade coffee. Actually green coffee beans worth between 275 and 295 DZD (Algerian dinar)/kg for Robusta and 290-320 DZD/kg for Arabica (Currently 1USD=77.87 DZD). Knowing that coffee grounds represent 3/5th of green coffee bean (Barbera, 1965), Algeria produces annually 75,000 tons of coffee-grounds which are usually thrown into the garbage.

Therefore, it became a necessity to find a way to recover the coffee-grounds. Many studies had been conducted in this direction to enhance their commercial value, as activated carbon and biosorbent for xenobiotic removal (Benrachedi et al., 2001, Abdebaki, 2010, Safaric et al., 2012), as organic fertilizer (Cruz et al., 2012, Gomes et al., 2013), for production of biodiesel (Ammerlaan et al., 2012, Caetano et al., 2012) and as a source of edible mushrooms (Mansour-Benamar et al., 2007, Ammerlaan et al., 2012).

Because of high price of coffee and the amount of coffee-grounds produced, the conversion of coffee-grounds into edible mushrooms will be a very suitable way of its valorization. In 2007, we demonstrated that the coffee-grounds could be valorized by the cultivation of a local strain of *Pleurotus ostreatus* (Jacq. ex Fries) Kummer (LPO) but the yields were low (Mansour-Benamar et al., 2007).

Since cereal straw is conventionally used as a basal substrate for edible mushrooms cultivation around the world (Laborde and Delmas, 1974, Chalaux et al., 1995, Savoie et al., 1995, Zervakis et al., 2001, Rahman et al., 2007, Norouzi et al., 2008) and in order to improve these yields, coffee-grounds was supplemented with wheat straw and calcium carbonate in the present work in order to improve the yield and efficiency of the process.

The life cycle of *Pleurotus* goes through two biological states: the vegetative phase during which the dicaryotic mycelium grows and the fruiting phase during which the mycelium condenses and forms fruiting bodies or carpophores (basidiocarps or mushrooms).

Environmental requirements of these two states are different (Olivier et al., 1991). Mushroom cultivation involves several operations: - Obtaining pure mycelium of the selected strain mushroom, - Spawn preparation, - Substrate preparation, - Inoculation of the substrate with the spawn (spawning), - Incubation and spawn running – and finally fruiting and yielding (Olivier et al., 2001, Benamar and Chavant, 2010, Sánchez, 2010, Yehia, 2012).

1. Oyster Mushroom Strains

Two strains of oyster mushrooms were used: a local strain of *Pleurotus ostreatus* (Jacq. ex Fr.) Kumm (LPO) and a commercial strain of *P. ostreatus* (CPO).

- The original dicaryotic mycelium of LPO was isolated in February 1993 under our care in Oued-Aissi (Tizi-Ouzou, Algeria) from fruiting bodies (basidiocarps). The mushroom had grown on a tree stump of castor-oil plants (*Ricinus communis* L.) cut in November 1992. It has been identified by morphological characters. The caps were grayish-brown, broad, with white decurrent gills moderately crowded; the stems were either absent or too short and lateral. Caps were growing in tight clusters.
- The dicaryotic mycelium of a commercial strain of *P. ostreatus* (P535) (CPO) coming from the "Royal Champignon" Society (France) in 1993.

The strains are kept in tubes on PDA (Potato-Dextrose-Agar) (2% dextrose, 20% potato extract, 2% agar). The mycelial culture are maintained and multiplied by sub-culturing them every 2-3 months. Once a year, mycelia are isolated again from new and fresh carpophores developed either on coffee grounds or olive pomace (Mansour-Benamar et al,. 2007, Benamar and Chavant, 2010) on sterilized PDA medium in Petri dish or tubes.

The quality of the mycelium is regularly checked by estimating the mycelial growth rate on solid culture medium after incubation for 8 days at 25°C (Mansour-Benamar et al., 2013).

2. Stages of the Cultivation

2.1. Spawn Preparation

To obtain inoculums or spawns, we used a method different from the previous one used in 2007 (Mansour-Benamar et al., 2007). After washing barley grains and boiling them in water they were allowed to drain. Once cooled, they were weighted and distributed in bags of polyethylene, mixed to 2% $CaCO_3$ (weight/weight) and then sterilized for 1 hour at 120°C in an autoclave.

To make mother spawn, each bag containing 100g of sterilized grains was inoculated by using mycelium-colony developed on PDA in a 9 cm Petri dish. The multiplication of the spawn was achieved from the mother spawn made by inoculating grain bags with 10 g of mother spawn. The spawn was obtained after incubation for 15 days and it was of good quality with barley grains well coated by a white root-like mycelium. The success of mushroom production depends, in great part, on quality of the spawn. Many substrates were tested for spawn production and mainly cereal grain are used as sorghum grains (Sánchez et al., 2011), wheat grains (Bisaria et al., 1987, Yehia, 2011), millet seeds (Velãzquez Cedeňo, 2005), rye grain (Velãzquez Cedeňo et al., 2004).

After many previous tests we had chosen barley grains that seem to give best results with LPO and CPO. The use of cereal grain makes easier to increase the spawn. The main limiting factors are pH, moisture and cereal grain sterilization.

2.2. Substrates Preparation and Thermal Treatment

Preparation of coffee-grounds (CG): Raw coffee grounds was gathered from home and cafeteria of Tizi-Ouzou. When not used immediately, it was dried either in the sun in summer or in an oven at 60%C in winter to avoid contamination by molds. The consumed coffee is either Robusta or Robusta-Arabica blend at the rate (8:2), currently there are rates of (7:3) and (6:4). A quantity of tap water was added to the substrate.

It was determined empirically by pressing the wet substrate in the hand. When water flows slightly between the fingers, it is estimated that substrate is sufficiently wet. Like most organic wastes, CG is lignocellulosic. The chemical composition of CG has been studied by Cruz (1983) and Mussatto et al. (2011).

Preparation of Wheat straw (WS): straw was purchased from "straw market" of Oued-Aissi. The WS had a golden color. It was previously chopped in pieces of 2 to 5 cm of length, soaked in water for a night and afterwards drained for 1 to 3 hours to allow the excess water to drop. WS is known to be poor in protein and minerals. Chemical composition of WS has been studied by Maréchal (2001) and Ouachem et al. (2008).

Preparation of the mixture CG-WS: From the raw substrate prepared previously, we had made mixture at the rate of (9CG:1WS) for CG-WS10 mixture and the rate (1:1) (50% of WS) for the CG-WS50 mixture.

pH improvement: 2% of $CaCO_3$ were added to CG, WS, CG-WS10 and CG-WS50.

Thermal treatment: Once prepared, the substrates were steamed in a traditional cooking steamer (couscousier) for15 to 20mn.

2.3. Inoculation, Incubation and Fruiting

Cultivation in bags (spawn running and fruiting): Once cooled the pasteurized substrates were aseptically sowed near the flame of two Bunsen burners, with the prepared spawn at the rate of 7% (weight/weight), then distributed into plastic bags of 500g each. Fifteen bags were prepared for each strain cultivated on each substrate.

Four bags were intended for the analysis of performance, nine were for the chemical analysis, and two were a reserve in case of contaminated bags. The incubation period was 23 days at 25±1°C and 70-80% relative humidity in air. The 7th day of incubation, the bags were perforated with a tin needle to allow aeration of the cultures.

When the primordia began to appear, the bags were submitted to cold shock by immersing them in water at 15°C for 15-20mn and then were removed and placed in the cultivation room to enhance fructification. The temperature was kept at 20°C by cooling the room with frozen water (4°C) and ambient moisture till 95% by the means of a humidifier.

3. MEASUREMENT OF SOME PARAMETERS DURING THE OYSTER CULTIVATION

With regard to the chemical analysis of the substrates CG, WS, CG-WS10 and CG-WS50, for each measurement, three culture bags were removed and mixed. From each mixture and for each analyze, three samples were taken to perform the different analyzes according to methods of Mathieu and Pieltain (2003). The results are gathered in tables numbered 1 to 2. Every value is the average of the three measurements and was accompanied by standard deviation. The measurements were performed at the beginning of the experiment, the 23rd day (the end of spawn running or end of incubation period) and at the end of the harvest in the 51th day of the mushroom cultures.

The results were submitted to multifactor variation analysis, ANOVA completed by the Newman-Keuls test when there were differences between the averages values (STATISTICA, version 5.1, 1997).

3.1. Evolution of pH in the Substrates

pH was measured using a pH meter (Inolab pH level1) in one volume of substrate mixed with 2.5 water volumes. Measurements were taken three times at 10-15 minutes intervals with three repetitions. The results are summarized in Table 1. In raw substrates, pH was acid except for WS that had a slightly basic pH; the lowest pH was in CG. Indeed, coffee-grounds are known for their acidity. When calcium carbonate was added, pH in the substrates was improved, but the addition of LPO and CPO spawn had reduced it. Nevertheless, initials pH values were still in favorable pH range reported by Olivier et al. in 1991 and Kibar and Peksen in 2011.

At the end of incubation period, pH was low in all the substrates.

Table 1. pH value (with standard deviation) before and after cultivation of Oyster mushroom LPO and CPO on coffee-grounds (CG), wheat straw (WS) and mixture CG + WS at two rates (9:1) (CG-WS10) and (1:1) (CG-WS50)

Substrate	pH00	pH0	pH1-LPO	pH1-CPO	pH2-LPO	pH2-CPO	pH3-LPO	pH3-CPO
CG	5.42 (0.02)	5.77 (0.02)	5.25 (0.05)	5.11 (0.04)	4.72 (0.02)	4.79 (0.03)	4.02 (0.05)	4.15 (0.04)
WS	7.88 (0.08)	8,19 (0.27)	7,58 (0.08)	7.30 (0.04)	4.93 (0.03)	5.01 (0.03)	5.79 (0.04)	6.04 (0.05)
CG-WS10	5.73 (0.02)	5.92 (0.05)	5.42 (0.01)	5.87 (0.05)	4.94 (0.03)	4.97 (0.06)	4.01 (0.04)	4.26 (0.06)
CG-WS50	6.03 (0.07)	6.44 (0.07)	6.22 (0.07)	6.41 (0.04)	4.87 (0.03)	5.05 (0.04)	4.36 (0.04)	4.56 (0.04)

pH00: pH in the substrate (S) alone at its reception in the laboratory, pH0: pH [((S) + 2% $CaCO_3$ (w/w) + water) = (S1)], pH1: pH [(S1) pasteurized + 7% LPO or CPO spawn (w/w)], pH2: substrate pH at the end of spawn running of LPO and CPO, pH3: substrate pH at the end of LPO and CPO cultivation. To avoid cluttering the table, the results of statistical analyzes are not shown.

The substrates acidification had probably resulted from the production of organic acids or by CO_2 dissolution in water associated with the activity of microorganisms (Olivier et al., 1991, Znaïdi, 2002). At the end of mushroom cultivation pH was continuously low except in WS. Indeed, pH had risen, which means that LPO and CPO activities had stopped (temporarily or permanently).

In the other cases with substrates based on CG, pH had continued to drop indicating that LPO and CPO were still in activity. The two oyster mushroom strains had probably not yet exploited all the nutrients contained in CG, CG-WS10 and CG-WS50 unlike in WS. Perhaps it was necessary to extend the incubation time beyond 23 days. According to Zervakis et al. (2001) growth of a mushroom must be slow in order to enable the mycelium to exploit the nutrient resources of the substrate.

3.2. Evolution of the Dry Matter, Mineral Matter and Organic Carbon in the Substrates

Moisture was determined after drying the sample at 60°C in an oven until complete stabilization of weight. Ash was determined by destruction of organic matter of dried samples at 550°C for 4 hours. Percentage of organic matter was estimated from the dry matter and ash. Percentage of organic carbon was estimated also from organic matter considering that organic material contains 58% carbon.

% Moisture (%H) = [(Initial fresh weight- Final dry weight)/(Initial fresh weight)]*100
% Dry matter (%DM) = 100% - % H
% Ash (%A) = [(Final weight after carbonization)/(DM before carbonization)]*100
% Organic matter (%OM) = % DM - % A
% Organic Carbon (%C) = 58% OM

The results are summarized in Table 2 for moisture (%H), dry matter (%DM), Ash (%A), organic matter (%OM) and organic carbon (%C).

In the substrates, WS retained more water than coffee-grounds leading to different moisture content.

Theses rates are sufficient to allow good mycelial development and are within the range described by Ahmed et al. (2013). During the mycelia development, the humidity fluctuated in the substrates between about 61 and 77% depending on the substrate and the strain except in CG-WS50 at the end of LPO incubation period were the moisture was about 40%. Although ambient humidity was of 80-95%, the moisture in the substrate had not exceeded 73%. This could be attributed to the consumption of water by the developing mycelium but also probably due to the protective layer (stroma) formed by the dense mycelium developed around the substrate. By the end of culture, watering had been stopped, so humidity decrease was normal.

Dry matter had evolved inversely to moisture and WS had presented less DM. Initially, in the substrates, the amount of ash was not very different but CG had the least quantity of ash. Inoculums of LPO and CPO had brought a lot of ash. Cultivation of LPO and CPO had favored straw enrichment with minerals, indeed, after fruiting; culture residue was rich in minerals. However, the initial ash rate in WS relative to the bibliographic data and compared to our previous work was to low (Mansour-Benamar et al., 2013). In the others substrates (CG, CG-WS10 and CG-WS50), the minerals were rather exhausted.

They had been probably used during the fruiting bodies formation. In general, dry matter, organic matter and consequently organic carbon had increased in the four substrates CG, WS, CG-WS10 and CG-WS50 during the culture of both strains of *P. ostreatus* LPO and CPO.

Pleurotus ostreatus is a saprophytic fungus. Then he needs a supply of organic matter for its development. As primary decomposers, *Pleurotus* species have the ability to degrade complex compounds such as wood in the rough. This is why it is cultivated on a large variety of organic substrates such as cereal straw and various residues from different industries like olive oil industry, fruit juice industry, coffee industry. At the end of the culture, there was a significant gain in organic matter, therefore in organic carbon except for WS where it was moderate.

Table 2. Substrate moisture (%H), dry matter (%DM), ash (%A), organic matter (%OM) and organic carbon (%C) contents (with standard deviation) before and after cultivation of Oyster mushrooms CPO and LPO on coffee-grounds (CG), wheat straw (WS), and mixture CG + WS at two rates (9:1) (CG-WS10) and (1:1) (CG-WS50)

	Substrate	T0	T1-LPO	T1- CPO	T2-LPO	T2- CPO	T3-LPO	T3- CPO
%H	CG	55.29 (0.08)	67.73 (0.48)	68.19 (0.52)	58.01 (0.05)	61.34 (0.86)	38.58 (0.61)	36.49 (0.64)
	WS	75.34 (0.08)	76.94 (0.14)	75.15 (0.80)	72.24 (0.23)	72.29 (0.60)	69.39 (0.49)	65.06 (0.47)
	CG-WS10	61.01 (0.08)	69.76 (0.30)	69.95 (2.55)	61.59 (0.42)	64.92 (0.64)	48.31 (0.67)	45.60 (0.30)
	CG-WS50	66.63 (0.34)	72.34 (0.64)	71.23 (0.71)	39.58 (0.96)	66.06 (0.63)	32.71 (4.41)	41.43 (4.89)
%DM	CG	44.71 (0.08)	32.27 (0.48)	31.81 (0.52)	41.99 (0.05)	38.66 (0.86)	61.42 (0.61)	63.51 (0.64)
	WS	24.66 (0.08)	23.06 (0.14)	24.85 (0.80)	27.76 (0.00)	27.71 (0.60)	30.79 (0.76)	34.94 (0.47)
	CG-WS10	38.99 (0.08)	30.24 (0.30)	30.05 (2.55)	38.41 (4.21)	35.08 (0.64)	51.69 (0.67)	54.40 (0.29)
	CG-WS50	33.37 (0.34)	27.66 (0.64)	28.77 (0.71)	60.42 (0.97)	33.94 (0.63)	67.83 (4.41)	58.57 (4.89)
%A	CG	2.16 (0.02)	2.78 (0.53)	2.35 (1.75)	2.70 (0.49)	2.41 (0.31)	1.08 (0.26)	2.39 (0.14)
	WS	2.25 (0.16)	5.44 (0.22)	4.65 (0.45)	7.72 (0.39)	6.56 (0.33)	10.61 (0.73)	9.93 (0.17)
	CG-WS10	2.47 (0.05)	3.68 (0.16)	3.71 (0.18)	2.24 (1.04)	2.61 (0.13)	0.47 (0.04)	1.88 (0.04)
	CG-WS50	2.59 (0.11)	4.55 (0.38)	4.09 (0.57)	3.14 (0.07)	3.25 (0.20)	1.69 (0.09)	2.75 (0.05)
%OM	CG	42.55 (0.06)	29.49 (0.55)	29.46 (2.10)	39.29 (0.45)	36.25 (0.94)	60.34 (0.36)	61.13 (0.58)
	WS	22.41 (0.11)	17.61 (0.36)	20.20 (0.36)	20.03 (0.62)	21.15 (0.92)	20.18 (1.37)	25.01 (0.63)
	CG-WS10	36.52 (00.7)	26.56 (0.46)	26.34 (2.61)	36.16 (5.13)	32.47 (0.64)	51.23 (0.66)	52.52 (0.25)
	CG-WS50	30.78 (0.44)	23.10 (0.43)	24.68 (0.68)	57.28 (1.04)	30.69 (0.44)	66.14 (4.41)	55.83 (4.91)
%C	CG	24.68 (0.03)	17.11 (0.32)	17.09 (1.22)	22.49 (0.26)	21.03 (0.55)	35.00 (0.21)	35.46 (0.34)
	WS	13.00 (0.07)	10.22 (0.21)	11.72 (0.21)	11.62 (0.36)	12.27 (0.53)	11.71 (0.79)	14.51 (0.37)
	CG-WS 10	21.19 (0.04)	15.40 (0.27)	15.28 (1.51)	20.98 (2.97)	18.83 (0.37)	29.71 (0.39)	30.46 (0.15)
	CG-WS 50	17.68 (0.25)	13.40 (0.25)	14.31 (0.40)	33.22 (0.60)	17.80 (0.26)	38.36 (2.56)	32.38 (2.85)

%H and %DM: in percentage of wet weight basis of the substrate (S). %A, %OM and %C: in percentage of (S) dry weight basis. T0: measures in $[((S) + 2\% CaCO_3 (w/w) + water) = (S1)]$; T1: measures in [(S1) pasteurized + 7% LPO or CPO spawn (w/w)], T2: measures in the substrates at the end of spawn running of LPO and CPO, T3: measures in the substrates at the end of LPO and CPO cultivation. To avoid cluttering the table, the results of statistical analyzes are not shown.

4. ESTIMATION OF YIELDS AND QUALITY OF THE FRUITING BODIES

Concerning the yields of the strains LPO and CPO based on the four substrates, the fruiting bodies were harvested daily at their maturity.

Four days after the cold shock the first fruiting bodies were harvested. The flushes were not well delimited; the fruiting bodies were formed continuously on the four substrates CG, WS, CG-WS10 and CG-WS50.

Three to four days were necessary for the maturation of fruiting bodies.

4.1. Size and Weight of Fruiting Bodies

Every fruiting body harvested was weighted with an analytical balance. Size of the cap and the length and width of the foot of each fruiting body were measured with a tape measure. Then average weight and average diameter of the caps and average length and width of the feet had been recorded. Only mushrooms whose weight was greater than 3g were taken account in the measures.

Fruiting bodies of LPO and CPO developed on WS were more numerous and smaller.

Globally LPO gave more fruiting bodies than CPO but CPO had developed larger fruiting bodies especially on CG-WS50 (Table 3). Same results had been obtained on solid olive mill wastes (SOMW) and SOMW+WS (Mansour-Benamar et al., 2013).

According to the weight, the fruit-bodies were similar to those formed by LPO and CPO on olive pomace alone but they were much smaller comparatively to those formed on SOMW +WS. The caps diameters were comparable, especially to those formed on mixture olive pomace - wheat straw. Respectively, the size of the caps and the length and the width of the feet of the fruit bodies of LPO and CPO developed were not significantly different on the substrates studied in this work.

4.2. Biological Efficiency

The Biological efficiency was calculated as the percentage yield of fresh mushroom in relation to the dry weight of each substrate at the beginning cultivation i.e., in the [substrat +2%CaCO$_3$+7% spawn]. Coffee grounds supplemented with 2% calcium carbonate seems to be a good cultivation substrate for the two strains with no significant difference in their BE.

The addition of wheat straw (50%) had enhanced significantly the yields and the biological efficiency of the two *Pleurotus* strains (the different results are gathered in Table 3) with highest BE for CPO. The highest BE for LPO was on WS. The LPO and CPO cultivation on coffee-grounds (supplemented or not supplemented by WS) was improved compared to cultivation conducted with the same mushroom strains in 2007.

CPO biological efficiency on CG-WS50 had exceeded BE obtained by Velăzquez Cedeňo et al. (2002) on the coffee pulp with cultivation of *P. ostreatus* and *P. pulmonarius*.

BE obtained on GC-WS10 with LPO cultivation and those of CPO and LPO cultivation on CG were comparable to the results of Patil (2012) with cultivation *P. sajor-caju* on soy-bean.

Table 3. Cultural characters of oyster mushrooms LPO and CPO on coffee-grounds (CG), wheat straw (WS) and mixture CG + WS at two rates (9:1) (CG-WS10) and (1:1) (CG-WS50)

Parameters	CG		WS		CGWS10		CGWS50	
Strains	LPO	CPO	LPO	CPO	LPO	CPO	LPO	CPO
Duration of the spawn running (Days)	23							
Total duration of the cultivation (Days)	51							
Substrate surface colonized by the mycelium	Totality							
Mycelial aspect	white, root-like, free of contamination							
Total fruit bodies	72.00	66.00	119.00	87.00	62.00	63.00	110.00	84.00
Fruit bodies total weight (g)	558.55	512.39	541.87	362,69	507.04	442.16	568.57	865.71
Average fruit bodies weight (g)	7.76 (1.50)^{ab}	7.76 (1.58)^{ab}	4.55 (0.70)^{b}	4.17 (0.35)^{b}	8.18 (3.61)^{ab}	7.02 (1.88)^{ab}	5.17 (1.70)^{ab}	10.31 (4.36)^{a}
Average diameter of the caps (cm)	6.07 (2.74)^{c}	5.02 (0.26)^{c}	4.27 (0.19)^{c}	4.06 (0.21)^{c}	4.88 (0.61)^{c}	5.16 (0.63)^{c}	4.99 (0.72)^{c}	5.10 (0.44)^{c}
Average length of the feet (cm)	2.15 (0.12)^{d}	2.19 (0.22)^{d}	1.74 (0.17)^{d}	1.75 (0.51)^{d}	2.00 (0.40)^{d}	1.85 (0.51)^{d}	2.22 (0.52)^{d}	1.76 (0.17)^{d}
Average width of the feet (cm)	0.95 (0.12)^{e}	0.96 (0.06)^{e}	0.76 (0.09)^{e}	0.84 (0.08)^{e}	0.87 (0.14)^{e}	0.93 (0.12)^{e}	0.90 (0.12)^{e}	0.96 (0.14)^{e}
Initial total dry matter in the substrate[*] (g)	645.40	636.20	461.20	497.00	604.00	601.00	553.20	565.40
BE (%)	86.54	80.54	117.49	72.98	83.84	73.57	102.78	153.11

In brackets: standard deviation; [*]Initial total dry matter in the substrate is calculated on the basis of dry matter in [(pasteurized (substrate + 2% $CaCO_3$ (w/w) + water)) + 7% LPO or CPO spawn (w/w)]. When followed by the same letters, the average are not significantly different (P=0.05).

CONCLUSION

In view of all the medicinal and nutritional values of Oyster mushrooms reported by many researchers around the world, and knowing that the cultivation of oyster mushrooms is reported to be among the easiest edible mushrooms technology and is the technique that requires the less investment, it would be wise for country such as Algeria develop large-scale cultivation of the two strains of *Pleurotus* species.

In the present work the potential for the use of wheat straw in mixture with coffee-grounds as substrate was shown as a promising method for producing mushrooms, both with an existing commercial strain of *Pleurotus ostreatus* or a wild isolate. The two strains were also shown to produce significant yields of good quality mushrooms when cultivated on substrates using solid olive mill wastes (Mansour-Benamar et al., 2013). By this way, these wastes could be valorized near the place of their production by generating human food and a complementary source of income. Outside the period of olive oil production, coffee grounds and wheat straw could be used as substrates to continue production and supply continuously the market with Oyster mushroom. Our work is a nice example of valorization of both local agro-industrial wastes and local biological resources.

In a near future, other agro-industrial residues might be used and diversification is envisaged with isolation of *Hericium erinaceus* or other local species.

ACKNOWLEDGMENTS

The authors wish to express their gratitude to Dr. Jean-Michel Savoie for all the help and reviewing this manuscript. They wish also to thank Mrs Samia Mebrek - Zaoui for her help with statistical analysis and Mourad Mansour for tables presentation.

Reviewed by Jean-Michel Savoie. INRA, UR1264 Mycologie et Sécurité des Aliments, CS20032, F-33882 Villenave d'Ornon Cédex, France. E-mail: jean-michel.savoie@bordeaux. inra.fr. +33 5 57 12 24 96.

REFERENCES

Abdebaki, R. (2010). Etude de l'adsorption de colorants organiques (rouge nylosan et bleu de méthylène) sur des charbons actifs préparés à partir du marc de café. *Thèse de Doctorat en Science en génie des procédés.* Université Mentouri-Constantine, Faculté des Sciences de l'Ingénieur, Département de Génie des Procédés, Algérie.

Ahmed, M., Abdullah, N., Ahmed, K. U., Bhuyan, M. H. M. B. (2013). Yield and nutritional composition of Oyster mushroom strains newly introduced in Bangladesh. *Pesquisa Agropecuária Brasileira, Brasilia*, 48, 197-202.

Ahmed, S. A., Kadam, J. A., Mane, V. P., Patil, S. S., Baig, M. M. V. (2009). Biological efficiency and nutritional contents of *Pleurotus florida* (Mont.) Singer cultivated on different agro-wastes. *Nature and Science*, 7, 44-48.

Aida, F. M. N. A., Shuhaimi, M., Yazid, M., Maaruf, A. G. (2009). Mushrooms as a potential source of prebiotics: a review. *Trends in Food Sciences and Technology*, 20, 567-575.

Akyüz, M. and Kirbað, S. (2010). Element contents of *Pleurotus eryngii* (DC. ex Fr.) Quel. var. eryngii grown on some various agrowastes. *Ekoloji*, 19, 10-14.

Ammerlaan, T., Barrière, V., Genest-Richard, P., Rabow, S. (2012). *Tales of a forgotten Bioresource: the recycling of spent coffee grounds*. Department of Bioresource Engineering, McGill University, Montréal, Canada.

Ayodele, S. M. and Okhuoya, J. A. (2007). Effect of substrate supplementation with wheat bran, NPK and urea on *Psathyrella atroumbonata* Pegler sporophore yield. *African Journal of Biotechnology*, 6, 1414-1417.

Bano, Z. and Rajarathnam, S. (2010). *Pleurotus* mushrooms. Part II. Chemical composition, nutritional value, post-harvest physiology, preservation, and role as human food. *Critical Reviews in Food Science and Nutrition,* 27, 87-158.

Barbera, C. E. (1965). L'utilisation du marc de café. *Revue « Café, Cacao, Thé »*, Vol. IK n 3, 206-217.

Benamar, M. and Chavant, L. (2010). *Guide illustré de la culture d'un champignon comestible: le pleurote en huître*. Editions El-Amel.

Benrachedi, K., Mekarzia, A., Messaoud Boureghda, M. Z. (2001). Valorisation du marc de café dans le domaine du traitement des effluents liquides. *La Tribune de l'Eau*, 50, 19-27.

Bisaria, R., Madan, M., Bisaria, V. S. (1987). Biological efficiency and nutritive value of *Pleurotus sajor-caju* on different agro-wastes. *Biological wastes*, 19, 239-255.

Caetano, N., Silva, V., Mata, T. M. (2012). Valorization of coffee grounds for biodiesel production. *Chemical Engineering Transactions*, 26, 267-272.

Chalaux, N., Libmond, S., Savoie, J.-M. (1995). A practical enzymatic method to estimate wheat straw quality as raw material for mushroom cultivation. *Bioresource Technology*, 53, 277-281.

Coste, R. (1989). *Caféiers et cafés. Edition Maisonneuve et Larose*. Paris.

Cruz, G. M. (1983). Residuos de cultura e indústrie. *Informe Agropecuário*, 9, 32-37.

Cruz, R., Baptista, P., Cunha, S., Pereira, J. A., Casal, S. (2012). Carotenoids of lettuce (*Lactuca sativa* L.) grown on soil enriched with spent coffee grounds. *Molecules*, 17, 1535-1547.

Daviron, B. and Lerin, B. (1990). Le café. Ed. Cyclope, *Economica*.

De Silva, D. D., Rapior, S., Hyde, K. D. (2012). Medicinal mushrooms in prevention and control of diabetes mellitus. *Fungal Diversity*, 56, 1-29.

Delmas, J. (1989). *Les champignons et leur culture, culture actuelle et potentielle des champignons supérieurs*. La Maison Rustique, Paris.

Direction Générale des Douanes Algériennes(2010). *Statistiques du commerce extérieur de L'Algérie* (Période: Premier trimestre 2010. Centre National de l'Informatique et des Statistiques, Ministère des Finances, Direction Générale des Douanes, République Algérienne Démocratique et Populaire.

El Enshasy, H. A. and Hatti-Kaul, R. (2013). Mushroom immunomodulators: unique molecules with unlimited applications. *Trends in Biotechnology*, 31, 668-677.

Fairtrade Foundation (2012). *Fairtrade and coffee*. Commodity briefing.

Gbolagade, J., Sobowale, A., Adejoye, D. (2006). Optimization of sub-merged culture conditions for biomass production in *Pleurotus florida* (mont.) Singer, a Nigerian edible fungus. *African Journal of Biotechnology*, 5, 1464-1469.

Gokulakrichnan, S., Chanddra, J., Sathyanarayana, K., Gummadi, N. (2013). Microbial and enzymatic methods for the removal of caffeine. *Enzyme and Microbial Technology*, 37, 225-232.

Gomes, T., Pereira, J. A., Ramalhosa, E., Casal, S., Baptista, P. (2013). Effect of fresh and composted spent coffee ground on lettuce growth, photosynthetic pigments and mineral composition, *IIV Congreso Ibérico de Agroingenieria Y Ciencias Horticolas*, Madrid.

Gregori, A., Švagelj, M., Pohleven, J. (2007). Cultivation techniques and medicinal properties of *Pleurotus* spp. *Food Technology and Biotechnology*, 45, 236-247.

Isikhuemhen, O. S. and Okhuoya, J. A. (1996). Cultivation of *Pleurotus tuber-regium* (Fr.) Singer for production of edible sclerotia on agricultural wastes. *Mushroom Biology and Mushroom Products*. Royse ed. Penn State University, 429-438.

Islam, M. Z., Rahman, M. H., Hafiz, F. (2009) Cultivation of Oyster mushroom (*Pleurotus flabellatus*) on different substrates. *International Journal of Sustainable Crop Production*, 4, 45–48.

Kariaga, M. G., Nyongesa, H. W., Keya, N. C. O., Tsingalia, H. M. (2012). Compost physico-chemical factors that impact on yield in button mushrooms, *Agaricus bisporus* (Lange) and *Agaricus bitorquis* (Quel) Saccardo. *Journal of Agricultural Science*, 3, 49-54.

Kariaga, M. G. (2005). Important factors in composting for production of high yields in button mushrooms and *Agaricus bitorquis* (Quel) Saccardo. *African Crop Science Conference Proceedings*, 7, 1273-1277.

Kibar, B. and Peksen, A. (2011). Mycelial growth requirements of *Lactarius pyrogalus* and *Lactarius controversus*. *African Journal of Microbiology Research*, 5, 5107-5114.

Laborde, J. and Delmas, J. (1974). Le pleurote. *Revue Horticole*, 145, 39-46.

Lindequist, U., Niedermeyer, T. H. J., Jülich, W. D. (2005). The pharmacological potential of mushrooms. *Evidence-Based Complementary and Alternative Medicine*, 2, 285–299.

Manimozhi, M. and Kaviyarasan, V. (2013). Nutritional composition and antibacterial activity of indigenous edible mushroom *Agaricus heterocystis*. *International Journal of Advanced Biotechnology and Research*, 4, 78-84.

Mansour – Benamar, M., Savoie, J.-M., Chavant, L. (2013).Valorization of a solid olive mill wastes by cultivation of a local strain of edible mushroom. *Comptes Rendus Biologies*, 336, 407-415.

Mansour-Benamar, M., Savoie, J.-M., Chavant, L., Lebsir, R. (2007). Valorisation du marc de café brut par la culture d'une souche locale de champignon comestible, *Pleurotus ostreatus*. *Sciences Technologies et Développement*, A.N.D.R.U., 2, 102–116.

Marechal, P. (2001). Analyse des principaux facteurs impliqués dans le fractionnement combiné de paille et de sons de blé en extrudeur bi-vis. Obtention d'agro-matériaux. *Thèse PHD*, INP. Toulouse.

Mathieu, C. and Pieltain, F. (2003). *Analyse chimique des sols- Méthodes choisies*. Edition TEC and DOC Lavoisier.

Ministère du Commerce Algérien (2011). Régulation du marché et observation des prix des produits de première nécessité et stratégiques, *Rapport de conjoncture du secteur du commerce au titre du premier semestre de l'année 2011, S/D des Statistiques et de l'information Economique*, Direction des Etudes de la Prospective et de l'Information Economique Direction Générale de la Régulation et de l'Organisation des Activités

Direction des Etudes de la Prospective et de l'Information Economique, Ministère du Commerce République Algérienne Démocratique et Populaire.

Mussatto, S. I., Machado, E. M. S., Martin, S., Teixeira, J. A. (2011). Production, composition and application of coffee and its industrial residues. *Food Bioprocess Technology*, 4, 661-672.

Norouzi, A., Peyvast, G., Olfati, J. (2008). Oilseed rape straw for cultivation of oyster mushroom. *Maejo International Journal of Science and Technology*, 2, 502-507.

Olivier, J.-M., Laborde, J., Guimberteau, J., Poitou, N., Houdeau, G., Delmas, J. (1991). *La culture des champignons*. Ed. Armand Colin.

Ouachem, D., Soltane, M., Kalli, A. (2008). Les pailles de céréales: Profil des fermentations et production de méthane. *Sciences and Technologie C*, 27, 23-28.

Patel, S., Goyal, A. (2012). Recent developments in mushrooms as anti-cancer therapeutics: a review. *3 Biotech*, 2, 1–15.

Patil, S. S. (2012). Cultivation of *Pleurotus sajor-caju* on different agro wastes. *Science Research Reporter*, 2, 225-228.

Philippoussis, A., Zervakis, G., Diamantopoulou, P. (2001). Bioconversion of agricultural ligno-cellulosic wastes through the cultivation of the edible mushrooms *Agrocybe aegerita*, *Volvariella volvacea* and *Pleurotus* spp. *World Journal of Microbiology and Biotechnology*, 17: 191–200.

Philippoussis, A. N. (2009). Production of mushrooms using agro-industrial residues as substrates. Sing nee' Nigam, P., Pandey, A. (eds.), *Biotechnology for agro-industrial residues utilization*. Springer Science+Business media B.V. pp. 163-189.

Rahman, M., Odhano, E. A., Haq, M. Z., Gul, S. (2007) Conversion of lignocellulosic wastes into Oyster mushrooms (*Pleurotus ostreatus*). *Journal of The Chemical Society of Pakistan*, 29, 251-255.

Safarik, I., Horska, K., Svobodova, B., Safarikova, M. (2012). Magnetically modified spent coffee grounds for dyes removal. *European Food Research and Technology*, 234, 345-350.

Sánchez, C. (2010). Cultivation of *Pleurotus ostreatus* and other edible mushrooms. *Applied Microbiology and Biotechnology*, 85, 1321-1337.

Sánchez, J. E., Moreno, L., Andrade-Gallegos, R. (2011). Pasteurization of substrate for growing *Pleurotus ostreatus* by selfheating. *Proceeding of the 7th International Conference on Mushroom Biology and Mushroom Products (ICMBMP7)*. pp. 398-405.

Savoie, J.-M., Chalaux, N., Olivier, J.-M. (1995). Variability in straw quality and mushroom production: Importance of fungicide schedules on chemical composition and potential degradability of wheat straw. *Bioresource Technology*, 41: 161-166.

Savoie, J.-M., Foulongne-Oriol, M., Barroso, G., Callac, P. (2013). Genetics and genomics of cultivated mushrooms, application to breeding of Agarics. F. Kempken (Ed.). *The Mycota XI, Agricultural Applications*, 2nd Edition, Springer-Verlag Heidelberg. pp. 1-33.

Shimelis, A. (2011). Optimization of coffee wastes for the cultivation of *Pleurotus ostreatus*. *Thesis of Master of Science in Biology*. Department of Biology, School of Graduate studies, Addis Ababa University.

Upadhyay, R. C. and Singh, M. (2010). Production of edible mushrooms. M. Hofrichteur (Ed.). *The Mycota X, Industrial applications*, 2nd Edition Springer-Verlag Heidelberg. pp. 79-97.

Velăzquez-Cedeňo, M. A (2005). Compétition entre *Pleurotus ostreatus* et *Trichoderma* sp en culture sur paille de blé: rôle des communautés bactériennes du substrat et des laccases de *Pleurotus*. *Thèse Doctorat*. de l'Université Paul Cézanne (Aix-Marseille III) en Biologie des Population et Ecologie. Ecole Doctorale des Sciences de l'Environnement.

Velăzquez-Cedeňo M A, Mata G, Savoie J M (2002) Waste-reducing cultivation of *Pleurotus ostreatus* and *Pleurotus pulmonarius* on coffee pulp: changes in the production of some lignolytic enzymes. *World Journal of Microbiology and Biotechnology*, 18: 201-207

Velăzquez Cedeňo, M. A., Farnet, A. M., Ferré, E. (2004). Variations of lignocellulosic activities in dual cultures of *Pleurotus ostreatus* and *Trichoderma longibrachiatum* on unsterilized wheat straw. *Mycologia*, 96, 712-719.

Wasser, S. P. and Weis, A. L. (1999). Medicinal Properties of Substances Occurring in Higher Basidiomycetes Mushrooms: Current Perspectives. *International Journal of Medicinal Mushrooms*, 1, 47-50.

Yehia, R. S. (2012). Nutritional value and biomass yield of the edible mushroom *Pleurotus ostreatus* cultivated on different wastes in Egypt. *Innovative Romanian Food Biotechnology*, 11, 9-14.

Zervakis, G., Philippoussis, A., Ioannidou, S., Diamantopoulou, P. (2001). Mycelium growth kinetics and optimal temperature conditions of the cultivation of edible mushroom species on lignocellulosic substrates. *Folia Microbiologica*, 46 3: 231-233.

Zied, D. C., Savoie, J.-M., Pardo-Giménez, A. (2011). Soybean the main nitrogen source in cultivation substrates of edible and medicinal mushrooms. *Soybean and Nutrition*, Prof. Hany El-Shemy (Ed.). pp. 433-452.

Znaïdi, I. E. K. (2002). Etude et évaluation du compostage de différents types de matières organiques et des effets des jus de composts biologiques sur les maladies des plantes. *Master of Science Degree Mediterranien Organic Agriculture*, C.I.H.E.A.M., Mediterranien Agronomic institute of Bari.

INDEX

#

21st century, 87

A

acarbose, 145, 146, 176
acetaminophen, 163, 168, 171
acetone, 177
acetylation, 58, 109
acid, 2, 41, 45, 47, 49, 58, 62, 64, 66, 67, 72, 79, 80,
    84, 85, 87, 95-98, 106, 108-111, 113, 124, 130,
    146, 147, 151, 158, 161, 164, 165, 168-170, 177,
    179, 180, 181, 185, 190, 193, 205, 213, 229, 232
acidic, 120
acidity, 232
activated carbon, 229
active compound, 144, 145, 208
activity level, 161
AD, 40
ADA, 39
adaptive immunity, 134
adenocarcinoma, 37, 38, 69, 110
adenosine, 121, 161, 167, 172
adenovirus, 204
adhesion, 206
adipocyte, 35
adiponectin, 150, 165, 176, 181
adipose, 22, 154, 190, 194
adipose tissue, 22, 154, 190
adjustment, 25
adolescents, 218, 222
adrenal gland, 66
adsorption, 237
adults, 31, 52, 131, 218, 220
adverse effects, viii, 2, 6, 22, 25, 29, 32, 50, 75
advertisements, 44
Africa, 210, 228

agar, 230
age, 30, 31, 32, 80, 193, 194
agencies, 219
age-related diseases, 32
aggregation, 112
aging process, 31
agonist, 69
agriculture, 116
Agrobacterium, 200
AIDS, ix, 2, 19, 21, 93, 191
alanine, 6, 158, 160, 163, 165, 167, 178, 179, 181,
    194
alanine aminotransferase, 6, 158, 160, 165, 167, 181,
    194
albumin, 192
alcoholic liver disease, 159
alcohols, ix, 119, 127, 136, 145
alertness, 228
algae, 152
Algeria, 228, 229, 230, 237
alkaloids, 153
allergy, 123, 124
Aloha, 211, 221
ALT, 6
amine, 96
amino, ix, 27, 78, 79, 107, 119, 120, 135, 160, 200,
    202, 203, 210, 228
amino acid(s), 27, 78, 79, 107, 160, 200, 202, 203,
    210, 228
amputation, 22
amylase, x, 113, 141, 143, 144, 146, 153, 154, 180
anaphylaxis, 123, 128
androgen, 11
angina, 29
angiogenesis, 158
angiosperm, 203
ANOVA, 232
antibiotic, 200, 201, 206, 208
antibody, 5, 21, 137

anti-cancer, 114, 134, 240
anticancer activity, 83, 96, 111, 124, 126
anticancer drug, 38, 122
antigen, 6, 9, 38, 110, 120, 124, 132, 134, 158, 166
antigen-presenting cell(s) (APCs), 6, 166
antioxidative activity, 161
antitumor, vii, ix, 1, 2, 4, 7, 8, 19, 21, 34, 35, 36, 37, 52, 58, 70, 77, 80, 83, 91, 93, 97, 98, 110, 115, 116, 118, 122, 125, 132, 138, 154, 214
antitumor agent, 70
antiviral drugs, 19
aorta, 192, 197
apoptosis, 14, 38, 110, 111, 147, 148, 158, 167
arginine, 79
arrest, 114, 163
arsenic, 167, 172
artery, 29, 160, 166, 172
arthritis, x, 157, 166, 173, 214
ascorbic acid, 10, 37, 38, 78, 87, 130, 191, 213
ASI, 112
Asia, 210, 229
aspartate, 6, 158, 163, 165, 167, 178, 179, 194
aspartic acid, 79
Aspergillus terreus, 191
assessment, 36, 176, 220, 223, 224, 225
atherosclerosis, 51, 193
atherosclerotic plaque, 192
ATP, 45, 69
autoimmune disease(s), 83, 120

B

backcross, ix, 119, 137
bacteria, 4, 5, 36, 49, 120, 160, 200, 205
bacterial fermentation, 84
bacterial infection, 19, 163
bacteriocins, 207
Bangladesh, 237
base, 160
beer, 89
Beijing, 141
beneficial effect, 32, 44, 51, 80, 83, 84, 113, 150, 178
benefits, vii, ix, xi, 1, 2, 7, 10, 22, 66, 81, 82, 83, 87, 88, 93, 209, 210, 216, 220, 223
benign, 14
benign prostatic hyperplasia, 14
beverages, 228
bile, viii, 44, 45, 47-50, 57, 60, 64, 66, 84, 193
bile acids, viii, 44, 45, 47, 48, 50, 57, 60, 84
bilirubin, 6, 164, 192
bioaccumulation, 86
bioactive extracts, vii, 1, 2, 33

bioassay, 90
bioavailability, 48, 85
biochemistry, 114
bioconversion, 228
biodiesel, 229, 238
biogas, 87
biological activity(s), vii, viii, ix, 1, 2, 34, 52, 57, 58, 63, 64, 75, 93, 96, 114, 196
biological anti-hyperglycemic agents, x, 141
biologically active compounds, 65
biomarkers, 159, 165
biomass, 172, 238, 241
biomolecules, x, 120, 141, 158, 205
biopolymer, 191, 197
biopsy, 9
bioremediation, 223
biosynthesis, 47, 53, 61, 62, 69
biotechnology, 86, 88
biotin, 79
Black Sea region, 88
bladder cancer, 202
blindness, 22, 184
blood circulation, 189
blood clot, 29
blood pressure, vii, 1, 26, 29, 31, 34, 35, 40, 51, 67, 83, 114, 151, 186
blood urea nitrogen, 168, 192
blood vessels, 29
blood-brain barrier, 168
body composition, 68
body fat, 30
body mass index (BMI), 31
body weight, 9, 10, 24, 30, 31, 52, 66, 68, 111, 113, 126, 148, 149, 158, 159, 165, 166, 176, 177, 179, 181, 182, 183, 190, 191, 192, 194, 201, 219, 220
bonds, 58
bone, 4, 9, 11, 36, 121, 122, 125, 135, 179, 222
bone marrow, 4, 36, 121, 122, 125, 135
brachytherapy, 11
brain, 17, 18, 118, 159, 160, 168, 172, 186
branching, 57, 58
breast cancer, 6, 7, 9, 36, 113, 182, 202
breast carcinoma, 5, 8, 110
breeding, 240
by-products, 69, 228

C

cadmium, 86, 219, 222, 225
caffeine, 228, 239
calcium, xi, 67, 80, 81, 108, 192, 212, 216, 217, 222, 227, 229, 232, 235
calcium carbonate, xi, 227, 229, 232, 235

Index

245

calorie, 32

cancer, vii, viii, 1, 3, 5, 6, 7, 8, 9, 10, 11, 13, 17, 18, 19, 21, 30, 34, 36, 37, 38, 41, 43, 44, 83, 91, 94, 97, 108, 110, 111, 114, 116, 120, 122, 126, 133, 135, 147, 149, 158, 171, 191, 214, 225

cancer cells, 5, 8, 10, 11, 13, 17, 18, 19, 34, 37, 38, 110, 111, 120

cancer death, 11

cancer progression, 8, 9, 10, 158

cancer therapy, 11, 225

canker sores, 131

capsule, 83, 152

carbohydrate(s), 31, 39, 64, 78, 79, 80, 81, 83, 94, 124, 126, 136, 144, 145, 148, 206, 212

carbohydrate metabolism, 39, 83

carbon, 72, 158, 164, 165, 167, 168, 169, 173, 233, 234

carbon dioxide, 72

carbon tetrachloride, 158, 164, 165, 167, 168, 169, 173

carbonization, 233

carcinogen, 7, 125

carcinogenesis, 3, 7, 8, 37, 110

carcinoma, 6, 7, 8, 36, 110, 114

cardiovascular disease(s), viii, ix, 2, 7, 29, 30, 32, 34, 40, 41, 65, 89, 93, 94, 108, 142, 195, 216

cardiovascular risk, 83

cardiovascular system, 184, 191

carotene, 87

carotenoids, 78

cartilage, 16, 17

cascades, 127

case study(s), 10, 24

catabolism, 62

CD8+, 8, 166

CDC, 142, 151

cell culture, 4, 5, 63, 138

cell cycle, 110, 111

cell death, 10, 11, 13, 14, 16, 18, 38, 165, 168, 170

cell differentiation, 4, 158

cell division, 127

cell line(s), 4, 20, 36, 38, 122, 126, 128, 133, 177, 206

cellular immunity, 5

cellulose, 51, 96, 176

ceramide, 3

cerebrospinal fluid, 200, 206

chemical(s), x, xi, 2, 22, 35, 72, 78, 81, 85, 89, 90, 91, 94, 95, 108, 109, 114, 116, 127, 142, 146, 157, 168, 195, 214, 227, 231, 232, 239, 240

chemical characteristics, 2

chemokines, 3, 34, 121

chemoprevention, 83

chemotherapy, 4, 8, 9, 10, 11, 15, 21, 37, 38

children, 31, 32, 130, 135, 218, 222

China, vii, 69, 76, 81, 89, 91, 93, 94, 115, 119, 141, 146, 153, 157, 175, 189, 199, 205, 210, 212

chitin, 48, 57, 58, 60, 64, 66, 79

chitosan, xi, 48, 49, 58, 60, 66, 67, 189, 190, 196

chlorine, 80

chloroform, 145, 177, 180

chromatography, 72, 94, 95, 96, 107, 109

chromatography analysis, 95

chromium, 41, 86, 88, 224

chyme, 48

CIA, 166

circulation, 27, 47, 62, 84

classes, 84

cleavage, 96

climates, 211

clinical examination, 150

clinical trials, viii, 5, 9, 30, 75, 86, 158

clone, 133

cloning, 135, 138

closure, 149

clusters, 230

CO_2, 63, 233

cobalamin, 79, 191

coenzyme, xi, 45, 61, 71, 189, 195

coffee, xi, 227, 228, 229, 230, 231, 232, 233, 234, 235, 236, 237, 238, 239, 240, 241

colitis, 117

collagen, x, 149, 157, 164, 166, 173, 183

collateral, 61

colon, 69, 111, 114, 202, 224

colon cancer, 111, 202, 224

color, 231

colorectal cancer, 149, 150, 151

coma, 22

combination therapy, vii, 1, 32, 42

combined effect, 11

commerce, 238, 239

commercial, xi, 133, 191, 214, 215, 227, 229, 230, 237

communication, 146

community(s), vii, 82, 94, 210, 211, 214

competition, 48

complement, 3, 121, 138

complete blood count, 6

complex carbohydrates, 145

complications, 20, 22, 24, 29, 32, 41, 142, 147, 148, 150, 151, 152, 184

composition, viii, 58, 68, 69, 72, 75, 78, 79, 81, 85, 86, 89, 90, 91, 94, 108, 112, 113, 146, 153, 159, 210, 213, 214, 221, 223, 231, 237, 238, 239, 240

composting, 239

compounds, viii, ix, x, 43, 44, 47, 48, 49, 50, 52, 57, 58, 60, 61, 63, 64, 65, 69, 78, 82, 83, 84, 85, 87, 88, 93, 94, 96, 97, 109, 110, 116, 119, 120, 133, 136, 141, 142, 146, 162, 170, 176, 180, 190, 205, 219, 222, 224, 225, 234
computational modeling, 200
computed tomography, 159
configuration, 94, 205
Congress, 69, 70, 90
connective tissue, 18, 19
conservation, 81
constipation, xi, 209, 214
constituents, vii, 50, 88, 93, 108, 113, 117, 118, 133, 145, 153, 164, 185, 210, 222, 223
consumers, 48, 220, 228
consumption, viii, xi, 41, 44, 48, 49, 75, 81, 84, 85, 86, 178, 209, 210, 211, 212, 213, 216, 217, 218, 220, 233
contaminated soil(s), 215, 225
contamination, 221, 231, 236
control group, 7, 8, 22, 23, 24, 32, 33, 50, 112, 149, 150
controlled studies, 21, 51
controversial, 11
cooking, 70, 81, 231
cooling, 231
coordination, 34
copper, 10, 80, 81, 97, 108, 182, 217, 221, 224
coronary arteries, 29, 192
coronary artery disease, 29, 40, 151
coronary heart disease, 31, 214
correlation(s), 39, 58, 108
cortical neurons, 160, 165
cost, 81, 228, 229
cotton, 212
coupling constants, 96
creatinine, 6, 31, 168, 183, 192
crude oil, 215, 222, 225
CSF, 5, 206
CT, 136
cultivation, vii, viii, xi, 53, 62, 63, 75, 77, 78, 81, 82, 83, 87, 90, 133, 187, 192, 196, 210, 211, 212, 214, 225, 227, 228, 229, 231, 232, 233, 234, 235, 236, 237, 238, 239, 240, 241
cultivation conditions, 187, 211
culture conditions, 148, 238
culture medium, 37, 230
cures, 142
CVD, 44, 47, 48
cycles, 63, 64
cyclooxygenase, 120, 128
cyclophosphamide, 15, 122, 126, 137
cysteine, 79, 161

cytochrome, 168
cytokines, 3, 5, 20, 34, 39, 111, 121, 123, 128, 131, 132, 137, 172, 177
cytotoxicity, 5, 16, 17, 37, 38, 110, 111, 117, 127, 130, 166, 172, 202
Czech Republic, 210, 225

D

damages, 9
deaths, 142
decay, 212
defects, 22, 190
deficiency, x, 2, 22, 120, 141, 175
degradation, 47, 58
Delta, 69, 222
dendritic cell, 3, 6, 20, 34, 36, 121, 124, 125, 136, 204
dengue, 204, 207
Department of Agriculture, 226
deposition, 190
deposits, 29
depression, 149
depth, 144
derivatives, vii, viii, 1, 22, 38, 43, 50, 51, 52, 53, 58, 95, 108, 109, 205
dermatitis, 114
desorption, 145
destruction, 20, 233
detoxification, 168
developing countries, 228
D-fraction, vii, 1, 2, 3, 4, 5, 6, 7, 8, 9, 10, 11, 13, 14, 15, 16, 17, 18, 19, 20, 21, 33, 34, 35, 36, 37, 38, 191
diabetes, vii, ix, x, 1, 2, 21, 22, 23, 24, 25, 26, 27, 29, 30, 32, 34, 39, 40, 41, 83, 84, 88, 89, 93, 94, 108, 113, 118, 141, 142, 144, 145, 147, 148, 149, 150, 151, 152, 153, 154, 175, 180, 184, 186, 215, 238
diabetic patients, viii, 2, 21, 22, 24, 25, 26, 29, 34, 39, 142, 149, 150, 151, 152, 184, 185
diacylglycerol, 45
diastolic blood pressure, 194
diesel fuel, 225
diet, viii, 22, 23, 29, 31, 32, 43, 44, 46, 49, 50, 51, 60, 67, 78, 80, 85, 86, 88, 120, 148, 159, 168, 172, 181, 182, 190, 191, 192, 193, 194, 195, 196, 214
dietary fiber, 58, 66, 70, 79, 84, 88, 142
Dietary Guidelines, 226
Dietary Guidelines for Americans, 226
dietary intake, 46, 218, 224
dietary supplementation, 149, 151, 193
diffusion, 47, 48

Index

digestion, viii, 43, 44, 45, 48, 53, 58, 60, 71, 145, 146
digestive enzymes, x, 141
dimerization, 61
direct bilirubin, 192
disease progression, 10
diseases, ix, 2, 4, 20, 30, 44, 76, 78, 83, 94, 214
distribution, 135, 221
diversification, 237
diversity, x, 70, 125, 133, 189, 199, 203, 222
DMMs, 60
DNA, 15, 31, 38, 116, 164, 165, 166, 171
DNA damage, 31, 171
DOC, 239
dominance, 6
dosage, 6, 23, 36, 50, 112, 177, 179, 183, 191, 201
double blind study, 150
down-regulation, 111, 146
drinking water, 122, 148, 177
Drosophila, 171, 205
drugs, 8, 10, 15, 16, 19, 20, 22, 30, 47, 60, 61, 84, 112, 134, 142, 150, 176, 184, 193, 195, 204, 205
dry matter, 79, 113, 118, 233, 234, 236
drying, 95, 116, 233
duodenum, 44
dusts, 212
dyes, 240
dyslipidemia, 181

E

earnings, 214
Eastern Europe, 65, 212
ecology, 86
economic status, 31
eczema, 114
edema, 111
editors, 38
education, 150
effluents, 238
Egypt, 241
elaboration, 27
electron, 85
ELISA, 27, 28
elucidation, 137, 138
e-mail, 209
emulsions, 50
encoding, 158, 164
endocarditis, 201, 208
endocrine, 32
endocrine disorders, 32
endogenous synthesis, viii, 44, 47
endothelial cells, 3

endothelial dysfunction, 89, 113
energy, vii, 52, 78, 79, 159, 210, 213
energy expenditure, 159
environment, 86
environmental conditions, 53
environmental control, 78
environmental management, 228
enzyme(s), viii, xi, 4, 6, 10, 14, 27, 38, 44, 47, 49, 53, 60, 61, 62, 67, 86, 122, 123, 124, 133, 144, 145, 147, 154, 158, 160, 161, 164, 165, 167, 168, 171, 178, 181, 182, 183, 189, 192, 194, 201, 203, 204, 215, 241
enzyme-linked immunosorbent assay, 27
eosinophils, 6
EPA, 220, 225
epidemic, 19
epithelial cells, 39
epithelium, 44
EPS, 148, 149
ergocalciferol, 53, 80
ergosterol, viii, ix, 43, 50, 51, 52, 53, 56, 62, 63, 69, 79, 84, 97, 110, 111, 113, 119, 146, 180, 193
ergosterol peroxides, viii, 43, 52
erythrocytes, 10, 167, 172
ester, 46, 47, 66, 97, 106
ethanol, 49, 58, 63, 96, 107, 109, 110, 111, 112, 113, 115, 146, 147, 159, 163, 165, 170, 173, 194, 212
ethyl acetate, 50, 111, 113, 146, 147, 166, 173, 177, 180, 192, 194
EU, 219, 220, 222
eukaryotic, 76
Europe, 210
European Union, 219, 221, 222
evidence, 36, 37, 80, 83, 84, 85, 86, 117, 153, 154, 167, 173, 206
excitotoxicity, 160
exclusion, 95
excretion, 45, 46, 48, 50, 51, 57, 168, 190, 192, 193
execution, 34
exercise, 32, 86, 162, 170
exopolysaccharides, 123, 136, 159, 172, 176, 181, 184, 185, 186
experimental condition, 22
exposure, 27, 28, 110, 122, 200, 220, 225
extraction, 58, 63, 64, 65, 70, 71, 72, 73, 96, 108, 115

F

families, 94, 210
FAS, 158
fasting, 24, 25, 26, 29, 149, 150, 151, 178, 190, 194

fat, 48, 50, 67, 79, 81, 154, 158, 159, 181, 190, 191, 192, 193, 194, 195, 196, 197, 212, 228
fatty acids, 45, 63, 66, 69, 72, 78, 79, 84
FDA, vii, 1, 9, 34, 44
feces, 197
female rat, 41, 183, 192, 193
fermentation, 84
fever, xi, 209, 214
fiber(s), vii, viii, xi, 41, 68, 75, 79, 84, 87, 189, 190, 191, 196, 210, 212, 228
fibroblasts, 3
fibrogenesis, 164
fibrosis, 158, 159, 164
filtration, 109
Finland, 94
fish, 80, 211
flame, 231
flavonoids, 85, 89, 131
flavor, vii, 76, 81, 210, 228
fluid, 37, 69, 72, 200
fluid extract, 72
fluorine, 80
folic acid, 79, 191, 213
food, viii, xi, 4, 7, 8, 31, 35, 43, 44, 46, 47, 48, 63, 65, 69, 75, 76, 81, 82, 83, 85, 86, 88, 116, 117, 148, 159, 178, 209, 210, 211, 213, 214, 215, 216, 218, 220, 222, 225, 226, 228, 229, 237, 238
food additive(s), 226
Food and Drug Administration, vii, 1
food industry, 44, 47, 63
food intake, 159, 178
food products, viii, 43
Ford, 41, 153
formation, 4, 30, 36, 38, 45, 47, 48, 57, 83, 122, 123, 127, 128, 131, 132, 161, 162, 163, 166, 167, 200, 212, 234
formula, 192
France, 69, 230, 237
free radicals, 10, 14, 37, 38, 85, 215
freezing, 124
fructose, 41
fruits, 44, 46
functional food, viii, ix, x, 43, 47, 60, 63, 65, 66, 75, 86, 87, 93, 112, 141
fungal immunomodulatory protein, ix, 119, 134, 135, 136
fungal metabolite, 35
fungi, 49, 60, 61, 70, 71, 76, 79, 80, 84, 88, 89, 90, 91, 145, 151, 154, 187, 195, 201, 203, 214, 215, 219, 221, 223, 228
fungisterol, viii, 43, 52, 53, 56, 63, 97
fungus, xi, 67, 76, 94, 114, 149, 151, 153, 202, 206, 208, 209, 211, 212, 222, 223, 224, 225, 234, 238

fusion, ix, 119, 123, 129, 130, 138

G

garbage, 229
gastritis, 113
gel, 50, 57, 96, 109, 194
gene expression, 47, 48, 50, 62, 63, 123, 125
genes, 46, 48, 66, 158, 164, 207
genetic factors, 88
genitourinary tract, 38
genomics, 240
genus, xi, 71, 209, 210, 211, 229
gill, 206
gland, 18, 19
glioma, 162
glucose tolerance, 24, 39, 175, 177, 178, 184
glucose tolerance test, 24, 177, 184
GLUT4, 26, 40, 151
glutamate, 160, 165, 171, 177
glutamic acid, 79, 107
glutamine, 160, 161
glutathione, 10, 14, 62, 122, 158, 159, 160, 161, 163, 165, 166, 167, 179, 180, 182, 183, 193, 194
glycans, 96
glycine, 107
glycogen, 79, 113, 146, 148, 177, 179, 180, 210
glycol, 201
glycoproteins, 124, 177
glycosylated hemoglobin, 24, 25, 150
gonorrhea, 214
grading, 9, 37
GRAS, 63
grasslands, 211
Greece, 69, 89, 221
growth, vii, xi, 1, 8, 11, 13, 15, 16, 18, 20, 21, 34, 38, 39, 53, 69, 78, 81, 110, 111, 122, 133, 162, 201, 202, 203, 209, 210, 211, 212, 215, 228, 230, 233, 239, 241
growth factor, 162
growth rate, 230
Guangdong, 141
guidelines, 151, 153

H

habitat(s), 90, 212
hair, 9
hair loss, 9
halogens, 85
harmful effects, 215
harvesting, 63, 228

Index 249

HBV, 20
HBV infection, 20
headache, xi, 209, 214
healing, 36, 84, 149, 183
health, vii, ix, 1, 2, 7, 10, 21, 31, 44, 47, 48, 64, 65,
68, 70, 76, 78, 80, 82, 83, 86, 87, 88, 93, 133,
142, 150, 154, 158, 168, 191, 207, 210, 218, 220,
221, 223, 224
health care, 21, 142, 150
health care system, 142
health effects, 70, 78, 83, 218
health expenditure, 142
health promotion, ix, 76
health risks, 86
health status, 31
heart attack, 30, 190
heart disease, viii, 30, 43, 65, 114, 214
heart failure, 31, 151
heavy metals, 210, 215, 222
hematocrit, 6
heme, 161
heme oxygenase, 161
hemisphere, 41
hemoglobin, 6
hepatic injury, 160
hepatic necrosis, 158, 163
hepatic stellate cells, 164
hepatitis, vii, x, 1, 2, 19, 20, 21, 35, 38, 157, 159,
169, 191
hepatocellular carcinoma, 134
hepatocytes, 20, 50, 158, 165, 167, 173
hepatoma, 4, 124, 169, 182, 201, 202
hepatotoxicity, 22, 161, 169, 171, 172
hepatotoxins, 168
herbal medicine, 33
herpes, 20, 204
herpes simplex, 20, 204
hexane, 110, 145, 146, 177
high blood cholesterol, 29
high blood pressure, 30, 31
high density lipoprotein, 113, 189, 191, 192, 194,
195
high fat, 190
highways, 214
histamine, 128
histidine, 107
histological examination, 9
histology, 67, 195
history, 76, 150
HIV, 2, 19, 20, 35, 38, 108, 113, 115, 182, 186, 193,
195, 201, 202, 203
HIV/AIDS, 19, 20
HIV-1, 108, 113, 115, 182, 186, 201, 202, 203

HLA, 125
HM, 133, 185
HO-1, 159
homeostasis, 46, 47, 66, 176
Hong Kong, 119, 141, 157, 175, 189, 199, 205
hormone, 62
host, 3, 4, 5, 20, 21, 84, 125, 160
HPV, 123
human body, vii, 84, 168
human exposure, 217
human health, viii, x, 75, 141, 169
human immunodeficiency virus, vii, 1, 2, 108, 113,
204, 206
human welfare, 169
humidity, 231, 233
humoral immunity, 5, 130
hybrid, ix, 119, 129, 130, 134, 136, 137, 138
hydrogen, 10, 37, 85, 109, 147, 152, 153, 163, 165
hydrogen peroxide, 10, 37, 109, 147, 152, 153, 163,
165
hydrolysis, 58, 64, 95, 107, 109, 144, 176
hydroxyl, 85, 110, 145, 163, 176, 182, 205
hydroxyl groups, 85
hyperandrogenism, 32
hypercholesterolemia, vii, 1, 2, 47, 66, 70, 193, 194,
195, 214
hyperglycaemia, 113, 148
hyperglycemia, 21, 30, 31, 145, 146, 150, 154, 175,
182, 185, 186, 214
hyperinsulinemia, 30, 32, 159, 190
hyperlipidemia, 30, 51, 68, 191
hyperplasia, 113
hypersensitivity, 121, 132
hypertension, vii, 1, 2, 29, 30, 31, 34, 40, 41, 80, 83,
142, 191, 214, 216
hypertriglyceridemia, 30, 190
hypertrophy, 125
hypotensive, vii, 1, 21, 29, 30, 83
hypothesis, 117

I

ID, 170, 171
identification, 86, 180, 186, 207
identity, 195
IFN, 3, 5, 6, 20, 136
IL-13, 5
IL-8, 3
immune function, 6, 36, 122, 186
immune response, 4, 5, 8, 84, 124, 136, 204
immune system, 3, 4, 9, 34, 36, 83, 84, 94, 120, 132
immunity, 6, 35, 38, 134, 138, 184
immunocompetent cells, 8, 9

immunoglobulin, 166
immunomodulation, ix, 66, 93, 124
immunomodulator, 5
immunomodulatory, vii, ix, 1, 2, 3, 4, 7, 8, 19, 20,
  21, 34, 57, 58, 83, 115, 119, 120, 121, 123, 124,
  125, 131, 132, 133, 134, 135, 136, 137, 138, 158,
  172, 184, 214
immunostimulatory, ix, 119, 121, 125
immunosuppression, 8, 37, 122, 137
immunotherapy, 11, 123
imports, 229
improvements, 9, 15, 20, 22, 25
impurities, 222
in situ hybridization, 14
in vitro, vii, x, 1, 4, 10, 11, 15, 19, 21, 27, 36, 37, 39,
  52, 53, 58, 60, 61, 66, 67, 68, 71, 84, 85, 86, 110,
  121, 123, 130, 131, 133, 136, 141, 144, 145, 146,
  147, 161, 162, 169, 170, 176, 182, 195, 201
in vivo, vii, x, 1, 4, 7, 8, 10, 21, 37, 50, 60, 65, 67,
  86, 110, 111, 117, 124, 135, 136, 141, 144, 161,
  170, 172
incidence, 7, 22, 44, 111, 148
income, 88, 237
incubation period, 231, 232, 233
incubation time, 233
Indians, 167
individuals, 6, 195, 210
Indonesia, 229
induction, 14, 42, 111, 132, 136
industrial wastes, 237
industrialized countries, 44, 47, 65
industry(s), 61, 87, 214, 234
INF, 6
infancy, 211
infection, 2, 19, 20, 36, 193, 204, 208
infertility, 32, 33
inflammation, x, 31, 89, 116, 117, 147, 157, 158,
  159, 164, 169, 172, 177
inflammatory disease, 120
inflammatory mediators, 111, 128
inflammatory responses, 69
influenza, 19, 20, 21, 39, 113, 204
influenza a, 19
influenza virus, 20, 21, 39, 113
ingestion, 220
ingredients, viii, ix, 63, 64, 75, 93, 97, 117
inhibition, 7, 8, 19, 20, 35, 47, 48, 62, 63, 66, 69, 84,
  108, 109, 111-113, 133, 143, 145, 152, 158, 206
inhibitor, xi, 53, 61, 70, 71, 84, 112, 117, 146, 147,
  151, 153, 189
injections, 158, 165, 176, 179
injury(s), 7, 169, 170, 171, 172, 173
inoculation, 4

INS, 28
insulin, viii, x, 2, 21, 22, 23, 24, 25, 26, 27, 29, 30,
  31, 32, 34, 35, 39, 40, 83, 113, 114, 141, 142,
  146, 147, 148, 149, 150, 152, 154, 159, 165, 172,
  175, 176, 177, 178, 179, 180, 181, 184, 185
insulin dependent diabetes, 175
insulin resistance, 22, 27, 28, 29, 30, 31, 32, 34, 39,
  40, 142, 148, 149, 150, 152, 154, 159, 165, 172,
  176, 181, 185
insulin sensitivity, 22, 24, 26, 31, 180, 184
insulin signaling, 40, 154
insulinoma, 148
integrity, 160
interferon, 3, 20, 35, 120, 121, 123, 124, 125, 128,
  131, 133, 138, 164, 167
interferon-γ, 3, 121, 128, 131, 167
intervention, 142
intestinal tract, 48
intestine, 45, 47, 112
intima, 192
intoxication, 168
intravenously, 7
intrinsic viscosity, 95
invertebrates, 200
Investigational New Drug (IND), vii, 1, 9
investment, 237
iodine, 80
ion-exchange, 57, 96
ions, 97, 202
iron, 10, 67, 80, 81, 86, 108, 165, 166, 171, 217
irradiation, 163, 166, 171
ischemia, 160, 166, 172
Islam, 134, 136-138, 152, 185, 196, 224, 228, 239
isoflavone, 152
isoflavonoids, 177
isolation, 72, 117, 118, 134, 184, 206, 237
issues, 22, 84, 225
Italy, 70, 90

J

Japan, vii, 9, 48, 51, 94, 122, 210
Japanese women, 33
jejunum, 159
joints, 166

K

Kenya, 228
keratinocyte, 109
kidney(s), 17, 18, 20, 51, 147, 168, 178, 182, 184,
  192, 194, 201

kidney failure, 184
kill, 14, 21, 37
killer cells, 5, 36
kinase activity, 26, 146, 155
kinetics, 47, 145, 241
Korea, 87, 224

L

labeling, 38, 158
lactate dehydrogenase, 158, 194
lactic acid, 22
Lactobacillus, 160
lactose, 206
larvae, 162
Latin America, 229
LDL, viii, 29, 31, 43, 44, 46, 47, 48, 49, 50, 51, 52, 62, 65, 68, 89, 183, 189, 190, 191, 193
lead, 4, 22, 30, 32, 33, 48, 57, 86, 175, 225
leishmaniasis, 204
lens, 147, 153, 181
leptin, 181, 190
lesions, 121, 193
leucine, 107
leukemia, 9, 18, 124, 136, 201, 202, 206
leukocytes, 70, 166
life cycle, 229
ligand, 28, 47, 124, 126
light, 162
lignin, 94, 108, 113, 115, 164, 173, 212
linoleic acid, 51, 79, 145
lipases, 44
lipid metabolism, 7, 30, 34, 40
lipid peroxidation, 31, 67, 84, 87, 108, 109, 122, 158, 161, 165, 167, 182
lipids, vii, 1, 30, 32, 34, 35, 44, 51, 60, 67, 192, 193, 195, 210
lipoproteins, 46, 47, 190
Listeria monocytogenes, 4, 36
liver, ix, 5, 7, 8, 9, 17, 18, 22, 30, 35, 39, 45, 46, 47, 50, 51, 62, 69, 84, 93, 108, 113, 114, 158, 159, 161, 164, 165, 167, 168, 169, 170, 171, 172, 173, 178, 180-182, 185, 187, 190, 192, 193, 194, 214
liver cancer, 5, 9
liver cells, 160, 161, 164, 168
liver damage, 158, 159, 167, 170, 172
liver disease, ix, 93, 114, 159, 165, 170, 181, 185, 214
liver failure, 22, 168
locomotor, 159
lovastatin, xi, 47, 61, 63, 67, 71, 87, 189, 190, 194, 195

low-density lipoprotein, viii, 29, 43, 44, 46, 67, 178, 191, 192, 193
luciferase, 111
lumen, 45, 47, 48
lung cancer, 9, 37, 113
Luo, 69, 153
lupus, 83
lycopene, 87
lymph, 36, 45, 122, 132, 166
lymph node, 36, 122, 132, 166
lymphocytes, 3, 5, 6, 112, 123, 124, 127, 132, 133
lymphoid, 138
lymphoid tissue, 138
lymphoma, 18, 19
lysine, 107
lysis, 5

M

macrophages, 3, 4, 5, 6, 8, 20, 21, 34, 36, 69, 111, 112, 120, 121, 122, 123, 125, 126, 127, 128, 129, 130, 131, 132, 135, 136, 138, 163
magnesium, 67, 80, 81, 108, 192, 212, 216
major histocompatibility complex, 5, 124
majority, 2
malaria, x, 157, 160, 204, 208
Malaysia, 170
malignancy, 38
malignant tumors, ix, 93
mammalian cells, 38, 69
man, 218
management, 142, 148, 151, 153, 154
manganese, 80, 81, 86, 108, 217
mannitol, 79
manufacturing, 215
manure, 87
marketing, 86
mass, 72, 96, 107, 116, 145, 147, 190, 220
mass spectrometry, 72, 145
materials, 81, 90, 218
matter, 154, 233, 234, 236
MB, 38, 110
measurement(s), 78, 232
meat, 51, 68, 79, 211, 214
media, 21, 240
median, 218
medical, 30, 31, 39, 41, 91, 152, 211, 215
medical care, 39
medication, 23, 29, 32
medicine, ix, 30, 76, 83, 86, 93, 114, 142, 184, 225
medium composition, 192
melanin, 97, 117
melanoma, 7, 111

252 Index

mellitus, x, 21, 40, 113, 141, 142, 175, 184
melon, 214, 225
membranes, 45, 53
memory, 159, 172
meningitis, 200, 206
menstrual cycles, 33
menstruation, 32
mercury, 80, 86, 220, 222, 223, 224, 225
Metabolic, 30, 41, 146, 154
metabolic changes, 33
metabolic disorder(s), viii, 2, 21, 30
metabolic disturbances, 31
metabolic pathways, 61
metabolic syndrome, 31, 34, 41, 165
metabolism, viii, 23, 29, 30, 31, 34, 44, 48, 52, 62, 63, 66, 71, 86, 149, 151, 177, 187, 189, 195, 215
metabolites, 61, 72, 85
metal ion(s), 10
metals, 37, 85, 86, 88, 215, 220, 221, 223, 225
metastasis, 8, 9, 10, 11, 34, 37, 122, 158
metastatic disease, 10
meter, 232
metformin, 22, 39, 152, 176, 177, 183, 185
methanol, 50, 51, 60, 61, 63, 109, 111, 145, 147
Mexico, 68
MHC, 5, 122, 135, 166
microenvironments, 3
micronutrients, 210, 216, 217, 220
microorganisms, 120, 159, 233
microsomes, 62
migration, 149, 183
MIP, 3
mitochondrial DNA, 166
mitogen, 127, 128, 132, 138, 159, 162
mixing, 44, 63, 214
models, 84, 136, 144, 148
modifications, 11, 66, 95, 96, 118
moisture, 212, 213, 219, 231, 233, 234
moisture content, 213, 233
molar ratios, 94, 95
molds, 231
molecular mass, 58, 96, 112, 177, 191, 208
molecular structure, 57
molecular weight, 2, 20, 21, 49, 58, 61, 64, 94, 95, 96, 97, 109, 116, 134, 166
molecular weight distribution, 96
molecules, 45, 46, 49, 52, 58, 61, 84, 95, 110, 120, 124, 134, 199, 205, 215, 238
monocyte chemoattractant protein, 165, 181
monomers, 58
monosaccharide, 94, 95
Moon, 116, 117, 170
morphology, 113

mortality, viii, 43, 44, 65, 162, 170
MR, 71, 171, 208
mRNA(s), 50, 51, 61, 63, 68, 111, 121, 126, 163, 167, 172, 179, 190, 192
mucoid, 45
multiple factors, 22
multiplication, 230
mumps, 214
muscles, 30
mussels, 200
mycelium, 37, 50, 112, 135, 146, 170, 171, 172, 180, 186, 229, 230, 233, 236
mycology, 88
myelosuppression, 4

N

National Academy of Sciences, 71
natural compound, 146
natural food, 86, 220
natural killer (NK) cell(s), 3, 36, 121, 122, 126, 130, 131, 132
natural resources, 108
nausea, 9
necrosis, 14, 39, 123, 125, 128, 133
nematode, 204, 208
neoplasm, 111
nephropathy, 22
nerve, 162
nerve growth factor, 162
nervous system, 184
Netherlands, 90
neuroblastoma, 162
neuronal cells, 171
neurons, 162, 168
neuropathy, 22, 24
neurotoxicity, 165, 171, 172
neutral, 50, 95, 178
neutrophils, 3, 121, 125
New England, 66, 151
niacin, 41, 79, 213
nickel, 220
nicotinamide, 180
nicotine, 73
nicotinic acid, 50, 79
Nigeria, vi, vii, xi, 209, 210, 211, 214, 216, 219, 220, 221, 222, 224, 225, 228
nitric oxide, 4, 85, 111, 120, 125, 126, 127, 128, 130, 131, 132, 159, 162, 163, 164, 177, 180, 202
nitric oxide synthase, 4, 128, 162, 163, 177
nitrogen, 60, 122, 241
NK cells, 3, 5, 6, 9, 34, 36
NMR, 96, 108, 145

nodes, 166
non-enzymatic antioxidants, 158
North America, 94
Nrf2, 161, 171
nuclear magnetic resonance, 200
nutraceutical, 88
nutrient(s), xi, 53, 77, 85, 87, 209, 211-213, 233
nutrition, 79, 80, 81, 224

O

obesity, vii, 1, 2, 22, 29, 30, 31, 32, 40, 41, 172, 196
occlusion, 160, 166, 172
octane, 61
oil, 44, 72, 191, 193, 212, 230
Oklahoma, 225
oleic acid, 145
oligomers, 58, 66
oligosaccharide, 161
olive oil, 8, 234, 237
operations, 81, 229
opportunities, ix, 93, 151
optimization, 169, 186
organ(s), 8, 26, 158, 168, 183, 223
organic food, 210
organic matter, 233, 234
organic solvents, 72
organism, 57, 146
overnutrition, 31
overweight, 32, 148
ovulation, 32, 33, 41, 42
ox, 50
oxidation, 62, 85, 89, 148, 177
oxidative damage, 165, 168, 173
oxidative stress, 10, 13, 14, 31, 38, 89, 109, 147,
    153, 162, 165, 169, 170, 177, 186, 187, 196
oxygen, 38, 147
oyster, xi, 49, 51, 61, 67, 68, 77, 87, 136, 150, 151,
    170, 186, 193, 194, 195, 197, 205, 208, 209, 211,
    228, 230, 233, 236, 237, 240

P

Pacific, 223
pain, xi, 9, 29, 209, 214
Pakistan, 240
pancreas, 30, 44, 113, 146, 148, 178, 179, 182
pantothenic acid, 79
parasite(s), xi, 94, 160, 199, 200, 204
participants, viii, 2, 6, 25, 32, 194
pathogenesis, 185
pathogens, 4, 5, 20, 34, 200

pathology, 36
pathophysiological, 83
pathways, 26, 83, 112, 127, 132, 136, 150
PCP, 134
penicillin, 200
pepsin, 44
peptidase, 176
peptide(s), ix, 5, 107, 112, 115, 120, 122, 132, 133,
    137, 138, 160, 171, 172, 182, 185, 186, 200, 201,
    202, 203, 205, 206, 207, 208
periodontitis, 114
peripheral blood, 5, 121, 123, 124, 125, 126, 127,
    131, 132, 136, 169
peripheral blood mononuclear cell, 124, 125, 127,
    131, 136
peritonitis, 200
permeability, 128
permeation, 96
peroxidation, 13, 38, 109, 178, 192
peroxide, ix, 69, 84, 97, 107, 110, 111, 113, 119,
    126, 146, 147, 165, 166, 180
peroxynitrite, 163
personal communication, 229
pests, 78
petroleum, 111
pH, xi, 44, 86, 124, 200, 227, 231, 232, 233
phagocytosis, 3, 4, 121, 128
pharmaceutical(s), 22, 47, 61, 76, 113, 214, 215
pharmacokinetics, 37
pharmacology, 114
phenolic compounds, 78, 85, 89, 109, 164
phenotype, 120
pheochromocytoma, 162
Philadelphia, 39
phosphate, 192
phosphatidylcholine, 44, 62
phosphatidylethanolamine, 62
phospholipids, 45, 50, 192
phosphorus, 80, 81, 108, 212
phosphorylation, 27, 28, 40, 125, 127, 132, 146, 161
physical exercise, 120
physical inactivity, 31
physicians, 21
physicochemical properties, 116
physiology, 238
phytosterols, viii, 43, 48, 66, 69
PI3K, 26, 127, 161
pilot study, vii, 1, 9, 18
pioglitazone, 24
placebo, 6, 51, 68, 130, 150, 151, 152, 154, 176, 185
plant diseases, 88
plant sterols, viii, 43, 45, 47, 48, 52, 66
plants, 108, 145, 152, 230

254 Index

plaque, 40, 132
plasma levels, 177, 179, 194
plasma membrane, 13, 26, 179
platelet aggregation, 89, 107, 112, 115
playing, 146
Pleurotus mushrooms, xi, 213, 224, 227, 238
pneumonia, 200
Poland, 88, 90, 94, 221, 223, 224
polarization, 120, 138
pollutants, 85
pollution, 81
polymer(s), 58, 114, 148, 149, 154, 179, 180, 187
polymerization, 94, 97
polymorphisms, 44
polypeptide(s), 85, 203, 207
polyphenols, ix, 93, 97, 105, 109, 116, 117, 164, 191
polyunsaturated fat, 13, 46, 79
polyunsaturated fatty acids, 13, 79
population, 6, 41, 66, 86, 142, 151, 220
potassium, 80, 83, 108, 192, 212
potato, 205, 230
precancer, 121
precipitation, 48, 58, 96
predators, 200
pregnancy, 32
preparation, 2, 49, 71, 81, 112, 229
preservation, 85, 238
prevention, viii, ix, 2, 21, 22, 26, 30, 34, 37, 76, 83,
   86, 88, 89, 112, 117, 142, 144, 147, 151, 205, 238
primary function, 14
principles, x, 147, 164, 175, 180
probability, 9
probiotic(s), 160
prognosis, 10, 25, 37
pro-inflammatory, 3, 111, 120, 125, 126, 184
project, 34
proliferation, 4, 5, 8, 18, 112, 116, 121, 122, 124,
   127, 128, 131, 132, 148, 163, 164, 182, 202, 204,
   206
promoter, 110
propagation, 133
prophylactic, 204, 214
prophylaxis, 114
prostaglandins, 111
prostate cancer, 9, 10, 11, 14, 15, 17, 38
prostate carcinoma, 38
prostatectomy, 9
protection, x, 34, 157
protein synthesis, 61
proteinase, 112
proteins, x, xi, 40, 44, 45, 46, 48, 79, 81, 84, 111,
   112, 121, 123, 127, 131, 133, 134, 138, 141, 146,
   163, 199, 203, 204, 205, 208, 210, 228

proteoglycans, 133, 137, 181
protons, 96
pseudopodia, 125
psoriasis, 114
public health, viii, 43
pulp, 235, 241
purification, 152
pyridoxine, 79
pyrophosphate, 61

Q

quality of life, vii, 1, 9, 10, 21, 151
quercetin, 85, 147

R

radiation, 168, 170
radicals, 10, 38, 85, 89, 109, 176, 182
radiotherapy, 11
rape, 240
RE, 165, 186
reactions, 123
reactive oxygen, 4, 31, 122, 127, 159, 163, 165, 166
reactivity, 161
reagents, 58, 131
reception, 232
receptor sites, 62
receptors, x, 3, 66, 112, 141, 148
recognition, 4, 5, 35, 145
recommendations, 150
recovery, 228
recurrence, 9
recycling, 81, 238
red blood cells, 6
regeneration, 38, 149, 183
regions of the world, xi, 209, 211
regression, 9, 40, 84
regulations, 48
remediation, 215
remission, 9
renal failure, 22, 142
renin, 31, 180
repair, 148
repetitions, 232
replication, 20, 168, 204
reproductive age, 32
reproductive organs, 113
requirements, 53, 58, 213, 229, 239
researchers, viii, 75, 83, 86, 228, 237
residues, 26, 27, 60, 124, 126, 130, 146, 228, 234,
   237, 240

Index

255

resins, 57
resistance, 20, 22, 27, 30, 32, 34, 38, 39, 40, 84, 177
resources, xi, 151, 227, 228, 233, 237
respiratory syncytial virus, 204
response, 4, 5, 6, 8, 9, 11, 20, 36, 39, 57, 72, 111, 121, 124, 131, 201, 204
reticulum, 45, 168, 169
retina, 147
retinopathy, 22, 24
reverse transcriptase, 108, 113, 182, 186, 201, 202, 203, 206
RH, 72, 135, 171
rheumatoid arthritis, 83, 166
riboflavin, 79, 213
ribonucleotide reductase, 204
ribosome, 133, 202, 203, 206
risk(s), viii, 4, 9, 21, 29, 30, 40, 41, 43, 44, 48, 65, 75, 86, 88, 148, 151, 153, 190, 195, 216, 220, 223, 224
risk factors, viii, 31, 43, 44, 151
RNA, 128
root(s), 153, 201, 207, 230, 236
root rot, 201
routines, 32
RPR, 61
Russia, 94, 113

S

safety, vii, ix, 1, 21, 25, 34, 67, 76, 150, 218
saliva, 44
salivary gland(s), 146
Salmonella, x, 157, 163, 170
salts, 44
sawdust, 77, 212
scavengers, 47, 85
science, 67, 81, 116
secrete, 5
secretion, x, 5, 22, 44, 67, 84, 124, 125, 126, 128, 141, 147, 148, 152, 177, 190
seed, 225
selectivity, 154
selenium, 62, 66, 80, 86, 186
senescence, 53
senses, 46
sensitivity, 24, 49, 142, 193
sensitization, 26
septic shock, 22
serine, 26, 27, 107
serum, viii, 6, 9, 10, 24, 27, 30, 35, 43, 44, 46, 47, 48, 49, 50, 51, 57, 60, 65, 66, 67, 69, 110, 113, 121, 126, 133, 148, 160, 161, 164, 165, 167, 168, 180, 181, 182, 183, 190, 191, 192, 193, 194, 223

serum albumin, 133
sesquiterpenoid, ix, 119, 127, 136
shape, xi, 95, 209
shelf life, 81
shock, 164, 231, 235
shortage, 228
showing, 30, 51, 53, 63, 121, 203
Siberia, 114
side chain, 53, 58, 145
side effects, viii, 4, 8, 9, 20, 21, 34, 66, 75, 113
signal transduction, viii, 2, 26-29, 34, 40, 146
signaling pathway, 127, 138, 154, 158, 161
signals, 96
silica, 50, 194
silicon, 108
silver, 225
skeletal muscle, 27
skin, 7, 53, 110, 113, 183
skin cancer, 7, 113
small intestine, 45, 57
smooth muscle, 164
SMS, 153
sodium, 62, 80, 83, 91, 108, 111, 117, 192, 194, 212, 216
solubility, 47, 48
solution, 8
solvents, 63
somatic cell, 171
South Asia, 151
SP, 35, 72, 169, 170, 172, 186
Spain, 43, 65, 70, 72
speciation, 88
spectroscopy, 200
spiders, 200
spleen, 5, 112, 121, 124, 128, 129, 132, 163, 167, 201, 204
sporophore, 49, 53, 238
Sprague-Dawley rats, 26, 31, 50, 51
Spring, 172
SS, 41, 134, 136, 137, 138, 185
stabilization, 233
standard deviation, 12, 15, 194, 215, 232, 234, 236
starch, 142, 145, 146, 215
state(s), 10, 27, 31, 84, 120, 169, 211, 229
statin, 61, 63
sterile, 94, 114
steroids, 85, 94, 97, 107, 109, 110, 205
sterols, 48, 50, 53, 63, 69, 72, 116
stimulant, 208, 228
stimulation, 20, 21, 128, 170
stock, 11
stomach, xi, 9, 17, 44, 94, 209, 214
stomatitis, 20

storage, xi, 30, 81, 133, 160, 209, 211
stress, 13, 41, 168, 169, 172
stroke, 31, 190
stroma, 233
structural characteristics, 72
structure, 3, 35, 53, 58, 85, 96, 117, 118, 129, 145, 172
substitutes, 211
substitution, 51, 109
substrate(s), xi, 26, 53, 61, 62, 78, 81, 85, 86, 146, 206, 212, 215, 225, 227, 228, 229, 230, 231, 232, 233, 234, 235, 236, 237, 238, 239, 240, 241
sucrose, 31
sugar beet, 68
sulfate, 111, 117
sulfonylurea, 22, 176
sulfur, 80, 108
Sun, 37, 69, 113, 118, 122, 136, 138, 153, 171, 172, 173, 186, 187
supplementation, 50, 62, 66, 67, 68, 87, 149, 150, 159, 172, 178, 190, 192, 196, 227, 238
suppliers, 4
suppression, 4, 62, 84
surgical removal, 122
surveillance, 10
survival, 4, 36, 111, 124, 158, 160, 163, 166
survival rate, 4, 111, 163, 166
susceptibility, 14, 47, 120
swelling, 128, 214, 215
Switzerland, 226
symptoms, 9, 20, 30, 31
syndrome, 2, 31, 32, 33, 41, 42, 120, 148
synergistic effect, 35, 78
synthesis, viii, 43, 44, 47, 50, 60, 61, 65, 84, 97, 148, 162, 181, 185
systolic blood pressure, 29, 180, 194

T

T cell(s), 4, 5, 6, 7, 8, 20, 112, 120, 123, 125, 166
T lymphocytes, 5, 128
target, vii, 1, 5, 14, 27, 38, 61, 147, 148
tartrate-resistant acid phosphatase, 179
tau, 159
T-cell receptor, 5
techniques, 81, 223, 239
technology(ies), 60, 63, 64, 71, 72, 87, 90, 150, 228, 237
technology transfer, 87
temperature, 33, 64, 69, 95, 212, 231, 241
terpenes, 85, 205
testing, 16, 86
testosterone, 33

texture, vii, 76, 81, 210
Th cells, 5, 120
Thailand, 91
therapeutic agents, 158
therapeutic use, 2, 83
therapeutics, 142, 146, 207, 240
therapy, 9, 20, 22, 24, 33, 37, 38, 62, 86, 184, 195, 205
thermal treatment, 95
thermostability, 137, 200, 201, 206
threonine, 26, 79, 107
thrombosis, 112
thymus, 132
thyroid, 62
Tibet, vii, 210
tin, 231
tincture, 114
tissue, 29, 71, 135, 147, 159, 183, 184, 190, 201, 211
TLR, 127
TLR2, 121, 138
TLR4, 125
TNF, 3, 5, 20, 21, 31, 39, 110, 111, 112, 121, 126
TNF-α, 3, 5, 110, 111, 112, 121
tocopherols, 78, 79
total cholesterol, 6, 29, 50, 51, 60, 63, 84, 113, 149, 178, 179, 180, 182, 183, 190, 191, 192, 193, 194
toxic effect, 4, 111, 215
toxic metals, 86, 216, 217, 220, 223
toxicity, viii, 4, 6, 36, 75, 85, 126, 147, 165, 169, 173, 200, 201
toxicology, vii, 1, 9
toxin, 161
TPA, 110
trace elements, 80, 83, 85, 86, 215, 224
trade, 229
traditions, vii, 210
transaminases, 164, 178
transcription, 46, 123, 125, 161
transformation(s), xi, 48, 223, 227
translation, 202, 203
translocation, 26, 40, 127, 132, 146, 161
transplantation, 186
transport, 66, 148, 151, 177
trial, 6, 10, 23, 25, 29, 36, 37, 38, 41, 42, 49, 51, 68, 149, 150, 151, 152, 176, 185
triggers, 20, 47
triglycerides, 6, 29, 30, 34, 50, 51, 179, 192, 193
tuberculosis, ix, 93, 94, 114
tumor, 3, 5, 6, 7, 8, 9, 10, 20, 36-39, 83, 96, 110, 111, 117, 118, 120-128, 130, 131, 132, 134, 136, 137, 160, 161, 164, 166, 206
tumor cells, 8, 111, 121, 125, 137, 206
tumor growth, 5, 7, 8, 36, 83, 127

Index

tumor metastasis, 8

tumor necrosis factor, 3, 39, 120, 121, 122, 123, 125, 126, 128, 130, 131, 132, 160, 161, 164, 166

tumors, 7, 38, 84

Turkey, 190, 195

turnover, 44, 67, 147

type 1 diabetes, 25, 168, 175

type 2 diabetes, 22, 24, 25, 29, 39, 40, 41, 113, 117, 151, 152, 153, 175, 176, 179, 185

tyrosine, x, 26, 27, 97, 107, 141, 143, 146, 154

U

ubiquitin, 203, 206

UK, 91, 187, 218, 225

ulcer, 113

ultrasonography, 33

ultrasound, 70

umbilical cord, 4, 36, 186

United Nations, 88, 224

United States (USA), 1, 37, 11, 142, 224

universe, 36

urban areas, 210, 214

urea, 31, 168, 183, 238

uric acid, 192

US Department of Health and Human Services, 226

USDA, 216, 226

UV, 68, 69, 108

UV irradiation, 68, 69

UV-irradiation, 69

V

vacuum, 95

valine, 79

valorization, 227, 229, 237

vanadium, 187

vancomycin, 36, 200, 201

variations, 78

varieties, xi, 77, 83, 86, 112, 209, 210

VCAM, 126

vegetables, 46, 79

vein, 164

very low density lipoprotein, 49, 189

vessels, 8, 30

viral diseases, 199

viral infection, vii, 1, 19, 21

viral pathogens, 3

virus infection, 21, 38, 39

viruses, 5, 20, 34, 113, 168, 204

viscosity, 48, 49, 66, 67, 96

vitamin B1, 81

vitamin B2, 79, 81

vitamin C, vii, 1, 10, 16-19, 37, 38, 80, 158, 194, 228

vitamin D, 53, 68, 69, 90, 191

vitamin E, 158, 194

vitamins, vii, viii, 75, 79, 80, 81, 83, 210, 213, 228

VLDL, 49, 50, 51, 62, 189

W

Washington, 226

waste, xi, 81, 90, 212, 227

web, 153

weekly intake, xi, 209, 219

weight control, 32

weight gain, 32, 191, 214

weight loss, 31, 32

welfare, 76, 133

well-being, 20

West Africa, 214

western blot, 149

Western Siberia, 94

wood, xi, 70, 169, 209, 211, 212, 234

workers, 211

World Health Organization (WHO), viii, 43, 88, 142, 154, 213, 219, 220, 224, 226

worldwide, vii, viii, x, 10, 19, 20, 41, 75, 76, 77, 78, 175, 210, 215, 228

worms, 94

wound healing, 149, 153, 180, 184, 185

Y

yeast, 184

yield, 64, 87, 207, 212, 229, 235, 238, 239, 241

young women, 51

Z

zinc, 80, 81, 86, 108, 182, 221